VALÉRIE WORTH-STYLIANOU

CONFIDENTIAL
STRATEGIES

The Evolving Role
of the *Confident* in French Tragic Drama (1635-1677)

LIBRAIRIE DROZ S.A.
11, rue Massot
GENÈVE
1999

ISBN: 2-600-00339-8
ISSN: 1420-7699

Copyright 1999 by Librairie Droz S.A., 11, rue Massot, Genève.

Travaux
du Grand Siècle

N° XII

CONTENTS

Acknowledgements ix
Note on the text...xi

INTRODUCTION 1

PART I: FAMILIAR PRACTICES AND CRITICAL VOICES: FROM *MÉDÉE* TO THE *QUERELLE DE SOPHONISBE*

Chapter One: Before the *Querelle de Sophonisbe*: the example of Pierre Corneille..**13**
    (i) The identity and distribution of *confidents* 14
    (ii) Disguising the imparting of information: opening scenes 16
    (iii) Receiving confidences and giving advice: the later acts....................25
    (iv) Some early variations on the *confident's* role................................35
        (1) The *confident* given a monologue..35
        (2) The *confident* turned conseiller...37
        (3) The *faux confident*..38
        (4) The shared *confident* 41
        (5) The absent *confident*...42

Chapter Two: Theoretical debates: a renewed interest in the *confident(e)* **45**
    (i) Judging the *confident's* role: d'Aubignac, *La Pratique du Théâtre*.....45
    (ii) Polemical positions in the *Querelle de Sophonisbe* 47
    (iii) The evidence of the plays: a comparison between Corneille's *Sophonisbe* and Mlle Desjardins's *Manlius*..56

PART TWO: NEW STRATEGIES

Chapter Three: The eclipse of the *confident* **67**
    (i) Successfully marginalising the *confident*: Rotrou's *Venceslas* 68
    (ii) Eliminating the *confidents* from polymythic plots: Pierre Corneille from *Pertharite* to *Pulchérie* 73
    (iii) Taking up the challenge: Racine's *La Thébaïde* and *Alexandre*........81

Chapter Four: The rebirth of the active *confident*..................................**93**
    (i) The high profile of the *confidents* in *Andromaque* 94
    (ii) *Camma* and *Pausanias*: different strategies and different ends.........101
    (iii) *Tite et Bérénice* and *Bérénice*: confirming the *confidents'* place......106

Chapter Five: The *confident* turned *conseiller* **121**
(i) The legacy of the *conseiller* upon whom the plot turns: Rotrou's *Cosroès* 123
(ii) Tacitean tragedies: the "arcana imperii" in P. Corneille's *Othon* 127
(iii) Tacitean tragedies: the courtiers of Nero in Gilbert's *Arie et Pétus* and Racine's *Britannicus* 135
(iv) An epilogue: the *conseiller* in Racine's biblical tragedies 143

Chapter Six: The strategic exclusion of the *confident* **147**
(i) Heightening suspense in tragi-comedies: Th. Corneille's *Timocrate*..149
(ii) The climate of doubt: Quinault's *Bellérophon* 154
(iii) The climate of suspicion: Racine's *Mithridate* and Pierre Corneille's *Suréna* 159

Chapter Seven: Crossing boundaries: protagonists as *confident(e)s* **175**
(i) The model of tragi-comedies: Magnon's *Tite* 177
(ii) The protagonist as unwilling false *confident(e)*: Racine's *Bérénice* and Thomas Corneille's *Ariane* 179
(iii) Overplaying the role of false *confidente*: Racine's *Bajazet* compared with Pradon's *Phèdre et Hippolyte* 189
(iv) Rejecting the role of the false *confidente*: Racine's *Iphigénie*.........197

Chapter Eight: Conclusions **203**
(i) Evaluating the evolution of the *confident's* role 203
(ii) A final test of confidential strategies: Racine's *Phèdre* 205

Appendices **217**
Appendix One: the use of *confidents*/equivalent characters in Corneille's tragedies and related genres 219
Appendix Two: the use of *confidents*/equivalent characters in Racine's tragedies 223

Bibliography **227**
Primary texts 227
Secondary works 229

Indexes **235**
Index of plays 235
Index of characters 237
General index 243

Acknowledgements

My abiding interest in seventeenth-century French tragedy was born when I was introduced to Racine by Cecily Coney. Like the best teachers of her generation, she combined rigorous scholarship with a great passion for her subject.

Since 1990 I have been privileged to teach seventeenth-century French drama to many undergraduates at King's College London, and to share in lively discussions with my colleagues in the French Department. I owe an earlier debt of gratitude to David Maskell, Marie-Claude Canova-Green, Michael Hawcroft and Sarah Hendry, with whom I took part in "'Monday night play readings" in Oxford for several years. These enjoyable occasions brought home to me the significance of the minutiae of dramaturgical construction, and the relevance of secondary roles, including the *confident(e)s*.

I am particularly grateful to David Clarke and Michael Hawcroft for generously reading a large part of the final draft of this book, and for sharing with me their insights and wise counsel.

I must also express my gratitude to other colleagues at King's College London for their interest and encouragement, especially Professors Richard Griffiths and Simon Gaunt. Without the support of the King's College Centre for Computing in the Humanities (in the person of its Director, Harold Short), the final preparation of the disk would have defeated me.

When I was writing up my research I was fortunate to have a term's sabbatical leave from King's College London and then a British Academy Research Leave Award. In preparing the text for publication, I have been awarded generous financial support by the Modern Humanities Research Association and by the School of Humanities and the Principal, King's College London.

It is a pleasure to record my gratitude to all the libraries which I have used while working on this project, and most particularly to express my thanks to the staff of the Taylor Institution Library, Oxford, for their unfailing co-operation and goodwill.

For errors and shortcomings which remain, I alone am responsible.

Finally, I would like to record my personal thanks to my husband and our children. To be able to draw on a classicist's breadth of knowledge and good judgement has been of immense benefit, while Anastasia and Christopher have shown remarkable patience with my demands for "time to think".

King's College London, 1999

Note on the text

I use self-explanatory short forms of titles throughout (with the year of publication included on the first appearance of a work in the text). Full bibliographical details are given in the Bibliography.

When quoting from a seventeenth-century text, I use the edition listed in the Bibliography. Where I have occasion to refer to more than one edition of a given text, I specify which edition I am citing. In the case of seventeenth-century editions, I have followed the usual conventions of distinguishing *u* and *v*, *i* and *j* and of resolving ampersands, but have retained the original punctuation. In transcribing from modern editions I have followed the conventions of the editor.

For the works of Pierre Corneille and Racine, except for the few occasions where I have specifically indicated to the contrary, I quote from the following editions (selected because most readers are likely to have access to them):

Pierre Corneille, *Œuvres complètes*, ed. G. Couton, 3 vols. Bibliothèque de la Pléiade, Gallimard, Paris, 1980-87.

Jean Racine, *Théâtre complet*, ed. J. Morel and A. Viala, Classiques Garnier, Paris, 1995.

INTRODUCTION

There are few scenes in French classical tragedy which can surpass the poignancy of Andromaque's vivid evocation of the sack of Troy:

> *Songe, songe, Céphise, à cette nuit cruelle*
> *Qui fut pour tout un peuple une nuit éternelle.*
> *(Andromaque, ll.997-8)*

Equally, there are few which haunt us so memorably as Phèdre's terrible resolve to destroy the love of Hippolyte and Aricie:

> *Non, je ne puis souffrir un bonheur qui m'outrage,*
> *Œnone; prends pitié de ma jalouse rage;*
> *Il faut perdre Aricie, il faut de mon époux*
> *Contre un sang odieux réveiller le courroux.*
> *(Phèdre, ll.1257-60)*

If asked to name the most dramatic scenes in either play, we might opt for Hermione's order to Oreste to kill Pyrrhus, or for Thésée's banishment of Hippolyte: in other words, scenes between two main protagonists. Yet it is often the encounters between a main character and *confident(e)*, like those just cited, which are most crucial to the expression of tragic emotions. Without such scenes, classical tragedy would be less able to afford us that uniquely painful pleasure of being the intimate witnesses to human suffering.[1] The *confident(e)* is, quite simply, instrumental to the tragic design.

Claudel became rhapsodic about Racine's *confidents*; he celebrated the "superbe économie" which their roles lent to both the exposition and development of the plays.[2] Yet his is largely a voice in the wilderness. For many critics, from Voltaire onwards, the *confident* has been perceived as an unfortunate artifice, whose ubiquitous presence dispenses us from closer comment except in such rare cases as Narcisse or Œnone, who are raised to the status of individualised characters contributing significantly to the development of the plot.[3] In sharp contrast, the servants in classical comedy are commonly

---

[1] For a concise yet searching appreciation of this paradox, see P. Nurse, "Towards a definition of *le tragique racinien*" (1967).

[2] P. Claudel, *Conversation sur Jean Racine* (1956), p.8.

[3] Voltaire's commentaries on Pierre Corneille's tragedies are peppered with criticisms of the roles of *confidents*. The negative approach has been perpetuated by some twentieth-century critics such as L. Lockert, who dismissed the four *confidents* of *Andromaque* as: "those insipid, colorless figures peculiar to pseudo-classical drama, who have no personality of their own but

acknowledged to be a major factor of a play's success, and thus to justify critical scrutiny. J. Émelina's substantial monograph on the subject, *Les Valets et les servantes dans le théâtre comique en France de 1610 à 1700*, provides more than adequate proof of its rich interest. In comedy servants can be at the epicentre, as the titles of Pierre Corneille's *La Suivante* (1633-4?) or Molière's *Les Fourberies de Scapin* (1671) demonstrate.[4] We would never find a classical tragedy bearing the name of a *confident*.[5] Yet if the *confident* is never the primary focus of a tragedy, nor even the most obvious key to our estimation of the play, it is salutary to remember that the most successful tragedies of the period all share in common the skilful deployment of certain *confident* scenes.

If we look to studies on the material circumstances of Parisian theatres, the significance of *confidents*' roles is again clear. On the basis of S.W. Deierkauf-Holsboer's research, we know that the troupe of the Hôtel de Bourgogne numbered at least eleven actors and actresses throughout the period 1635-80, and usually twelve,[6] while the Théâtre du Marais had a minimum of ten in its troupe between 1648 and its closure in 1673.[7] Given the increasingly strong tendency to limit the number of principal characters in tragedies, we can deduce that either troupe was regularly able to furnish both several male and several female *confidents* if a playwright so desired.[8] What of those playing these roles? One unsympathetic critic, the Abbé d'Aubignac, complained that the *confidentes* were usually played by the worst actresses,[9] and it is true that gazetiers often lavish praise on those in leading roles while passing over the *confidents* in silence. However, H. C. Lancaster's research into the *Repertoire des Comedies françoises qui se peuvent jouer en 1685* furnishes evidence of the seriousness with which troupes at the end of the period provided for the *confidents*.[10] For the plays of Racine which he lists, there is a regular pattern as to which actor or actress plays certain types of secondary role,[11] and there is

---

exist solely to listen to their respective principals, to inform them, advise them, and sympathize with them, and to do their bidding." (*Studies in French Classical Tragedy*, 1958).

   [4] Émelina highlights the significant increase in (male) servants who have the leading role in comedies between 1651-1700, drawing statistics from some 400 surviving comedies of this period: *Les Valets et les servantes* (1975), pp.153-170.

   [5] Nor - as far as I am aware - have modern French playwrights been tempted to write a Gallic equivalent of *Rosencrantz and Guildenstern are Dead*.

   [6] *Le Théâtre de l'Hôtel de Bourgogne*, vol. II (1970).

   [7] *Le Théâtre du Marais*, vol. II (1958).

   [8] Scherer points out that several actors in a troupe would probably have performed only comedies (*La Dramaturgie classique*, 1948, p.37), but this would still have left at least eight to ten actors to cover the main and secondary roles, with "gagistes" employed where necessary for very minor parts.

   [9] See p.50.

   [10] *Actors' Roles at the Comédie Française* (1953).

   [11] For example, Guérin plays a *confident* in 6 of the 9 tragedies listed in the *Repertoire*, as well as understudying another; and la Poisson is *confidente* in 7 of the 9.

usually an understudy for the *confidents*,[12] suggesting that the performance of these roles was considered integral to the success of the play. Furthermore, there are various cases of established actors and actresses who normally secured main parts also on occasion playing the role of a *confident(e)*.[13] In other words, by 1685 actors, like playwrights and audiences, considered the *confident* an essential and respected constituent of the dramatic repertoire.

Given the nearly-ubiquitous presence of *confidents* in French classical tragedy, it is surprising that to date no full-length study has been devoted to an assessment of their evolving role. This lack may in part reflect critics' overwhelming preference for talking about the subject matter and "meaning" of plays rather than their structure. In his recent genetic study of Corneille's theatre, G. Forestier makes the point that most of his predecessors have concentrated on Corneille's *ideas*, whether political, psychological or other, and concludes: "il y a là l'idée que chez Corneille, plus que chez tout autre écrivain, le sens préside à la forme."[14] On the one hand, Forestier suggests that genetic criticism offers the tantalising possibility of entering "l'atelier de l'écrivain, <pour> appréhender les conditions de la fabrique de l'œuvre."[15] When we are studying a period for which almost no manuscripts or revised drafts have come down to us, such an undertaking is, as Forestier admits, "une vaste hypothèse de travail"[16] but it is none the less rewarding for the fresh insights it offers. Secondly, and most significantly from our viewpoint, he argues that for Corneille the structure (*la forme*) precedes the meaning (*le sens*) of the work, and that what most distinguishes Corneille from less successful contemporaries is not his ideas but his masterly exploitation of *la forme* in which they are encased. This approach does not imply that dramaturgy and interpretations of substance are two entirely separate disciplines, but rather that it is by starting from the structural perspective that we can most accurately reach an understanding of the finished work. If we transpose this argument to the work of Racine, we might recall Louis Racine's remark that his father took great pains over the original *canevas* in prose, but saw the subsequent composition in verse as a mere trifle.[17] While few critics would now take Louis

---

[12] For example la Guiot understudies a *confidente* in 6 of the 9 tragedies, and Raisin L 3 out of 9 *confidents*.

[13] Thus le Comte, who in 4 tragedies has the second principal female role, plays a *confidente* (Ismène) in *Phèdre*. La Thuillerie, who plays 4 secondary protagonists (Pharnace, Oreste, Ulysse and Étéocle), also takes on the *confident* roles of Burrhus and Paulin.

[14] *Essai de génétique théâtrale. Corneille à l'œuvre* (1996), p.21.

[15] *Ibid.*, p.13.

[16] *Ibid.*, p.14

[17] *Œuvres de Jean Racine*, ed. P. Mesnard, vol. I, p.268.

Racine at his word, the evidence of the one remaining fragment of *canevas*, the draft for the first act of *Iphigénie en Tauride*, adds credence to the view that Jean Racine worked out the structure in minute detail.[18] Similarly, Racine's annotations of plays of Sophocles and Euripides show his keen interest in the mechanics of entrances, exits, reports of offstage action, and so forth.[19]

The study of a playwright's dramaturgy allows us to understand these creative processes. We are dismantling an entity which we normally perceive only as a completed and unified whole; yet our understanding of the assembly of the machine undoubtedly contributes to our fuller appreciation of why certain scenes are so successful, why certain plays hold the audience rapt through five acts. If we look to seventeenth-century theorists for confirmation of this, even the Abbé d'Aubignac, who put an absolute premium on the playwright maintaining the illusion of reality for the duration of the performance, concedes the interest of our subsequently unravelling "l'ingénieuse économie" of the work.[20]

The seminal analysis of dramaturgy in classical French theatre remains J. Scherer's *La Dramaturgie classique*. It is a tribute to the fullness of Scherer's study that half a century later it has not been totally superseded. Rather, a number of studies have developed our understanding of specific aspects of the dramaturgical process: the use of monologues and *récits*,[21] *stances*,[22] and so forth. The present work fulfils the same brief with regard to the *confident*. Scherer had devoted part of a chapter to the subject, sketching out some of the main stages in the development of the *confident* and highlighting some milestones.[23] However, his analysis is necessarily schematic and suggestive rather than comprehensive, and, as we shall see shortly, he does not ask some of the questions which seem to me most significant. In addition, since Scherer's work, critics have become increasingly sensitive to the significance of rhetoric in classical tragedy.[24] I would argue that an appreciation of the dramaturgical function of the *confident* must now necessarily be accompanied by an analysis of the characters' patterns of discourse.

On a smaller scale, there are four articles providing broad analyses of the *confident* in French classical tragedy or in the work of Racine. Together they indicate a variety of approaches, some very fruitful, others less so, and I wish to

---

[18] It is noteworthy that the role of a *confident* is included in the draft.

[19] R. Knight, who has studied Racine's marginal annotations closely, concludes, "c'est la dramaturgie que Racine place ici au premier plan." (*Racine et la Grèce*, 1974 edition, p.212.)

[20] *Dissertations contre Corneille*, ed. N. Hammond and M. Hawcroft (1995), p.10.

[21] N. Ekstein, *Dramatic Narrative: Racine's récits* (1986).

[22] M.-F. Hilgar, *La Mode des stances dans le théâtre tragique français, 1610-87* (1974).

[23] *La Dramaturgie classique*, pp. 39-50.

[24] Among recent studies we might cite M. Fumaroli on Corneille (*Héros et orateurs*, 1990), and M. Hawcroft (*Word as Action: Racine, Rhetoric and Theatrical Language*, 1992) and H. Phillips (*Racine: Language and Theatre*, 1994) on Racine.

establish at the outset to what extent I shall draw upon them. The earliest is J. Fermaud's, which seeks to challenge the view that as a character the *confident* is "invraisemblable". His argument is summed up in his claim that: "ce confident de la tragédie classique n'est pas une *utilité*, mais bel et bien une réalité vivante."[25] By reference to memoirs of the late Renaissance and early seventeenth century, he shows how historical figures had functions analogous to those of *confidents* in later plays. On the one hand, his approach reminds us that the rise of the *confident* may echo social *mores* of the period, but on the other hand it has the distinct limitation of refusing to admit a possible divorce between reality and fictional/dramatic conventions.

This problem does not arise in H. Lawton's study, "The Confidant in and before French Classical Tragedy"(1943). Lawton's purpose is twofold: to trace the history of the confidant through Greek, Roman and Renaissance tragedy, and to define the essence of the *confident*'s function in French classical tragedy. His historical survey remains useful for its thoroughness, demonstrating that the *confident* is present in Greek plays, especially those of Euripides, as well as the Latin tradition of Seneca and Renaissance reworkings of classical tragedy.[26] However, his aim of showing a historical continuum is weakened by the jump he makes from the late Renaissance to Corneille and Racine, with only the briefest allusion to Hardy and Mairet. On the tragedies of the earlier seventeenth century, Scherer is more helpful, and refines Lawton's assumption that the rise of the *confident* is simply coincidental with the demise of the chorus.[27] As far as the function of the *confident* is concerned, Lawton observes that the role serves particularly "to exteriorize the interior debate" of a main protagonist.[28] With this statement, we can generally agree. However, in expanding upon his thesis Lawton joins a critical tradition of assuming that the *confident*'s identity is limited to that of a "double" of the protagonist, for he argues that the *confident* regularly represents one side of the main character. This seems to me too restrictive a definition of the secondary role.[29] In that protagonists face dilemmas, *confidents* must on occasion necessarily support a particular case corresponding to one side of the protagonist's own arguments, but this does not mean that the *confident* can normally be reduced to an allegorical cipher.[30] Such a theory does not do justice to either the

---

[25] "Défense du confident" (1940), p.340.

[26] I shall discuss in chapters 3 and 4 the relationship between Racine's conception of the *confident* and the chorus/secondary characters of Greek tragedy.

[27] See Lawton, *art.cit.*, p.19 and Scherer, *La Dramaturgie classique*, pp. 39-40.

[28] *Ibid.*, p.28

[29] Compare the criticism of Lawton's theory in J. Lapp, *Aspects of Racinian Tragedy* (1955), p.9.

[30] Claudel furnishes another example of critics perpetuating this reductive definition, when he enthuses over the *confident*'s role as a "reflet évocateur" and "un écho" (*Conversation sur Jean Racine*, p.9).

dramaturgical or rhetorical variations which are evident in successful tragedies of the period.

Fermaud and Lawton are both concerned to produce a synthesis, and do not provide detailed analysis of individual plays. In contrast, two other critics concentrate on particular aspects of the Racinian *confident*.[31] M. Olga's article "Vers une esthétique du confident racinien" (1964) promised to be the first stage in a fuller evaluation of the Racinian *confident*, but the project was not taken further. Olga's initial premiss is one with which I agree fully: that Racine renewed the tradition of the *confident*, as he did other elements of tragedy. Although the article appears to overlook some earlier publications,[32] contains some inaccuracies,[33] and leaves out of account Racine's first two plays,[34] it nonetheless establishes some important lines of approach. In particular, Olga shows how Racine skilfully employs *confidents* as a dramaturgical device to increase our appreciation of the tragic outcome, and argues that some scenes with *confidents* achieve more subtle effects than a meeting between main protagonists could have done. On one essential point, however, I would question Olga's judgement. The article proposes that "Par ses questions et ses commentaires, le confident devient le spectateur idéal, notre délégué sur la scène".[35] Like Fermaud's idea that we should see the *confident* as epitomising one side of a character, Olga's thesis puts the *confident* in a straitjacket. Certainly the *confident* may contribute to the exposition of what the spectator wishes to discover, but *confidents'* acts of speech are determined by the context of a particular scene. The *confident* must be perceived to be participating in a dialogue, not standing above it.[36] Some *confidents'* views are more naive than those of the spectator; other *confidents* have their own purposes which determine their response. Thus Olga's article is significant for our work in its

---

[31] An article by M. Monaco appears from its title to offer promising insights into the Racinian *confident*: "Racine's naming of 'Greek' confidantes and handmaidens" (1961). However, Monaco's comparisons between classical works Racine may have read and the significance of the names of his *confidentes* remain highly speculative. For different reasons, I mention only in passing here C.J. Gossip's account of the function of some of the *confidents* in one play by each of Mairet, Pierre Corneille and Racine. Despite its broad title ("The Language of *confidence* in French Classical Tragedy", 1992) the article draws on only a narrow range of examples.

[32] Notably Lawton and Scherer.

[33] *Pulchérie* is not the only play of Pierre Corneille to omit the *confident* (*art.cit.* p.3); *Pertharite* also did.

[34] Olga does not perceive their crucial interest for our understanding of Racine's reaction to the *Querelle du confident*. See below.

[35] *Art.cit.*, p.10. The term "notre délégué sur la scène" had already been used by G. Le Bidois in *La Vie dans la tragédie de Racine* (6th edition 1929), p.156.

[36] H. Phillips explores the way in which the acts of speech of all of Racine's characters are shaped by the context in which they occur: *Racine, Language and Theatre*, chapter 2.

definition of an area ripe for fuller study, but the lines of argument pursued are of unequal merit.

The other article to attempt an overview of the Racinian *confident* is G. Schrammen's "Zur Funktion des *confident* bei Racine" (1970). Schrammen is well acquainted with earlier critical literature on the subject, but proposes a fresh thesis. He does not see the Racinian *confident* as an echo or double of his master, but rather as a character designed to articulate opposition. Through a close analysis of *Andromaque*, he establishes how the *confident* systematically argues against the protagonist by exposing the viewpoint of another character.[37] Selected examples from other plays support this theory, but Schrammen prudently refrains from claiming that he has uncovered a single or universal formula. What he has done is to bring to the fore the significance of the principle of opposition or conflict in Racine's handling of the *confident*.

Additionally, we should not overlook the fact that many studies of leading playwrights, especially of Racine, have broached the issue of the *confident* at least in passing.[38] At the turn of the century, G. Le Bidois devoted a sensitive and sympathetic chapter of *La Vie dans la tragédie de Racine* to the Racinian *confident*, arguing that it is peculiar to Racine's theatre that *confidents* not only contribute to the revelation of the protagonists' states of mind and feelings, but also actively influence their conduct. Subsequently J. Lapp, R. Barthes and O. de Mourgues, among others, have devoted short sections to the secondary role.[39] M. Hawcroft's recent work on Racine's handling of the rhetorical category of *dispositio* includes a chapter on the speeches of the *confidents*.[40] While Hawcroft acknowledges that a full study of the Racinian *confident* is not within his scope, he advances our understanding considerably. His main argument complements the conclusions of Schrammen, by demonstrating the interest of the *confidents'* argumentative strategies.

In brief, earlier critics have established some overviews of the classical *confident*, surveyed the use of analogous devices in tragedies of Greek and Roman Antiquity and the Renaissance, and given detailed accounts of the workings of the *confident* in isolated plays. With the exception of a brief discussion in Hawcroft's book,[41] however, none has looked closely at the impact of seventeenth-century debates on the *confident*, and this is one of the major

---

[37] E.g. Cléone speaks to Hermione using the same arguments as Oreste would do.

[38] Cornelian criticism has accorded *confidents* less attention. I would suggest that this reflects both the general view that Cornelian *confidents* play a less significant role, and the fact that the scope and diversity of Pierre Corneille's tragic *œuvre* make reductive generalisations particularly difficult.

[39] See respectively: *Aspects of Racinian Tragedy*, pp.83-87; *Sur Racine* (1963), pp.55-57; *Racine or the Triumph of Relevance* (1967), pp. 105-111.

[40] *Word as Action*, pp.160-182.

[41] *Ibid.* , pp.162-7.

reasons why I believe this study offers a new starting point, as well as a fuller account of what I shall term "confidential strategies".

In the decades when the conventions of classical tragedy were becoming established in France, the *confident* was regularly employed by most playwrights, but was not the subject of sustained critical scrutiny. While debates raged over issues of *bienséance*, or the exact observance of the unity of time or the rule of the *liaison des scènes*, the *confident* escaped closer attention. An overview of Pierre Corneille's tragedies from *Médée* to *Nicomède* in Chapter 1 demonstrates the recurrence of certain regular functions fulfilled by *confidents*, but also the degree of freedom enjoyed by the playwright in his exploitation of this dramaturgical tool. It is only in the *Querelle du confident*, part of the *Querelle de Sophonisbe* of 1663, that the *confident* comes to occupy centrestage. For a brief while, in a kind of "Alice in Wonderland" scenario, *confidents* eclipse main characters in terms of critical interest. In analysing the debate in Chapter 2, I both identify key statements on the role of *confidents*, and also consider the wider import of the exchanges. Just as the *Querelle du Cid*, born of a rivalry between Scudéry and Pierre Corneille, afforded playwrights, critics and audiences the opportunity to re-evaluate the balance between the aesthetic and moral functions of literature, so in 1663 the *Querelle de Sophonisbe* went beyond the long-standing differences separating d'Aubignac and Corneille to embrace a series of reflections on the nature of dramatic illusion. The debate probably had some effect upon Corneille's conception of the *confident* in his subsequent tragedies, but it is above all the work of Racine which suggests that the *Querelle* fuelled a desire for experimentation with an unpromising role.

As chance had it, it was in 1663 that Racine was about to commence the composition of *La Thébaïde*. Although we do not have his correspondence from this period to inform us of his reading, he could hardly have failed to be aware of the debate. The evidence that he perceived some of the challenges posed by d'Aubignac's criticisms is, I believe, furnished by his handling of the *confident* in his own plays. In Chapter 3, I argue that the minimal role accorded to *confidents* in *La Thébaïde* and the total elimination of such characters in *Alexandre* can be read as a direct response to the *Querelle*. Yet the dramaturgical experiments brought new problems: if *confidents* were not to be used, alternative strategies were necessary, some more cumbersome than the device they replaced. The absence of *confidents* was a bold move in *Alexandre*; equally bold, and far more successful, was the reintroduction of not one or two but four *confidents* in *Andromaque*. From *Andromaque* to *Athalie*, *confidents* continue to occupy a key place in each Racinian tragedy. However, as I explore in Chapters 4-7, Racine does not follow a static formula or simply the established practices of his predecessors. Instead, influenced by his admiration for Greek tragedy and by his study of Sophocles' and Euripides' use of the chorus and secondary characters, he reinvests the *confident* with a new energy and vigour, and experiments with a variety of high-profile strategies. While critics have long acknowledged the power of the characters of Narcisse, Burrhus and Œnone, I wish to argue that Racine uses nearly all his *confidents* in a particularly thoughtful and exciting fashion.

The reappraisal of this element of Racine's dramaturgy is one of the main purposes of this study. Hence Chapters 4-7 are grouped around the development of key patterns in Racine's work. I respect broadly the chronological order of his tragedies, but do not suggest that he follows one single line. Thus, I look at *Bérénice* together with *Andromaque* as examples of the "rebirth of the active *confident*" (Chapter 4). In the following chapter I return to *Britannicus* in the context of a full investigation of the interface between the roles of *confident* and political *conseiller*. In Chapter 6, I look ahead to *Mithridate* to illustrate how the isolation of a main character is achieved by the strategic exclusion of a *confident*. *Bajazet* is then grouped with *Iphigénie* (Chapter 7) to explore the romanesque device of a protagonist taking on a false role as *confident(e)* to a rival. Finally *Phèdre* provides an ultimate test for fresh readings of the *confident* in Chapter 8. Racine's religious tragedies lie outside the chronological scope of this volume by some ten to fifteen years, and raise quite unique dramaturgical issues by virtue of their choruses. However, their use of *confidents* demonstrates some intriguing parallels with *Britannicus*, and so they feature briefly in an epilogue at the end of Chapter 5.

It will be evident that on the one hand I see this book as a contribution to Racinian studies. On the other hand it is impossible to reassess Racine's work in isolation. Thus, my second and complementary aim has been to explore how far the use of *confidents* contributed to the dramatic or thematic interest of other tragedies of the period. In each of Chapters 3-8 I have compared Racine's approach with a number of plays which rely on similar dramaturgical patterns.[42] My discussion has concentrated upon the close reading of selected tragedies and I have not attempted a large-scale statistical survey.[43] While some scholars such as J. Émelina[44] or G. Forestier[45] have used the latter approach most fruitfully to further our understanding of theatrical trends in the seventeenth century, *confidents'* roles did not easily lend themselves to quantative analysis. However, in selecting the range of tragedies (and several

---

[42] For a full key to plays discussed, see the Index.

[43] However, the two Appendices at the end of this work provide statistics on the use of *confidents* in all the tragedies of Pierre Corneille and Racine.

[44] *Les Valets et les servantes*.

[45] *L'Esthétique de l'identité dans le théâtre français (1550-1680)*, (1988).

tragicomedies) for discussion, I sought a balance between works representative
of widespread practices and others which merit inclusion precisely because they
are exceptional. It is always difficult to establish precise borrowings or debts
between seventeenth-century playwrights, but there is a general consensus that
in the decades 1660-1680 the best-known writers observed each other's
fortunes closely, even jealously. As far as confidential strategies are concerned,
Racine both sets the pace, being imitated by others (including Pierre Corneille
in some of his later works), but also reworks some ideas suggested by the plays
of his predecessors and rivals, notably Rotrou and Thomas Corneille. It is by
considering Racine alongside such authors as Boyer, Pierre and Thomas
Corneille, Mlle Desjardins, Gilbert, Magnon, Pradon, Quinault and Rotrou that
we can best measure general developments in the use of the *confident* in the
period. And on this basis we can make an informed judgement about the ways
in which confidential strategies could be fundamental to a play's success.

PART I.

FAMILIAR PRACTICES AND CRITICAL VOICES: FROM *MÉDÉE* TO THE *QUERELLE DE SOPHONISBE*

CHAPTER ONE

BEFORE THE *QUERELLE DE SOPHONISBE*: THE EXAMPLE OF PIERRE CORNEILLE

It would be impossible to draw a blueprint of "the universal *confident*", even before the *Querelle de Sophonisbe* in 1663. Precisely because the role was perceived as a dramaturgical tool, playwrights were free to adapt it to their requirements. Nonetheless we can identify some recurrent patterns in tragedies composed in the preceding thirty years. In this chapter I propose to draw upon the tragedies from the earlier part of Pierre Corneille's career –from *Médée* (1635) to *Nicomède* (1651)[46]– to explore both the standard functions of the *confident* and some of the more interesting ways in which the role could be extended. The choice of Corneille has several obvious advantages, not least that his plays will be sufficiently familiar to most readers to allow me to make comparisons across the range of his work. More substantially, it was Corneille's vision of tragedy which prompted d'Aubignac's attack in the *Querelle de Sophonisbe*, and the latter's specific criticisms of the *confidentes* of *Sophonisbe* (to be discussed in Chapter 2) are best understood within the broader context of Corneille's dramaturgy. Finally, for playwrights of the period 1660-1680, the earlier tragedies of Pierre Corneille remained a particularly powerful model.

It is important to establish at the outset that this discussion of Pierre Corneille's earlier works is necessarily partial. In later chapters of this study I shall be focusing on individual plays by various dramatists (including several later tragedies by Corneille) in order to examine ways in which our appreciation of confidential strategies can open up new readings of a *whole* work. In this chapter, however, I am concerned for the most part with single scenes, selected because they allow us to examine the detailed processes of dramaturgical construction. This angle may sometimes seem distant from the nub of Cornelian tragedy, but it is through the successful assembly of such constituent parts that the machinery of tragedy can effect its sway over the minds and emotions of the audience.

---

[46] Unless otherwise indicated, all dates throughout this study relate to the first performance rather than the publication of a play.

(i) THE IDENTITY AND DISTRIBUTION OF *CONFIDENTS*

At the start of our analysis we need to ask which characters can be classed as *confidents*, and what patterns govern the distribution of their roles. Scherer addressed both issues in *La Dramaturgie classique*, but could produce only approximate answers. Characters acting as *confidents* bear a wide range of nomenclatures, and the examples to be discussed from Cornelian tragedy will reveal some of the complexities. On the frequency with which tragedies use *confidents*, Scherer summarised his findings in the following pithy phrase: "Après le confident triomphant, le confident honteux".[47] The period 1635-45 is singled out as the heyday when "l'enthousiasme pour le confident est à son comble".[48] Since this is the decade which coincides with the rise of French classical tragedy, one might argue that the parallel rise of the *confident* simply marks the acceptance of one of the many conventions of the genre. What is less predictable in Scherer's schema is the *confident*'s fall from grace. He does not date the change in taste precisely,[49] still less account for it. My research leads me to agree that *confidents* generally become less numerous, or play less significant parts, in tragedies of the mid 1640s and 1650s. I shall use Pierre Corneille's tragedies to develop this observation and to suggest some possible reasons for it.

All of Corneille's tragedies from 1635-1651 contain various characters who can be considered to fulfil functions akin to a *confident*.[50] The one exception according to the list of *dramatis personae* is the last of these plays, *Pertharite*, to which I shall return in chapter 3. As Scherer reminds us, the fluctuations in the names for secondary roles equivalent to *confident* do not necessarily allow us to read great significance into the chosen nomenclatures.[51] If we look at Cornelian tragedies of this earlier period, we find (leaving aside characters whose function is strictly limited to that of silent attendant or messenger): [52]

---

[47] J. Scherer, *La Dramaturgie classique en France*, p.46

[48] *Ibid.* p.46

[49] The observation that "Après la Fronde les choses ont bien changé" (*ibid.* p.47) is too imprecise to help.

[50] I do not include *Andromède* in the present discussion since as a machine play it posed quite different dramaturgical challenges (nor, for the same reason, *La Toison d'Or* when I discuss Corneille's later works). However, I do include *Don Sanche*, Corneille's first *comédie héroïque*, which is dramaturgically closer to his tragedies. (On the genre of *Don Sanche* see A. Stegmann, *L'Héroïsme cornélien*, 1968, vol. II, p.608.)

[51] *La Dramaturgie classique*, p.40. Compare Émelina's discussion of the range of terms used to designate servants in classical comedy (*Les Valets et les servantes*, pp.19-55). S. Dosmond's recent article on "Les confident(e)s dans le théâtre comique de Corneille" (1998) takes into account the nomenclatures: *domestique, écuyer, femme de chambre, nourrice, servante, suivante, valet.*

[52] For example Polyclète and Évandre, the *affranchis* of Auguste and Cinna, or Fabian and Cléon, the *domestiques* of Sévère and Félix.

affranchi: Euphorbe in *Cinna*.

ami: Amyntas in *Héraclius*.[53]

capitaine des gardes: Araspe in *Nicomède*.

confident(e): Julie in *Horace* (styled "dame romaine confidente de Sabine et de Camille");[54] Fulvie in *Cinna*; Stratonice and Albin in *Polyeucte*; Paulin and Stéphanie in *Théodore*; Laonice in *Rodogune*; Cléone in *Nicomède*.

dame d'honneur: Charmion in *La Mort de Pompée*; Blanche in *Don Sanche*.

gouverneur/gouvernante: Cléone in *Médée*; Léonor in *Le Cid*; Timagène in *Rodogune*.

suivante: Nérine in *Médée*; Elvire in *Le Cid*.[55]

Each of these characters can be considered akin to a *confident* in at least some respects. For ease of reference, I shall therefore use the general term *confidents* in the subsequent discussion to include all of those designated above.

What all these secondary characters share in common is their relationship with a main protagonist. Conventionally each *confident*-type character exists exclusively in relation to one main character. Hence *confidents*' appearances are mainly confined to occasions when they accompany the designated protagonist, unless they have a message to deliver or are used to narrate a death offstage in the last act.[56] Most significantly, such characters have no interest for the spectator in their own right; their fortunes depend on those of the characters they serve. Their appearance is a dramaturgical device which is justified only if it is not abused and if the scenes in which they appear carry dramatic or emotional force.

In plays of this period there is not an accompanying *confident* for every main protagonist. The symmetry of four main characters plus four *confidents* which distinguishes Racine's *Andromaque* or Corneille's *Tite et Bérénice* is unknown.[57] Corneille's earlier plays have a relatively large cast; almost all the

---

[53] The term *ami(e)* must be treated with caution, however, since it can refer either to a purely functional secondary character or to a major character of interest in his/her own right. For example in *Polyeucte* Néarque is styled "seigneur arménien, ami de Polyeucte".

[54] On the potential significance of the epithet "dame romaine" see S. Doubrovsky, *Corneille et la dialectique du héros*, p.138.

[55] Elvire was styled *suivante* in the 1637 text, but in response to the criticisms expressed in the *Sentiments de l'Académie*, Corneille elevated her to *gouvernante* in editions from 1660.

[56] On the latter point see Scherer, *La Dramaturgie classique*, p.46.

[57] On these later plays see Chapter 4. The nearest we come in the earlier period of Corneille's theatre is *Polyeucte*, in which Félix, Sévère and Pauline have *confidents*, but Polyeucte and Néarque do not.

tragedies before 1660 list at least nine named characters.[58] Hence, not all main characters require or could sustain a *confident*. Some confide in another protagonist, others appear sufficiently infrequently that we need learn no more about them. We can thus draw the preliminary conclusion that Corneille creates secondary characters only where they have a clear function.

The essence of the *confidents'* roles may be summarised under four headings:

(1) Facilitating the exposition, especially of political complexities.

(2) Receiving confidences which serve to reveal the thoughts and passions of the main character, and (on occasions) offering confidential advice.

(3) Bearing messages.

(4) Delivering a final *récit* of offstage action, especially of the death of a main character.

These third and fourth offices are not specific to the *confident*; the task could be (and often was) performed by a main character. I shall not therefore examine them further in their own right at this juncture.[59] It is the first and second functions which constitute the mainstay of the *confidents'* purpose, but which, by the same token, were even in the 1630s and 1640s the source of some anxiety.

(ii) DISGUISING THE IMPARTING OF INFORMATION: OPENING SCENES

Scherer claims that it is standard for tragedies to open with a scene between a main character and *confident*,[60] and this is paralleled by Émelina's findings for comedies of this period.[61] Yet even if we allow for the blurring of the distinction between *confident* and *ami*, only four of Corneille's tragedies from *Médée* to *Nicomède* conform to this conventional opening,[62] and of these *Polyeucte* employs the pairing of Néarque and Polyeucte, whose relationship will be one of the main sources of dramatic interest as the play unfolds. Looking back at *Médée* with the accumulated wisdom of some twenty years,

---

[58] The exceptions are *Rodogune* which has 7, *Nicomède* which has 8 and *Pertharite* which has 6.

[59] See p.113 on the bearing of messages in Racine's *Bérénice*.

[60] *La Dramaturgie classique*, p.46.

[61] His statistics show that opening scenes between master and male servant were the most common, followed by those between mistress and female servant.

[62] Pollux and Jason in *Médée*, Sabine and Julie in *Horace*, Polyeucte and Néarque in *Polyeucte*, and Placide and Cléobule in *Théodore*. The last two cases use an *ami* whose importance goes beyond that of a *confident*.

Corneille ponders in the *Examen* on the disadvantages of employing a protactic character for the exposition. His comments are central to our discussion since they highlight general as well as particular dramaturgical problems. The fact the the *confident* must assume a passive role as listener is identified as the key weakness of such expository scenes:

> *Pollux est de ces Personnages protatiques qui ne sont introduits que pour écouter la narration du Sujet.*[63]

In our analysis of the way in which dramatists respond to the *Querelle de Sophonisbe*, we shall see that the drive to make the *confident* an active participant is crucial.

On a second level, Corneille is alert to the difficulty of creating a situation in which it is *vraisemblable* for the main character to rehearse past events at length.

> *Je pense l'avoir déjà dit, et j'ajoute que ces Personnages sont d'ordinaire assez difficiles à imaginer dans la Tragédie, parce que les événements publics et éclatants dont elle est composée sont connus de tout le monde, et que s'il est aisé de trouver des gens qui les sachent pour les raconter, il n'est pas aisé d'en trouver qui les ignorent pour les entendre.*[64]

In the case of *Médée*, the problem is resolved by recourse to the traditional device of a character returning from a journey.[65] Thus, in his initial meeting with Jason, the protactic character can ask a series of questions, starting with:

> *Quoi! Médée est donc morte à ce compte? (l.7)*

> *Dieux! et que fera-t-elle? (l.9)*

Likewise he can express surprise at the changes which have occurred since his departure:

> *Il <Pélie> est mort! (l.43)*

In his critical edition of *Médée*, A. de Leyssac points out that Corneille has eschewed a simple imitation of either Euripides' opening scene with the Nurse or the tirade of Seneca's Medea. Nonetheless, the invented scene is evidently contrived. Its effectiveness depends entirely upon our interest in the portentous events recounted, for the exchange between characters lacks vigour.[66]

---

[63] P. Corneille, *Œuvres complètes*, vol. I, p.538.

[64] *Ibid.*, p.538.

[65] On the use of this by other dramatists see Scherer, *La Dramaturgie classique*, p.57.

[66] For example, Pollux warns Jason about the dangers of incurring Médée's wrath, but only in the most tentative terms: "Bien que de tous côtés l'affaire résolue/ Ne laisse aucune place aux conseils d'un ami,/ Je ne puis toutefois l'approuver qu'à demi." (ll.138-40).

In his next two tragedies, Corneille opts for the formula of an opening scene between a main character and a *confidente*. This presents an obvious obstacle: how the exposition can be made convincing when both characters present already know the facts. In the introduction to his critical edition of *Le Cid*, Forestier points out that this is a key concern of theoreticians in the 1650s, including d'Aubignac. But twenty years earlier, the Académie was equally troubled by the same issue. Corneille's first version of *Le Cid* had a short opening scene of 32 lines between Elvire and Don Gomès. However, it was judged inappropriate to the dignity of a tragedy that a mere *suivante* should discourse on the possible marriage of her mistress with the Comte. In 1660, Corneille eliminated this scene, and had the play open with the conversation between Elvire and Chimène. In the revised edition he resorts to the rather clumsy device of making Chimène ask Elvire to repeat her account of the interview with Don Gomès:

> *Dis-moi donc, je te prie, une seconde fois*
> *Ce qui te fait juger qu'il approuve mon choix.*
> *(1660: ll.7-8).*

Elvire duly obliges Chimène (and the spectator), providing a résumé of what had been said in the original version of the opening scene (1660: ll. 17-52). One gain in the later version, noted by Forestier,[67] is the shift towards deliberative rhetoric, since Elvire's speech is designed to reassure rather than merely inform Chimène. Such a preference for deliberative rather than demonstrative language is characteristic of many of the most successful expositions in French classical tragedy.

In *Horace*, from the first version Corneille concentrates not on the imparting of news but on the expression of a critical state of mind and feeling. The scene is carried along by the force of Sabine's contradictory sentiments, as wife of Horace, yet daughter of Alba, and her opening line sets the tone with the plea to Julie:

> *Approuvez ma foiblesse, et souffrez ma douleur.*

In her account of her conflicting loyalties, Sabine conveys the background to us without losing the emotional momentum. Her impassioned apostrophe to Rome and Alba in turn[68] shows the heights to which the exposition can be taken. We should note, though, that the *confidente* is still little more than a passive listener, however great the declamation to which she is witness. Julie ventures several comments to prompt further speeches from Sabine, but the drama of the scene does not lie in the exchange between characters.

---

[67] P. Corneille, *Le Cid 1637-1660* (1992), p.XXXVI.

[68] "Albe, mon cher pays, et mon premier amour..." (ll.30-32) and "'Rome, si tu te plains que c'est là te trahir..." (ll.33-60). For a fuller discussion of the style and emotional impact of this scene, see S. Harwood-Gordon, *The Poetic Style of Corneille's Tragedies* (1989), pp.72-73.

Corneille's dramaturgical experiments do not often follow an uninterrupted path. Thus, while intervening plays exploit alternative formulae for the opening scene, it is not until *Rodogune* that he returns to the use of the *confident*, but this time with a surprising difference, namely that the exposition is spoken between two *confidents*.[69] As Corneille turns to increasingly less well-known and complex plots, so the exposition becomes more difficult to construct.[70] Certainly Laonice's report to her brother Timagène does justice to the intricacies of the situation; indeed, it could hardly fail to do so since it occupies two long scenes (I.1 has 71 lines, I.4 has 88). However, as Corneille reluctantly acknowledges in the *Examen*, his critics had grounds for censure;[71] a less dynamic opening would be hard to imagine, and he cannot deny that it lacks *artifice*.[72] First, it is not *vraisemblable* that Timagène should depend upon his sister Laonice's report of the developments which have taken place in his absence, and in this respect the opening of *Rodogune* compares unfavourably even with the contrived exposition to *Médée*, as Corneille acknowledges in the *Examen* to the later play. Secondly, and here we return to the main problem encountered in *Médée*, the exchanges are no more than the passive transmission of information. This is betrayed by Timagène's use of the verb *apprendre*:

> *Pour le mieux admirer trouvez bon, je vous prie,*
> *Que j'apprenne de vous les troubles de Syrie.*
>   *(ll.23-4)*

and Laonice's use of the imperative *Sachez*:

> *Sachez donc que Tryphon après quatre batailles...*
>   *(l.43)*

Perhaps aware that he had too much material to convey in a single scene of this nature, Corneille has Laonice interrupt her *récit* after some 28 lines with the words:

> *Je vous achèverai le reste une autre fois,*
> *Un des Princes survient.*
>   *(ll.70-71)*

---

[69] A strategy which Scherer suggests belongs primarily to comedy (*La Dramaturgie classique*, p.60). Émelina oberves, however, that opening scenes between two servants are not common (*Les Valets et les servantes*, pp.80-81).

[70] Corneille voices this concern in the *Examen* to *Cinna*, distinguishing between his "<pièces> simples" and the "pièces embarrassées, qu'en termes de l'Art on nomme *implexes*, par un mot emprunté du Latin, telles que sont *Rodogune* et *Héraclius*."

[71] "On a fait tant d'objections contre la narration de Laonice au premier acte, qu'il est malaisé de ne donner pas les mains à quelques-unes."

[72] "J'avoue qu'elle est sans artifice, et qu'on la fait de sang-froid à un personnage protatique...".

The appearance of Antiochus and then Séleucus injects considerable interest
into the first act, but upon their departure Timagène and Laonice are allowed
only four lines of comment before the conclusion of the expository *récit* is
requested and duly delivered:

> TIMAGÈNE
> *Mais de grâce, achevez l'histoire commencée.*
>
> LAONICE
> *Pour la reprendre donc où nous l'avons laissée,*
>   *Les Parthes au combat par les nôtres forcés ...*
>   *(ll.215-7)*

Her long, uninterrupted account (ll.216-88) is designed to sustain the
audience's curiosity about Cléopâtre, whose entrance is cleverly delayed until
Act II. However, in his *Examen* Corneille acknowledges that the exposition does
not engage the audience's emotions:

> *La narration ne laisse pas de demeurer froide comme celle-ci, parce qu'il ne
> s'est encore rien passé dans la pièce qui excite la curiosité de l'auditeur, ni qui
> lui puisse donner quelque émotion en l'écoutant.*[73]

The key phrases here are *demeurer froid(e)* and *donner quelque émotion*, which
are precisely the grounds on which Corneille's opponents will attack his use of
confidents in the *Querelle de Sophonisbe*. If Corneille's own *Examens*
anticipate the criticisms of d'Aubignac and others, it is a clear sign of a new
critical focus emerging around 1660.

      The foregoing examples demonstrate the problems presented by the use of
a *confident* to open a play, but what of the alternatives? Do they have obvious
advantages, and to what extent does Corneille still rely on scenes with *confidents*
later in the first Act? The tragedies before *Pertharite* illustrate several common
devices. That closest to the *confident* is the use of two main characters related to
each other. This at once makes the meeting plausible and affords a degree of
intimacy to the exchange, but at the same time it is not easy for the dramatist to
give the characters good reason for labouring over old terrain. Corneille
employs this device in the two tragedies which followed *Rodogune*, *Héraclius*
(1646/7) and *Don Sanche* (1649/50). In *Héraclius* Phocas analyses his fears
and receives the counsel of Crispe, his *gendre*. Although Crispe is scarcely more
than a protactic character, saying little in the rest of the play, and being
confined essentially to the function of a messenger,[74] in the *Examen* Corneille
defends this exposition in contrast with that of *Rodogune*:

---

[73] P. Corneille, *Œuvres complètes*, vol. II, p.201.
[74] He brings Léontine to Phocas in IV.4, and announces the triumph of Exupère in V.4.

> *Cette tragédie a encore plus d'effort d'invention que celle de Rodogune ... Sa conduite diffère de celle-là, en ce que les narrations qui lui donnent jour sont pratiquées par occasion en divers lieux avec adresse, et toujours dites, et écoutées avec intérêt, sans qu'il y en ait pas une de sang-froid, comme celle de Laonice.*[75]

The *Examen* underlines the fact that there is a genuine exchange between Phocas and Crispe. Phocas conveys to Crispe and the spectator his strong sense of foreboding, while Crispe responds with urgent advice, underscored by his use of imperatives: "Mais pressez cet Hymen" (1.63), "Qu'il vous laisse un neveu" (1.70), and "Il faut agir de force avec de tels esprits" (1.87).[76] The exposition between the Queen of Aragon and her daughter provides *Don Sanche* with an equally vigorous opening. A dramatic conflict is established at the outset as mother and daughter debate the choice of husband for the princess. There is a significant difference between this *comédie héroïque* and most of Corneille's other plays, however, in that the plot is fictional and thus the focus is on the affairs of the heart. Background matters of state can be summarised cursorily, so that the challenge of the exposition is simpler.

Most expository scenes are confined to two characters (we shall consider the rare exceptions below). Effectively this leaves the dramatist with four options: *confident*-main character; *confident-confident*; two related main characters; two unrelated main characters. The last of these is the least commonly employed by all playwrights, even though we might imagine it would offer the most interesting confrontation. However, such a scene requires not only that the dramatist contrive a meeting between the two protagonists, but also that their exchange be at once comprehensible to the audience and sufficiently dramatic. We may suspect that many playwrights preferred to avoid firing their big shots first.[77] Racine, the consummate master of rationing scenes between main characters so that we savour them to the full, never opens a play with two unrelated main characters on stage. Corneille does so on only two occasions in his earlier tragedies, namely with Néarque and Polyeucte, and with Nicomède and Laodice. We have already established that as an *ami* Néarque is at once a

---

[75] P. Corneille, *Œuvres complètes*, vol. II, p.358.

[76] This is in sharp contrast to the tentative advice proffered by Pollux in the exposition of *Médée*. See above.

[77] Émelina observes that it is rare for comedies to open with scenes between major protagonists. However, Molière provides an interesting exception to the rule: 14 out of his 29 plays do *not* use a servant in the opening scene (*Les Valets et les servantes*, pp.86-87).

confident to Polyeucte, and yet of significance in his own right.[78] The tone of the scene is similar to that of the opening of *Héraclius*: Polyeucte expresses his fears (occasioned by Pauline's dream) and Néarque vigorously argues against them, using forceful imperatives.[79] The conflict of Polyeucte's divided loyalties is thus the focus for the exposition. A fuller account of the public situation is not forthcoming until Albin (Félix's *confident*) reports Sévère's achievements to Pauline in I.4. Corneille makes little attempt to justify Albin's fairly long récit (ll.281-316), for Félix simply bids him:

> *Mais, Albin, redis-lui ce que ces gens t'ont dit.*
> *(l.280)*

The contrivance can escape notice, however, since, as Corneille notes, we are aware that Pauline listens willingly to the praises of Sévère. Arguably, it is more *vraisemblable* for the playwright to orchestrate a scene in which a protagonist listens to an expository *récit* from a *confident* rather than the reverse.[80]

Nicomède sees one of Corneille's boldest experiments, bringing Laodice and Nicomède together, alone, in the opening scene.[81] Since only two characters (Prusias and Arsinoé) have the equivalent of a *confident* (Araspe and Cléone respectively), scenes between main characters dominate the play. In the dialogue between Nicomède and Laodice Corneille creates both the framework for a political exposition (based upon the hero's unauthorised return from the army) and a climate of high emotions. Laodice's concern for Nicomède's safety is prompted by her love, declared in the opening couplet of the play:

> *Après tant de hauts faits , il m'est bien doux, Seigneur,*
> *De voir encor mes yeux régner sur votre cœur.*

Nicomède's first speech (ll.18-38) may be dense with references to the prevailing hostilities between Bythinia and Rome, and it may largely repeat familiar information to Laodice,[82] but the presentation of historical background is achieved through an appeal to Laodice's emotions. Both Nicomède and Laodice move away from the predominantly declarative statements of demonstrative rhetoric to interrogatives, imperatives and hypotheses, the language of conflict and persuasion. In this way Corneille transcends simple

---

[78] This is in contrast to *Théodore*, in which Cléobule (who shares the opening scene with Placide) is described as "ami de Placide". Cléobule's arguments have more weight in the later acts than those of a low-ranking *confident*, but his own fate is not of significance.

[79] "Rompez ses premiers coups, laissez pleurer Pauline." (l.65); "Il ne faut rien aimer qu'après lui <Dieu>, en lui-même" (l.74); "Hâtez-vous donc de l'être <chrétien>" (l.93); and finally the repeated injunction "Fuyez" (ll.103-4).

[80] The device of the *confident* listening to an expository *récit* from a main protagonist is one of d'Aubignac's main subjects of criticism in the *Querelle de Sophonisbe*. See p.50.

[81] The comparison must be made with Rotrou's dramatic opening scene between main protagonists in *Venceslas*. See p.70.

[82] Tellingly, the main verb "Je sais que.." governs lines 19-26.

exposition to capture the spectator's attention. But, as with *Polyeucte*, he still relies on a slightly later scene with a *confidente* (I.4, Arsinoé, Cléone) to complete the exposition.[83] We can provisionally conclude that for Corneille an opening scene between two main characters affords dramatic tension, but requires that some of the exposition be delayed, and conveyed through later scenes, generally involving a *confident*.

The long opening scene of *La Mort de Pompée* (212 lines) is also unusual, presenting a council of war between four characters. However, the formality of this setting lends itself to clear exposition since each of the characters speaks in turn, uninterrupted, with Ptolomée then bringing the deliberations to a conclusion. In the *Examen* Corneille drew attention to the particularly high register of this play:

> *Pour le style, il est plus élevé en ce Poème qu'en aucun des miens, et ce sont sans contredit les Vers les plus pompeux que j'aie faits.*[84]

In I.1 the contributions of Photin, Achillas and Septime all follow impeccably the rules of formal forensic oratory.[85] Corneille establishes a majestic tone, which suits his reworking of a celebrated passage from Lucan's *Pharsalia*.[86] D'Aubignac condemned the absence of any vigorous exchange between the characters,[87] but this was to overlook Corneille's priorities. The historic moment at which this play opens makes the scene effective here, and audience of the 1640s undoubtedly appreciated the eloquent adaptation of Latin epic for the French stage. However these specific circumstances meant that the opening of *La Mort de Pompée* was in a class of its own, and defied general imitation.[88]

---

[83] This scene with the *confidente* allows Arsinoé to deliver a *récit* to Cléone outlining the hostilities between Rome and Hannibal and their political repercussions (ll.295-323), but also to reveal her secret plans for Nicomède's downfall. It is essential that she should disclose the latter if we are to follow the development of the play, and it could not be revealed to any character other than a *confidente*.

[84] P. Corneille, *Œuvres complètes*, vol. I, p.1077.

[85] For a discussion of the style of this particular scene see S. Harwood-Gordon, *The Poetic Style of Corneille's Tragedies*, p.78. M. Hawcroft discusses forensic oratory in general, including council scenes, in Chapter 2 of his study *Word as Action*.

[86] Couton reminds us that in editions of *Pompée* from 1644-1655 Corneille had the lines of Lucan which he had imitated most closely printed at the bottom of the page. Couton judges this to be "une très remarquable nouveauté dans la présentation", calculated to emphasise the unusually close relationship between the French play and its Latin model. See P. Corneille, *Œuvres complètes*, vol. I, p.1713.

[87] *La Pratique du théâtre*, p.309.

[88] We might compare the formal council scene in Racine's *Alexandre*. However this does not occur until II.2, allowing Racine to exploit tensions between the characters which have already been revealed.

At the other end of the spectrum is the opening of *Cinna*, in which Corneille allows his heroine to take centre-stage alone, with a monologue of 52 lines, before she is joined by her *confidente* in I.2. Although Scherer suggests that by this date the monologue was becoming outdated in tragedy, particularly in the exposition,[89] there was a celebrated recent precedent in Tristan l'Hermite's *La Mariamne* (1636), and the acclaimed "fureurs d'Hérode" are a clear model for the "ardents transports" of Émilie. However, Corneille also achieves a variant on the successful expository strategy of *Horace*: Émilie's monologue is structured by the expression of contradictory feelings (hatred for Auguste and love for Cinna), just as Sabine's exchange with Julie was. As Barnwell reminds us, in both plays Corneille introduces in the opening scene the major character who is his own creation,[90] and it is this character who must engage the audience's emotions. The deliberative rhetoric of scene 1 of *Cinna* is marked out by the use of exclamation, apostrophe and several rhetorical questions. Relatively little of the historical background is imparted, and, interestingly, the following scene with Fulvie continues the deliberative mode as *confidente* and main character debate whether Émilie should pursue her vengeance. It is thus not until I.3, in which Cinna gives Émilie a detailed account of his meeting with his fellow conspirators, that we fully grasp the political situation. This strategy of delaying a substantial part of the exposition is the exception rather than the rule,[91] but an exception upon which Corneille congratulates himself in the *Examen*, for despite the length of Cinna's *récit* (ll.157-248), both characters (and therefore the spectators, too) are fully absorbed by it.[92]

From this survey of Corneille's practice, we can conclude that the *confident* is normally integral to either the opening scene of the exposition, or the following scenes. By the time of the *Examens* Corneille displays an acute critical sensitivity to the problem of interesting both characters and spectators in *récits* of past actions. His earlier practice was not always founded on the same priorities. Among his most successful opening scenes were those which established a sense of conflict within a main character. Such scenes often privileged deliberative rhetoric. The sense of conflict will be fundamental to another solution to the exposition which Racine develops: however, in his case

---

[89] *La Dramaturgie classique*, p.59.

[90] *The Tragic Drama of Corneille and Racine* (1982), p.100.

[91] *Polyeucte* follows a similar pattern, but Albin's exposition in I.4 is justified by the discovery, *after* the start of the play, that Sévère is still alive.

[92] "Émilie a de la joie d'apprendre de la bouche de son Amant avec quelle chaleur il a suivi ses intentions; et Cinna n'en a pas moins de pouvoir lui donner de si belles espérances de l'effet qu'elle en souhaite. C'est pourquoi, quelque longue que soit cette Narration sans interruption aucune, elle n'ennuie point."

the conflict will be foregrounded in the exchange *between* the protagonist and the *confident*.

(iii) RECEIVING CONFIDENCES AND GIVING ADVICE: THE LATER ACTS

Protactic characters, like Pollux in *Médée*, who have been introduced to facilitate an exposition may be entirely or almost entirely absent from the rest of the play. The same is not true of *confidents* or their equivalents, who reappear at certain intervals. A major feature of Corneille's tragedies up to *Nicomède* is that all have one or more female characters who act as *confidente*, but not all have a male character with a parallel function.[93] This is exactly the mirror image of comedies of the same period, in which male servants outnumber female ones and tend to have the more significant roles.[94]

Play	Female characters equivalent to *confidente*	Male characters equivalent to *confident*
Médée	Nérine Cléone	Pollux
Le Cid	Léonor Elvire	(none)
Horace	Julie	(none)
Cinna	Fulvie	Euphorbe
Polyeucte	Stratonice	Albin Fabian
La Mort de Pompée	Charmion	Philippe
Théodore	Stéphanie	Paulin
Rodogune	Laonice	Timagène
Héraclius	(none)	Amyntas
Don Sanche	Blanche	(none)
Nicomède	Cléone	Araspe

---

[93] As discussed above (p.14) I exclude from this category *domestiques*, *gardes*, messengers and the like, who are silent or only message-bearers. Equally I am not concerned here with figures of noble rank who are independent of the main protagonists (e.g. Exupère in *Héraclius*) or who interest us in their own right (e.g. Néarque in *Polyeucte*).

[94] See Émelina, *Les Valets et les servantes*, p.132.

This unequal distribution is largely explained by the fact that in Corneille's earlier tragedies there are more secondary male roles. The hero is thus brought into contact with other protagonists in whom he can confide, whereas more heroines depend upon the offices of their *confidentes*. For example, in *Le Cid* Rodrigue has a key scene with his father at the end of Act III, and in *Cinna* the eponymous hero unburdens himself to Maxime in two successive acts (II.2 and III.2), whilst Auguste confides initially in Cinna and Maxime (II.1) and then, after learning of Cinna's betrayal, in Livie (IV.3). In addition, while the Cornelian hero of this period has the opportunity to act, the heroine is often thrown (against her will) into a *reactive* role, in which the analysis of passions plays a larger part. It follows from this that my discussion in the remainder of this chapter pertains especially to the *confidente*, and it is significant that d'Aubignac's criticisms of *Sophonisbe* expose the weaknesses of the female role.

To assess the significance of the *confident(e)s'* role beyond the exposition, we can first distinguish between (a) scenes in which the *confident(e)* participates in the dialogue, and (b) "walk on" appearances where he/she accompanies the main character, but says nothing for the duration, and departs with that character. Such a role can last for several scenes,[95] and may either fulfil the dictates of *bienséance*,[96] or demonstrate the main character's rank.[97] Hawcroft suggests Racine is unusual in having most of his *confidents* speak in at least half the scenes in which they appear.[98] If we compare this with Corneille's practice in the earlier period, we can see that Corneille's *confidents* are more frequently silent spectators:[99]

- Nine speak in half or over half the scenes in which they appear (Nérine and Pollux in *Médée*; Elvire and Léonor in *Le Cid*; Julie in *Horace*; Euphorbe in *Cinna*; Albin in *Polyeucte*; Laonice and Timagène in *Rodogune*).

---

[95] One of the longest examples is Charmion, *dame d'honneur* to Cléopâtre in *La Mort de Pompée*, who is present without speaking for the duration of IV.2-IV.5 (272 lines) and then again for V.2-V.5 (267 lines).

[96] This is especially true of scenes between lovers. See Scherer, *La Dramaturgie classique*, pp.44-45.

[97] For example, Félix and Sévère are accompanied by Albin and Fabian respectively through almost the whole of *Polyeucte*. On some occasions protagonists are also surrounded by non-speaking *gardes, courtisans*, etc. as a sign of their rank (see D. Maskell, *Racine. A Theatrical Reading*, 1991, p.48).

[98] *Word as Action*, p.168.

[99] See Appendix I for further details.

- Twelve speak in fewer than half the scenes in which they appear (Cléone in *Médée*; Fulvie in *Cinna*; Fabian and Stratonice in *Polyeucte*; Charmion and Philippe in *La Mort de Pompée*; Paulin and Stéphanie in *Théodore*; Amyntas in *Héraclius*; Blanche in *Don Sanche*; Araspe and Cléone in *Nicomède*).

It is obvious at a quick glance that the silent *confident* scene becomes more commonplace in the tragedies from *Polyeucte* onwards.[100]

Since the scene, unlike the act, is an imprecise yardstick, however, we need to refine this information by also taking into account the length of appropriate scenes. In Appendix 1 I give a full breakdown of:

(a) the length of the scenes in which the *confident* speaks, and the ratio of his/her contribution

(b) the length of the scenes in which the *confident* is completely silent.

From this we can weigh up both the percentage of the play for which the *confident* is on stage and the percentage of the play in which he/she speaks. Throughout this period of Corneille's career, it is common for one of more *confidents* to be present on stage for over a third of the play:[101]

Play	*Confident(e)*	Percentage of the play present
Médée	Nérine	41.83%
Le Cid	Elvire	40.57%
Horace	Julie	35.77%
Cinna	Fulvie	46.46%
Polyeucte	Stratonice	36.49%
Pompée	Charmion	44.87%
Théodore	Paulin	51.43%
	Stéphanie	45.7%
Rodogune	Laonice	60.47%
Don Sanche	Blanche	50.6%
Nicomède	Araspe	41.42%

[100] *Rodogune* is an exception to this general trend. For various reasons, we may consider Corneille's use of the *confident* in this play to be experimental. See p.19 above on the exposition, and p.40 below on the double role of Laonice.

[101] The exception is *Héraclius*, in which the only *confident*-type character, Amyntas, is present for a mere 15.61% of the play.

Not surprisingly, female characters dominate this list, both because *confidentes* are more numerous than their male counterparts, and because *bienséance* keeps them closer to their mistresses. Far less even is the share of discourse apportioned to each of the characters above:

Play	Confident(e)s	Percentage of the play in which the characters speak
Médée	Nérine	7.63%
Le Cid	Elvire	5.2%
Horace	Julie	7.2%
Cinna	Fulvie	2.75%
Polyeucte	Stratonice	6.84%
Pompée	Charmion	1.71%
Théodore	Paulin	9.19%
	Stéphanie	4.25%
Rodogune	Laonice	11.66%
Don Sanche	Blanche	5.03%
Nicomède	Araspe	1.94%

This table invites two observations. First the discrepancies between the most loquacious and the most taciturn of *confidents* are striking. Secondly, these figures corroborate the general impression that, as Corneille's career progresses, individual *confidents* have less to say. If we add together the contributions in each play of all the characters I have classed as *confidents*, the trend is even more marked:

Play	*Confident(e)*	Perecentage of the play in which the characters speak
Médée	Cléone, Nérine and Pollux	14.12%
Le Cid	Elvire and Léonor	8.52%
Horace	Julie	7.2%
Cinna	Euphorbe and Fulvie	6.23%
Polyeucte	Albin, Fabian and Stratonice	13.51%
Pompée	Charmion and Philippe	4.52%
Théodore	Paulin and Stéphanie	13.44%
Rodogune	Laonice and Timagène	15.4%
Héraclius	Amyntas	1.72%
Don Sanche	Blanche	5.03%
Nicomède	Araspe and Cléone	2.64%

In the last three plays the role of the *confidents* is minimal, and in the following play, *Pertharite*, there are no *confidents* at all. Here is the evidence in the work of Pierre Corneille of "le confident honteux" of which Scherer spoke. But this demise of the *confident* is accompanied by the extension of an alternative role, which I shall term the *para-confident*, a main character who also acts as a *confident* to another protagonist.[102]

With reference to the earlier tragedies, what can be defined as characteristic of a *confident*'s role as both listener and speaker? In scenes where several main protagonists are present, it is the exception rather than the rule for *confidents* to speak, unless in their capacity as messenger. Their voice can only rarely be allowed to interrupt the discussion engaged between main characters.[103] However, when alone with the main character, the *confident* facilitates the revelation of the character's true thoughts and feelings both by listening and by commenting (and thereby provoking further reflections). Scherer gives little credence to the notion that scenes with a *confident* are simply an alternative to a

---

[102] The term *para-confident* is my own, but compare J. Prophète's use of the form *para-personnages* (to designate characters referred to in Racinian tragedies, but never present on stage): *Les Para-personnages dans les tragédies de Racine*, (1981).

[103] Julie in *Horace* is something of an exception, but her status as a *dame romaine* justifies interventions such as those in I.3 and III.3.

monologue by the main character.[104] Some playwrights of this period use the virtual monologue, or what Scherer terms "le monologue devant le confident" - the main character speaking as though unaware of the *confident*'s presence - but in Pierre Corneille this is very rare.[105] We may suspect this is due in part at least to Corneille's liberal use of monologues proper in his plays up to *Cinna*.[106] Even in his subsequent plays, he does not show a strong taste for the virtual monologue. We can cite as an isolated example Cornélie's impassioned speech in V.1. of *La Mort de Pompée*, delivered in front of Philippe (her dead husband's *affranchi*, who has borne his ashes).[107] At the start (ll.1453-7) and conclusion (ll.1481-4), she addresses Philippe, but his reply must wait, and he is ignored as she launches into her elegy to Pompée and her oath of vengeance.[108] However, once this is pronounced, Philippe delivers a long *récit* of Pompée's death (ll.1485-1536), with only one interruption from Cornélie (l.1517).[109] His function in the scene is thus transformed from the passive role of witness to the active one of informant.

In almost all scenes which take place solely between a *confident* and a main character, Corneille has both sides speak. What varies is the balance between the two parties, and the nature of their exchange. If we are looking for standard strategies, there are two which stand out:

(1) self-analysis by the main character, which the *confident* merely sustains by brief questions or comments

(2) revelation of the main character's love or evolving passions, with the *confident* (or, more frequently, the *confidente*) playing a fuller role in the exchange.

Scenes with a main protagonist and a *confident* in which the *confident* makes only a very minimal contribution are rare in Corneille's tragedies. However, one example (selected in part for its brevity so that it can quoted it in

---

[104] *La Dramaturgie classique*, pp.42-43.

[105] *Ibid.*, p.255.

[106] *Ibid.*, p.259.

[107] Even Voltaire was won over despite himself by the power of the scene: "Par quel art une scène inutile est-elle si belle?" (*Remarques sur Pompée* in *Œuvres complètes de Voltaire*, vol. IX, p.460).

[108] She apostrophises the urn/ashes three times ("Ô vous, à ma douleur objet terrible et tendre", l.1458; "Je jure donc par vous, ô pitoyable reste", l.1469; "Ô cendres, mon espoir aussi bien que ma peine", l.1478). The physical presence of the object in her hands makes the spectator aware that her thoughts are totally concentrated upon her dead husband, to the exclusion of the *confident*.

[109] Philippe speaks for 49.04% of the scene.

full here) will provide a focus for our analysis. Since one of d'Aubignac's recommendations in the *Querelle de Sophonisbe* will be precisely that *confidentes* should say as little as possible, Corneille's handling of the taciturn *confident(e)* is particularly interesting. In the last scene of Act III of *Théodore*, following the confrontation between Marcelle and Placide in III.5, there is a scene between Marcelle and her *confidente*, Stéphanie. This is part of a standard sequence: first a scene between two main characters, during which one or two *confidents* are present but silent, followed by a scene between a main protagonist and a *confident* to reveal the protagonist's reactions to the preceding scene. The exchange between Marcelle and Stéphanie relies upon another common structure. There is a contrast between the perspective of the *confidente*, who had judged the scene at face value, and that of the heroine, who can now reveal feelings which she had earlier concealed.

> STÉPHANIE
> *Enfin vous triomphez de cet esprit rebelle?*
>
> MARCELLE
> *Quel triomphe!*
>
> STÉPHANIE
>   *Est-ce peu que de voir à vos pieds*
> *Sa haine, et son orgueil enfin humiliés?*
>
> MARCELLE
> *Quel triomphe, te dis-je! et qu'il a d'amertumes!*
> *Et que nous sommes loin de ce que tu présumes!*
> *Tu le vois à mes pieds pleurer, gémir, prier,*
> *Mais ne crois pas pourtant le voir s'humilier,*
> *Ne crois pas qu'il se rende aux bontés qu'il implore;*
> *Mais vois de quelle ardeur il aime Théodore,*
> *Et juge quel pouvoir cet amour a sur lui,*
> *Puisqu'il peut le réduire à chercher mon appui.*
> *Que n'oseront ses feux entreprendre pour elle,*
> *S'ils ont pu l'abaisser jusqu'aux pieds de Marcelle,*
> *Et que dois-je espérer d'un cœur si fort épris,*
> *Qui, même en m'adorant, me fait voir ses mépris?*
> *Dans ses submissions vois ce qui l'y convie:*
> *Mesure à son amour sa haine pour Flavie,*
> *Et voyant l'un et l'autre en son abaissement,*
> *Juge de mon triomphe un peu plus sainement,*
> *Vois dans son triste effet sa ridicule pompe.*
> *J'ai peine en triomphant d'obtenir qu'il me trompe,*
> *Qu'il feigne par pitié, qu'il donne un faux espoir.*
>
> STÉPHANIE
> *Et vous l'allez servir de tout votre pouvoir?*

MARCELLE
Oui, je vais le servir, mais comme il le mérite.
Toi, va me l'amuser dedans cette visite,
Et de tout ton pouvoir donne loisir au mien.

STÉPHANIE
Donc ...

MARCELLE
          Le temps presse, va, sans t'informer de rien.
                    (ll.1080-1106)[110]

Despite the obvious predominance of Marcelle in the exchange, Corneille
has succeeded in infusing Stéphanie's role with some interest. It is the
confidente who initiates the scene, pressing Marcelle for an explanation through
two questions, introduced by the persuasive "Enfin" and "Est-ce peu que".
Marcelle's reply is far removed from a virtual monologue, for she uses the
imperative to command Stéphanie's attention no fewer than eight times. The
repetition of "vois" and "juge" in particular underlines the interest the
confidente (and the audience) should take in Marcelle's explanation. In short,
this is a strong example of deliberative rhetoric, at a dramatic moment of the
play. The *confidente* has thus fulfilled the very basic function of drawing
information from the protagonist. Yet despite the fact that Stéphanie has only
four lines in the scene, the dramatist has avoided making her appear a purely
passive vehicle. Even her last line, with the device of *interruptio*, works to
convey the urgency of the situation.

It has been a commonplace of Cornelian criticism, dating back at least to Le
Bidois, to maintain that Corneille's *confident(e)s* - unlike their Racinian
counterparts - speak little, and when they do, only concur with their
masters/mistresses. Such a view is based upon the assumption that the "strong"
Cornelian hero or heroine requires no support and brooks no interference.[111]
Yet the evidence does not support such a theory. It is far easier in the earlier
plays of Corneille to point to scenes in which *confidentes* speak between a
quarter and half the lines. Such scenes allow Corneille to portray the inner
turmoils of his heroines, and the *confidentes* are far from passive. To appreciate
both the difficulties and the opportunities these scenes present to the dramatist,
we can compare two examples, one from *Le Cid*, in which the dramaturgical

---

[110] I quote the 1646 text. In later editions lines 1104-5 are amended to read: "Toi, va par
quelque adresse amuser sa visite,/ Et sous un faux appas prolonger l'entretien."

[111] "Mais que pourraient tenter sur ces volontés altières des âmes basses ou sans force? Dans
un semblable théâtre, les confidents n'ont qu'un emploi, celui d'écouter, et, s'ils parlent, de se
mettre autant que possible à l'unisson de leurs maîtres."(*La Vie dans la tragédie de Racine*, p.158).

joints are less well oiled, and one from *Horace* in which Corneille has mastered the technical challenges superbly.

Act V of *Le Cid* has two successive *confidente* scenes, the first between the Infante and Léonor (V.3) and the second between Chimène and Elvire (V.4). These scenes suspend the action: while Rodrigue fights the duel with Don Sanche, the audience observes the state of mind and feeling of the two heroines. In both cases, the *confidentes* play a significant role. The share of the scenes is as follows:

Infante:	23/48 lines	= 47.92%
Léonor:	25/48 lines	= 52.08%
Chimène:	35/60 lines	= 58.33%
Elvire:	25/60 lines	= 41.67%

The Infante has a monologue before her scene with Léonor, which supports Scherer's argument that *confident* scenes do not merely replace monologues. In her *stances* (ll.1575-1606), the Infante has delivered a set-piece debate on the respective claims of duty and love, before reaching the noble conclusion that she cannot stand between Rodrigue and Chimène. The arrival of Léonor (l.1607) does not bring any new information (as the audience might have anticipated), nor, surprisingly, are fresh arguments set forth. Instead, this scene allows the Infante to repeat to Léonor the arguments and the conclusions she had already reached in her monologue. On the one hand, if we expected the play to move forward, we are disappointed. Léonor merely validates the Infante's decision, herself formulating the arguments that Chimène's love for Rodrigue cannot be denied after having endured so much,[112] and that the Infante's noble birth makes Rodrigue an unsuitable husband.[113] On the other hand, if we look at the affective qualities of the scene, it might be argued that it allows the audience to appreciate more fully the suffering involved in the Infante's sacrifice. In particular, Corneille achieves a strong contrast between Léonor's fairly brusque arguments and the Infante's use of the stylised vocabulary of the passions, studded with exclamation and rhetorical questions:

> *Et toi qui vois les traits dont mon cœur est percé*
> *(l.1653)*

> *A quoi me résoudrai-je, amante infortunée?*
> *(l.1639)*

Still, the Infante was not one of Corneille's best received creations, and stasis is scarcely appropriate to Act V. If this part of the act is flawed, I suspect that the

---

[112] Lines 1599-1602 in the Infante's monologue and ll.1621-1636 in Léonor's exchange with her.

[113] Lines 1575-1582 in the Infante's monologue and ll.1640-1641 in Leonor's exchange with her.

fault lies at least as much in the artificiality of the set-piece monologue as in the construction of the scene with the *confidente*.

Similarly, we might question the device of having another scene with a *confidente* to follow immediately upon V.3. This is in clear violation of the *liaison des scènes*, but we must remember that Corneille did not claim to adhere to this principle until *Horace*. In *Le Cid* the disposition of scenes invites the audience to contrast the sufferings of each heroine in turn. The exchange between Elvire and Chimène differs in several important respects from that between the Infante and Léonor, almost always to the advantage of the later scene. Elvire's voice contradicts rather than supports Chimène. We witness a conflict as she first assumes (naively) that the duel will resolve Chimène's dilemma, and then argues strongly that if Rodrigue is victorious Chimène should lay aside thoughts of revenge. Where the Infante reiterated her position, approved by Léonor, at the end of V.3,[114] Chimène's divided loyalties build up to a crescendo in V.4 until the scene is dramatically interrupted by Don Sanche's arrival. This *confidente* scene has allowed the audience privileged insight into the unrelieved anguish of the heroine. The scene between the Infante and her *confidente* was of minimal relevance to the action, serving only to confirm her decision taken in V.2. The scene between Chimène and Elvire, on the other hand, is crucial if we are to understand Chimène's continued reaffirmation of her position even in the last scene of the play. In short, Act V of *Le Cid* illustrates the gap between the ornamental and the well-integrated *confidente* scene.

Another reason for the success of V.4 is the exploitation to dramatic and affective purpose of the time which elapses as action is completed offstage. Scenes with *confidents* may traditionally be employed to fill time, but dramatists vary in how skilfully they can sustain the tension created by the break in the action. Corneille uses a parallel situation in the second example I wish to consider here, the scene between Sabine and Julie in III.2 of *Horace*. This act is punctuated by the suspense as battle is commenced, stopped and rejoined. In the *Examen*, Corneille refers proudly to the construction of this Act as "un des plus artificieux". At the start of the act, he employs the familiar sequence of a monologue followed by a scene with a *confidente*, but he directs the two scenes to very different ends. Sabine's long monologue (ll.711-764) examines her conflicting loyalties. Despite initially setting out a clear dilemma:

> *Prenons parti, mon âme, en de telles disgrâces:*
> *Soyons femme d'Horace, ou sœur des Curiaces.*
> *(ll.711-2)*

this speech does not advance the action, for Sabine cannot, of course, arrive at a conclusion. The monologue is thus only a disguised act of deliberation, for its

---

[114] "Viens me voir achever comme j'ai commencé." (l.1654)

real effect is to move to the audience to pity Sabine. It is the *confidente* scene which resolves the stasis, as Julie provides the essential link with the action offstage.[115] The *confidente*, acting as messenger, has the larger share of the discourse.[116] However, we perceive the report through Sabine's eyes, and, prepared by III.1, share her successive reactions of impatience for news, then relief and hope. The contrast with our relative lack of interest in the Infante is striking, and if Corneille is right to explain it in part by the better integration of Sabine within the plot,[117] we might add that it is also aided by the tighter dramaturgy.

The following two scenes of *Horace* offer a further contrast with Act V of *Le Cid*. Instead of a second confidente scene, Corneille has Camille join Sabine and Julie, and the two heroines are subsequently left alone. Thus the revelation of Camille's state of mind and feelings is achieved primarily through her exchanges with Sabine, in which the relative sufferings of each are keenly argued. What we perceive here is a more reflective use of the confidente, and a closer orchestration of the diverse possibilities afforded by monologue, dialogue with confidente, and dialogue between main characters. In this respect *Horace* remained a key model for dramatists of the next generation.

(iv) SOME EARLY VARIATIONS ON THE *CONFIDENT*'S ROLE

We have established the most significant ways in which *confidents* are regularly employed throughout this earlier period of Corneille's writing. In conclusion to this chapter, I want to look briefly at some departures from these practices, which are suggestive of other possibilities the role can afford. Apart from their obvious interest as evidence of Corneille's dramaturgical flexibility, these examples have been selected because they are, in embryonic form at least, crucial to the reworking of confidential strategies in the period following the *Querelle de Sophonisbe*.

(1) THE *CONFIDENT* GIVEN A MONOLOGUE

We have already referred to the general decline of the monologue in the period 1630-60. If we look at *Médée* (1635), there are six monologues, spoken by four characters, and for the most part they are *bravura* pieces giving each actor or actress their chance to shine. By *Pertharite* (1651) there are only two, both delivered by the same character (Garibalde), and necessary solely to reveal

---

[115] Compare the structure of Act IV of *Cinna*. Auguste in his famous monologue (IV.2) fails to resolve his doubts, and it is the counsel of Livie (brought on for the first time in the play in IV.3 and acting as a *para-confidente*) which provides the impetus for the play to move forwards.

[116] Julie has 48 lines (72.73% of the scene), Sabine 18 lines (27.27%).

[117] See the *Examen* to *Horace*: P. Corneille, *Œuvres complètes*, vol. I, p.841.

motives and reactions which have been kept secret from other characters.[118] In the earliest plays, two *confidentes* are given monologues: Nérine one of 32 lines in III.1 of *Médée*,[119] and Julie one of 12 lines, which served as the original epilogue to *Horace* but was dropped in 1660. In both plays, the monologue underlines the significance of the role accorded to the *confidente*.[120]

Nérine's monologue falls into two sections: first she recalls the dreadful powers of Médée (ll.701-20), and then she excuses her own part in Médée's crimes (ll.721-32). The earlier section of the monologue sets an ominous tone as Médée's revenge is approaching. But the second section is the more interesting here in that it establishes, at least in passing, the *confidente*'s independent existence as a moral character. Nérine serves Médée through fear, but wishes she had the courage to disobey her:

> *Moi, bien que mon devoir m'attache à son service,*
> *Je lui prête à regret un silence complice,*
> *D'un louable désir mon cœur sollicité*
> *Lui ferait avec joie une infidelité.*
>   *(ll.721-24)*

Scherer suggests that at the time of Racine the *confident* will be given "un véritable caractère".[121] Corneille has taken a first step with *Médée*.

Julie, in *Horace*, is a *confidente* set apart by her status, and it is a sign of her authority that in the original text Corneille used her to close the play. Her concluding monologue spells out the paradoxical truth of the oracle in an apostrophe to the dead Camille:

> *Camille, ainsi le ciel t'avait bien avertie*
> *Des tragiques succès qu'il t'avait préparés.*

Julie uses the first person plural three times in the following ten lines to refer to Camille and her family: "Il semblait *nous* parler"; "En *nous* cachant"; "en trompant *notre* sens". Her reflection on the incomprehensible workings of the heavens is thus related to the private tragedy of Camille. In contrast, the revised version of the scene (in 1657) resites Camille's individual tragedy within the broader political context: it is the king not the *confidente* who pronounces the reconciliation of the public and private as he decrees that Camille and Curiace shall be buried together.[122] One effect of the rewriting was to allow Corneille

---

[118] *Pertharite* II.3 and III.6.

[119] Cut to 28 lines from 1660.

[120] Over a century later, Voltaire was unequivocal in his condemnation of Nérine's monologue: "C'est ici un grand exemple de l'abus des monologues. Une suivante, qui vient parler toute seule du pouvoir de sa maîtresse, est d'un grand ridicule." (*Remarques sur Médée* in *Œuvres complètes de Voltaire*, vol.IX, p.349).

[121] *La Dramaturgie classique* , p.48.

[122] See S. Doubrovsky, *Corneille et la dialectique du héros*, pp. 182-4.

discreetly to reduce the role of a *confidente* at a period when tastes had changed.[123]

(2) THE *CONFIDENT* TURNED *CONSEILLER*

The adviser is a recurrent character in political tragedies as we observe rulers making decisions under pressure and looking for guidance. One of the contributors to J. Truchet's volume *Recherches de thématique théâtrale: l'exemple des conseillers des rois dans la tragédie classique* observes that "On n'est jamais d'emblée conseiller, on le devient".[124] The study establishes that *conseillers* can be drawn from any class or rank, but since the *conseiller* is essentially an episodic character whose appearances are dictated by a clear function, the *confident* is well situated to take on this office. In one sense, it could be argued that most *confidents* are *conseillers* in that they listen and advise. However, some are more clearly raised to a status of trusted *political* adviser. An example of an early form of the *confident/conseiller* is furnished by Araspe in *Nicomède*.

Araspe appears in the list of *dramatis personae* as *capitaine des gardes*, and is effectively *confident* to Prusias. He is one of many examples in a line of *conseillers* who give bad advice and suffer their just desserts. In II.1, his only scene alone with the king, Araspe apparently defends Nicomède's virtue,[125] but the real tenor of his discourse is a categorical warning of the danger of over-powerful subjects. Thus, he uses four times the phrase "tout autre" to remind Prusias what a less virtuous character than Nicomède might do:

> *Mais tout autre que lui devrait être suspect.*
> *(l.369)*

> *C'est ce que de tout autre il faudrait redouter,*
> *Seigneur, et qu'en tout autre il faudrait arrêter.*
> *(ll.397-8)*

> *Pour tout autre que lui je sais comme s'explique*
> *La règle de la vraie, et saine Politique.*
> *(ll.431-2)*

The subtext is all too clear, summed up in the machiavellian maxim of the next couplet:

---

[123] Compare Voltaire's dismissal of the original ending, showing again the eighteenth-century's suspicions of both the monologue and the *confident*: "Ici c'est une confidente inutile qui dit une chose inutile." (*Remarques sur les Horaces* in *Œuvres complètes*, vol. IX, p.396.)

[124] (1981), p.76.

[125] Lines 367, 400, 441.

Aussitôt qu'un Sujet s'est rendu trop puissant,
Encor qu'il soit sans crime, il n'est pas innocent.
(ll.433-34)

Although he may appear at the outset of each speech to be tempering Prusias's anger at Nicomède's unauthorised return, Araspe effectively fuels Prusias's resentment and fears.[126] Araspe's function as *conseiller* ends with this scene,[127] and his death in Act V does not interest the audience as does, say, that of Racine's Narcisse. The report of Araspe's death (ll.1748-1754) serves instead to increase the dramatic tension as Prusias, Arsinoé, Attale and Laodice wait to learn what role Nicomède has played in the revolt.

If Araspe is no more than a shadow of the *mauvais conseiller* which the *confident* will become in some later plays, we can look back to *Cinna* for an example of the intervention of the *confident/conseiller* in the action, a subject which also leads us on to our next category, the *faux confident*. The *conseiller* is free to act either in the main character's interests or against them (although Truchet's team concludes that the *mauvais conseiller* is the more common figure in tragedy).[128] But with the *faux conseiller*, the trust between main character and *confident* is irreversibly breached.

(3) THE *FAUX CONFIDENT*

The examples selected earlier in the chapter to show the role of the *confident* in the exposition and in the revelation of the mind and feelings of a main character all had one thing in common: the *confident* had no secret to hide. In these cases the relationship between character and *confident* was transparent, at least in so far as any relationship based on linguistic exchange can be said to be so, and the scenes were primarily a means for the audience to learn the truth. The *confident(e)* adopts a different kind of role, however, when he or she deliberately and secretly contravenes the wishes of the main character, a subject to which I shall return in detail in Chapter 5. In *Médée*, Nérine's monologue implied that Nérine would have wished to do so, but this is never translated into action. However, in both *Cinna* and *Rodogune* the very workings of the plot depend on a *confident(e)* who betrays the protagonist's trust. This does not necessarily mean that the *confident(e)* is seeking to further his/her own interests nor that the betrayal has negative consequences in the eyes of the

---

[126] Jacques Delon goes so far as to refer to him as an "agent double" on the basis of this scene (*Recherches de thématique*, ed. J. Truchet, p.42), but I doubt whether we have the evidence in the play to know that Araspe is definitely working for Arsinoé.

[127] Although Araspe accompanies Prusias in a number of other scenes, he speaks again only in III.7 and V.5, both times very briefly, and to deliver a message.

[128] *Recherches de thématique théâtrale*, p.87.

audience.[129] Indeed, we shall see that the example of Laonice in *Rodogune* demonstrates the *confidente* to be on the side of moral principle. But the *faux confident*'s independence both undermines the trust on which the relationship with the main character is based, and also raises the possibility that the *confident* might become a significant character in his/her own right.

Scherer cites *Cinna* as an early example of a *confident* "jouant le rôle d'agent de renseignement", which he sees as a prelude to the full-blown *confident/agent double*.[130] Euphorbe's betrayal of Maxime is a halfway stage in that Maxime is already inclining in the direction Euphorbe takes. In the first encounter between the two (III.1), Euphorbe argues strongly for Maxime to betray Cinna (ll.730-4), and such is his influence upon Maxime that by the end of the scene the debate has moved from the theoretical principle of betrayal to the question of whether Maxime can hope for tangible benefits. Characterised by his determination, a disregard for higher principles and a convenient perspicacity,[131] Euphorbe acts without Maxime's consent, a strategy which allows the dramatist to avoid painting too black a picture of one of the main characters.[132] Like Racine, who will have Œnone accuse Hippolyte offstage between acts, Corneille avoids showing Euphorbe's act of denunciation on stage. However, as Act IV opens with Auguste's reaction to what he has just heard, one part of Euphorbe's *récit* is delayed so that the spectator hears it: the lie that Maxime has drowned himself in remorse (ll.1103-14). The deception is not exposed until IV.5, when Maxime appears to Émilie and tries to persuade her to escape with him. The lie on stage creates additional suspense and permits a *coup de théâtre* when Maxime appears; it also allows Émilie's fidelity to be put to the test. But the price Corneille pays is our uncertainty (both in IV.1 and later) of how far, if at all, Maxime was aware of Euphorbe's intentions. Maxime bitterly blames his *confident*'s pernicious influence in both his soliloquy in IV.6,[133] and his confession to Auguste in V.3,[134] but the precise sequence of events between III.1 and IV.1 is never detailed. Unlike Araspe, Euphorbe is spared (in keeping with the new reign of tolerance) at Auguste's orders.[135] He

---

[129] This distinction is examined futher in *Recherches de thématique*, ed. J. Truchet, pp.113-117.

[130] *La Dramaturgie classique*, p.49.

[131] Twice in III.1 Euphorbe is used to predict that Auguste will show clemency (ll.733-34, l.764)

[132] For a discussion of the use of the *mauvais confident* to exculpate a main protagonist in other plays, see p.125. Voltaire overlooked this function of Euphorbe when he condemned his role ("On ne peut nier que ce lâche et inutile mensonge d'Euphorbe ne soit indigne de la tragédie." *Remarques sur Cinna*, p.413).

[133] "Euphorbe, c'est l'effet de tes lâches conseils" (l.1407). Maxime attributes Euphorbe's *fourbe* to his lowbirth (l.1416), and wishes to kill his *affranchi* to expiate his own crime.

[134] He repeats his wish to see Euphorbe punished by death (l.1687).

[135] "Qu'Euphorbe de tous trois ait sa grâce à son tour" (l.1739).

does not appear in the final scene: his function, that of *precipitating* action which will affect main characters, has been completed.

Laonice similarly transmits information, in breach of confidence, which is essential to the progress of the plot. However, where Euphorbe worked against the interests of higher principles, Laonice works for them. Her official title is *confidente de la Reine*, a function which she fulfils in their exchange in II.2 and by accompanying Cléopâtre silently in other scenes of the play. Yet we learn that Laonice had also been entrusted with guarding Rodogune during her captivity.[136] As Cléopâtre reveals her true motives and thirst for power, we are made aware that Laonice is hearing these dreadful secrets for the first time.[137] She is also a silent witness to Cléopâtre's subsequent interview with the princes (II.3), in which their mother promises the throne to the one will kill Rodogune. It is after this that Laonice opens Act III by betraying Cléopâtre's confidence to Rodogune. The betrayal is better motivated than that of Euphorbe, and also charged with suspense, for Laonice twice refers to her fears lest Cléopâtre should discover her act:

> *Le cœur gros de soupirs, et frémissant d'horreur,*
> *Je romps une foi due aux secrets de ma Reine.*
> *(ll.770-1)*

> *Je vous parle en tremblant, si j'étais ici vue,*
> *Votre péril croîtrait, et je serais perdue.*
> *(ll.791-2)*

Euphorbe's betrayal was crucial to the dénouement (the scene was followed immediately by Auguste's reflections on his reign and the policy of severity). Laonice's, on the other hand, opens the way for the next stage in the action: as a result of the new information, Rodogune will counter Cléopâtre's demand with her own for the queen's life (III.4). The symmetry which is essential to the play's structure is thus achieved through the work of the *fausse confidente*.[138]

In both *Cinna* and *Rodogune*, the single breach of confidence interests us for the effect it will have on the course of the plot, but we are not further interested in the *faux confidents* themselves. However, Corneille has opened up

---

[136] Cléopâtre reminds Laonice of this: "Quand je mis Rodogune en tes mains prisonnière" (1.504).

[137] E.g. LAONICE "Je vous connaissais mal." CLÉOPÂTRE "Connais-moi tout entière." (1.503).

[138] Voltaire typically criticises this dramatic role afforded to a *confidente*, and suggests that Corneille should have had Rodogune learn the truth about Cléopâtre from the princes themselves. Yet this is to overlook the dramatic *evolution* which structures Act III.

a new active role for the *confident*, and one which will be developed in a number of plays of the 1660s.[139]

(4) THE SHARED *CONFIDENT*

One of the obvious implications of the *faux confident* is that *confidents* are authorised to speak with a main character other than their own master/mistress. This is a further extension of the confident's role, in which he/she may be shared between several characters. *Confidents* are frequently called upon to deliver messages to a third party, and we have already referred to the fact that in many instances a *confident* relates a death *récit* to surviving characters. In other words, there is nothing surprising in *confidents* delivering some of their lines to a third party.

In earlier plays Corneille makes use several times of a variation on this device: namely, a third party coming upon the *confident* by surprise. Jason interrupts Nérine's monologue (*Médée* III.2) and seeks to persuade the *confidente* to make Médée give her robe to Créuse. In this case the scene has little significance beyond demonstrating further to the audience Jason's deceitful rhetoric.[140] We may suspect that it is motivated in part by the need to contrive an encounter between Jason and Médée. Thus as Jason detains Nérine, Médée can come towards her *confidente* and prevent him from leaving.

Much more dramatic is the encounter between Elvire and Rodrigue in III.1 of *Le Cid*. The scene derives from a stock *comic* situation: the protagonist arriving unbidden and being hidden by the servant as another protagonist returns. Elvire's role here and in III.3 is strangely like that of the traditional servant/*entremetteuse*, who both scolds the comic hero yet facilitates the ultimate union of the lovers. Like other dramatic moments of *Le Cid*, what could verge on the comic is of course saved by the tragic emotions at stake. We are struck in III.1 by the force of Elvire's language. In the 19 lines she speaks, she uses 7 rhetorical questions and 8 imperatives, expressing her outrage and fear for Chimène's honour. Equally interesting is III.3, in which Elvire speaks ostensibly to Chimène but with the knowledge that their exchange is overheard by Rodrigue. Although Chimène speaks for the greater part of the scene, Elvire's contributions, showing her incomprehension of Chimène's values, are important to sustain the heroine's revelations. She also comes increasingly to take what she assumes to be Rodrigue's part, initially questioning Chimène's

---

[139] There may be some cross-fertilisation between tragedies and comedies as far as this kind of role is concerned. Among the limited examples of the "serviteurs-traîtres" in seventeenth-century comedy, Émelina cites several early comedies by Pierre Corneille, and the two versions of *La Mère Coquette* (by Donneau de Visé and Quinault) of 1665: *Les Valets et les servantes*, pp.116-9.

[140] For example, his disguised blackmail that Médée should give up her robe in return for the safety of her children (ll.763-82).

sentiments,[141] but then (again we note the imperatives) commanding Chimène to forget her pursuit of vengeance:

> *Quittez, quittez, Madame, un dessein si tragique,*
> *Ne vous imposez point de loy si tyrannique.*
>   *(ll.839-40)*

> *Ne vous obstinez point en cette humeur étrange.*
>   *(l.851)*

Like the famous scene of *Britannicus* in which Junie speaks at once to Britannicus and the hidden Néron, so here Corneille has Elvire speaking to Chimène but for the benefit of Rodrigue..

In several other plays the formula of a shared *confident* is present from the outset, notably in *Horace* and *Rodogune*. We have seen that Corneille has only one *confident*-type character in *Horace*, Julie,[142] and she is shared between Sabine and Julie. As our earlier analysis of scenes from this play has shown, the sharing of the *confidente* is carefully planned. By not giving Sabine and Camille separate *confidentes*, Corneille strengthens our sense that this is a tragedy in which no character can stand isolated.[143] Similarly, in *Rodogune*, where the princes both share Timagène as their *gouverneur*, it is significant that neither prince can rely exclusively on any other character. Antiochus is accorded one scene alone with Timagène and Laonice (I.2), but no lengthy confidences are forthcoming. Thereafter, the princes have recourse only to each other or Rodogune. What we observe here is the closing off of one aspect of the traditional relationship with the *confident*, in which the latter is concerned exclusively with the destiny of the one character to whom he/she is bound. The intimacy of the *confident* scene is one of its greatest strengths, but, paradoxically, the removal of this intimacy may accentuate the protagonists' tragic isolation. To share a *confident* is already to sacrifice something of the intimacy; it is one stage towards the exclusion of the *confident*.

(5) THE ABSENT *CONFIDENT*

In a play which uses *confidents*, the dramatist may be making a deliberate statement by depriving one or more characters of a *confident*. Although, as I discuss in Chapter 6, this argument is more compelling in the case of the mature Racine, who uses the *confident*/main character pairing more systematically,[144] it throws new light on some of Corneille's earlier plays. If we look back to the

---

[141] Lines 819 and 835.

[142] A disposition explained by the large number of main and secondary protagonists, as discussed above.

[143] See the discussion by D. Clarke of the importance of the social group in Corneille's conception of tragedy: *Pierre Corneille* (1992), p.112.

[144] See R. Barthes, *Sur Racine*, pp.55-57.

table of *confident*-type characters, we could draw up an alternative table of the characters without *confidents*. This would have to include a majority of the heroes: Rodrigue, Horace, Cinna, César, Héraclius, Carlos and Nicomède. We can omit Jason, Polyeucte and Placide from this list on the basis that Pollux, Néarque and Cléobule, though all styled *ami*, function as *confidents*. However, for the other characters listed above the absence of a personal *confident* may increase our perception of their isolation at key moments of the play.

Even when there is another main character acting as a *para-confident* in whom a hero may confide, the relationship will often be fraught with greater complexities than that with a *confident*. Don Diègue is overjoyed to see his son in III.6 of *Le Cid*, but he speaks more than he listens, such is his concern to advise Rodrigue. Similarly in the first private exchange between Cinna and Maxime (*Cinna*, II.2), the tone of the scene is one of urgent debate, with each character seeking to impose his will. Even in their susequent encounter in Act III, in which Maxime invites Cinna to explain his sufferings,[145] and refers to himself as a "confident discret" (l.864), Maxime responds to Cinna's confidences by restating his own political arguments. It is only in his monologue in the following scene that Cinna lays bare his soul. *Horace* also furnishes proof of the tragic inadequacy (from the hero's perspective) of main protagonists to replace *confidents*. After his killing of Camille, Horace has to encounter in turn wife, father and king, none of whom listen to him as a *confident* might. In contrast, at the start of Act V of *Héraclius* the hero is praying to be delivered from the bewildering isolation in which he delivers his monologue, and the arrival of Pulchérie, now recognised as his sister, is greeted with relief.[146] Another playwright might have given either Horace or Héraclius a *confident* with whom to share these scenes. Yet the absence of one can create the solitude in which the hero must confront his dilemma.

The five different strategies which I have outlined suggest that even in this earlier phase of classical tragedy the *confident* is not a mechanical device limited to one type of scene. Where it suits the dramatic situation and the affective pattern, the *confident* can either be given an enhanced role or be effaced. There is evidence that as Corneille becomes a more experienced playwright, his technical dramaturgical control is refined (a development particularly evident in the movement from *Le Cid* to *Horace*), and this is shown in his increasingly varied use of the *confident* over the plays from *Horace* to *Rodogune*. However, in the later plays of his first period of literary activity, we

---

[145] "D'un penser si profond quel est le triste objet?" (1643-57), later amended to "Puis-je d'un tel chagrin savoir quel est l'objet?".

[146] "O Ciel! quel bon Démon devers moi vous envoie,/ Madame?" (ll.1555-6).

CHAPTER TWO

THEORETICAL DEBATES: A RENEWED INTEREST IN THE
CONFIDENT(E)

The years 1657-1663 saw a distinct quickening of pace and tempers in theatrical debates. While the outstanding success of Molière's early plays in Paris resulted in a challenge to the previously accepted supremacy of tragedy, the very nature and form of the latter were being held up to renewed public scrutiny. The first major contribution was the publication in 1657 of d'Aubignac's *Pratique du Théâtre* (which had been composed for the most part around 1640).[147] In this the *confident* is not discussed at length, but we shall see that many of d'Aubignac's general remarks on the exploitation of characters and the observance of the rules bear upon traditional confidential strategies. *La Pratique* was followed shortly by Corneille's *Discours*, which, together with the *Examens* of 1660, give a veiled response to d'Aubignac as well as establishing Corneille's own alternative agenda. In Chapter 1 of this study we saw that Corneille in his turn raises some issues pertaining to the *confident* in these *Examens*. However, it is when d'Aubignac returns to the offensive with his series of four *Dissertations* in 1663 that the spotlight comes to rest on the *confident*, and especially the *confidente*. In the following years, we may expect that dramatists were acutely aware of the challenges and pitfalls such characters represented.

(i) JUDGING THE *CONFIDENT(E)*'S ROLE: D'AUBIGNAC, *LA PRATIQUE DU THÉÂTRE*

La Pratique may be considered a didactic rather than a polemical work, valuable (despite its undeniably pedantic tone) as a rare attempt at a synthesis of what made for good drama.[148] D'Aubignac's governing concerns are his much-

---

[147] For a succinct account of the genesis of *La Pratique* and an evaluation of its relationship with Corneille's theoretical writings, see H. Barnwell, *The Tragic Drama of Corneille and Racine*, pp.134-5.

[148] See the positive appraisal of d'Aubignac's work in the introduction to d'Aubignac's *Dissertations contre Corneille*, ed. N. Hammond and M. Hawcroft (1995), p.xii.

discussed insistence on verisimilitude at all cost,[149] and the priority he accords to the pleasure of the spectator.[150] In adopting this optic he assumes that the quality of pleasure is directly associated with the avoidance of unclarity. Thus he addresses, for example, the question of how many characters can appear on stage at one time by taking as his touchstone "l'intelligence des Spectateurs":

> Il faut donc dire, à mon avis, Que l'on peut mettre et faire agir dans une Scéne tant d'Acteurs que l'on voudra, pourveû que le nombre, et leurs discours ne confondent en rien l'intelligence des Spectateurs.[151]

Similarly, he believes that the dictates of clarity should govern the introduction of a new character on stage:

> ... le Poete ne doit mettre aucun Acteur sur son Theatre qui ne soit aussi-tost connû des Spectateurs, non seulement en son nom et en sa qualité: mais encore au sentiment qu'il apporte sur la Scéne: autrement le Spectateur est en peine.[152]

The highest achievement of an author who respects d'Aubignac's rules is to move the spectator, an effect equated metaphorically with the heating of the passions. Conversely, the danger a playwright must avoid is failing to engage the audience's emotions, a situation expressed by images related to *froideur*.[153] We can note immediately that d'Aubignac is speaking in the same idiom as Corneille, even if they approach the problem from different angles.[154]

The role of the *confident* is subsumed implicitly and explicitly within this general framework. For d'Aubignac, it is one of a number of devices which, if employed with due regard for verisimilitude, can aid the spectators' appreciation of the play. This is illustrated if we look at the contexts in which he specifically alludes to the *confident* in the fourth book of *La Pratique*.

(1) A main character must be clearly identified on his/her first appearance: he praises the classical device of using a *confident* to declare the identity.[155]

---

[149] Barnwell offers a detailed appraisal of the differences between d'Aubignac's and Corneille's treatment of verisimilitude in *The Tragic Drama of Corneille and Racine*, pp.72-77.

[150] Hammond and Hawcroft argue that this aspect of d'Aubignac's critical approach merits closer attention than it has traditionally received: *Dissertations contre Corneille*, pp.xix-xxi.

[151] *La Pratique du Théâtre*, ed. P. Martino (1927), p.271.

[152] *Ibid.* p.272.

[153] For example, speaking of long *récits*, d'Aubignac observes, "mais ce qu'il y a de particulier en cette conjoncture est, qu'alors le Theatre est *dans la chaleur* de l'action et dans l'empressement des Incidens que ces longues Narrations *refroidissent* et relâchent." (my italics).

[154] Compare the appraisal of H.M. Davison, who argues that d'Aubignac and Corneille start out from a common rhetorical framework ("La vraisemblance chez d'Aubignac et Corneille: quelques réflexions disciplinaires", 1992).

[155] *La Pratique*, p.273.

(2) The unity of place must be respected and actors should always have a reason for being in the determined place: he cites as an example that if the scene is a camp, the queen cannot step outside her tent solely to bemoan her lot to her *confidente*.[156]

(3) Main characters should appear as frequently and for as long as possible, and secondary characters (including *confidents*) should not occupy centre-stage more than absolutely necessary: "autrement le Theatre languira".[157]

(4) *Narrations* (i.e. *récits* as opposed to action seen on stage) lose the spectators' interest if they are too long or unnecessary. D'Aubignac cites as an example of bad practice the expository scenes of *Rodogune*.[158]

(5) The character listening to a *narration* should have good reason for doing so: again, the opening scene of *Rodogune* provides a counter-example as d'Aubignac formulates the principle, "je ne puis approuver qu'on fasse entretenir des valets, par une simple curiosité, sur les aventures d'un grand Prince."[159]

All but the first of these points serve as a warning against an overuse of *confidents*. There is the general assumption that secondary characters, played by the least distinguished actors, are inherently less interesting.[160] And even when minor characters are tolerated, d'Aubignac demands that their presence and contribution should satisfy the stringent demands of verisimilitude.

(ii) POLEMICAL POSITIONS IN THE *QUERELLE DE SOPHONISBE*

The principles of verisimilitude and of the pleasure of the audience remain the guiding force behind d'Aubignac's onslaught on *Sophonisbe*. Corneille had not gratified d'Aubignac by any acknowledgement of the publication of the *Pratique du théâtre*, and his own *Discours* and *Examens* challenged head-on the centrality d'Aubignac had accorded to verisimilitude and *bienséance*. In 1662 Corneille was reported to have contributed to the criticisms of *Manlius*, a

---

[156] *Ibid.*, p.274.

[157] *Ibid.*, p.279.

[158] *Ibid.*, p.300. Note however that d'Aubignac is generally balanced in his judgement of Corneille in *La Pratique*. Shortly before this example he had praised the exemplary exposition of *Théodore* (ibid., p.299).

[159] *Ibid.*, p.302.

[160] The reverse, of course, often prevailed in comedy, with playwrights tailoring the leading role of a servant to suit a successful actor. See Émelina, *Les Valets et les servantes*, p.186.

tragedy by d'Aubignac's protégée, Mlle Desjardins.[161] When Corneille's *Sophonisbe* met with an indifferent public reception, d'Aubignac seized the opportunity to reiterate his principles, this time clearly at Corneille's expense. Unlike *La Pratique*, his four *Dissertations* of 1663 are increasingly hostile and personal in their attack. As a result we need to extrapolate the essence of the criticisms from the agressively censorious tones in which they are couched.

However, d'Aubignac was neither the only nor the first to publish his criticisms of *Sophonisbe*. The young Donneau de Visé's appeared in the third volume of his *Nouvelles nouvelles* (a series of fictitious discussions among journalists) in February 1663, just under a month after *Sophonisbe* had been staged. D'Aubignac's *Remarques sur Sophonisbe*, presented in the form of a letter to Madame la Duchesse de R**, followed very closely.[162] In a period when criticisms circulated freely before being published, there is nothing surprising in the fact that Donneau de Visé and d'Aubignac should arrive at similar conclusions. Couton suspects that Donneau de Visé was in fact echoing d'Aubignac's views.[163] Certainly Donneau de Visé plays a less-than-straightforward role in the whole *Querelle*, for thereafter he changes sides and becomes the defender of Corneille on the dubious pretext that when he published his initial views he had not read *Sophonisbe* closely enough! In reality we may guess that the future editor of *Le Mercure galant* knew that for every argument there is a counter-argument, and found Corneille's camp the more interesting to support.

The initial criticisms of Donneau de Visé[164] concentrated on the main characters and on the reasons for which the play failed to arouse the emotional response of the audience. He notes, but only in passing, the weakness of the scenes with the two *suivantes*:

> *qui sont d'autant plus ennuyeuses qu'elles <les suivantes> n'ont point d'intérêt en la pièce.*[165]

It is d'Aubignac who develops the issue substantially. His *Remarques* start with the basic grounds for criticism: the failure of the play to engage the passions of the audience. The analysis then falls broadly into two sections, the flaws in the construction of the play and the unsatisfactory nature of the main characters. While this latter section is similar to the criticisms of Donneau de Visé, the analysis of the dramaturgical devices is far more detailed, and it is in this context that d'Aubignac enumerates at length the shortcomings of the

---

[161] See G. Couton, *La Vieillesse de Corneille*, pp.48-51. We rely for our information on an imprecise reference in Tallemant des Réaux, *Historiettes* II, p.905.

[162] For a discussion of the uncertainties surrounding the publication, apparently without d'Aubignac's permission, see *Dissertations contre Corneille*, pp.xvii-xviii.

[163] *La Vieillesse de Corneille*, p.48.

[164] Reproduced in Granet, *Recueil de dissertations*, vol. I, 1739, pp.116-33.

[165] Granet, *Recueil*, vol. I, p.129.

suivantes. Having taken Corneille severely to task for failing to respect the criterion of verisimilitude in his observance of the unities of time and place,[166] d'Aubignac launches into a much longer analysis of the *suivantes*. At first sight, we might be surprised by the energy with which he attacks minor characters for their role in a mere two scenes of *Sophonisbe* (I.2 between Herminie and Sophonisbe and II.1 between Barcée and Éryxe). However, it becomes evident that the case of *Sophonisbe* is the pretext for a much fuller general discussion of this question. We should note in this section d'Aubignac's repeated use of phrases conveying the wider import of his argument:

> *C'est un défaut pour lequel j'ai <u>toujours</u> eu de l'aversion ... Davantage ces Suivantes, ne récitant <u>jamais</u> que de légères considérations sur la fortune d'autrui, et qui sont <u>ordinairement</u> assez mal reçues dans les passions qui occupent l'esprit des Grands, elles ne sont <u>jamais</u> animées, et leur discours ... est <u>toujours</u> froid.[167]*

After his cutting remark that scenes with *suivantes* are generally of so little interest that the audience treat them as an interval,[168] d'Aubignac uses the specific example drawn from *Sophonisbe* as support for his general thesis:

> *Il n'en faut point d'autres preuves que le mauvais succès de ces deux narrations.[169]*

Clearly the flaws of *Sophonisbe* had touched a raw nerve, and d'Aubignac felt entitled to establish some general principles. It is these broader issues which I now propose to examine, before returning in the last section of the chapter to an assessment of the validity of d'Aubignac's judgements on *Sophonisbe* itself.

The criticisms of the *suivantes* in *Sophonisbe* are briefly summarised by d'Aubignac at the outset:

> *Les deux principales narrations qui doivent donner les lumières à l'intelligence du sujet, et le fondement à tous les événements de la Scène, sont faites par deux Reines à deux Suivantes, qui n'agissent point dans la conduite du Poème, qui n'ont point une confidence avec leurs Maîtresses, et qui demeurent sans aucun intérêt à tous les Accidents du Théâtre, pour qui le Spectateur ne désire ni ne craint, et qui ne font aucune impression sur son esprit. [170]*

His objection is very similar to Corneille's own admission in the *Examen* to *Médée* about the problem of relying on a protactic character such as Pollux for

---

[166] *Dissertations contre Corneille*, pp.7-8.

[167] *Dissertations contre Corneille*, pp.8-9. The underlinings are mine.

[168] "C'est le temps que les Spectateurs prennent pour s'entretenir de ce qui s'est passé, pour reposer leur attention, ou pour manger leurs confitures". *Dissertations contre Corneille*, p.9.

[169] *Dissertations contre Corneille*, p.9.

[170] *Dissertations contre Corneille*, p.8.

the exposition.[171] However, d'Aubignac is swift to link this unsatisfactory use of the device to his theory of verisimilitude. For him, the serious obstacle is the impossibility of the spectator believing that queens would really choose to confide in "de simples Suivantes". In the case of *Sophonisbe*, Corneille has compounded the *invraisemblance* in each scene by having the Queen repeat to her *suivante* information which both parties already know. In other words, the intelligent spectator cannot but be aware of the contrivance, which breaks the circle of illusion.[172] Thus d'Aubignac is appealing to his other touchstone, the pleasure of the spectator. This lies behind another general criticism he voices: that the words of *suivantes* are ordinarily devoid of passion and so fail to move the spectator, a fact which is exacerbated since:

> les Femmes qui jouent ces Rôles, sont ordinairement de mauvaises Actrices
> qui déplaisent aussitôt qu'elles ouvrent la bouche.[173]

In the context of such damning criticism, what advice can d'Aubignac offer? Strangely, two conflicting lines emerge, the one raising the prominence of the role, the other lowering it. If *suivantes* are unsatisfactory because they are too peripheral to the action, the playwright should take pains to integrate them:

> Il faudrait auparavant avoir bien établi le mérite et la suffisance d'une Fille de
> cette qualité, avec la nécessité de la consulter: Enfin il en faudrait faire un
> personnage de l'action du Thêâtre, et non pas un simple ornement pour le
> remplir.[174]

Yet a little later, as though ignoring this possibility, d'Aubignac praises at length the classical tradition of not allowing such characters to speak:

> Et le meilleur avis que l'on pourrait donner à nos Poètes, ce serait de suivre en
> cela l'exemple des Anciens, et de ne point faire parler leurs Suivantes, si elles
> ne se trouvent engagées dans les affaires de la Scène, et qu'elles ne soient des
> Actrices nécessaires.[175]

We might argue that the phrases "si elles se trouvent ... et qu'elles ne soient ..." provide an escape clause, but the thrust of the argument is clear. D'Aubignac is recommending that playwrights should give as few lines as possible to *suivantes*.

This raises an important point, which appears to have been overlooked by other critics. In this section of the *Remarques* d'Aubignac is concerned almost exclusively with the inappropriate use of *female* characters. Of Bocchar and

---

[171] See p.17.

[172] D'Aubignac accepts that in reflection after the performance the spectator may take pleasure in unravelling the playwright's clever dramaturgical construct, but he insists that at the time the suspension of disbelief should be absolute (*Dissertations contre Corneille*, p.10).

[173] *Dissertations contre Corneille*, p.9.

[174] *Ibid.*, p.9.

[175] *Ibid.*, p.9.

Mézétulle, the male equivalents to Herminie and Barcée, there is not a word of criticism. Perhaps this is in part because their function is primarily that of messengers rather than full-blown *confidents*. But d'Aubignac takes exception not only to the *suivantes* but also to the heroines of *Sophonisbe*, because the latter have been allowed to discourse on politics:

> On ne souffre pas volontiers des Femmes faire ainsi les Catons, et l'on souhaiterait qu'elles fissent un peu plus les Femmes.[176]

D'Aubignac's conception of drama is binary: the heroes should be active, political and military leaders; the heroines should be content to discourse on their passions.[177] Correspondingly, the *suivantes* or *confidentes* should be muted, for if the heroines themselves are to be exiled from the political domain, there is little hope that their followers may have an active role.

In his unauthorised defence of Corneille, Donneau de Visé devotes a substantial section to the *confidente* in his turn,[178] adding in conclusion that he has only treated the role at such length since d'Aubignac had done so. What has subsequently been termed the *Querelle du confident* (perhaps it would be more apt to call it the *Querelle de la confidente*) is thus engaged, with d'Aubignac's challenge being taken up. The comments in the *Defense de Sophonisbe*, like those of the Abbé, transcend the immediate context and concern the role of the *confident(e)* in general.

Before responding to the two major thrusts of d'Aubignac's attack, Donneau de Visé questions d'Aubignac's use of the term *suivantes* for Herminie and Barcée, whom Donneau de Visé styles *confidentes*. He defends the verisimilitude of scenes between mistress and *confidente* with the argument that queens must confide in those "que l'on peut appeler leurs créatures"[179] because they may need to hide secrets from those of their own rank. If we bear in mind the tense relationship between the two queens of *Sophonisbe*, the remark is well founded. The encounters between Sophonisbe and Éryxe (I.3, II.3, III.3, V.4) are marked by thinly veiled hostility; mutual trust is absent.

---

[176] *Ibid.*, p.10. In his reappraisal of *Sophonisbe* ("Corneille in 1663: the tragedy of *Sophonisbe*", 1984), H. T. Barnwell argues (pp.576-7) that other contemporary critics, including Saint-Evremond, appreciated Corneille's vigorous portrayal of his heroine.

[177] On the inversion of male and female roles in Corneille's theatre, and the particular case of *Sophonisbe*, see the fine analysis by S. Doubrovsky, *Corneille et la dialectique du héros*, pp.355-9. However, Doubrovsky concentrates on the main characters and does not comment on the *confidents*.

[178] *Deffense de la Sophonisbe de Monsieur de Corneille* in Granet, *Recueil*, vol. I, pp.154-194 (pages 167-173 concern the *confidente*).

[179] Granet, *Recueil* vol. I, p.169.

Donneau de Visé has put his finger on a central function of *confident(e)* scenes
in tragedy of the 1660s. They allow the audience to discover truths which
cannot be spoken before other characters. There are, of course, earlier examples
of the primacy of such scenes, such as Cléopâtre's speech to Laonice in
Rodogune,[180] but with the peak of interest in "cloak and dagger" plays of
suspense and disguised identity, the *confident(e)* was, in some circumstances,
almost indispensable. Certainly in *Sophonisbe* Corneille's queens each have a
secret which they will confide only to a *confidente*: namely, Sophonisbe's
jealousy if Massinisse should marry Éryxe, and Éryxe's love for Massinisse
(which Éryxe's pride prevents her from acknowledging publicly).

Donneau de Visé also offers an answer to the other main charge of
invraisemblance, that the *confidentes* already know what the queens tell them.
He argues that Sophonisbe's and Éryxe's speeches are differently motivated:
they do not inform their *confidentes* in order to seek advice, but rather they are
making "une réflexion sur l'état de leurs affaires". Although Donneau de Visé
is here defending Corneille's *confidentes*, we should note that his claim
effectively reduces them to a passive role of listener. Indeed he compliments
Corneille on using only five or six lines by *confidentes* to prompt admirable
speeches from main characters. In this he is also meeting d'Aubignac's
stricture concerning the lack of interest and passion aroused by *confidentes*. For
Donneau de Visé, the fact that we are interested in the fate of a protagonist
justifies the use of her *confidente*. His argument makes the two characters
inseparable:

> *Vous voyez par-là que l'intérêt de ces Confidentes est confondu avec celui de*
> *leurs Maîtresses.*[181]

It could be argued that this defence of the *confidente* is paradoxically achieved
at the *confidente*'s expense, and certainly does not by allow for any expansion
of the role.

These two texts constitute the main exchanges of the *Querelle*, but there are
indications that the subject remained topical in the following months. The
anonymous author of the *Lettre sur les remarques qu'on a faites sur la*
Sophonisbe de Monsieur Corneille (a response parallel to Donneau de Visé's,
though briefer and less heated) confines himself to supporting d'Aubignac's
view that the *suivantes* need to be involved in the plot.[182] As for Corneille
himself, in the "Au Lecteur"of *Sophonisbe* (published in 1663), while
declining to mention d'Aubignac by name, he does respond vigorously to a
number of his criticisms. The issue of the *confidentes* is not in itself broached,

---

[180] See p.40.
[181] Granet, *Recueil*, vol. I, p.170
[182] Granet, *Recueil*, vol. I, p.200

perhaps because Corneille recognised that d'Aubignac was in part justified in
his criticisms, perhaps also because he had no overview to state. However, we
may perceive a connection between the *Querelle* and Corneille's defence of
Éryxe, a character of his own invention. He feels obliged to add a warning that
Massinisse's declarations of love to her in II.2 are "un équivoque dont le sens
caché regarde cette autre reine". If spectators could have failed to understand
the implications of this scene,[183] it is reasonable to ask how they could have
followed the play at all had they not had the benefit of the expository scenes
between the queens and their *confidentes*.

D'Aubignac did not let the *Querelle* fade away so soon. He returned to the
issue in his second *Dissertation*, treating Corneille's previous play, *Sertorius*.[184]
It seems probable that d'Aubignac had composed this piece at roughly the
same time as his attack on *Sophonisbe*; when he came to publish both
Dissertations himself, he appended to the criticisms of *Sertorius* a response to
Donneau de Visé's defence of *Sophonisbe*.[185] In the discussion of *Sertorius*, he
confines himself to one specific criticism of the role of a *suivante*, judging
Sertorius's confession to Thamire of his love for Viriate inappropriate and
unnecessary:

> *Thamire lui donne conseil de ce qu'il doit faire: mais ce grand Homme en
> devait prendre ailleurs, ou le Poète devait donner quelque couleur à cette
> confidence, et à la suffisance de cette sage Conseillère.*[186]

Once again, the scene which d'Aubignac has singled out is one which relies on
a *confidente* for the revelation of secret passions. The majority of the epilogue
to this *Dissertation* is devoted to the next instalment of the *Querelle du
confident*.[187] D'Aubignac presumes (wrongly) that the defence of *Sophonisbe*
came from Corneille's own pen, and so addresses his increasingly acerbic
riposts directly to the playwright. The main focus of his remarks is one we
might think of as secondary, at least from the dramaturgical point of view: the
use of the term *suivantes* for the *confidentes*. However, in an age preoccupied
by social titles and etiquette, nomenclatures were undoubtedly of importance.

---

[183] Does Corneille imply that some of his critics did so wilfully: "tant d'autres *ont voulu* s'y
méprendre ..."?

[184] D'Aubignac intended to work backwards through Corneille's *œuvre*, subjecting each play
to rigorous criticism, but the project petered out after his third *Dissertation*, on *Œdipe*.

[185] See *Dissertation contre Corneille*, pp.xxii-xxiii.

[186] *Ibid.*, p.56.

[187] In the *Dissertations contre Corneille*, the epilogue occupies pp.61-67, of which pp.63-
66 deal with the *suivantes/confidentes*.

D'Aubignac also associates the point with his repeated criticism that the role of such characters is ill-defined and prejudicial to the structure of the play:[188]

> *Et M. Corneille ne faisant point connaître la condition de Thamire, non plus que des autres Femmes de sa* Sophonisbe, *on ne saurait les considérer autrement que comme une suite inutile introduite seulement pour la pompe, et qui pour cela ne peuvent agir que très faiblement au Théâtre.[189]*

Corneille had not taken account of the Abbé's remarks on the scenes with Barcée and Herminie when first revising *Sophonisbe*, but this time there is evidence that he was stung by the rebuke, especially since it concerned his own inconsistency in having used the term *suivantes* in earlier plays. The 1668 edition of *Œdipe* carefully renames Nérine and Mégare "dame d'honneur" and "fille d'honneur" respectively, and the term *suivante* never appears in the cast list of Corneille's subsequent tragedies.

Donneau de Visé kept up the momentum of his self-publicising "press campaign" by publishing an unsolicited defence of *Sertorius*.[190] On the *confidentes*, he offers little more of substance, but cannot resist an ironic remark that d'Aubignac missed his opportunity to include them as a further example of Corneille's *polymythie*.[191] His remarks show that the battle lines are now fixed: d'Aubignac is the detractor of the *suivante/confidente*, Donneau de Visé their defender. D'Aubignac's third *Dissertation* (on *Œdipe*), a piece concerned mainly with demonstrating the horrific lack of verisimilitude in Corneille's reworking of the myth, suggests that here an additional *confident(e)* scene might have been appropriate. But the remark is laden with irony. D'Aubignac professes shock that Dircé should have remained with Thésée to listen to the récit of Œdipe's death (V.9), and returns to a principle of *La Pratique*, that a *narration* must always be made to a suitable person, even a *confident(e)* if necessary:

> *En vérité c'est être bien stérile en inventions que de ne pas trouver à qui conter une aventure, et je m'en étonne de M. Corneille qui tant de fois l'a fait par les entretiens des Suivants et des Suivantes.[192]*

In effect, d'Aubignac is scoring two points at once: reminding us of Corneille's over-reliance on *confident* scenes elsewhere, and challenging the playwright's statement in the *Examen* to *Œdipe* (1660) that Dircé's presence is an example

---

[188] The second *Dissertation* was concerned primarily with the unity of action, and what d'Aubignac terms the "polymythie" of *Sertorius*, in which he finds five plots.

[189] *Dissertation contre Corneille*, p.65.

[190] *Deffense du Sertorius de Monsieur de Corneille*, in Granet, *Recueil*, vol. I, pp. 295-360.

[191] "et si vous aviez aimé les Suivantes, Confidentes, ou Dames d'honneur, vous auriez sans doute dit, que l'on aurait pû faire un Poeme dramatique, du personnage de Thamire, qui est Dame d'honneur de Viriate; et je crois qu'il aurait fallu appeler ce Poeme *la Suivante* ou *la Dame d'honneur*..." (Granet, *Recueil*, vol. I, p.314).

[192] *Dissertations contre Corneille*, p.97.

of dramatic considerations taking priority over verisimilitude.[193] Of the
"unnecessary" or *invraisemblable* use of *confidents*, d'Aubignac is as
intolerant as ever. He specifically criticises two scenes of *Œdipe*. Dircé's scene
with Mégare (II.2) produces the familiar complaint that:

> *Ce sont des vers inutiles et du temps mal employé durant lequel le Théâtre
> languit.*[194]

In this case the scene is the more reprehensible in the Abbé's eyes because of
the unacceptable freedom with which the heroine discourses on her passion
(another example of the connection between d'Aubignac's attacks on the
confidente and the moral limitations he would impose on the nature of the
heroine). The criticism of Nérine's role in II.3 is rather different: d'Aubignac
is unhappy that the account of Laius's apparition should have been entrusted to
a mere *suivante*.[195] He is hereby questioning another of the essential functions
of the *confident*, that of bearing reports of offstage action.

We can only speculate on how d'Aubignac would have expanded his
criticisms of the *confident(e)* had he fulfilled his intention of scrutinising each
of Corneille's earlier plays. As it was, the *Querelle* was not pursued, d'Aubignac
being occupied with revising *La Pratique*,[196] and Corneille with an in-folio
edition of his works in 1663 and then returning to the regular production of
new plays for the remaining ten years of his career as a dramatist. So what had
the *Querelle du confident* achieved? Its impact on Corneille must be judged by
developments in his dramaturgy in this later period. For other playwrights,
d'Aubignac and Donneau de Visé had drawn attention to what had previously
been no more than one in a repertoire of devices and had made it - briefly - a
subject of critical controversy. D'Aubignac expressed in the *Troisième
Dissertation* a perception of the surprising fruitfulness of some theoretical
debates:

> *Les disputes d'érudition sont comme les cailloux qui se choquent et qui font
> naître du feu où jamais on n'eût pensé d'en rencontrer ...*[197]

The best proof that the time had been ripe for a full debate on confidential
strategies lies in the various experiments with the *confident* which characterise
the plays of the next fifteen years, and which will be discussed in Part II of this

---

[193] "C'est une incommodité de la représentation qui doit faire souffrir quelque manquement à
l'exacte vraisemblance." (*Œuvres complètes*, vol. III, p.21).

[194] *Dissertations contre Corneille*, p.100.

[195] *Ibid.*, p.100.

[196] D'Aubignac never published the revised edition he was preparing but Martino's critical
edition shows how his draft had expunged the earlier laudatory references to Corneille.

[197] *Dissertations contre Corneille*, p.77.

study. First, in conclusion to this chapter I propose to return a detailed reading of *Sophonisbe* and a comparison with Mlle Desjardins's *Manlius*.

(iii) THE EVIDENCE OF THE PLAYS: A COMPARISON BETWEEN CORNEILLE'S *SOPHONISBE* AND MLLE DESJARDINS'S *MANLIUS*

D'Aubignac's comments on the scenes with *confidentes* in *Sophonisbe* use this play as a pretext for a thorough-going criticism of the device. He seems determined to present *Sophonisbe* in the most negative light possible, for example limiting his remarks on the *confidentes* to the two weakest scenes of the play, despite the fact that Herminie speaks in two other scenes. For a more balanced appraisal of the use of *confident(e)s* in *Sophonisbe*, one must therefore probe further, asking such questions as whether *Sophonisbe* shows a less skilful deployment of the *confident(e)* than Corneille's earlier tragedies or those of his contemporaries. What is specific to Corneille in 1663 can be thrown into clearer relief by a brief comparison with *Manlius*, the tragedy of Mlle Desjardins, staged the previous year, which d'Aubignac held up as an example of the judicious reworking of historical material in explicit contrast to the *dénouement* of *Sophonisbe*.[198]

If we compare *Œdipe, Sertorius* and *Sophonisbe* with the tragedies which Corneille had composed previously, we are struck by several points. First, there are more characters potentially equivalent to *confidents* in these three later plays (four characters in each case).[199] Secondly, whereas the number of lines spoken by *confident(e)s* in his plays of the late 1640s and early 1650s had fallen sharply, in the new plays these characters are restored to a more active role. In *Œdipe* Cléante, Dymas, Mégare and Nérine together account for 9.05% of the play, with Nérine having the largest single role (4.28%). In *Sertorius*, Arcas, Aufide, Celsus, Thamire similarly occupy 9.02%, with Aufide having 4.64% and Thamire 3.54%. Surprisingly, in view of d'Aubignac's strictures, the four characters of *Sophonisbe* who are broadly equivalent to *confidents* speak rather less than their counterparts in *Œdipe* and *Sertorius* (only 7.2% of the play), and none of them has more than 42 lines in total. Apparently d'Aubignac would have found more ammunition had he started with the two preceding plays.

To concentrate initially, as d'Aubignac does, on the female roles of *Sophonisbe*, we need to look at what the *confidentes* say and at the confidences which they receive. D'Aubignac did not take issue with any of the scenes in which *confidentes* were simply silent witnesses to conversations between main

---

[198] *Ibid.*, p.13.
[199] See Appendix I.

characters. Thus their main function went unchallenged.[200] It is the expositions which drew the weight of the Abbé's disapproval on the grounds of the *confidentes*' failure to engage the audience's interest and of the lack of verisimilitude. However much we may agree that the audience required the information imparted by Sophonisbe to Herminie in I.2, it is hard to argue that Corneille has done more than recycle a familiar strategy - the *confidente* listening and prompting with the occasional question. In his analysis of the rhetoric of *confidents* in Racine, M. Hawcroft looks back to *Sophonisbe* and comments that the scene does not lend itself to an analysis of persuasive devices, wherein lies its failure; "there is no persuasion".[201] We might, like Donneau de Visé, respond that our interest is in Sophonisbe herself, not in her relationship with her *confidente*, but Herminie's repeated expressions of incomprehension are a very artificial device for eliciting information.[202]

Her other scenes alone with Sophonisbe (II.5 and V.1) also depend on a conventional contrast between the *confidente*'s lack of perspicacity and the main character's clearer understanding of the passions, but here the contrast has an element of conflict, with each side adopting persuasive language. II.5 is important if the audience is to understand that Éryxe is not indifferent to Massinisse's proposal to Sophonisbe (as Herminie thinks), but is in fact disguising her jealousy. The discussion with the *confidente* allows for hidden sentiments to be analysed, a particularly important concern given that Éryxe is an invented character whose motivation we cannot otherwise know. In V.1 Corneille employs another standard strategy, but again to good effect: the *confidente* and anxious heroine speak together while they are awaiting news of an event offstage (Massinisse's interview with Scipio). We recognise a familiar pattern: the *confidente* is encouraging and optimistic, while the heroine has a presentiment of tragedy.[203] Whereas Hawcroft rightly criticised I.2 for a lack of interaction between the two characters, in V.1 Corneille has Sophonisbe and Herminie engage in argumentative strategies, including *interruptio*,[204] and the scene provides a suitable prelude to the dramatic arrival of Mézétulle with the letter and poison. We may conclude that in his criticisms of Herminie, d'Aubignac overlooked the two-thirds of the evidence which did not suit his

---

[200] Barcée is in fact present for 44.13% of the play, although she speaks for only 1.04%. Herminie is present for 56.59%, speaking for 2.31%. This high ratio of silent presence on stage is comparable with that of their counterparts in earlier tragedies of Corneille (see Appendix I).

[201] M. Hawcroft, *Word as Action*, p.166.

[202] "Madame, ou j'entends mal une telle prière,/ Ou ..." (l.35); "J'ai peine à concevoir que ..." (l.83); "Je comprends encor moins ..." (l.101).

[203] The scene opens with Sophonisbe exclaiming "Cesse de me flatter d'une espérance vaine" (l.1517).

[204] Lines 1525 and 1541. D'Aubignac took Corneille to task for excessive use of this device in his criticisms of *Sertorius* (*Dissertations contre Corneille*, pp.51-52), but here I would suggest that it adds to the speed of the debate.

case. In these later scenes Corneille was not breaking any new ground in his use of the *confidente*, but they demonstrate that a familiar strategy still had a dramatic application.

In the case of Éryxe and Barcée, we must form our opinion on the evidence of a single scene, their exchange in II.1. Although d'Aubignac's comments imply that this is a replica of I.2, serving the exposition,[205] this view is hard to sustain. Between Acts I and II fortunes have been reversed in battle, and the purpose of II.1 is both to inform the audience of the defeat of Syphax and to explore Éryxe's reactions to this turn of events. Donneau de Visé's general defence therefore seems apt: Barcée is a necessary mechanism to allow Éryxe "une réflexion sur l'état de <ses> affaires". Nor is the scene devoid of all persuasive devices. In fact, it is closer to V.1 than to I.2. Barcée's role is to argue against Éryxe's negative assessment, and this she does in two speeches (lines 415-422 and 469-479). Again, we can conclude that d'Aubignac's comments apply primarily to I.2 not II.1. Indeed, his criticism of the later scene is better understood as a function of his general criticism of Éryxe herself as a superfluous character.[206]

In contrast, when we turn to Bocchar and Mézétulle, the male characters who approximate to *confidents*, we note that they are used primarily as messengers. Bocchar is listed as the "lieutenant de Syphax", but appears in only one scene with the latter, I.4, and then only as a silent witness to Syphax's exchange with Sophonisbe. Bocchar's main function has been to act *for* Syphax at the start of the play by delivering a report of the battle to Sophonisbe. He concludes this *récit* with an acknowledgement that he is speaking as his master's proxy.[207] His language is that of demonstrative rhetoric. All the sentences are declarative statements, and although the spectator is left in no doubt of the importance of the battle, Bocchar does not seek to engage Sophonisbe's emotions. It is therefore only in the following scene with her *confidente* that Sophonisbe can reveal to the audience the personal and affective dimension of the situation. I would suggest that the opening *récit* constitutes no less obvious a use of a convenient device than the ensuing scene with the *confidente*, but one which escapes censure in that it allows the playwright to establish a dramatic situation with brevity.[208] Bocchar is a protactic character, absent from the remaining four Acts of the play. Indeed, rather than reintroduce him, Corneille makes Lépide,

---

[205] He does not distinguish between Herminie and Barcée: "Les *deux* principales narrations qui doivent donner les lumières à l'intelligence du sujet ... sont faites par *deux* Reines à *deux* Suivantes..." (*Dissertations contre Corneille*, p.8; my italics).

[206] *Dissertations contre Corneille*, pp.15-16.

[207] "Voilà ce que le Roi m'a chargé de vous dire." (I.27).

[208] Voltaire, otherwise a very harsh critic of *Sophonisbe*, praised the concision of this scene: "Vous voyez que l'exposition de la pièce est bien faite: on entre tout d'un coup en matière, on est occupé de grands objets." (*Remarques sur Sophonisbe* in *Œuvres complètes de Voltaire*, vol. IX, p.612).

who is officially Syphax's guard, take on the role of *confident* in III.7, so that
the audience may savour the pathos of the preceding interview between Syphax
and Sophonisbe.

Mézétulle, the "lieutenant de Massinisse", on the other hand, is present in
four of the five acts. Yet he is not employed as a conventional *confident* either;
on two occasions he, too, functions as a messenger. In III.1 he brings Massinisse
a report of the preparations for the wedding, and of Éryxe's reactions. The
arrival of Éryxe herself precludes any development of the exchange between
Mézétulle and Massinisse, and in this case the information imparted by
Mézétulle is not essential in itself but serves rather to alert the spectator to the
state of mind and feelings of Éryxe. In V.2, however, Mézétulle is charged with
the dramatic role of bearing the letter with the poison from Massinisse to
Sophonisbe. His language is of a different rhetorical order from that of III.1,
for he assumes the role of defender of Massinisse, using a series of rhetorical
questions and hypotheses.[209] When these fail to move Sophonisbe, he paints an
eloquent picture of Massinisse's distress in composing the letter.[210] His rhetoric
does not achieve its objective: Sophonisbe scornfully sends the poison back. Yet
the proud irony with which she delivers her message to him shows that she has
engaged in this contest of wills as clearly as if she were speaking to Massinisse
himself.[211] Thus the *confident* is raised from the role of messenger to that of
substitute for the main protagonist. It is a development which other dramatists
will take further. D'Aubignac was concerned with the impropriety of
Sophonisbe's behaviour in the play as a whole and especially in the
dénouement,[212] whereas Corneille was proud of his heroine. By pitting her
against Mézétulle rather than contriving a final scene with Massinisse, he had
given maximum weight to Sophonisbe's authority on stage.[213]
Characteristically, Corneille had opted for dramatic effect where d'Aubignac
would have accorded priority to the creation of an exemplary moral character.

Compared with Corneille's earlier plays, *Sophonisbe* thus offers few new
departures as far as the *confident(e)* is concerned. Herminie and Barcée lack the
vigour of their earlier counterparts such as Nérine, Elvire or Julie, but play a
standard if unexciting role. The male *confident* had never been such a regular
feature of Corneille's dramaturgy. Rather, he draws on the tradition of the
messenger in employing Mézétulle and Bocchar to provide a link with offstage

---

[209] Lines 1565-9, 1575-7, 1582-4.
[210] "... et par ce peu de mots/ Qu'ont arrosé ses pleurs, qu'ont suivi ses sanglots" (ll.1587-8).
[211] "Reportez, Mézétulle, à votre illustre Roi/ Un secours dont lui-même a plus besoin que moi." (ll.1605-6).
[212] "Sophonisbe <en> est l'Héroine; mais hélas, quelle Héroine! elle n'a pas un seul sentiment de vertu." (*Dissertations contre Corneille*, p.13).
[213] Note her interruption of Massinisse with the single imperative "Donnez." (l.1589). Once the letter and poison are handed over, Mézétulle is afforded no further opportunity to defend Massinisse.

action. A striking contrast to this is afforded by Mlle Desjardins's *Manlius*, where a male *confident* enjoys a prominent role, both receiving confidences and offering advice.

*   *   *

The comparison between *Sophonisbe* and *Manlius* is interesting not simply because the tragedies appeared within a year of each other, but also because it is generally assumed that d'Aubignac, as mentor of Mlle Desjardins, probably advised her on the composition of *Manlius*.[214] There is no doubt that the Abbé held it up as a counter-example to point out what he saw as flaws in Corneille's conception of tragedy. In the *Préface* to *Sophonisbe*, Corneille obliquely responded to d'Aubignac's criticism that his heroines were too political by criticising prevailing taste. He prides himself on having avoided:

> *d'avoir effeminé mes héros, par une docte et sublime complaisance au goût de nos délicats, qui veulent de l'amour partout.*[215]

a statement which Couton believes is a specific allusion to Mlle Desjardins's *Manlius*.[216] In short, we may surmise that for d'Aubignac and Corneille *Manlius* and *Sophonisbe* characterised two different visions of tragedy. If we extend the comparison bewtween these plays to the level of dramaturgy, we may ask to what extent Mlle Desjardins respected d'Aubignac's views on the relationship between *bienséance*, verisimilitude and the role of the *confident(e)*, and how far the *confident(e)s* of *Manlius* differ from those of *Sophonisbe*.

Mlle Desjardins provides the equivalent of a *confident* for three of her four main characters, the exception being Manlius himself. Interestingly, whereas Omphale has a *suivante* (Phénice), Camille is given a male adviser, the *licteur* Pison. Iunius, who accompanies Torquatus, is styled *ami*, a title which reflects his status and his right to speak freely to Torquatus. Manlius does not require a *confident* in that he is an "open" character (unlike Torquatus). Although his love for Omphale is initially a secret, when Camille reveals that she knows it (III.2) Manlius's only concern is to protest his virtuous conduct. Furthermore, his heroic stature is increased by his isolation. In a play which has six monologues, quite contrary to the prevailing fashion, two are by Manlius. The first (III.3), following Camille's revelation that his father is his rival for Omphale, is designed to secure our sympathy for the *jeune premier* crossed in

---

[214] On the debate over the exact part d'Aubignac may have played in advising Mlle Desjardins on *Manlius*, see Couton, *La Vieillesse de Corneille* p.48.

[215] *Œuvres complètes*, vol. III, p.384.

[216] *La Vieillesse de Corneille*, p.51.

love.[217] The second (III.5), following the passionate scene with Omphale, is briefer but exposes a classical dilemma, the conflict between "*Les desirs de ma gloire et ceux de mon amour.*" Manlius chooses the noble path of duty, and thereafter the events of the play are out of his hands; our interest in Act IV and most of Act V is centred on Torquatus's decision and the influences brought to bear by Omphale and Camille. Manlius, then, has no need of a *confident*, for his path is fixed, and it remains only for him to follow it with a stoic courage of which d'Aubignac undoubtedly approved.

Phénice is an illustration of the taciturn *suivante* d'Aubignac is prepared to tolerate (at least in the light of the attack on *Sophonisbe*). She accompanies Omphale in 13 scenes,[218] but is alone with her in only two, speaking four lines in I.4 (a scene of 39 lines) and listening in silence to Omphale in I.6 (20 lines). The first scene with Phénice allows Omphale to express her pride and anger after Torquatus's declaration of love to her. Mlle Desjardins has anticipated d'Aubignac's general point that queens would not seek advice from a mere *suivante*, by having Omphale stress her trust in Phénice:

> O toy qui sçeus toûjours le secret de mon ame,
> Phénice cher témoin d'une plus belle flâme. . .

Phénice's short intervention simply prompts further confidences; it does not establish any debate. This scene in fact illustrates Donneau de Visé's claim that we are prepared to accept the *confidente* as a mechanism to allow us insight into the heroine. Omphale's virtual monologue in I.6. is addressed to Manlius,[219] following his reaffirmation of his love in I.5, and Phénice is no more than a spectator. This is her role through the remainder of the play, where she faithfully accompanies Omphale but speaks no further.[220] D'Aubignac could have found little to disapprove of here.

Camille is afforded an active *confident* in Pison in the opening scene of the play, when he bring her news of Manlius's love for Omphale. The scene would satisfy d'Aubignac's concern for verisimilitude and moral propriety in that the widow relies on the trusted adviser of her dead husband.[221] Yet, Pison has no further scenes with Camille, and does not reappear until Act V. Camille is

---

[217] The speech is studded with *précieux* conceits, such as the long prayer to the gods that all other mortals may be blind to Omphale's beauty.

[218] In the copy of the play I have consulted (Claude Barbin, Paris, 1662: Taylor Institution Library Oxford, Vet.Fr.I.A.5 38(3)) she is, strangely, not listed as present in I.3 when Omphale speaks to Torquatus. I suspect this is a printer's error, and Phénice should be present in 14 scenes.

[219] The first 16 lines continue a dialogue with the absent Manlius. A general statement on the benevolence of the gods (ll.17-20) allows the transition to the first person plural ("Allons donc dans ce temple...") as Omphale and Phénice leave the stage together.

[220] She is present even in V.3 when Omphale has asked to be left alone with Manlius.

[221] Pison makes clear his duty to speak to her:"Pour moy que les bontez de vostre Illustre Espoux,/ Iusques à mon trépas attacheront à vous...".

effectively left without a *confident* for the remainder of the play.[222] However,
she is portrayed as a very strong character, concerned to act upon Torquatus
rather than examine her own state of mind. Her privileged position as a widow
allows her to move freely between the main characters, and her determination
leads her to seek out both Omphale and Manlius as well as Torquatus.[223] Thus,
in her treatment of both the main female characters - who have excellent
dramatic roles - Mlle Desjardins has made a significant step towards the
possibility of eliminating the *confidente*.

The only character for whom a *confident* remains essential is Torquatus,
who has two major scenes with Iunius.[224] Torquatus is hiding a guilty secret, his
love for Omphale. As we established in Chapter 1, it is when there is deceit that
the *confident* becomes a particularly valuable device. In II.4 Iunius presses
Torquatus, forcing him to confront his less honourable motives:

> *Que diroit-on de vous si le chef du Senat,*
> *Mesloit son interest à celuy de l'Estat?*

Mlle Desjardins takes pains to make Iunius justify the freedom with which, as an
old friend, he advises Torquatus.[225] The result is a scene of keen debate as
Iunius both argues Manlius's case and questions Torquatus's motives. Both
characters employ deliberative rhetoric effectively, although we are aware that
the question cannot be resolved at this stage.[226] In IV.4 Iunius continues his
unambiguous defence of moral conscience above expediency. He expresses his
position without fear[227] and in a speech of 37 lines argues that Torquatus must
listen to his inner conscience. The use of such a strong *confident/conseiller* in
these scenes of debate both adds to the dramatic strengths of *Manlius* - I think
Mlle's Desjardins's talent merits greater critical interest - and ensures that the
voice of morality is heard. Like d'Aubignac, Mlle Desjardins undoubtedly

---

[222] Donneau de Visé criticises the fact that Camille's love is mentioned only in the exposition (Granet, *Recueil*, pp.157-8). I suspect that the absence of a traditional female *confidente* precluded a fuller development of it.

[223] She initiates interviews with Torquatus in I.2, IV.2 and V.4 (he expresses surprise at her presence on the first two occasions), and with Omphale in II.6 and Manlius in III.2.

[224] II.4 has 100 lines and IV.4 has 137. In other scenes Iunius's role is purely functional: he acts as a messenger in II.2, IV.3 and V.5, and in V.7 he comments in two and a half lines on the struggle within Torquatus.

[225] Iunius defers to Torquatus's authority at the start of each of his last three speeches. He explains his concern for Torquatus by reference to "Le précieux honneur que j'eus dés vostre enfance/ De prendre toûjours part à votre confidence."

[226] Donneau de Visé criticises the "perpétuelles irrésolutions de Torquatus" (Granet, *Recueil*, vol. I, pp.157-8). Mlle Desjardins obviously accorded a higher priority to vigorous moral debate than to the unerring development of the plot.

[227] "Vous m'avez ordonné, Seigneur, expressément/ De vous dire tousjours quel est mon sentiment;/ De grace pardonnez ce discours à mon zele;/ Je serois moins hardy, si j'estois moins fidelle."

believes that the theatre should demonstrate the triumph of morality, and she is prepared to use the *confident* to this end. This is in keeping with her rewriting of history so that Manlius is finally spared, ensuring the triumph of *nature* or family bonds – and thus providing an implicit critique of some of Corneille's most celebrated plays.[228]

If the role of Iunius is exploited effectively through dramatic conflict, Mlle Desjardins is less successful in resolving another challenge posed by the character of Torquatus. The latter cannot confide in Iunius his ignoble designs, and particularly his deception of his son. Mlle Desjardins falls back on the monologue and another outmoded device, the aside, for the audience to understand Torquatus's intentions. In I.2 Torquatus disguises from Camille his horror at learning that Manlius loves Omphale, but he utters three asides, the last of which is more reminiscent of comic than tragic style:

> *Feignons de ne pas croire une telle nouvelle.*

Even more unexpected in a tragedy is the strategy employed in V.2, where, as Omphale begs for a private interview with Manlius, Torquatus whispers at the end:

> *Tâchons sans estre vû, d'écouter leurs discours.*

He eavesdrops on the following scene, providing, perhaps, one of the models for Racine's scene with Néron spying on his rival. In *Manlius* the situation is not so cleverly exploited, and we can judge that the absence of a *confidente* has obliged the playwright to have recourse to a more obviously artificial device.

Manlius is not a blueprint of the Abbé's recommendations for the *confident(e)*, but it does present some radical contrasts with *Sophonisbe*. Phénice has a minimal role; Camille has no *confidente*: the dangers of the *suivante* are thus circumvented. In contrast, although Pison and Iunius do both function as messengers, as did Mézétulle and Bocchar, Iunius is also promoted to the far weightier office of *conseiller*, and contributes to the moral debate. It is conflict which is the key to the most exciting scenes of *Manlius,* whether between Iunius and Torquatus or between protagonists. To generate this conflict, Mlle Desjardins orchestrates an unusually high number of meetings between principal characters. In this she participates in the trend towards the eclipse or elimination of the *confident* which we shall examine in chapter 3. The example of *Manlius* makes it clear that this alternative strategy brings with it certain obstacles as well as some rewards.

---

[228] In her other tragedy, *Nitetis*, she offers an explicit reworking of the dilemma of *Le Cid*. The heroine refuses to marry the man she loves once he has killed her brother.

PART TWO.

NEW STRATEGIES

CHAPTER THREE

THE ECLIPSE OF THE *CONFIDENT*

Dramaturgical devices are rarely cast in stone. *Stances* had enjoyed several decades of popularity before largely disappearing from the tragic repertoire of the 1660s and 1670s.[229] Similarly the monologue, once *de rigueur*, is of minimal importance in many plays of this period.[230] By the same token, if the *confident* was perceived as a tired device, disliked by the spectator, we might expect a significant number of playwrights to eliminate the role. Yet when we look at the repertoire from *Le Cid* to *Phèdre*, we can produce very few plays without any immediate equivalent of a *confident* or *confidente*,[231] and of these Pierre Corneille's *Pertharite* (1651) predates the *Querelle du confident*. Only Racine's *Alexandre* (1665) is likely to be (in part at least) a direct reaction to it. Corneille's *Pulchérie* (1672) is written some nine years after the debate, and its structure is explained, as we shall see, by other considerations.[232]

This small tally of three plays would suggest that most playwrights (and Corneille and Racine for the greater part of their *œuvre*) realised that the *confident* was, at the least, too useful a dramaturgical tool to dispense with, or, in the best cases, that it could be positively exploited to dramatic and tragic effect. We may compare this with the nearly ubiquitous presence of servants in seventeenth-century comedies.[233] My purpose in this chapter is therefore to look at these plays as isolated experiments, weighing the gains brought by the

---

[229] See M.-F. Hilgar, *La Mode des stances dans le théâtre tragique français 1610-87* (1974), pp.15-21.

[230] See Scherer, *La Dramaturgie classique*, pp.256-9.

[231] We should note here that Boyer's *Oropaste* (1662) lists one *confidente*, but the character scarcely fulfils a *confidente's* functions; instead Boyer depends heavily on *para-confidents* (see p.148). Tristan L'Hermite's *La Mort de Sénèque* (1645) lists one *confident*, but he has a silent role; however, there are a large number of minor secondary characters among the conspirators (see p.135).

[232] Although *Pulchérie* is entitled a *comédie héroïque*, as *Tite et Bérénice* had been, I follow critical tradition in considering both plays as essentially part of Corneille's tragic œuvre. For a fuller discussion of the genre of the *comédie héroïque*, see C. Gossip, "*Tite et Bérénice*: a coherent *comédie héroïque*?" (1982).

[233] For the period 1610-1700, Émelina cites only 8 out of 250 plays with no servants (*Les Valets et les servantes*, p.17).

elimination of the *confident*, the alternative strategies adopted to replace such a role, and the problems these may occasion.

To broaden the scope of enquiry, I also include in my discussion several plays which use only one or two *confidents*, these having limited roles. Such a strategy corresponds to one of the main thrusts of d'Aubignac's advice in the *Querelle*, namely that the less a *confident(e)* speaks the better.[234] However, it is not clear that d'Aubignac's influence is responsible for this trend. Three plays of Pierre Corneille preceding *Pertharite* (*Héraclius*, 1646/7; *Don Sanche*, 1649/50; *Nicomède*, 1651) demonstrate that, in his case at least, the *confident*'s role had been reduced long before the *Querelle*. The same is true of Rotrou's *Venceslas* of 1647.[235] Furthermore, my survey of major playwrights in the 1660-70s suggests that there was no universal tendency to reduce the role of the *confident* in the wake of the *Querelle de Sophonisbe*. One significant exception will be treated here, however: the eclipse of the *confident* in Racine's first tragedy, *La Thébaïde*.

(i) SUCCESSFULLY MARGINALISING THE *CONFIDENT*: ROTROU'S *VENCESLAS*

It was only at the tail end of his prolific career that Rotrou gained fame as an author of tragedies. However, both Corneille - his main rival in the 1640s - and Racine were clearly influenced by several of his plays.[236] Various critics have commented on the similarities between the dark passions of Ladislas in *Venceslas* and those of Racine's heroes.[237] Rotrou's reputation rests in no small measure on his dramaturgical skill, and the construction of *Venceslas* with a minimum of *confident* scenes also foreshadows a number of strategies we shall find exploited in later plays. Since *Venceslas* maintained an honourable place in the tragic repertoire for the remainder of the century, its significance as a possible model should not be underestimated.[238] A comparison with *Iphigénie* (1641) and *Cosroès* (1648),[239] reveals that in these tragedies Rotrou gave *confidents* a more substantial role. This leads us to ask what small part

[234] See p.50. We must remember that the Abbé had never suggested a wholescale rejection of the device.

[235] Although originally published as a *tragicomédie*, *Venceslas* is taken by modern critics to belong to the genre of tragedy.

[236] The most obvious parallels are between *Cosroès* (1648) and *Nicomède* (1651), and Rotrou's *Iphigénie* (1641) and Racine's version of the Greek myth. On the relationship between Corneille and Rotrou, see R. Garapon, "Rotrou et Corneille", 1950.

[237] E.g. L. Lockert, *Studies in French Classical Tragedy*, p.187; D. Watts' introduction to his edition of *Venceslas* (1990), p.XXIV.

[238] Watts states that Molière's troupe performed the play at least 14 times between 1659-69, and the Comédie Française gave 84 performances of it between 1680 and 1701 (*op.cit.*, p.V).

[239] For a discussion of *Cosroès* see Chapter 5.

confidents do retain in *Venceslas*, and to what effect Rotrou uses alternative strategies for the greater part of the play.

The characters of both the Infante (Théodore) and her *suivante* (Léonor) are invented by Rotrou. The role of the latter is minimal.[240] In the first three acts she delivers but one line, announcing Alexandre's arrival.[241] In other words, she plays no part in the exposition. Nor does she act as *confidente* to her mistress's passions until IV.1, when she adopts a traditional, reassuring stance as Théodore awakens from the dream which heralds her brother's death.[242] Apart from reporting the delivery of Théodore's letter in V.1, and the briefest aside in V.8, Léonor's role is complete. She has in sum total two brief appearances as a messenger, and one scene receiving her mistress's confidences. Almost the same is true of Octave, styled *gouverneur de Varsovie*, and in effect *confident* to Ladislas. At the end of Act I, after the Prince's first outburst, we have the type of *confident* scene we might regularly expect: Octave urges Ladislas to hide his anger, but Ladislas can think only of his jealous love for Cassandre. Yet for the remainder of the play Octave simply accompanies Ladislas,[243] and acts as messenger in V.7 (delivering the report of the popular uprising). He has in addition three brief asides in other scenes, an archaic device by which Rotrou seeks to heighten our anticipation of the tragedy. In total Octave delivers only 27 lines,[244] and taken together, he and Léonor speak for just 2.62% of the play.

Rotrou has marginalised the two *confidents* he has used, but statistically *Venceslas* is still on a par with two of Corneille's plays of this period, *Héraclius* and *Nicomède*.[245] What makes *Venceslas* different is Rotrou's systematic use of devices which clearly constitute alternative strategies to scenes with *confidents*. In this respect we should note that he opted to omit two secondary characters present in his Spanish source, a valet and the female servant of Cassandre.[246] Watts argues that the free and popular language of these characters, typical of Spanish *comedia*, would have been unthinkable in the French classical tradition.[247] This left Rotrou with the task of conveying the information Rojas had imparted through scenes with the servants by other means. In a play infused with an atmosphere of mistrust and secrecy, the eclipse of the *confident*

---

[240] She speaks in four scenes (II.5, IV.1, V.1, V.8), but has a total of only 23 lines, i.e. 1.23% of the play.

[241] Line 718.

[242] Léonor's speech in this scene retains hints of the bawdiness often associated with the *suivante* in comedy, as she remonstrates with Théodore that the prince is not of an age to spend the night sleeping alone in his own bed.

[243] In IV.2-3. Octave has saved the injured Ladislas and brought him to Théodore's appartments.

[244] i.e. he speaks for 1.45% of the play.

[245] In which *confidents* speak for 1.72% and 2.64% respectively.

[246] Coscorran and Clavela in Rojas's *No hay ser padre siendo rey*.

[247] *Venceslas*, p. XI.

is at first sight all the more surprising. I suggest there are three different techniques on which Rotrou relies.

First, the entire exposition is achieved through conflictual scenes between main characters. We cannot fail to be gripped by the power of the tempestuous opening between Venceslas, his sons and the Duke. The danger of using impassioned exchanges between main characters at the start of the play would be discussed by d'Aubignac,[248] but Rotrou keeps the audience's attention by varying the tempo. The summary dismissal of Alexandre after 3 lines - how many other classical tragedies *begin* by sending a main character offstage?[249] - is counterbalanced by the long speeches of Venceslas and Ladislas. Our interest is sustained over 266 lines not only by the exposition which the characters provide but also by the strategies through which each attempts to control the debate. Both Venceslas and Ladislas make repeated references to the acts of speaking and listening;[250] there is an attempted interruption by Ladislas to regain control (1.82), and Venceslas punctuates his son's speech with orders to continue (lines 195, 227). Scenes 2-5 move faster, with the emphasis on the gestures which accompany words: the embrace sealing the reconciliation between the brothers in I.2, the hesitant greeting between the Duke and Ladislas in I.4; the angry exit of the Duke at the end of I.4 and of Venceslas at the end of I.5.[251] As befits a first act, the tension between characters is implied and acknowledged, but never fully unleashed; the mood of smouldering conflict is coupled dexterously with a clear exposition.

The second device which renders *confidents* unnecessary ensures that we perceive the ironies even of the first scene: namely, the use of asides. Although d'Aubignac warns that the *à part* should be used sparingly and always in accordance with verisimilitude[252] for Rotrou, schooled essentially in the tradition of comedy and tragicomedy, it is a vital tool. From the start of Venceslas's speech in I.1, we know from Ladislas's aside that he is only humouring his father by listening:

> *Que la vieillesse souffre et fait souffrir autruy!*
> *Oyons les beaux advis qu'un flateur luy conseille.*
> *(ll.6-7)*

---

[248] *La Pratique*, pp. 280-1.

[249] We might note that the opening scene of Corneille's *Nicomède*, also a vigorous exchange between two main characters (see p.22), is centred upon Laodice's attempts to persuade Nicomède to leave. I am grateful to Dr David Clarke for drawing this parallel to my attention.

[250] Lines 4, 7, 8, 82, 131-7, 138, 140, 224, 249.

[251] D. Maskell has commented on the significant use of physical gesture throughout *Venceslas* in *Racine. A Theatrical Reading*, p.187.

[252] *La Pratique*, pp.255-61.

Similarly at the end of Ladislas's defence, Venceslas has an aside which prepares us for the fact that his generous reconciliation with his son is no more than a strategic move:

> LE ROY, *bas*
>
> *Que puis-je tenter, sur cette âme hautaine?*
> *Essayons l'artifice où la rigueur est vaine.*
> *(ll.247-8)*

The spectator thus sees each character playing out a role, creating a play within a play which will be continued as Venceslas oversees the embraces and entrances of characters for the rest of the act, much like a theatrical director. In such a world, open scenes with *confidents* would strike a dissonant note, threatening our pleasure in observing the layers of pretence.

Together with the device of the aside we must recognise the importance of the monologue in *Venceslas*.[253] In a number of cases the latter device is a clear alternative to a scene with a *confident*. Yet even Théodore, who has a *confidente*, is given a monologue. Her revelation of her shame when she believes that the Duke does not return her secret love (II.4) is rendered the more poignant because she is alone. Where the aside allowed Venceslas and Ladislas to create roles involving the complicity of the audience, the monologue is used by Rotrou's characters to question their sense of their own identity. Théodore's monologue is poised between affirmations of what she now believes to be fact (e.g. the repeated "Le Duc ayme Cassandre", lines 687, 691) and a series of questions as she attempts to make sense of the behaviour of the Duke. This culminates in the anxiety that she may have confused appearance and reality:

> *Sçais-je si mal d'amour expliquer le langage?*
> *Fais-je d'un simple hommage une inclination?*
> *Et formay-je un fantosme à ma presomption?*
> *(ll. 700-2)*

In the final monologue of Venceslas, as he has sent Ladislas to his execution, the king's dilemma is not the choice between two mutually exclusive truths, but rather the acknowledgement that he cannot preserve two identities.

> *Je ne puis rien pour luy, le sang cede à la loy,*
> *Et je ne luy puis estre et bon pere et bon Roy.*
> *(ll.1653-4)*

Another dramatist might well have replaced one or both of these monologues, and those of Alexandre in II.6 and the Duke in III.1, by a scene with a *confident*. Rotrou prefers to show each character alone in his or her suffering: ultimately his play is about the individual's sense of identity, a theme which

---

[253] Watts observes the high frequence of both, which he explains by the climate of mistrust (*op.cit.* p.XIII). I would suggest a connection with the virtual absence of *confidents*.

recurs frequently in his theatre. Dramaturgically Rotrou has much in common
with Pierre Corneille. He is not afraid to employ obviously artifical, even
archaic devices where they serve a specific dramatic function. We might argue
that both playwrights, unlike d'Aubignac, are confident that the audience will
prefer the skilful handling of dramatic illusion to the stringent demands of
verisimilitude.

On another level, Rotrou circumvents scenes with *confidents* by recourse to
a more discreet device, the scene with a *para-confident*. As we saw in Chapter 1,
if characters do not have their own *confidents* a dramatist may use their close
relationship with other main characters to fulfil the same ends. This can either
result in a totally open relationship, parallel to that between protagonist/
confident, or - more interestingly but also more problematically - in a situation
where characters are caught between conflicting loyalties. Théodore and
Fédéric are the characters who take on the role of *para-confidents* in *Venceslas*.
In Act II Théodore receives in turn the confidences of Cassandre, Ladislas and
Alexandre.[254] From her relatively detached role of adviser to her protégée and
to her profligate brother, Théodore is jolted, by a remark of Ladislas, into the
realisation that Cassandre may be her rival. Thus when Alexandre would
unburden himself and seek her support in II.6, Théodore is scarcely able to
listen. The audience still appreciates the import of Alexandre's confession of
his love for Cassandre, but Théodore retires "*appuyée sur Léonor*". Rotrou has
overcome the potential weakness of employing a *para-confidente* by drawing
Théodore into the emotional wheel: finally she who was the recipient of others'
confidences becomes the focus of our attention.

Fédéric is styled the "Favory" of Venceslas, but is effectively the *para-
confident* of Alexandre; he has no scenes alone with Venceslas. His role is
extended beyond the normal functions of a *confident* since he has allowed
Alexandre to shield behind his identity while courting Cassandre. Trusted
servants may traditionally be used to deliver the hero's messages of love,[255] but
the deception involved is unprecedented. As Watts points out, Alexandre's
motives for hiding his love remain obscure,[256] yet the confusion the secret
generates is essential to the plot, for it motivates the murder Ladislas commits.[257]
The spectator is left in further doubt initially about Fédéric's own sentiments in
III.2: he confesses to being in love but is ashamed to admit that it is Théodore

---

[254] Watts sees the use of Théodore as a *confidente* to Cassandre as a direct result of the
omission of the servants in the Spanish source (*op.cit.*, pp.X-XI).

[255] Racine will use Ephestion for this purpose in *Alexandre*.

[256] Watts, *Venceslas*, p.XVI.

[257] On the irony of this see J. Morel, *Jean Rotrou dramaturge de l'ambiguïté* (1968), p.23.

whom he aspires to marry.[258] Alexandre's suspicion that from being his *confident* the Duke has become his rival for Cassandre does not seem unreasonable, and although the Duke swiftly disabuses Alexandre, Rotrou has made us aware that a *para-confident could* cross the dividing line and become a suitor in his own right. It is a strategy that both Racine and Thomas Corneille will exploit as the mainstay of several plots.[259]

Venceslas had the most successful theatrical history of the plays which eclipsed the *confident*. Rotrou's strategy of maximising conflictual exchanges between main protagonists generates exciting theatre. This is probably the single most important lesson which the play demonstrated to later playwrights. The reliance on monologues and asides, and the ambiguity over the exact motivation of characters are the price he accepts for a structure which depends on suspense and unexpected twists. As Scherer has argued,[260] *Venceslas* shows that *invraisemblance* may paradoxically (and contrary to all d'Aubignac's theories) be a factor of a play's very success.

(ii) ELIMINATING *CONFIDENTS* FROM POLYMYTHIC PLOTS: PIERRE CORNEILLE FROM *PERTHARITE* TO *PULCHÉRIE*

There is a strange irony in the fact that the play whose failure precipitated the first retirement of Pierre Corneille should have used the same unusual strategy as *Alexandre*, the play which marks the first major success of Racine: both totally eliminate the *confident*. The irony is compounded by the fact that *Pertharite* is a key source of *Andromaque*,[261] the play in which Racine reintroduces *confidents* on a large scale. While S. Doubrovsky is right to emphasise the ideological distance between *Pertharite* and *Andromaque*,[262] the dramaturgical parallels cannot be lightly dismissed, and it is reasonable to wonder whether, among other things that he gleaned from *Pertharite*, Racine found fresh evidence of the pitfalls of the elimination of the *confident*.

The original failure of *Pertharite* is clearly documented, but the causes are still the subject of debate.[263] We cannot judge with certainty how far its fate was due to external political factors and how far as a play it disappointed audiences who had recently applauded *Nicomède*. However, if we look at the text itself afresh, we can perceive both some obvious shortcomings and some very

---

[258] The astute spectator might have guessed this from the oblique reference in the Duke's monologue (III.1) to "la Princesse" (l.780). However, Rotrou prolongs the suspense by not allowing the Duke to mention Théodore's name once in 24 lines.

[259] See Chapter 7.

[260] *Théâtre du XVIIe siècle*, ed. J. Scherer, Bibliothèque de la Pléiade (1975): vol. I, p.1349.

[261] See J. Racine, *Andromaque*, ed. R.C. Knight and H.T. Barnwell (1977), pp.12-15.

[262] *Corneille ou la dialectique du héros*, p.329.

[263] See the summary provided by A.-M. Desfougères, "L'échec de *Pertharite*" (1985), p.501.

dramatic scenes. The play hinges on the surprise return of Pertharite (presumed dead) in Act III, a *peripeteia* which marks a change in focus. Corneille admits in the *Examen* that this results in:

> *l'inégalité de l'emploi des personnages, qui donne à Rodelinde le premier rang dans les trois premiers actes, et la réduit au second ou au troisième dans les deux derniers.*[264]

It seems that *Pertharite* provides an early example of the problems of *polymythie*: the spectator has become interested in Rodelinde, only to find the plot has changed course. But it is possible that our unease is increased by the fact that Rodelinde is known to us entirely through her scenes with other main characters. With each character she is forced to be on her guard, arguing her position; at no point can she adopt a totally open stance as she might have done with a *confidente*.

On the one hand, this produces a well-paced exposition, as she confronts in turn Unulphe (I.1), Édüige (I.2) and then briefly Grimoald (I.3).[265] The first of these scenes is a skilful example of the use of deliberative rhetoric, with Unulphe trying in vain to defend Grimoald to Rodelinde. If we look at the rhetorical strategies which open each of their ten exchanges, we find three imperatives, one exclamation, one rhetorical question, and two concessive clauses, all proof of each speaker striving to control the debate. On the other hand, as A.-M. Desfougères has demonstrated,[266] at the critical point in Act III when Rodelinde demands that Grimoald kill her infant son, we are unsure of the precise motive for her ultimatum. Her behaviour shocks the spectator the more because we cannot know whether she is employing a desperate strategy to save her son, seeking to expose Grimoald's tyranny in all its horror, or is carried along by the force of her own pride. Since the news that Pertharite is alive cuts short this momentous scene, our doubts are never resolved. If we compare III.3 of *Pertharite* with IV.1 of *Andromaque*, we can measure what Racine has gained by the use of the *confident* scene. Andromaque's exchange with Céphise leaves us in no doubt of her motivation. With Rodelinde, the absence of a *confidente* produces a vigorous heroine who argues her ground impressively, but whose thoughts, like those of some of the characters in *Venceslas*, remain in part inscrutable.[267]

---

[264] P. Corneille, *Œuvres complètes*, vol. II, p.772.

[265] In the *Examen* Corneille singles out the exposition as one of the saving graces of the play: "la façon dont le sujet s'explique dans la première scène ne manque pas d'artifice" (P. Corneille, *Œuvres complètes*, vol. II, p.772).

[266] Although I find A.-M. Desfougères's analysis of the ambiguities in Rodelinde's position convincing (see "L'échec de Pertharite"), the second part of the article, offering a Lacanian analysis of Corneille's obsession with the "bad mother", is highly speculative.

[267] In one of the rare articles devoted to *Pertharite* ("*Pertharite*: a re-examination", 1965), J. W. Scott reaches a similar general conclusion about all the characters: "The protagonists of

Rodelinde was briefly indicated in Corneille's sources, although he has given her a far more important role. His other female character, Édüige, was mentioned but not named and there was no evidence of her disposition towards Grimoald, Rodelinde or Pertharite. Thus her role can be understood only from the context of the play. In that Édüige's motivation is not obscure, the absence of a *confidente* does not impede our comprehension.[268] However, she has a less sympathetic role than Rodelinde. Édüige is the spurned and bitter lover, who takes pleasure in humiliating her rival as far as is in her power. Her encounters with Rodelinde (I.2, III.2) are strangely reminiscent of Célimène's and Arsinoé's showdown in *Le Misanthrope*: cruel wit abounds, but tragic dignity may be lost in the process.[269] With Garibalde, Édüige is forced into bargaining her hand in return for revenge on Grimoald (II.1); and since Garibalde is motivated entirely by the desire for self-advancement, their exchanges have none of the pathos which Oreste's love for Hermione creates in *Andromaque*. The scenes between Hermione and Cléone will allow us some pity for Racine's heroine,[270] whereas Édüige, deprived of a *confidente* or any monologues, lacks the most obvious devices to appeal to the audience. This is another price to pay for the sacrifice of the *confident*.

The absence of a *confident* pure and simple for either Grimoald or Pertharite is unsurprising given that the heroes in a number of Corneille's earlier plays had none. Corneille has turned the omission to potential advantage by providing instead two *conseillers* who play a significant role in the plot. Both are accredited in Paul the Deacon's *Historia Langobardorum*, and Corneille builds on the contrast between their characters. The first mention of Grimoald in the excerpt from the *Historia* which Corneille cites refers to Garibalde's treachery.[271] Corneille develops Garibalde's role so that he is both the dishonest

---

Pertharite are often, in their confrontation scenes, *acting* in a game of love and politics." (p.356). He does not, however, make a connection between this observation and the absence of *confidents*.

[268] I disagree on this point with A. Stegmann. He finds the character of Rodelinde clear-cut, but suggests that psychological ambiguity is introduced via Édüige (*L'Héroïsme cornélien*, p.617).

[269] E.g. "ÉDÜIGE: Votre félicité sera mal assurée/ Dessus un fondement de si peu de durée./ Vous avez toutefois de si puissants appas ... RODELINDE: Je sais quelques secrets que vous ne savez pas,/ Et si j'ai moins que vous d'attraits, et de mérite,/ J'ai des moyens plus sûrs, d'empêcher qu'on me quitte." (ll.807-12).

[270] See p.96.

[271] "Mais Garibalde, usant de trahison envers son seigneur <Gondbert> ...". Corneille quotes the translation in Antoine du Verdier's *Diverses Leçons* in his *Au Lecteur* to *Pertharite* (*Œuvres complètes*, vol. II, p.716.).

adviser of Grimoald,[272] and also - Corneille's own invention - a rival for
Édüige's hand. In Acts II-IV Garibalde works upon Grimoald's hesitations,[273]
suggesting the ruthless blackmail of killing Rodelinde's son (II.3); presenting
Rodelinde herself with an ultimatum of choosing between immediately
marrying Grimoald or her son's death (III.1); and then, on Pertharite's
appearance, arguing that he is a mere imposter and should be executed (IV.1
and IV.3). Such is the significance of Garibalde's role that he is the only
character in the play to be given monologues.[274] He is in fact a more interesting
character than Grimoald, and here is perhaps the reason why the relationship
between the hesitant usurper and the machiavellian counsellor does not make
the play the success that *Cosroès* or *Britannicus* are. Quite simply, Grimoald
does not have the fascination of Racine's "monstre naissant". Neither is the
play primarily about the struggle between a ruler and powerful subject in the
way that, say, *Suréna* will be. This is but one of several undulating strands of the
plot.

Unulphe is given a far more prominent role than Garibalde in Corneille's
main source, where he is the model of the loyal *conseiller*. In *Pertharite* his role
is less satisfactory. In Acts I-II, he assumes Pertharite to be dead and so is the
spokesman for Grimoald with Rodelinde,[275] pressing the advantages of the
marriage. Apparently discredited in this lowly undertaking,[276] he is transposed -
without clear explanation - into the heroic protector of Pertharite (his role in the
Historia Langobardorum). His part in actively ensuring Pertharite's escape[277] is
essential to the dénouement, yet he is marginalised in the final scene, as the
focus shifts back to Pertharite and Grimoald. Unulphe's role absorbs some of
the functions of a *confident/conseiller*, but it also goes beyond this without his
clearly attaining the status of a main character equal to Garibalde. The strategy
of replacing *confidents* by two contrasting *conseillers* is significant in a number
of seventeenth-century tragedies, as we shall see in Chapter 5, but the plot of
Pertharite does not exploit the symmetry to full effect.

---

[272] A. Stegmann sees Garibalde as "une réplique enrichie de Photin", the machiavellian
conseiller of *La Mort de Pompée* (*L'Héroïsme cornélien*, p.615).

[273] In Antoine du Verdier's version of Paul the Deacon Grimoald is described as an "homme
facile à croire et bien souvent trop de léger" (P. Corneille, *Œuvres complètes*, vol. II, p.718).

[274] He has two monologues and in each reveals to the audience his immoral motives. In II.2
we learn that he seeks to marry Édüige only in order to gain the crown, and in III.6 he exposes his
plan to have Grimoald execute Pertharite.

[275] Édüige refers to him disparagingly as "ce confident si cher" (line 272).

[276] At the end of Act II Grimoald instructs Garibalde to take over Unulphe's role: "Achève,
Garibalde, Unulphe est trop crédule" (line 747).

[277] Reported in his *récit* to Édüige (ll.1527-40).

The absence of *confidents* is only one of a number of factors contributing to the status of *Pertharite* as a difficult play, and it can be argued that the experiment reaped some rewards in terms of dramatic effects. However, Corneille clearly felt more at ease with a conventional use of the *confident* (or the *confidente* in particular), and even after the *Querelle de Sophonisbe* did not immediately attempt to eliminate the role again. Rather, his initial response in the four tragedies from *Othon* (1664) to *Tite et Bérénice* (1670) was to forestall further criticism by taking greater pains to justify the presence and words of his *confidents*.[278] He also experiments with the *confidents'* roles, in ways which in general raise rather than lower their profile. The three *confidents* of *Othon* (Albiane, Albin and Flavie) speak for 9.44% of the play, the two of *Attila* (Flavie and Octar) for 10.46% and the four of *Tite et Bérénice* (Albin, Flavian, Philon and Plautine) for 13.42%. In each case this is greater than the 7.2% of *Sophonisbe* which had drawn d'Aubignac's fire. This general pattern is not the whole story, however. Corneille's interest in dramaturgical experimentation was rarely blunted,[279] and his handling of the *confident* is no exception. Alongside these later plays in which the *confidents* enjoy significant roles, there are three other plays which reduce their prominence. In *Agésilas* there is only one major *confident* (Xénoclès) and a second *confident* with a very minor role (Cléon): together they speak for only 3.63% of the play. *Pulchérie* has no *confidents*, and in *Suréna* the two *confidents* (Ormène and Sillace) are low-key (3.92%) - in a play in which the use and abuse of *confidence* is crucial.[280]

It is interesting to ask whether these apparently random fluctuations in Corneille's dramaturgy may be in part explained by reference to the work of Racine. While we must remember that the role of the *confident* had to be tailored in each play to suit the conception of the hero, the development of the plot, and perhaps the composition of the troupe who would perform it, it is hard not to see Corneille following some of Racine's more radical shifts. Racine eclipses the *confidents* in *La Thébaïde* (June 1664) and eliminates them totally from *Alexandre* (November 1665): *Agésilas* (February 1666) moves in the same direction.[281] *Attila* (March 1667) then marks a compromise: there are only two *confidents* for five main characters, but their role is not insubstantial.[282]

---

[278] For example in *Othon* Albin, the *ami* of Othon, opens the play with six lines excusing the freedom with which he will speak; he is strangely reminiscent of the hesitant Pollux in *Médée* (see p.17).

[279] See G. Forestier, "Une dramaturgie de gageure", (1985). He refers to "cette série de paris que constituent, chacune à sa manière, les tragédies qui se succèdent depuis *Œdipe*." (p.815).

[280] See Chapter 6.

[281] We know that Racine had read part of his first plays aloud to select *salon* gatherings prior to their first performance. This would have allowed Corneille time to digest the strategies of his new rival.

[282] It may be significant that this is the first tragedy of Corneille to be staged by Molière's troupe, which had originally put on *Alexandre*. *Attila*, like *Alexandre*, has three main male roles,

Racine sets the pace again with the reintroduction of the *confident* on a full
scale in *Andromaque* (November 1667) and *Britannicus* (December 1669):
Corneille matches the symmetry of *Andromaque* (four main characters plus
four *confidents*) in *Tite et Bérénice* (November 1670). The surprising absence
of *confidents* in *Pulchérie* (November 1672) has no obvious parallel with
developments in Racine. *Mithridate* (January 1673) has only two *confidents*, as
does Corneille's *Suréna* (December 1674).[283] At the very least we can state that
two leading playwrights were occupied with experimental strategies in the same
field at the same time. Some degree of convergence between them is probably
more than fortuitous.

When we compare these tragedies of Corneille and Racine, we also need to
take into account the fact that after *Alexandre* Racine used the Hôtel de
Bourgogne for all his plays, whereas in the same period Corneille moved
between the Hôtel de Bourgogne (*Sophonisbe, Othon, Agésilas*), the Palais-
Royal (*Attila, Tite et Bérénice* and the *tragédie-ballet, Psyché*), and the Marais
(*Pulchérie*), finally returning to the newly reconstituted Hôtel de Bourgogne
(*Suréna*). Thus, where Racine had a fair degree of continuity in the actors for
whom he was writing, Corneille may have had to adapt his dramaturgy to suit
different troupes.[284] I suspect this explains in part the small cast of *Pulchérie*.
The Marais was out of favour; Corneille had not used it since *Sertorius* in 1662,
and it would disappear the following year. We can assume it did not have the
resources of its rivals.[285]

*   *   *

---

two main female roles, and one secondary male role; Corneille introduces one further secondary
female role.

[283] The *première* of *Iphigénie* was in August 1674, and here the role of *confidents* is again
enhanced, but in subject and tone *Mithridate* was a more obvious model for Corneille to have
drawn on. Forestier argues that Corneille had been composing *Suréna* at the time of *Mithridate*'s
success: *Essai de génétique théâtrale*, p.35.

[284] Sadly, we have very little evidence of the casts for the first performances of Corneille's
later tragedies, which means that we can make only general conjectures upon the relationship
between a troupe's members and Corneille's conception of lesser roles. We can, however,
discount the possibility that the absence of *confidents* in *Pulchérie* was related to its genre, since
Tite et Bérénice, also a *comédie héroïque*, had each of the four protagonists accompanied by a
confident(e).

[285] In the *Au Lecteur* Corneille refers obliquely to his choice of the Marais: "... bien que cette
pièce ait été reléguée dans un lieu où on ne voulait plus se souvenir qu'il y eût un théâtre .... elle
n'a pas laissé de peupler le désert, de mettre en crédit des acteurs dont on ne connaissait pas le
mérite ..." (*Œuvres complètes*, vol. III, pp. 1171-2).

Like *Pertharite*, *Pulchérie* has only six named characters,[286] but where the omission of the *confident* in the earlier play produced some interesting developments, it is hard not to focus on the obstacles resulting from the strategy in *Pulchérie*. Critics are in agreement that it is a particularly static play: R. Knight suggests that "there is less action in this play than in any other Corneille wrote."[287] This means that there is little requirement for *confidents* to relay off-stage action, as the spectators' interest is focused entirely on the analysis of the shifting thoughts and feelings of the characters. Without *confidents*, these can be explored only in scenes between two or more protagonists.[288] With the exception of Aspar, no character is fundamentally deceitful, so the spectator's comprehension is not tested, but we are uncomfortably aware of the contrivances by which Corneille engineers revelations.

The two characters of his own creation, Justine and Irène, function as *para-confidentes*.[289] Corneille adopts the expedient device of making each the kinswoman of a main character, thus facilitating the exposition. While Pulchérie has declared her love to Léon with unprecedented openness at the very start of the play,[290] and elaborated upon the obstacles which stand in the way of their marriage, it is not until Léon's scene with his sister, Irène, in I.3 that he can speak freely of his fears. The spectator is made aware of the tight web in which the characters are caught: if Léon marries Pulchérie, the ambitious Aspar may marry Irène as sister of the Emperor; if not, Aspar may be a rival for Pulchérie's hand. The web is reminiscent of that of *Andromaque*, but is rendered far more complicated by the involvement of Justine and Martian.[291] In itself I.3 is effective: Irène has a substantial role, energetically advising her brother of the best course to follow.[292] Yet the relationship between Irène and Aspar, which has been analysed at length in I.3 and exposed in their meeting in I.5, then falls into the background. Irène is absent from Acts II and III, and as Pulchérie closes the play, the proposed marriage between Irène and Aspar is left in the balance:

---

[286] All the other tragedies of Corneille have between 7 and 12 named characters.

[287] *Corneille's Tragedies*, 1991, p.109.

[288] There is no use of the monologue, unless we count Irène's brief aside at the end of I.5.

[289] The point has been noted (in different terms) but not developed by several critics, including: A. Stegmann, *L'Héroïsme cornélien*, pp.644-5; R. Knight, *Corneille's Tragedies*, p.109.

[290] "Je vous aime, Léon, et n'en fais point mystère" (l.1).

[291] A. Stegmann attributes the failure of *Pulchérie* in part to this web: "Corneille, qui a voulu supprimer les confidents, est victime ici des liens qu'il a préalablement tissés entre ses personnages." (*L'Héroïsme cornélien*, p.647).

[292] Note the use of four imperatives and two rhetorical questions as she persuasively sets out her strategy (ll.216-236).

> *Mais j'ai donné deux jours à cet esprit flottant,*
> *Et laisse jusque-là ma faveur incertaine,*
> *Pour régler son destin sur le destin d'Irène.*
> *(ll.1756-8)*

More than a *confidente*, yet less than a main protagonist, Irène appears
uncomfortably like a creation of convenience.

The role of Justine is, at first sight, better integrated into the plot. She is both
the unassuming rival for Léon's hand and the daughter of Martian. Corneille
uses this strategy to justify a series of para-confidential exchanges in Act II:
scenes between Justine and Martian alternate with those involving first Aspar
and then Léon.[293] In order for the exposition to be complete, the spectator must
learn of Justine's and Martian's secret passions. Daughter and father each sigh
in turn, which provides the pretext in II.1 for their parallel confessions of love.
The symmetry which informs the scene is undisguised.[294] Yet in the later part of
the scene each character seems to be alone, listening but not responding to the
other's declaration. Martian articulates this delineation of roles at the end of his
long speech:

> *J'ai caché si longtemps l'ennui qui me dévore,*
> *Qu'en dépit que j'en aie enfin il s'évapore,*
> *L'aigreur en diminue à te le raconter,*
> *Fais-en autant du tien, c'est mon tour d'écouter.*
> *(ll.489-492)*

Justine needs no second bidding to take up her own tale: at her conclusion
Martian offers no sympathy, simply a brusque injunction that she is young
enough to choose another lover. A *confident* could hardly have done less, and
the artificiality of the parallel confessions would have been avoided.[295] But
perhaps the whole beauty of *Pulchérie* for Corneille lies in the surprising and
ironic parallels he creates. Justine and Irène have been invented precisely to
permit these.[296]

Both characters also function as *para-confidents* in relation to Pulchérie. As
trusted subjects, they are required to listen to the future Empress. Irène is no

---

[293] A common pattern of alternation between scenes with main characters and *confident*
scenes, as we established in Chapter 1 (see p.31).

[294] Again, one is struck in Corneille's "matrimonial plays" by exchanges which could derive
from the comic repertoire, e.g.: "MARTIAN: Aimerais-tu Léon? JUSTINE: Aimez-vous la
Princesse?" (1.402).

[295] Compare the very different effects achieved by Racine's exploitation of parallel
confessions to *confidents* in Act I of *Phèdre*.

[296] Even the most sympathetic of Cornelian critics have found it impossible to redeem
Pulchérie by reference to Corneille's treatment of familiar themes: e.g. A. Stegmann, *L'Héroïsme
cornélien*, pp.554-61; M. Descotes, *Dix promenades dans le cimetière cornélien* (1983), pp.
266-303. I agree with their final assessments, but suggest that we may come closer to Corneille's
original priorities if we focus on the *structure* of the play.

more than a cypher to advise Pulchérie on Léon's state of mind (IV.1). Potentially there is an interesting conflict between Pulchérie and Justine, with the latter serving as *para-confidente* yet being a secret rival.[297] This is precisely the same strategy as Racine had employed in *Bajazet* some ten months earlier. But whereas for Racine it had been crucial to the raw emotions of all three main characters, in *Pulchérie* it produces no more than passing pathos and irony (III.2, V.1). Corneille's play is centred on the dilemma of Pulchérie herself;[298] other characters simply weave intricate patterns around her. The elimination of traditional *confidents* is ultimately not significant. We are not made aware of an absence or lack, as I would argue we are in *Pertharite* and *Alexandre*, for their functions are subsumed by Justine and Irène. But Corneille is unable (or does not seek) to conceal the extent to which he has stretched the demands of verisimilitude by having such a polymythic plot depend on only six characters. We might point out the contrast with Racine's *Bérénice*, which is also confined to six characters,[299] but the disposition of three protagonists and three *confidents* produces strikingly different effects, as will be shown in Chapter 4.

(iii) TAKING UP THE CHALLENGE: RACINE'S *LA THÉBAÏDE* AND *ALEXANDRE*

Rotrou's *Venceslas* and Corneille's *Pertharite* represent important stages in experiments with the eclipse of the *confident*, but they surface as isolated moments rather than as a response to critical pressure. In both cases they are the works of mature, acclaimed dramatists who are accustomed to taking dramaturgical risks. *La Thébaïde* and *Alexandre* present a different scenario: they are the first plays of a young dramatist, and they coincide precisely with the conclusion of the *Querelle de Sophonisbe*.[300] Barnwell argues that the critical debate engendered by the *Dissertations* of d'Aubignac may have encouraged Racine to distance himself from some of the the hallmarks of Corneille's theatre, and in particular to create plays characterised by a new aesthetic of simplicity.[301] Hawcroft raises the further possibility that "in his first two plays Racine is experimenting and that, in particular, he is testing out

---

[297] In II.5 Martian extends this role to his own relationship with Léon, referring to "Les périls d'un amour <Pulchérie/ Léon> que nous avons vu naître,/ Dont nous avons tous deux été les confidents" (ll.714-5). However, he does not have any scenes alone with Léon during the course of the play.

[298] With the exception of Act II, she dominates the play.

[299] If we exclude the mesenger Rutile, whose role is minimal (he speaks only five lines in the whole play).

[300] Since we do not have any of Racine's correspondence from July 1662 to July 1663, we lack documentary evidence of his reaction to the stages of the *Querelle*.

[301] *The Tragic Drama of Corneille and Racine*, pp.134-7.

d'Aubignac's theories on confidants."[302] In that d'Aubignac does not advocate the wholesale suppression of the *confident*, *Alexandre* is not strictly a test of his theories, but, as I have argued elsewhere, many of the confidential strategies in Racine's first two plays can be interpreted as a practical and bold response to points raised in the *Querelle*.[303] In *La Thébaïde* only two *confidents* are used, each with a limited role; in *Alexandre* there are no *confidents* at all.

At first sight, this eclipse of the *confident* seems particularly surprising given the evidence of Racine's interest in both choruses and secondary characters in his annotations of the tragedies of Euripides and Sophocles.[304] R. Knight reminds us how unusual Racine's Greek scholarship was among contemporary playwrights, yet the influence of the Greek tragedies is neither immediate not all-pervasive in his own works before *Iphigénie* and *Phèdre*.[305] The treatment of secondary characters in Racine's first two works fits this general picture. However, in *La Thébaïde* the two *confidents* who are employed may owe something to Racine's reflections on Greek models.[306] I shall indicate several aspects of the treatment of Olympe in particular which may be traced to the Greek tradition, and which Racine will take up again in *Andromaque* and later plays.

The list of named characters in *La Thébaïde* represents a desire for simplification if we compare it for example with that of Rotrou's *Iphigénie* of 1641 (six main characters and five secondary characters), or with Corneille's *Sophonisbe* (five main characters and six secondary characters). Racine has six main characters, but only two secondary ones, both *confidents*. Barnwell has shown how Racine consistently reduces the number of main characters in his tragedies from *La Thébaïde* to *Bérénice*, which he interprets as a sign of

---

[302] *Word as Action*, p.168.

[303] See "La Querelle du confident et la structure dramaturgique des premières pièces de Racine", 1992. The remainder of this chapter is broadly based on this article.

[304] For a detailed discussion of these, see R. Knight, *Racine et la Grèce*, chapter XIX. More recently, H. Rossi has returned to the subject and follows Knight in observing Racine's particular interest in the functions and presence of secondary characters and choruses ("*Les Détours obscurs*". *Le annotazioni di Racine alle tragedie greche*, 1985, p.160). The study of Sophoclean themes and patterns in Racine's work by J. Stone (*Sophocles and Racine*, 1964), while valuable in other respects, does not shed any light upon Racine's conception of the *confident*.

[305] Knight would go so far as to argue that even though Racine claims in the prefaces to *La Thébaïde* and *Andromaque* that he has followed Euripides, these early plays in fact owe less to the Greek tragedian than to Homer, Virgil, Seneca and contemporary French sources (*Racine et la Grèce*, p.119).

[306] Knight warns that we cannot be sure of the exact dates of Racine's various annotations, although those on the Greek tragedies cannot have been made before 1662. In particular, we do not know whether the annotations of Euripides' *Phœnician Women* predate or postdate *La Thébaïde* (*Racine et la Grèce*, pp.222-3). I would agree with Knight (*ibid.*, p.257) that in either case they are still valuable as evidence of Racine's general reading of Euripides.

Racine's evolving quest for simplicity.[307] We should also note that *La Thébaïde* has fewer *confidents* than any of the other tragedies apart from *Alexandre* and *Mithridate*. On this level, simplicity is apparent from the outset of his career.

Neither of the two *confidents* of *La Thébaïde* has a direct counterpart in either Euripides' *Phœnician Women* or the extant fragments of Seneca's *Phœnissæ*.[308] They are Racine's own creations, and he allots them contrasting roles. Olympe, Jocaste's *confidente*, is closely linked to the action from the first scene. In this, Racine implicitly rectifies what he considered a flaw in the comparable expository scene between Antigone and the Tutor in Euripides.[309] Olympe twice brings news of the conflict offstage (I.1, III.1), and reports the words of the oracle in II.2. In the final act, she is also charged with the *récit* of what in the 1675-6 *Préface* Racine would call a "catastrophe ... un peu trop sanglante". Attale, Créon's *confident*, on the other hand, exists primarily to allow Créon to express his true motives. Racine has in fact reversed the pattern of *Sophonisbe*, where the *confidents* were largely messengers, and the *confidentes* passive listeners. The differences between Olympe and Attale can be seen as a factor of the essential contrast between Jocaste and Créon. The Queen has nothing to hide; the dreadful truth of the house of Oedipus is all too well known. Jocaste does not therefore require a traditional *confidente*. In contrast, Racine has endowed Créon not only with ambition but also with a secret passion for Antigone.[310] While Jocaste and Antigone divine Créon's pride and ambition in I.5, Antigone is taken in when he pretends to desire peace in Act III. It is only in the scene with Attale (III.6) - the first between Créon and his *confident* - that the spectator learns that this is no more than a ruse on the part of Créon. As we have observed in other plays, the *confident* becomes indispensable when a character practises deceit. Rotrou might arguably have used a monologue in such a situation. Racine is sparing of this device in *La Thébaïde*;[311] he prefers the alternative of a scene with a *confident*.

If we look at the words of Attale, Racine has not created a character markedly more interesting than the stereotypes criticised by d'Aubignac. In III.6 Attale prompts Créon's confidences by expressing naive surprise at Créon's apparent change of policy, and then concludes his contribution with a moral platitude resembling the gnomic sentences of the chorus in Greek tragedies:

[307] *The Tragic Drama of Corneille and Racine*, p. 148.

[308] The two sources cited in the 1676 preface to *La Thébaïde*.

[309] He noted at line 120: "Tout ceci n'est point de l'action; mais le poète a voulu imiter une chose qui est belle dans Homère..." (J. Racine, *Œuvres*, ed. P. Mesnard, vol. VI, pp.260-1).

[310] Knight suggests that Racine, having criticised Euripides for making Créon unexpectedly antipathetic at the end of *The Phœnician Women*, wanted to show his Créon harbouring a destructive passion from early in the play.

[311] There are only two monologues in *La Thébaïde*: Jocaste's in II.2 and Antigone's *stances* in V.1.

> *Vous n'avez plus, Seigneur, à craindre que vous-même,*
> *On porte ses remords avec le diadème.*
> *(ll.891-2)*

Attale's part in the scene is strictly limited; instead, our interest is totally focused on Créon, who condemns himself from his own mouth. De Visé's defence of the *confidente* might be applied here. Spectators can overlook the artificiality of the device when they are sufficiently interested in the revelations made by the main character. There is only one other scene (V.4) between Créon and Attale, and again Attale says relatively little; instead he provides a foil for Créon.[312] Whereas III.6 corrected our (potential) misreading of the previous scene, in V.4 it is Créon who misreads what has preceded. As Antigone leaves, having refused Créon's hand, Attale gives a first prompt in the form of a question:

> *... Son courroux serait-il adouci?*
> *Croyez-vous la fléchir?*
> *(ll.1420-1)*

With overweening pride Créon expresses his confidence that his dreams will be fulfilled. Attale's next prompt confirms the repugnance Créon evokes in the spectator. As the voice of moral reason, Attale assumes Créon's pleasure is outweighed by his grief for his sons, but Créon affirms that the satisfaction of his ambition takes precedence. The few lines of Attale have sufficed to show us the evil face of Créon. Yet with his suicide in V.6 Racine suddenly makes Créon into the last, tragic victim of a cursed family. The reversal is too swift, the grief of Créon at Antigone's death scarcely credible after his machiavellian stance. The fault does not lie, however, in the role of the *confident*, but rather in Racine's wish to make his first tragedy as overwhelming as possible.

The economy of speech we noted with Attale is characteristic also of Olympe.[313] It is as though in both cases Racine is concerned to avoid censure for allowing the *confidents* any unnecessary lines.[314] With Olympe he has achieved the additional goal set by d'Aubignac, integrating the *confidente* within the action. After the first scene, Olympe is not the traditional *confidente* who simply listens; she is the active observer and participant on behalf of Jocaste and Antigone. The opening scene of *La Thébaïde* reveals all Racine's theatrical powers in the urgency with which Olympe reports on the battle. In just six lines, she repeats "*J'ay veu*" three times, stressing her authority as a witness of the impending conflict. Here she recalls the Tutor in Euripides'

---

[312] Attale speaks only 30 lines in the whole play. In III.6 and V.4 - his main contribution - he speaks only 15 and 7 lines respectively out of 92 and 42, i.e. 16.42% of these scenes.

[313] She has only slightly more lines in the whole play (49), and again speaks a very low proportion of the lines in the scenes in which she is involved. See Appendix 2.

[314] Compare the attention which Racine pays in his annotations on Sophocles and Euripides to the need for playwrights to avoid unnecessary deviations from the unity of action.

Phœnician Women, who leads Antigone to the rooftop to survey the battle
below. But Racine has combined this, I think, with the effect of the Messenger's
speech in Seneca's *Phœnissæ* (ll. 387-402).[315] The latter galvanised Jocasta to
seek out her warring sons. As a direct result of Olympe's report, Racine's
Jocaste takes two decisions (ll.15-18), sending immediately for Antigone and
declaring her determination to separate her sons or perish in the process. This
rapid, dramatic scene illustrates Racine's eclectic use of Greek and Latin
sources as a starting point for a *confident* scene.

Later in the play, Racine implicitly meets a further challenge which had
emerged from the *Querelle de Sophonisbe*: to create a *confidente* personally
touched by the fate of the characters, whose role will engage the audience's
attention. In his annotations on Greek tragedies, Racine makes a striking
number of references to the occasions on which the chorus participates in the
tragic emotions.[316] For example at line 120 of Sophocles' *Electra* (one of the
plays which he annotated most fully) he observes:

> *Chœur de filles qui viennent pour la consoler.- Le chœur est de filles d'Argos,*
> *qui approuvent la douleur d'Électre, qui détestent comme elle le crime de sa*
> *mère, mais qui sont plus timides qu'elle, et qui n'osent parler librement.[317]*

I would suggest that this is one of the most important ways in which Greek
models influence Racine's conception of the *confident*. When Olympe reports
the words of the oracle to Antigone and Hémon, her fear presages that of the
characters and spectators:[318]

ANTIGONE

Eh bien! apprendrons-nous ce qu'ont dit les oracles?
Que faut-il faire?

OLYMPE

   Hélas!

ANTIGONE

      Quoi? qu'en a-t-on appris?
Est-ce la guerre, Olympe?

OLYMPE

      Ah! c'est encore pis!

---

[315] R. Tobin analyses Racine's debt to Senecan themes in *La Thébaïde*. However he does not
look in detail at the roles of Olympe and Attale: *Racine and Seneca*, 1971, pp. 79-85.

[316] On this aspect of the Greek chorus, see for example the introductory comments of R.
Burton on the choruses of Sophocles' *Ajax* or *Electra*: *The Chorus in Sophocles' Tragedies*
(1980), pp.6-7 and p.41.

[317] *Œuvres*, ed. P. Mesnard, vol. VI, p.225.

[318] Compare the similar expressions of pity in the speech of the messenger charged with the
reporting the brothers' death in Euripides' *Phœnician Women*, ll.1334-5, l.1346.

HÉMON

Quel est donc ce grand mal que leur courroux annonce?

OLYMPE

Prince, pour en juger, écoutez leur réponse.
                    (ll.388-92)

Similarly, when she comes on stage in V.5 to announce the death of Antigone, Créon comments, *"Dieux! elle est tout en larmes"* (1.1462).[319] Her récit is brief, but the expression of her grief is worthy of a main character:[320]

> *J'ai senti son beau corps tout froid entre mes bras,*
> *Et j'ai cru que mon âme alloit suivre ses pas,*
> *Heureuse mille fois, si ma douleur mortelle*
> *Dans la nuit du tombeau m'eût plongée avec elle!*
>   *(ll.1475-8)*

From the start to the end of the play, Olympe is shown to be intimately involved in the sufferings of the house of Œdipus. Long before Phèdre and Œnone, Racine has created a *confidente* whose emotional bond with her mistress (and her mistress's daughter) is essential to the spectator's appreciation of the tragedy.[321] In spirit, Olympe owes much to the Greek chorus, such as that of Euripides' *Phœnician Women*. Both *confidente* and chorus are moved by the tragedy, and give lyrical expression to it at moments of greatest poignancy.

With one *confident* who is justified on a functional plane and another whose role is a small dramatic triumph, Racine has given no more than 4.77% of the play to the words of secondary characters. Because of the extraordinary nature of his subject, in which his six main characters are all related to one another, he can orchestrate exchanges between them without recourse to any other secondary characters, and without violating the principle of verisimilitude. But I think a second element is at play in Racine's choice not to introduce other *confidents*. He has perceived - as Rotrou and Pierre Corneille knew and had demonstrated - that good theatre depends on conflict,[322] and he maximises the opportunity for engagement between protagonists. Only the couples Jocaste/Antigone and Antigone/Hémon are non-conflictual, and interestingly

---

[319] On the use of tears as a visual symbol in other plays, see D. Maskell, *Racine. A Theatrical Reading*, pp.81-82.

[320] M. Edwards draws our attention to "la sensibilité et la tendresse du monde féminin" in Olympe's description of Antigone's death (*La Tragédie racinienne*, 1972, p.70).

[321] We should note that in contrast Attale does not have such a role. His exclamation of horror (1.1493) as Créon is about to kill himself in the last scene is purely conventional.

[322] I. Heyndels has attempted a psychological and semiotic study of the theme of conflict in Racine (*Le Conflit racinien*, 1985), but I do not find the particular approach taken enlightening.

Racine makes little use of the mother-daughter pairing (which could have lent itself to a simple *para-confidente* relationship of the kind Corneille would invent in *Pulchérie*). Their exchanges in Act I (I.2 and I.6) are very brief, and in their only substantial scene (III.3) it is their conflicting reactions to the suicide of Ménécée (Antigone's hope, Jocaste's fear) on which Racine concentrates. Even Antigone and Hémon are accorded but one meeting (II.I.1-2).[323] It is evident that Racine's real interest lies in the violent passions which bring characters into conflict, and which of course find their culmination in the single meeting of Étéocle and Polynice in Act IV. But the successive meetings of the sons with Jocaste (I.3 and II.3) prepare the ground. These scenes are crucial to the exposition, which is achieved through the tense debates we witness as Jocaste argues in vain for the brothers to be reconciled. All the rhetorical strategies we associate with deliberation are present: rhetorical questions, exclamations, imprecations, supplications abound.[324] Racine has certainly avoided the flatness d'Aubignac criticised in the exposition of *Sophonisbe*, but by his heavy reliance on one alternative, conflictual scenes between main characters, there is another risk. The tension has been set at such a sustained pitch from so early in the play that, as Hawcroft has argued, Racine left little in reserve for the later acts.[325] However, the experimental strategy is taken further before Racine is convinced enough of its limitations to change course.

* * *

Had Racine written no other plays after *La Thébaïde* and *Alexandre*, we should probably have been struck primarily by the divergences between his first two tragedies. There is only one death in *Alexandre*, and that is of less interest than Alexandre's act of *générosité* towards Porus; the accursed family of Greek legend is abandoned for a quasi-Cornelian world of the political hero; love and *galanterie* are introduced on a large scale (*à la Quinault*). But if we look at the dramaturgy underlying these two works, there are signs that Racine is still charting broadly the same course, while effecting some further simplifications. The number of main characters is reduced by one; there is only one secondary character; the plot is less loaded than that of *La Thébaïde*;[326] and *confidents* are totally eclipsed. How has Racine achieved this last feat, and can we discern any

---

[323] Compare Racine's remark in his Préface of 1675-6: "L'amour, qui a d'ordinaire tant de part dans les tragedies, n'en a presque point ici; et je doute que je lui en donnasse davantage si c'était à recommencer."

[324] See for example ll.111-129 (Jocaste/Étéocle) and ll. 471-505 (Jocaste/Polynice).

[325] *Word as Action*, p.116. Compare d'Aubignac's warning of the dangers of trying to "mettre en chaque Acte un notable Evenement et une forte Passion" (*La Pratique du théâtre*, p.67).

[326] The role of Taxile, as Barnwell has shown, cleverly unifies its two separate strands. See *The Tragic drama of Corneille and Racine*, p.140.

inherent disadvantages which may explain why in his next tragedy *confidents* are restored to a position of prominence?

The one character who might have been the equivalent to a *confident* is Ephestion, the general and ambassador of Alexandre, but he is never given a scene alone with Alexandre. His role falls into two stages: before and after the arrival of the Alexandre. In the first stage, he acts as proxy for the absent hero. On a political level he has a powerful presence. Having summoned Taxile and Porus to meet with him, he presides over the council scene (II.2), and it is he who breaks it off by standing up and interrupting Porus. Quite unlike Attale and Olympe, he is given a significant proportion of the lines.[327] Furthermore it is his veiled threats and challenge which provoke Porus into engaging battle against Alexandre's forces between Acts II and III. Ephestion's role here is a far cry from the colourless, insignificant remarks which d'Aubignac associates with *suivantes*.[328] More debatable in the eyes of Racine's audience of 1665 was Ephestion's role as proxy for Alexandre the lover.[329] Various critics, not least Saint-Évremond,[330] censured Racine for making Alexandre into a sighing prince rather than the conqueror of half the world. Ephestion's role in II.1 as the self-styled:

> Fidèle confident du beau feu de mon maître
> (l.349)

is a consequence of this *galant* conception of the hero. The interview between Ephestion and Cléofile apparently does litle more than prefigure her meeting with Alexandre in Act III, but it is significant in that it permits Cléofile to express her doubts about the permanence of Alexandre's love and her fears for Taxile. Nevertheless, there is something *invraisemblable* in a general discoursing on love on behalf of his ruler and listening to the amorous confessions of the heroine. Ephestion has been forced awkwardly into the role of *para-confident* precisely because Cléofile has no *confidente* to whom she might speak instead.

Once Alexandre arrives, Ephestion's role becomes essentially that of a messenger. He briefly reports the disappearance of Porus in III.7 and then delivers the *récit* of Taxile's death in V.3. The latter is a dignified rhetorical exercise, but devoid of any personal commentary. The muted tragic tone of the

---

[327] The scene has 152 lines: Ephestion has 47, Porus 73, Taxile 32.

[328] See Hawcroft's analysis of the rhetorical qualities of all three speakers in the scene: *Word as Action*, pp.77-83.

[329] We need to remember that although the episode of Alexandre's liaison with Cléofile is historical in origin, Racine has departed from his sources in making it coincide with Alexander's campaign against Porus. Hence the uneasy conjunction of Ephestion's two functions as proxy. On Racine's adaptation of history, see *Alexandre*, ed. M. Hawcroft and V. Worth, pp.X-XI.

[330] *Dissertation sur le grand Alexandre* in *Œuvres en prose*, ed. R. Ternois, vol. II, pp.69-109.

ending depends solely on Cléofile's grief;[331] Racine does not repeat the effect achieved by Olympe at the end of *La Thébaïde*. In summary, Ephestion remains a secondary character, memorable only for his strong stage presence in II.2.

By what means does Racine avoid introducing *confidents* for any of the five main characters? Unlike *La Thébaïde, Alexandre* is not a play about kinship. Racine adapts his historical sources to make Taxile and Cléofile brother and sister,[332] but the one totally fictional character, Axiane, is not given any convenient kinsman or kinswoman in whom to confide. Meetings and confidences between main characters thus require alternative strategies. Even in the opening scene, in which Racine relies on the close relationship between Cléofile and Taxile to achieve the exposition, what emerges most clearly (and is reminiscent of *La Thébaïde*) is the atmosphere of conflict. It does not match the force of the first scene of Rotrou's *Venceslas*, but Cléofile's initial speech establishes a tone of vigorous debate, with an exclamation, a long rhetorical question and three imperatives:

> *Quoi? vous allez combattre un roi dont la puissance*
> *Semble forcer le ciel à prendre sa défense,*
> *Sous qui toute l'Asie a vu tomber ses rois,*
> *Et qui tient la fortune attachée à ses lois?*
> *Mon frere, ouvrez les yeux pour connaître Alexandre:*
> *Voyez de toutes parts les trônes mis en cendre,*
> *Les peuples asservis, et les rois enchaînés,*
> *Et prévenez les maux qui les ont entraînés.*
> *(ll.1-8)*

She has provided the same information as a messenger might have done, yet it is disguised by the use of deliberative rhetoric as she tries to persuade Taxile to seek an alliance with Alexandre. In this way Racine has overcome one of d'Aubignac's objections to the expositon of *Sophonisbe*: that the characters had no reason to repeat information which both speaker and listener already knew. Taxile is familiar with the facts Cléofile cites, but we are not aware of a lack of verismilitude because she is voicing them to support an argument. The same holds true for her analysis of her relationship with Alexandre, which in turn gives Taxile cause to set out his alternative priorities.[333] However, we may suspect that Racine was too eager to complete the exposition at a single stroke while he had on stage the two characters concerned by every aspect of the plot,

---

[331] Lines 1539-44.
[332] See *Alexandre*, ed. M. Hawcroft and V. Worth, p.XI.
[333] Lines 65-73.

for he also has Cléofile inform Taxile of Axiane's love for Porus. In his only
play which does not open with a *confident* scene, Racine has achieved a lucid if
overloaded exposition. Like Rotrou in *Venceslas* and Corneille in *Nicomède*
and *Pertharite*, he shows that a conflictual opening scene between two main
characters can heighten our initial grasp of the tensions between the various
characters, and create a sense of fear in anticipation of the tragedy which looms.

Conflictual exchanges provide the key to the dramaturgical structure of the
rest of *Alexandre*, and, as in *La Thébaïde*, they provide the main mechanism
through which Racine can avoid recourse to *confidents*. One very clear example
is the scene between Axiane and Cléofile at the start of Act III, when both are
anxiously awaiting news of the battle. The situation is a commonplace of
tragedy, with the difference that a heroine awaiting news of developments
offstage is often accompanied by her *confidente*. Instead Racine brings together
the two rivals (ignoring the *invraisemblance* of Axiane being held prisoner in
Taxile's camp).[334] We are not led to sympathise wholly with one or other, as a
scene with a *confidente* might have allowed, but rather caught up in the crossfire
as each tries to prove her superiority. It is as though the battle between
Alexandre and Porus is being fought out in words between Cléofile and Axiane.
In scenes alone with their lovers, either heroine can move the audience to
pity.[335] But in their exchanges with each other, and with Taxile, they strike us by
their ruthless cruelty. Similarly, neither Taxile nor Porus can win the audience's
sympathy through the focus a *confident* scene would afford. Their two scenes
alone together (I.2, II.3) are entirely antagonistic, their interests at variance.[336]
Rejected by Axiane and Porus, scorned by Cléofile, Taxile stands alone. He is
given only one short monologue (ll.1261-68) to assert his heroism before he
goes into the battle where he will meet his death. Otherwise, there is no device to
replace the *confident*, no means to ensure the tragic victim of the play the pity
which we accord to an Oreste.

Our analysis of *Venceslas* and *Pertharite* has demonstrated that the other
possible weakness caused by the omission of *confidents* is the inscrutability of
some characters' thoughts and actions. In that there are no fundamentally
dishonest characters in *Alexandre*, Racine has obviated the pressing need for a
confident which we saw with Créon in *La Thébaïde*. True, Cléofile delays telling
Taxile of Porus's return in IV.4, and Porus holds back the information that
Taxile is dead in V.3, but these deceits are short-lived and calculated. Yet the
characters of *Alexandre* are not completely open; there are some aspects of
their behaviour which seem incoherent. For example, as with Rodelinde in

<hr>

[334] Louis Racine points out this flaw in his *Examen d'Alexandre*, in *Œuvres de Louis Racine*,
vol. V, p.323.
[335] E.g. Axiane/Porus, II.5; Cléofile/Alexandre, III.6, V.1.
[336] This is in stark contrast to the *générosité* which unites the princes of *Rodogune* or the
two kings of *Attila*, making the Cornelian pairs sympathetic *para-confidents*.

Pertharite, we are unsure of the exact motivation of Cléofile: we see her only as she presents herself to argue her case, be it to Taxile, Alexandre or Axiane, but never in a neutral situation. Thus we remain unsure of the significance of her relationship with Taxile. On the one hand she claims to Alexandre that she depends on her brother;[337] and at the end of the play she grieves bitterly for him:

> *Seigneur, que vous peut dire un cœur triste, abattu?*
> . . . .
> *en l'état où je suis,*
> *Je ne puis que me taire et pleurer mes ennuis.*
> *(ll.1539-44)*

Yet she has been cruelly scornful of Taxile from the opening scene, and she taunted him to return to the battle at the end of Act IV.[338] We cannot tell whether this contradiction is a flaw in Racine's characterisation, or an attempt at a more complex, enigmatic character.[339] On several occasions the absence of a *confident* leads Racine to a different compromise, as verisimilitude is disregarded in the interests of our fuller understanding of a character. For example, Alexandre is twice made to listen to Axiane's defence of Porus. In IV.2 this has at least the dramatic merit of establishing a comparison between the virtues of Alexandre and Porus, even if the victor on the battlefield would have been unlikely to appreciate the pæon from his enemy's mistress. In V.2 we may assume Racine himself realised that it was inappropriate for Alexandre to listen to Axiane's renewed declarations of love, for in 1672 he excised some 40 lines from the scene. By this time, however, Racine had re-espoused the conventional wisdom that *confidentes* can serve the revelation of the mind and feelings of the heroine - although he did not forget some of the lessons he had learned in his experiments with their elimination.

From *La Thébaïde* and especially from *Alexandre*, Racine seems to have concluded that the game was not worth the candle. To eliminate all *confidents* must lead, in some scenes at least, to awkward contrivances, an incomplete revelation of a character's thoughts and passions, and - perhaps most seriously - to a failure to engage the audience's sympathy for a protagonist. The experience of *Pulchérie* can but have reinforced these conclusions. However, *Venceslas, Pertharite, La Thébaïde* and *Alexandre* all lay bare the dramatic potential afforded by some alternative strategies. They demonstrate the power

---

[337] "Seigneur, vous le savez, je dépends de mon frère." (l.929).

[338] Similarly, Hawcroft draws our attention also to Cléofile's puzzling defence of Porus in V.1: *Alexandre*, ed. M. Hawcroft and V. Worth, p.XXX.

[339] See the study of Taxile by C. Spencer, *La Tragédie du prince* (1987), pp. 161-175.

CHAPTER FOUR

THE REBIRTH OF THE ACTIVE *CONFIDENT*

Nearly two years elapsed between the *première* of *Alexandre* and that of *Andromaque*, and by November 1667 the *Querelle de Sophonisbe* had been definitively consigned to a chapter of literary history. Apart from Racine's falling out with Port-Royal in the *Querelle des Imaginaires*,[340] we know almost nothing of his activities preceding and during the composition of *Andromaque*, and have no documents to aid our understanding of the way in which he conceived the play. The outstanding success of the first performances brought in its wake an inevitable battery of critics and snipers, but they leave us little the wiser as far as Racine's dramaturgy is concerned. Instead, if we look for example at Subligny's attack in *La Folle Querelle* and Racine's ripost in his first *Préface*, attention is focused on the nature of the tragic hero, the playwright's reworking of history, and the minutiae of *bon usage*. No-one commented on the surprising fact that after eliminating all *confidents* from *Alexandre*, Racine had reintroduced a *confident* for each of the four main characters in *Andromaque*. True, Subligny has cause to refer to each of the *confidents* by name at least once in *La Folle Querelle*, but not to comment on their role *per se*. And Racine was not likely to draw attention to it, for playwrights of this period rarely discussed details of the dramatic construction of their works unless to reply to critics.

I would argue, however, that the use of a full complement of *confidents* was no less experimental on Racine's part than his reduction or elimination of them in his first two plays. But this time he was setting the pace, rather than responding to established critical pressure. There are few other classical tragedies before *Andromaque* which use the structure of four (or more) main characters *each* accompanied by a *confident*. It is the exact symmetry of *Andromaque* which is so striking. If we look at Racine's predecessors and rivals, we can cite Cyrano de Bergerac's provocative *libertin* tragedy of 1653(?), *La Mort d'Agrippine*, as a parallel example,[341] but other playwrights rarely sought

---

[340] See R. Picard, *La Carrière de Jean Racine* (1961: 1st ed. 1956) pp. 119-125.

[341] However, Cyrano's *confidents* have a much lower profile than those of *Andromaque*, and their integration into the play is perfunctory to the point where we may even ask whether Cyrano

such a precise balance. For example, we have seen that Pierre Corneille's *Sophonisbe* had five main characters and only four secondary characters; Thomas Corneille's *Camma*, which will be examined below, had 4 main protagonists and only 3 secondary characters. Quinault's *Stratonice* (1660), which may well have influenced Racine's composition of *Andromaque*, did have four main characters and four *confidents*, but also included another secondary protagonist and a *courtisan*. Similarly Thomas Corneille's *Maximian* (1662) had four main characters and four *confidents* but also two other secondary protagonists. Yet the year following *Andromaque*, Quinault's *Pausanias*, a play whose clear debt to some other aspects of *Andromaque* has been recognised,[342] adopts the strict symmetry of four protagonists and four *confidents*. Pierre Corneille also tries out the formula in his first play after *Andromaque*, *Tite et Bérénice* (November 1670) - at the same time as Racine produces his only other work to observe a strict symmetry between main protagonists and *confidents*, his *Bérénice* (three main characters and three *confidents*).[343] In the previous chapter we discussed the reasons for which a total absence of *confidents* might have been considered unsatisfactory. We shall here examine to what extent Racine's reintroduction of the *confident* is a strategy to meet these challenges, and how his conception of the role avoids some of the weaknesses exposed during the *Querelle du confident*. Comparisons with other plays of the same period, notably *Camma* and *Pausanias,* will allow us to measure what is unique to Racine, while a comparison between Racine's *Bérénice* and Pierre Corneille's *Tite et Bérénice* will demonstrate ways in which the structural model of *Andromaque* is developed.[344]

(i) THE HIGH PROFILE OF THE *CONFIDENTS* IN *ANDROMAQUE*

The reintroduction of the *confidents* in *Andromaque* may in part derive from Racine's return to a subject of Greek tragedy. His immediate classical models (Euripides' *Andromache* and Seneca's *Troades*) employ both secondary characters and chorus, and in part the role of the *confidents* in *Andomaque* can be understood as a reworking of these elements. However, the use of a *confident* for each protagonist seems a deliberate choice by Racine in a play in which we are aware of the potentially tragic fate of all four main

---

is deliberately flouting tragic conventions. See C. J. Gossip's assessment of the *confidents'* reduced role in his edition of the play (*La Mort d'Agrippine*, 1982, p. XVII).

[342] See É. Gros, *Philippe Quinault* (1928), p.328.

[343] I defer discussion of Racine's intervening tragedy, *Britannicus*, until chapter 5, since this does not observe the same symmetry, and raises different issues.

[344] Racine's only comedy, *Les Plaideurs*, followed *Andromaque*, and, in accordance with comic tradition, the servants play a substantial role in it. However I have discovered no evidence that it influenced Racine's subsequent handling of the tragic *confident*.

characters. The scenes between protagonist and *confident* allow us to focus on each destiny in turn, seeing the character's lot in isolation from the mechanism of which it is a part. For the duration of such a scene, we can empathise fully with the character in question. In achieving this concentration, Racine is using the *confident* in a way which, as we established in Chapter 3, corresponds to one of the functions of the chorus in Greek tragedy.[345]

What is significant in *Andromaque* is not the crude statistic of how many scenes there are between each protagonist/*confident*, but the point at which they are introduced and the effect they achieve.[346] Thus Pylade and Oreste have three substantial meetings situated almost exactly at the beginning, middle and end of the play: I.1, III.1 and V.5. They correspond to the three stages of Oreste's growing despair: his forebodings at the outset of his embassy, his black *fureur* when Pyrrhus has announced his renewed decision to marry Hermione, and his final madness. In contrast, the two substantial scenes between Andromaque and Céphise are concentrated at the end of Act III and the start of Act IV. Previous to these scenes we have seen Andromaque only in relation to Pyrrhus and Hermione.[347] In III.8 and IV.1 we witness Andromaque facing her agonising choice, and then resolved to sacrifice her life. In her scenes with Céphise, the spectator sees the play as the tragedy of Andromaque. That her plan to sacrifice herself is never executed is almost immaterial: it is her attitude to the dilemma and the decision she takes which confirm her tragic status.[348] No further scenes with Céphise would serve any purpose. Pyrrhus has only one substantial scene with Phœnix, and that fairly early in the play (II.5). If we wish to account for the relative under-exposure of this pairing of protagonist/*confident*, there are two possible reasons. First, Pyrrhus's position as king gives him reason to speak to each of the other three main characters in turn, and he is already shown from three dimensions in his interaction with them. Secondly, of the four protagonists, his sentiments are the most transparent even when he is confronting another character, thus obviating the need for further *confident* scenes. Quite the reverse prevails for Hermione, whose volatile thoughts and feelings are revealed to us in four major scenes with Cléone.[349] The pattern is similar to that of Oreste and Pylade; Hermione is alone with Cléone at regular

---

[345] See p.85.

[346] I. McFarlane is one of the few critics to acknowledge that in *Andromaque* a "greater burden is placed on the confidants, so far as preservation of tone and momentum is concerned." He observes that this is reflected in the considerable number of variants introduced in their parts between 1668-97: "Reflections on the variants in *Andromaque*" (1982), p.113.

[347] Her exchange with Céphise in III.5 is but a very brief prelude to the metting with Pyrrhus in III.6.

[348] Like many critics I disagree with L. Goldmann who argued (*Le Dieu caché*, 1959, p.361) that the compromise implicit in Andromaque's plan removes the play from the realm of tragedy.

[349] I do not count IV.2 here, since Hermione utters only half a line in it. The scene is calculated to make us suspicious of Hermione's true feelings rather than to expose them to us.

intervals, in fact once in each of Acts II-V.[350] Three of these scenes correspond to Hermione's greatest moments of suffering and jealousy (Acts II, IV, V), one to her brief, illusory hope that Pyrrhus has returned to her. I would suggest it is this prominence accorded to Hermione's passions, revealed through her scenes with Cléone, which makes her such a powerful figure in the tragedy.

The disposition of the *confident* scenes allows us to conclude that Racine did not deploy his four protagonists/*confidents* mechanically. This view is borne out by the essential distinctions he draws between the four *confidents* in terms of their status. Like many other playwrights, including Pierre Corneille, he prefers to assign a specific title to the male characters who fulfil the function of *confident*. Thus Pylade is the "ami d'Oreste" and Phœnix the "gouverneur d'Achille, et ensuite de Pyrrhus". Both characters are drawn from classical sources,[351] and, significantly for a play so imbued with history and personal memories, both are associated with the past of Oreste and Pyrrhus. For example, Phœnix uses a comparison between Pyrrhus and Achilles to congratulate Pyrrhus on overcoming his passion for Andromaque:

> C'est Pyrrhus, c'est le fils et le rival d'Achille,
> Que la gloire à la fin ramène sous ses lois,
> Qui triomphe de Troie une seconde fois.
> *(ll. 630-32)*

Although Phœnix himself is drawn from Homer rather than Euripides, the title of *gouverneur* sets him in an established dramatic tradition.[352] It also justifies the tenor of his exchanges with Pyrrhus: as a former *gouverneur*, Phœnix is destined to dispense sound political advice, yet be brushed aside by the impatient Pyrrhus.[353] The framework for conflict between protagonist and *confident* is established by their respective roles.

In Pylade's relationship with Oreste Racine falls back on the stock variation on the *confident*, the *ami*. Many other dramatists, from Pierre Corneille's *Médée* onwards, had used friends who have just been reunited to provide the exposition. In his annotations on Aeschylus's *Chœphori* and Sophocles' *Electra*, Racine had noted that Pylades is the silent companion and even accomplice of Orestes, a role also assigned to him in Euripides' *Orestes* (on which we have no annotations by Racine). Racine's Pylade, however, is no protactic or silent character. His friendship with Oreste stands the most severe of

---

[350] II.1 before receiving Oreste; III.3 after triumphantly assuring Oreste she will accept Pyrrhus's renewed offer of marriage; IV.4 when she resolves that Pyrrhus shall die; and V.2 while awaiting his murder.

[351] See R. Knight, *Racine et la Grèce*, pp. 280-1.

[352] Compare the *gouverneur* of Orestes in Sophocles' *Electra*, a role on which Racine remarked several times in his annotations (see *Œuvres*, ed. P. Mesnard, lines 1330ff.).

[353] Note the use of *interruptio* on two occasions as Pyrrhus cuts Phœnix short to rejoin Andromaque: 1.257 and 1.1391.

tests: in III.1 he wants to arrange Oreste's secret departure, spiriting Hermione away,[354] and in V.5 he comes to conduct Oreste in safety from the palace. He may be seen as a figure of authority in a world of chaos.[355] From his actions, it is clear that Pylade is broadly Oreste's social equal. Unlike the other three *confidents*, he is never present in a scene as a silent listener, another clear indication that he is not subservient to Oreste, and a marked departure from the Greek tragic tradition of a silent Pylades. Subligny was not slow to criticise Racine for the inconsistencies over Pylade's status: his presence at Pyrrhus's court is never explained;[356] his intimate knowledge of the secret passages in Pyrrhus's palace is inappropriate;[357] and, most seriously, it is incongruous that Oreste should use *tu* to Pylade, while Pylade replies with *vous*.[358] Subligny succeeds in catching Racine out as far as details of verisimilitude are concerned, but Racine's use of the *tu/vous* distinction seems indicative of his dramatic priorities. In Pylade, he seeks to create a character whose role and authority is greater than than of a simple subaltern, yet who remains a secondary character, an accessory to the tragedy, not himself an actor in it. Dramaturgically, Pylade has a role equivalent to a *confident*, but perhaps Subligny's criticisms hit home, for in later plays Racine avoids the ambiguous category of *ami*.

From the list of *dramatis personæ*, Céphise and Cléone have identical status; both are called *confidentes*. Although Racine has avoided the unflattering term *suivantes*, he has made no attempt to disguise his reintroduction of the female *confidente*. In this way *Andromaque* constitutes a direct challenge to the proposals of d'Aubignac in the *Querelle de Sophonisbe*. Neither *confidente* has a named counterpart in classical tragedy, but Euripides' *Andromache* gives the eponymous heroine a handmaiden and Hermione a Nurse.[359] For Cléone, the audience needs only to be aware that Hermione trusts her and on occasions even heeds her advice. Hermione's first words in the play acknowledge that she has deferred to Cléone in agreeing to see Oreste:

> Je fais ce que tu veux; je consens qu'il me voie.
>   (l.385)

Céphise has a clearer identity, for she is a representative of the Trojan women in exile. She shares Andromaque's fate of captivity at the court of Pyrrhus, and she is bound to her mistress by affections born of their common

---

[354] *Andromaque*, ll.786-794. A plan which momentarily transports us to the world of heroic romance, which Racine judged an inappropriate model for tragedy!

[355] In saying this, I take issue with M. Edwards's negative interpretation of Pylade's final speech ("Les derniers vers sauvent Oreste de l'univers supérieur de la tragédie pour le réintégrer dans un monde plus banal, celui du confident.") in *La Tragédie racinienne*, p.112.

[356] "On demanda quel mestier Pilade faisoit à la cour de Pirrhus." *La Folle Querelle*, p.28.

[357] *Ibid.* p.72.

[358] Subligny returns to this point three times: *ibid.*, p.32, p.36, pp.37-38.

[359] Unusually, Knight overlooks this detail (*Racine et la Grèce*, p.161).

sufferings.[360] The intimacy and complicity between them in III.8 and IV.1 is exceptional. In this, Céphise resembles Euripides' handmaiden, but also reminds us of the tradition of the Greek chorus identifying with certain heroines.[361] Andromaque's use of the formula "(Ma) chère Céphise" is no mere convention;[362] it is Céphise she would charge with the last sacred rites:

> *Céphise, c'est à toi de me fermer les yeux.*
> *(l.1100)*

Céphise responds to Andromaque's planned suicide by expressing the wish to follow her mistress to the grave:

> *Ah! ne prétendez pas que je puisse survivre...*
> *(l.1101)*

At the end of this scene, like Olympe in *La Thébaïde*, Céphise is described as weeping.[363] Her tears anticipate the emotions the scene arouses in the audience.

Should we infer from the example of Céphise that the *confidents* of *Andromaque* are, as some critics have traditionally presumed of the role in general, the embodiment of the spectator, expressing his/her reactions?[364] I would contend that this is far too limited a description. Certainly there are key moments in the play where this is the case. Apart from the example of Céphise cited above, we can quote such instances as Cléone's questioning of Hermione's ominous silence in IV.2 (ll.1130-1142). But equally important is the principle of opposition, the role of the *confident* in conflict with the will of the main character. As Schrammen has shown in his detailed study of *Andromaque*, there is a symmetry as three *confidents* argue the case of another character: Phœnix puts Hermione's case to Pyrrhus, Céphise puts Pyrrhus's to Andromaque, and Cléone puts Oreste's to Hermione.[365] Although Pylade does not speak for a single other protagonist, he also regularly opposes Oreste's will.[366] Racine thus uses a balance between the *confident* in conflict and the *confident* in sympathy. We have already noted in respect of *La Thébaïde* and *Alexandre* that Racine employs conflictual exchanges between main characters

---

[360] Andromaque recognises her fidelity: "Ta foi, dans mon malheur, s'est montrée à mes yeux." (l.1075).

[361] See for example the handmaiden's speech in *Andromache*, ll. 87-90.

[362] *Andromaque*, l.1037, l.1073.

[363] "On vient. Cache tes pleurs, Céphise ..." (l.1127).

[364] See for example my discussion in the Introduction of M. Olga, "Vers une esthétique du confident racinien". The chorus of Greek tragedy had this as *one* function among others, as Burton observes (*The Chorus in Sophocles' Tragedies*, pp.2-3).

[365] G. Schrammen, "Zur Funktion des *confident* bei Racine", pp.386-9.

[366] *Ibid.*, p.389.

to avoid a flat exposition or imparting of information. Similar conflictual strategies are at the heart of his regeneration of the *confident*, and set his use of the role apart from that of many of his contemporaries. Hawcroft draws a helpful distinction, contrasting this use of conflict between *confident* and protagonist with the conflicts between two main characters. He suggests that in the former case Racine engineers "a conflict between the two characters, not a deep-rooted conflict, but one which lasts usually just for the duration of the scene".[367] Such conflicts never risk alienating protagonist and *confident* definitively in *Andromaque*, but we must be convinced the *confident* has a case to argue if we are to appreciate the full dilemma of the protagonist. Again, Racine's development of this strategy may in part derive from his admiration of the chorus of Greek tragedy. Within acts, the chorus would traditionally engage in dialogue with the protagonists, including spirited disagreement. It is interesting that Sophocles' *Electra*, which Racine annotated so closely, contains just such a scene, described by Burton as "a contest in which one participant tries, and fails, to persuade another".[368] Racine had noted the contrast between Electra and the Chorus earlier in the play.[369] It is this kind of tense exchange which may have provided a model for Racine to accord the *confident* a more dynamic role.

As Hawcroft has also observed, Racine's *confidents* speak in an unusually high percentage of scenes, suggesting that they are very active advocates.[370] Our closer analysis of the share of the discourse for each character in *Andromaque* reveals one particularly significant figure: if we put together the lines spoken by the four *confidents*, they account for 17.51% of the play. This is more than even, say, the 15.4% of *Rodogune* (the highest percentage for Pierre Corneille's tragedies before 1651) or the 13.42% of *Tite et Bérénice* (the highest percentage among Corneille's later plays, and directly comparable to *Andromaque* in having four *confidents*). We must assume that Racine believes his *confidents* have a particularly important role to play. It is easy to point to scenes in which the protagonist and *confident* engage in one of the "temporary" conflicts which Hawcroft identifies: Phœnix urging Pyrrhus to forget Andromaque (II.5), Céphise pressing Andromaque to accept Pyrrhus (III.8), and so forth. However we need to look more closely not only at the rhetorical strategies through which the *confidents* seek to impose their

---

[367] *Word as Action*, p.168.

[368] *The Chorus in Sophocles' Tragedies*, p.195.

[369] See p.85 on his annotation of line 120.

[370] *Ibid.*, p.168. In the volume *Recherches de thématique théâtrale* (ed. J. Truchet), J. Delan observes (pp.47-49) that the *confidents* in *Andromaque* are unusually active, but he does not develop the point.

viewpoint,[371] but also at the ways in which on occasions they attempt to control a protagonist's discourse.

Critics generally agree on the primacy of language in Racine's theatre; it is the medium through which action is effected and experienced. It follows that controlling another character's speech is one crucial way to influence his/her actions.[372] Hence, at a simple level, in II.5 Phœnix uses the privileges of a *gouverneur* to dictate what Pyrrhus may *not* speak about (Andromaque):

> *Commencez donc, Seigneur, à ne m'en parler plus.*
> *(l.664).*

And at the end of the same scene, he also presumes to tell Pyrrhus how he should address Hermione:

> *Oui, voyez-la, Seigneur et par des vœux soumis*
> *Protestez-lui ...*
> *(ll.707-8)*

His use of three imperatives in these lines, two referring to how Pyrrhus should speak, is revealing of the strategy by which he seeks to assume control. Similarly, at the crucial moment of III.6, when we wait to see whether Andromaque will deign to stop Pyrrhus as he goes to Hermione, it is Céphise who orders her mistress to speak:

> *Qu'attendez-vous? Forcez ce silence obstiné.*
> *(1668-87: l.895)[373]*

Andromaque does reluctantly accept Céphise's injunction, and as soon as they are alone again in III.8, she attributes the development in her situation to her *confidente*'s words:

> *Hélas! de quel effet tes discours sont suivis!*
> *(l.979)*

Like Hermione when she claimed to see Oreste only at Cléone's bidding, Andromaque is seeking to lay the repsonsibility for her actions on another's shoulders, but in both cases it is undeniable that the *confidentes* have contributed to the progress of the situation.[374] Racine has met one of d'Aubignac's objections: his *confidentes* are integrated in the action of the

---

[371] Hawcroft analyses several examples from *Andromaque* (*Word as Action*. pp.175-7).

[372] H. Phillips examines what he terms "substitution" of voice in Racine, i.e. occasions where one character speaks for another (*Racine, Language and Theatre*, chapter 3). What I am discussing here might be seen as a variant of, or prelude to, full "voice substitution".

[373] Amended to "Qu'attendez-vous? Rompez ce silence obstiné." in 1697.

[374] J. Delan draws the conclusion that "En définitive, tous les quatre <confidents> échouent dans leurs efforts de persuasion." (*Recherches de thématique théâtrale*, p.49). While the *confidents* are powerless to prevent the ultimate tragedy, I would argue that Delan's statement undervalues their contribution at earlier points in the play.

play. We might see this as the first stage in a process which will lead to Œnone replacing Phédre's voice in her calomny of Hippolyte.

The *confidents* of *Andromaque* do not themselves speak untruths, but on several occasions they press the protagonists to do so. In the first scene of the play, Pylade's advice on Oreste's embassy to Pyrrhus requires that Oreste use language to obtain the opposite of his stated purpose, effectively practising an act of deception:

> *Pressez, demandez tout, pour ne rien obtenir.*
> *(l.140)*

In the 1668 version, in Act III Pylade uses a metaphor of speech to persuade Oreste to conceal his true feelings:

> *Faites taire, Seigneur, ce transport inquiet.*
> *(1668-76: l.719)*

From 1687, Racine replaces "Faites taire" by "Dissimulez", but the meaning is unchanged. In speech, actions and appearance, Oreste must deceive those around him.[375] The advice is paralleled by Cléone's command to Hermione in III.4 to hide her triumph from the approaching Andromaque:

> *... Dissimulez. Votre rivale en pleurs*
> *Vient à vos pieds, sans doute, apporter ses douleurs.*
> *(ll.855-6)*

There are classical models, including one intervention of the chorus in Sophocles' *Electra* (annotated by Racine),[376] in which the chorus gives a protagonist similar advice. Racine is thus working within established parameters and has not yet undermined the traditional bond of trust between protagonist and *confident(e)* by having the *confident(e)s* be false to their own master/mistress. However, the way has been opened for the *confident(e)*'s contribution to cease to be associated with transparency and truth.

(ii) *CAMMA* AND *PAUSANIAS*: DIFFERENT STRATEGIES AND DIFFERENT ENDS

The significance of the roles accorded to the *confidents* in *Andromaque* is thrown into relief if we look back to Thomas Corneille's *Camma* (1661), a tragedy whose plot has marked similarities with *Andromaque*, and therefore

---

[375] An injunction repeated at the end of the scene: "Dissimulez, Seigneur; c'est tout ce que je veux." (l.800).

[376] At line 213 Racine notes, "Le Chœur l'avertit de dissimuler sa douleur" (*Œuvres*, ed. P. Mesnard, p.225).

furnishes a useful comparison.[377] *Camma* also has four main characters, but uses only two *confidents*, Phædime and Phénice, plus the "Capitaine des gardes", Sosime, who functions essentially as a messenger. One immediate result of this disposition is that neither Hésione nor Sostrate[378] has a personal *confident*, and the number of meetings between main protagonists is necessarily increased. It follows that Thomas Corneille could not easily turn our undivided attention to each of the characters as Racine does in *Andromaque*. If we set the plays side by side, this lack is most keenly felt in the contrast between Hermione and Hésione. We perceive the latter only in her meetings with Camma, Sostrate and Sinorix, and she is not present at all in Act V. It is as though in the final working out of the tragedy Thomas Corneille has overlooked the suffering of his fictional heroine. Our interest is focused instead on the other characters, whom we know more intimately through their scenes with secondary characters.[379]

Phædime has the most substantial of these secondary roles. It is not just that he speaks with Sinorix in three scenes (I.1, II.2, III.1), but that he is cast as the unscrupulous, machiavellian adviser, who expresses political views which would ill-become the moral character of a reigning monarch, even a usurper.[380] Phædime's share in the exchanges with Sinorix is significant: he speaks 68 of the 204 lines in the three scenes (i.e. 33.33%), and does not hesitate to give advice using imperative forms[381] and other strategies associated with deliberative rhetoric. Only one line, however, touches upon how Sinorix should speak (to Camma):

> *Menacez, contraignez, rien ne luy peut déplaire.*
> *(l.809)*

Phædime does not otherwise seek to influence his master's discourse. His concern is more broadly with Sinorix's vacillations and guilty conscience. Ironically, as Watts has observed, Phædime's advice does not persuade Sinorix; the usurper instead falls prey instead to further doubts and self-questioning as a result of Phædime's words, especially in his monologue in III.2.[382] After this point, his *confident* has no more to say. Thomas Corneille's strategy is very

---

[377] In his critical edition of *Camma* (1977), D.A. Watts concludes "il est donc fort possible que Racine, au moment de la composition de son premier chef d'œuvre, ait relu avec profit cette tragédie dont le succès récent aurait peut-être suffi pour attirer son attention." (p.XXX).

[378] These two characters are Thomas Corneille's invention; they are not present in his source, Plutarch. See D. Watts' edition of *Camma*, p.XIV.

[379] Sosime fulfils a role parallel to a *confident* when he listens to Sostrate's declaration of his love for Camma in V.1 (ll.1630-44). Since Sostrate is Thomas Corneille's invention, the audience need such a device in order to learn his true feelings.

[380] "Phédime ... est le mauvais génie de Sinorix, ou plutôt le serait volontiers si la conscience de l'usurpateur n'était si délicate." (*Camma*, ed. D. Watts, p.XV).

[381] Lines 35, 802, 809, 843.

[382] *Camma*, ed. D. Watts, p.XXV.

different from that which Racine will adopt: Phædime serves to provide the voice of amoral political pragmatism and to allow Sinorix to reveal his hidden thoughts and feelings. Our pity for the protagonist builds up only after the *confident* has been relegated to the role of a silent attendant.

Phénice has just two scenes alone with her mistress (I.3 and IV.1), in which her questions and interventions permit Camma to reveal in her turn her secret passions and designs. Phénice is not the taciturn *confidente* that d'Aubignac would recommend: at several points she makes quite forceful suggestions as to how Camma might act. Her first speech in the play is typically direct:

> *Si dans vos déplaisirs la vengeance vous flate,*
> *Pour en jouir, Madame, il est temps qu'elle éclate,*
> *Sinorix menaçant rien n'est à négliger.*
>   *(ll.233-5)*

However, unlike the comments of the *confidentes* of *Andromaque*, Phénice's suggestions never bear directly on how Camma should speak, only how she might act; and they do not at any point determine Camma's course of conduct. Nor is Phénice instrumental in invoking the spectator's pity for Camma. Rather, she serves Camma's desire for revenge by anticipating the obstacles the Queen's various plans may encounter. Where Racine is concerned above all in *Andromaque* to move the spectator to pity his characters, and uses the *confidentes* to this end, Thomas Corneille relies on the power of suspense and drama. One direct comparison is particularly revealing of these different ends. Racine has Andromaque confess her "innocent stratagème" to Céphise in IV.1; as a result we are moved by her determination to safeguard her son while preserving her loyalty to Hector. Thomas Corneille did not have Camma tell Phénice - or any other character - of her plan to poison the wedding chalice. The dénouement of *Camma* relies precisely on the *coup de théâtre* which takes the other characters and the audience by surprise.

Camma and *Andromaque* are both very powerful plays in their individual ways. If Racine uses his *confidents* in the more innovative and interesting fashion, it is because he understood that they could contribute to his overall conception of tragedy. Thomas Corneille's dramatic priorities were different, and did not require the same exploitation of the *confident*. Once *Andromaque* had won public acclaim, however, there was a new model for playwrights to draw upon. When we turn to Quinault's *Pausanias*, in which the echoes of *Andromaque* are unmistakable, we cannot avoid direct comparisons with Racine's handling of the *confident*. The plays are produced at an interval of some twelve months, and both are performed by the Hôtel de Bourgogne. I suspect that *Pausanias* is the first of a number of the plays written in Racine's shadow which emulate some of his confidential strategies.

*   *   *

The symmetry of the four protagonists and four *confidents* in *Pausanias* suggests an essential structural parallel with *Andromaque*.[383] This is in contrast to the fact that, with the rare exception of *Stratonice*, Quinault is usually economical in his deployment of secondary characters.[384] The cast list of *Pausanias* describes all four secondary characters as *confident(e)*, but both Eurianax and Sophane stand out as friend and political adviser respectively, recalling the roles of Pylade and Phœnix. When confessing his true passions to Eurianax, Pausanias justifies his openness with a reference to their friendship:

> *Notre amitié m'en presse, il te faut tout apprendre.*
> *(l.192)*

Sophane's trusted status is shown by Aristide's account of his political machinations in I.5, and in their next exchange (III.1) we realise that Sophane is himself active on Aristide's behalf. He brings reports of troops ready to take Aristide's side against Pausanias (ll. 699-702); and at the end of the scene he returns to their supporters with a couplet indicating that he will himself be involved in the action:

> *Et vais de mon côté disposer nos amis,*
> *A tenter hautement ce qu'ils nous ont promis.*
> *(ll.741-2)*

It is of course possible that Quinault is following general dramatic practice, rather than *Andromaque* in particular, in giving the male *confident* a more active role. However, the parallel with Racine's dramaturgy is particularly obvious with regard to the female roles. Charile is the regular personal attendant of Demarate (like Cléone to Hermione), while Stratone, like Céphise, can be presumed to have accompanied her mistress into exile as a prisoner. Quinault does not exploit this bond in the way that Racine does, however, for his captive princess secretly returns her captor's love, and does not require Stratone's intimate complicity or support. They have only the one scene alone (II.1), and Stratone's role is that of the traditional, passive listener, who is not closely touched by the passions of her mistress. This distinction between *Andromaque* and *Pausanias* holds true for the whole play. Where Racine relies on *confidents'* emotional reactions to convey the pathos of the fates of Andromaque and Oreste in particular, Quinault keeps his *confidents* detached

---

[383] The first act consists of alternating scenes between protagonist/*confident(e)* and two protagonists, introducing us to Demarate/Charile (I.1), Pausanias/ Eurianax (I.3) and Aristide/Sophane (I.5). Cléonice/Stratone open Act II, so that by II.1 the parallel with the structure of *Andromaque* is evident.

[384] See W. Brooks, "The Evolution of the Theatre of Quinault" (unpublished Ph.D. thesis, 1968), Chapter 4.

from the tragedy. Eurianax and Sophane are involved on the political level
rather than personally,[385] and neither of the two *confidentes* comments on how
the developing situation touches herself. On this level Quinault has followed
Racine's outer structure, but not turned it to the same ends.

Another aspect of the exchanges between protagonists and *confidents* may
owe more to *Andromaque*, or at least *Andromaque* and *Pausanias* may both
draw on a common set of assumptions. Quinault makes some vigorous use of
conflictual dialogues, which we saw as essential to the dynamism of
Andromaque. This is particularly true of the opening scene between Demarate
and Charile, and I.3 between Eurianax and Pausanias. If we compare *Pausanias*
with *Astrate*, Quinault's highly acclaimed tragedy of 1664/5, we note that in the
earlier play Quinault had exploited a tense, conflictual opening, but between
two main characters (Agenor and Astrate), while the subsequent *confident* scene
was almost entirely occupied by an expository declaration by Agenor. The new
reliance on early *confident* scenes, characterised by deliberative rather than
demonstrative rhetoric, may arguably be an emulation of the success of
Andromaque. For example, in I.1 Charile combats Demarate's doubts over
Pausanias's affections by adopting his defence.[386] This is similar to the strategy
Schrammen identified with regard to the *confidents* of *Andromaque* arguing
against their master/ mistress. Charile's speeches are also marked by a series of
rhetorical questions as she seeks to persuade Demarate that her interpretation of
Pausanias's behaviour is mistaken.[387] When Eurianax is alone with Pausanias,
the same pattern is adopted. The *confident* first takes Demarate's part:

> *De si beaux sentiments, où tant d'amour s'exprime,*
> *Méritent bien, Seigneur, tout au moins votre estime.*
> *(ll.175-6)*

Then, on Pausanias confessing his love for Cléonice, Eurianax tries to dissuade
his master/friend by basing his speech (ll. 197-208) on five rhetorical questions.
As the play develops, the exchanges between Eurianax and Pausanias continue
to be characterised by argumentative strategies, similar to those between
Racine's heroes/*confidents*. There is a particular echo of the relationship
between Pyrrhus and Phœnix in V.3 of *Pausanias*, where Eurianax tries to
argue that Pausanias is blinded by his love, but twice Pausanias cuts him short.[388]
Like *Phœnix*, Eurianax fails to persuade his master to heed his warning as the
crisis looms.

---

[385] E.g. Eurianax's plea to the dying Pausanias: "Vivez pour tous les Grecs." (l.1575).

[386] E.g. "Son embaras l'excuse, il est chef d'une armée,/ Jalouse de son rang et de sa
renommée." (ll.59-60).

[387] For example, lines 27-31 contain four rhetorical questions.

[388] Lines 1409, 1411. Compare the use of *interruptio* in *Andromaque* at lines 257, 1391.

Conflictual exchanges are less dominant in the later scenes between
Demarate and Charile, for here Quinault has other priorities. The main function
of II.5 and IV.4 is to allow Demarate to reveal her secret intentions to Charile -
and the spectator.[389] Where Hermione fascinates us by Racine's subtle portrait
of a mind constantly divided between love and hatred, Quinault creates a
heroine who moves steadily from love to jealousy to vengeance. Hermione's
scenes with Cléone allow us to perceive the conflict within the heroine;
Demarate's with Charile serve to inform us of the next stage in the heroine's
plans for revenge.[390] Both heroines occupy centre-stage at crucial moments by
virtue of their scenes with the *confidentes*, but the scenes achieve quite different
effects.

We may conclude that *Pausanias* takes up some of the successful
confidential strategies employed in *Andromaque*, and in particular relies on the
symmetry of four secondary characters/four main protagonists to accomplish
the complex exposition. However, it is telling that, overall, Quinault's *confidents*
have only approximately half the share of discourse which Racine accorded to
his.[391] They are neither such a central nor such a constant resource as in
Andromaque. And in one particular way, Quinault's tragedy is no different
from *Camma*: at no point do the *confidents* attempt to influence the
protagonists' discourse, nor do their words directly affect the course of the
action. In this respect *Andromaque* stands alone in its integration of the
confidents into the tragic mechanism.

(iii) *TITE ET BÉRÉNICE* AND *BÉRÉNICE*: CONFIRMING THE CONFIDENTS' PLACE

After the discreet hommage paid by *Pausanias* to Racine's new conception
of the *confident*, other playwrights can also be seen to appropriate certain
Racinian strategies. Pierre Corneille's *Tite et Bérénice*, provides a particularly
interesting case. This *comédie héroïque*[392] has, of course, frequently been
compared with Racine's *Bérénice*, not least by its earliest audiences who were

---

[389] As with Eurianax-Phœnix, so with Cléone-Charile there is one strikingly close parallel.
In IV.2 of *Andromaque*, Cléone remarks on Hermionne's silence and a "calme si funeste"
(l.1141); this is shortly before Hermione delivers her order for Oreste to kill Pyrrhus. In
Pausanias, after Demarate's meeting with Pausanias in IV.3, Charile remarks on her mistress's
self-control ("J'admire que votre âme ait tant pû se contraindre."), just before Demarate reveals
her decision to avenge herself. In both cases the *confidentes'* remarks on the heroines' self-
control precede the dramatic revelations of their plans to punish the errant lover.
[390] W. Brooks suggests that Quinault's later plays revolve precisely around questions of
information and deception ("The Evolution of the Theatre of Quinault", chapter 5).
[391] Together, the *confidents* of *Pausanias* speak 146 lines in a play of 1588 lines, i.e.
9.19%.
[392] On the implications of the genre, see C.J. Gossip, *"Tite et Bérénice: a coherent comédie héroïque?"*.

able to see both versions within a week. Yet as far as the *confident* is concerned, it is the comparisons with *Andromaque* and *Britannicus* which are the more telling, since these are the models with which Corneille was familiar when writing his work, and which he was seeking to rival. Corneille had written no play since *Attila*, which had been staged in March 1667, some six months before *Andromaque*.[393] *Tite et Bérénice* is thus his first work which might reflect the influence of the new Racinian *confident*. On a superficial level, there is an immediate parallel with *Andromaque*: the four protagonists are each given a *confident* - a symmetry identical to *Pausanias*. The *confidents'* total share of the discourse in *Tite et Bérénice*, 13.42%, is notably greater than in any other post-1660 work of Corneille. Both these features suggest a shift in Corneille's handling of the *confident*.

It is possible that Corneille was moving partly in this direction on his own initiative, perhaps still exploring an answer to d'Aubignac's criticisms. Whereas *Agésilas* (February 1666) had reduced the two *confidents'* roles to a minimum, *Attila* the following year had exploited a pair of servants whose role clearly owed much to the comic tradition, as Autrand has pointed out in one of the rare articles dealing with Cornelian *confidents*.[394] Not only do Octar and Flavie speak for 10.46% of the play, but their own sentiments are capital to the way in which they serve the protagonists. Octar regularly relays Attila's confidences to Honorie through the intermediary of Flavie, whom he wishes to marry.[395] Honorie twice explicitly makes Octar's betrayal of Attila a condition of her permitting his marriage to Flavie, and even threatens to inform Attila of Octar's secret love if he does not do her bidding.[396] The strategy of a parallel between the protagonists' and the servants' love affairs is standard in the comic tradition,[397] and the device of one servant betraying a protagonist to serve the master/mistress of his/her lover is also familiar. To this extent, Corneille may have been doing no more than providing a plausible motive for Octar to disclose information essential to the plot's progression. Certainly Corneille stops well short of one essential of the comic tradition, scenes with the two

---

[393] On Corneille's absence from the stage after *Attila*, see G. Couton, *La Vieillesse de Corneille*, pp.159-68.

[394] M. Autrand, "Stratégie du personnage secondaire dans l'*Attila* de Corneille. Étude dramatique." (1985).

[395] In particular, in V.2 we learn that it is Octar who has warned that Attila plans to have Valamir and Ardaric killed. (Honorie: " Octar aime Flavie et l'en vient d'avertir.", l.1495).

[396] IV.1 (ll.1085-8), V.5 (ll.1702-4 and 1715).

[397] Molière's *George Dandin*, staged the following year, is one of the many examples of this structure. Émelina appears to overlook *Attila* when he categorically dismisses the possibility of a love interest between servants in tragedy (*Les Valets et les Servantes*, p.111).

servants alone on stage. Yet as Autrand argues,[398] he comes very close to breaching the dividing line between the tragic and the comic in IV.3 when Attila makes the outrageous threat that he will humiliate Honorie by having her marry Octar.[399] Such exceptional situations are the essence of Cornelian drama, and the symmetry between the loves of the secondary and main characters is less surprising if we think of the importance of parallel structures in Corneille's work as a whole.[400]

While *Attila* raised the profile of its two *confidents* by elevating them momentarily to the status of characters with their own tale, it still circumscribed the overall role of secondary characters. Neither Ardaric, Valamir nor Ildione is accorded a *confident*. Instead, Corneille has the two kings function as *para-confidents* for each other in a number of scenes. By contrast, in *Tite et Bérénice*, for the first and only time in a serious play of Pierre Corneille, no protagonist is left without a *confident*. How does the way in which the four *confidents* are exploited compare with the distinctive features of Racine's reintroduction of the role?

Corneille's secondary characters are all described as *confident(e)*, with the distinction that Philon is "ministre d'Etat, confident de Bérénice". There are precedents for the use of a male *confident* for a female personnage including, as we have seen, Mlle Desjardins's *Manlius* and Thomas Corneille's *Camma*. But in the case of *Tite et Bérénice* the choice corresponds to a deliberate wish to focus the exchange between heroine and *confident* on politics rather than affairs of the heart. In other respects, too, Corneille avoids the passive *confidentes* of *Sophoisbe*. The secondary characters of *Tite et Bérénice* are close to the recent Racinian model in that their views are often in (temporary) conflict with those of the main characters, and each *confident* has a distinctive voice. Philon is the political adviser, initially in III.3 providing a more positive interpretation than Bérénice of Tite's formal reception of her,[401] then in IV.1 reporting the unfavourable opinions he has heard among the Roman people. In the latter scene he remains neutral, citing the populace verbatim in two speeches,[402] and allowing the Queen to draw her own conclusions. Philon's report contributes to the evolution of the play in that Bérénice's pride leads her

---

[398] "Stratégie du personnage secondaire", pp.524-9.

[399] "Et s'il faut un Sujet à qui dédaigne un Roi,/ Choisissez dans une heure, ou d'Octar, ou de moi." (ll.1235-6).

[400] *Rodogune* provides the most famous example, but *Attila* runs a close second in the careful balancing of the fates of the two kings, Valamir and Ardaric.

[401] Lines 894-899.

[402] Lines 1065-1080 and ll.1093-1102.

to challenge the Roman people and seek the support of Domitian, but she acts independently, neither in response to nor contradiction of her *confident*.

Plautine, the *confidente* of Domitie, is far more outspoken. Although a large part of the opening scene is taken up by the expository *récit* of Domitie,[403] we also observe Plautine challenging Domitie's litany of grievances. Without going so far as to become Tite's advocate, Plautine draws our attention to the fact that Domitie blames Tite for marrying without passion while she herself is prepared to do exactly the same:

> La chose est bien égale, il n'a pas tout le vôtre,
> <votre cœur>
> S'il aime un autre objet, vous en aimez un autre.
> (ll.47-48)

Plautine's reproaches show her to be actively involved in the exchange with Domitie. Indeed, her rebuke to Domitie momentarily approaches the harrying tones of the *nourrice* of comedy:

> Que ce que vous avez d'ambitieux caprice,
> Pardonnez-moi ce mot, vous fait un dur supplice!
> (ll. 55-56)

Domitie's replies indicate that she is listening carefully to her *confidente*. The first lines of each of her speeches respond preceisely to Plautine's words, even echoing the *confidente*'s exact words in several cases.[404] In this conflictual role, Plautine resembles the *confidents* of *Andromaque*, but the effect achieved is not the same. Corneille uses the divergent viewpoints primarily to focus our minds on the dilemma which Domitie faces, rather than to arouse our pity.

Both the male *confidents* also question the protagonists' judgements. The differences between the characters of Tite and Domitian lead to a fine distinction between the tones in which Flavian and Albin deliver their advice. Flavian's role is little more than that of a listener in his earliest scene with Tite (II.1),[405] for the Emperor is himself painfully aware of the conflict between his *cœur* and his *raison*, which he exposes at length. When Tite decides in Act V to follow the dictates of his heart, Flavian acquires a new importance for he represents the moral imperative of Tite's duty to the state. The parallel with

---

[403] This is justified in a rather clumsy fashion (ll. 71-78). Although Corneille establishes that Plautine is hearing the account for the first time, he takes little trouble to convince the spectator that this is the best occasion for Domitie to deliver it, and does not allow Plautine to respond to it at any length before the arrival of Domitian. One of the earliest criticisms of the play, the Abbé de Villars's *La Critique de Bérénice. Seconde Partie*, comments very negatively on the opening scene. The Abbé finds it too long and full of "narrations purement épisodiques" (Granet, *Recueil*, p.219).

[404] E.g in response to Plautine's words at line 47, Domitie starts her speech with "Ne dis point qu'entre nous la chose soit égale ..." (l.51).

[405] Flavian speaks only 16 of the 115 lines in the scene.

Paulin in Racine's *Bérénice* is obvious, but there are also echoes of Phœnix's advice to Pyrrhus in II.5 of *Andromaque*:[406]

> TITE
>
> *Ne perds plus de raisons à combattre ma flamme,*
> *Les yeux de Bérénice inspirent des avis,*
> *Qui persuadent mieux que tout ce que tu dis.*
>
> FLAVIAN
>
> *Ne vous exposez donc qu'à ceux de Domitie.*
>   *(ll.1468-71)*

Flavian also gives a number of warnings to Tite about the dangers of neglecting Domitie's anger,[407] which recall Phœnix's vain attempts to make Pyrrhus heed the wrath of Hermione.

Domitian's *confident*, on the other hand, stands apart from Racinian models. Albin not only meets the vacillations of Domitian with positive advice (a conventional strategy), but expands his arguments to offer insights into universal human nature, almost as a *moraliste* might. The ironic detachment of the *confident* is surprising, although perhaps less out of keeping in a *comédie héroïque* than it would have been in a tragedy. In I.3, as S. Doubrovsky has remarked,[408] Albin resembles La Rochefoucauld:

> *Seigneur, s'il m'est permis de parler librement,*
> *Dans toute la Nature aime-t-on autrement?*
> *L'amour-propre est la source en nous de tous les autres,*
> *C'en est le sentiment qui forme tous les nôtres,*
> *Lui seul allume, éteint, ou change nos désirs,*
> *Les objets de nos vœux le sont de nos plaisirs.*
>   *(ll.277-282)*

It is not until he has expounded his general philosophy of *amour-propre* that he relates it directly to Domitian's situation.[409] For the Abbé de Villars, who judged *Tite et Bérénice* purely according to the conventions of tragedy, such a "joyeuse morale" had no place, particularly not when expressed by a *confident* "qui n'y doit faire aucune figure que pour la connexion des Scénes".[410] Even more unexpectedly, after Domitian's humiliating encounter with Domitie in

---

[406] Compare this speech also with the reference to the power of Andromaque's eyes in III.6 of *Andromaque*.

[407] Lines 415-426, line 1474 (almost a verbatim echo of the advice of line 426), lines 1487-8, line 1593.

[408] *Corneille et la dialectique du héros*, p.407.

[409] Such a movement away from the immediate situation would be foreign to Racine's *confidents*. For example, when Acomat refers to the lessons of old age to explain his lack of passion for Atalide, we see that it is the particular which authorises a brief general statement, not the reverse (*Bajazet*, ll.177-181).

[410] Granet, *Recueil*, p.218.

IV.3, Albin provides a ten-line analysis of the behaviour of "les fières beautés", using Domitie's behaviour to illustrate a general principle:

> *Seigneur, telle est l'humeur de la plupart des femmes*
>
> ....
>
> *Domitie a pour vous ces communs sentiments*
> *Que les fières beautés ont pour tous leurs Amants.*
>> *(ll.1283-1294)*

Perhaps partly because of the flexibility afforded by the genre of the *comédie héroïque*, the Cornelian *confident* is here given a new lease of life. The combined examples of Octar and Flavie in *Attila* and Albin in *Tite et Bérénice* suggest that in creating the *confidents* of these later works Corneille was looking back to the comic vein in which he had first excelled. Such roles have a new interest for the spectator, but risk interrupting our focus upon the unique situation of the protagonist.[411]

On another level the case of Albin shows Corneille integrating the *confidents* into the unfolding of the plot, as Racine had. It is on Albin's initiative that Bérénice's unexpected return rekindles Tite's latent passion:

> *Et si je vous disais que déjà Bérénice*
> *Est dans Rome, inconnue, et par mon artifice?*
> *Qu'elle surprendra Tite ...*
>> *(ll.343-5)*

And later in the play Albin confides that he has ensured the Senate will approve the marriage of Tite and Bérénice:

> *Pour le Sénat, n'en soyez point en doute,*
>
> ....
>
> *Et je l'y tiens déjà, Seigneur, tout préparé.*
>> *(ll.1300-6)*

Corneille's *confident* has crossed the boundary to become a political force in his own right, perhaps in the footsteps of Burrhus and Narcisse. Certainly Domitian accepts his *confident*'s authority, for IV.4 closes with the protagonist acknowledging the value of Albin's advice :

> *... Je suivrai ce que ton zèle en dit.*
>> *(l.1326)*

Plautine also influences events, albeit that Domitie, like the heroines of *Andromaque* is quick to reproach her *confidente* for her advice. She attributes her visit to the Emperor (II.3), which ironically coincided with Bérénice's arrival, to Plautine's influence:

---

[411] Compare this with Gilbert's introduction of a much longer philosophical debate between the *confidents* of *Arie et Pétus*. See Chapter 5.

> *Non, non, tu l'as voulu, Plautine, que je vinsse*
> *Désavouer ici les vanités du Prince...*
>   *(ll.655-6)*

On this evidence, the *confidents* of *Tite et Bérénice* not only speak more lines than their counterparts in other later plays of Corneille but they are also more closely drawn into the plot.[412]

One final comparison with Racine's theatre needs to be established: the extent to which the *confidents* of *Tite et Bérénice* seek to control the protagonists' discourse as well as their actions. In both Corneille and Racine, the story of Bérénice is exceptionally lacking in any external action, and the spoken word must be the prime subject. While Racine makes the act of speaking (or failing to speak) the single turning point, Corneille makes it one among several others, but he too recognises that the *confidents* can play an effective role only if they can influence what is said. In this, *Tite et Bérénice* is closer to the Racian model than, say, *Pausanias* was. From the opening scene Plautine presses Domitie to dissimulate.[413] Albin's counsel to Domitian two scenes later revolves around how he should speak to Tite:

> *S'il s'émeut, redoublez, dites que l'on vous aime,*
> *Dites qu'un pur respect contraint avec ennui*
> *Une âme toute à vous à se donner à lui.*
> *S'il se trouble, achevez, parlez de Bérénice.*
>   *(ll.320-3)*

The repetition of the imperatives "dites" and "parlez" underlines the urgency of the advice. If Albin sees speaking of Bérénice as the ultimate weapon, Flavian gives Tite very different advice; like Phœnix, he wants to forbid his master to speak to the object of his desires:

> *Et sur tout de la Reine évitez l'entretien.*
>   *(l.1594)*

How far Corneille is borrowing Racine's techniques in these interventions of the *confident* is difficult to judge, but we can conclude that at the very least both dramatists have perceived that an active *confident* has the power of controlling discourse.

*   *   *

Racine's *Bérénice* does more than simply re-employ the familiar devices of his previous two tragedies. Because of the extreme economy of its characters, it

---

[412] I thus disagree with Le Bidois's claim that *Tite et Bérénice* provides a clear demonstration of "l'impuissance des confidents de Pierre Corneille" (*La Vie*, p.161).

[413] "Du moins à l'Empereur cachez cette tristesse." (l.16).

is one of the plays in which the role of the *confidents* is most crucial. This is illustrated by the fact that the three *confidents* share 17.12% of the lines.[414] The single most important development in the use of the *confident* is Racine's strategy of using Antiochus, a major protagonist, as a *para-confident* for Titus - while he is simultaneously and secretly Titus's rival in love. This crossing of boundaries between the roles of *confident* and protagonist will be examined in Chapter 7, but for the present we can note that Antiochus's double status highlights the significance of all the *confidents'* functions.

As in *Andromaque*, the *confidents* themselves are both active in their arguments, and essential to the workings of the plot. The control of discourse is again a central feature, but with a difference: the *confidents* of *Bérénice* rarely tell the protagonists what to say; more importantly, they are explicitly charged with the function of speaking *for* them. The movement of the play depends entirely upon whether one protagonist will speak to another, yet - and this is paradoxically the dramatic strength of *Bérénice* - Racine is economic in the extreme with meetings between protagonists. In Acts I-IV, each of the three protagonists meets each other protagonist only twice: Antiochus and Bérénice in I.4 and III.3; Titus and Bérénice in II.4 and IV.5; and Antiochus and Titus in III.1 and IV.7. It falls to the *confidents* to mediate so that either characters may be brought together, or messages conveyed. The unglamorous traditional role of the messenger thus takes on a new dimension.[415]

Each of the first four Acts opens either with a protagonist requesting a *confident* (or *para-confident* in Act III) to bear a message, or with a protagonist awaiting the return of the messenger. In the opening scene Arsace is sent to Bérénice to request that she speak with Antiochus. When Arsace returns to announce that his mission has been successful, his statement is the first indication of the power *confidents* will have to act for protagonists:

> *Vous la verrez, Seigneur: Bérénice est instruite*
> *Que vous voulez ici la voir seule et sans suite.*
> *La reine d'un regard a daigné m'avertir*
> *Qu'à votre empressement elle allait consentir.*
> (*ll. 63-66*)

At the start of Act II, Paulin has apparently done no more than transmit a message that Titus wishes to speak to Antiochus.[416] The significance of the message emerges, however, in the course of the private interview between Titus and Paulin:

---

[414] Rutile functions only as a messenger, appearing in two scenes (II.3, IV.8), and speaking 5 lines in total.

[415] H. Phillips analyses in some detail the voice of the message-giver in Racine. However, he does not differentiate substantially between the use of the *confidents* and the protagonists (*Racine. Language and Theatre*, pp.36-37).

[416] Lines 327-331.

> *J'attends Antiochus pour lui recommander*
> *Ce dépôt précieux que je ne puis garder!*
> (ll. 485-6)

The meeting between Titus and Antiochus, strategically delayed until III.1, sees Antiochus, the *para-confident*, ironically charged with bearing the fateful news to Bérénice. It is perhaps no coincidence that Titus has used the phrase "de ma part" to both Paulin and Antiochus:

> *A-t-on vu de ma part le roi de Comagène?*
> (l.327)

> *Employez le pouvoir que vous avez sur elle:*
> *Voyez-la de ma part.*
> (ll.700-1)

The Emperor's reluctance to speak makes him rely on his messengers as proxies. For Bérénice, the opposite pertains: she asks only to speak to Titus, but, denied access to him, she must rely on Phénice to convey her request. At the start of Act IV she is alone, and her isolation and vulnerability are compounded by the fact that her happiness depends on the return of a *confidente*. Twice in her monologue she repeats "Phénice ne vient point?" (lines 953 and 957). Her fate depends essentially on her *confidente*'s performance,[417] for Phénice must not only deliver a message but move Titus as Bérénice herself would do. From Phénice's report in IV.2, she has represented Bérénice's case with consummate skill:

> *Oui, je l'ai vu, Madame,*
> *Et j'ai peint à ses yeux le trouble de votre âme.*
> *J'ai vu couler des pleurs qu'il voulait retenir.*
> (ll.963-5)

And, like Arsace in Act I, she has brought about the meeting which was asked of her.

As Barthes has observed, *confidents* move with a freedom denied to the main protagonists.[418] Not only can they gain access to other main characters, but they are also employed to observe events offstage. This is the essential role of Paulin, who - like Corneille's Philon - is the spokesman for the voice of Rome. Titus uses the metaphor of Paulin acting as his ears and eyes,[419] and concludes:

---

[417] Herein lies an essential difference from V.1-2 of *Andromaque*, where Hermione awaits the news of Pyrrhus's fate. Cléone does no more than report what she has witnessed; Phénice must play an active role offstage.

[418] *Sur Racine*, pp. 55-56.

[419] Line 362. In "The Power of the Spoken Word in *Bérénice*", (1976) J.A. Dainard has established the close links between the semantic fields relating to vision and speech throughout *Bérénice* (art.cit. pp.159-161).

> *Je veux par votre bouche entendre tous les cœurs.*
> *(l.358)*

While Corneille had Philon quote the Romans' views verbatim, in Racine Paulin's report represents his own interpretation of public opinion. He is poised between the traditional *confident* and the *conseiller*, at once the intimate and trusted servant, and also the political adviser who is given the freedom to voice his opinion. Indeed, Titus claims to have chosen him precisely because his sincerity will make him a good "interpète" of others (line 364). Paulin's long speech (ll.371-419) is a forceful example of how deliberative rhetoric can be used to turn background history into urgent argument. There is a similarity with the strategies of Agrippine's mighty *tirade* in IV.2 of *Britannicus*.[420] The *confident* commands the full attention of both the protagonist and the audience. Unlike Agrippine's, Paulin's speech produces the effect he desired. While it alone has not determined Titus's course of action, Titus acknowledges it as confirmation of the decision that he has reluctantly reached:

> *Mon cœur en ce moment ne vient pas de se rendre.*
> *Si je t'ai fait parler, si j'ai voulu t'entendre,*
> *Je voulais que ton zèle achevât en secret*
> *De confondre un amour qui se tait à regret.*
> *(ll.447-450)*

At the end of Act IV, when Titus hesitates between going to Bérénice or to the Senate, Paulin's entreaties (lines 1249-51) again prevail. Titus is poised between the conflicting arguments of Antiochus and Paulin, as Néron is between Burrhus and Narcisse in Act IV of *Britannicus*.[421] In *Bérénice*. Paulin is a worthy successor to Burrhus, acting as a *confident/conseiller* who has, at least temporarily, a definable impact on the turn of events.

The relationship between Titus and Paulin demonstrates the degree to which the Racinian hero/heroine relies upon the *confident* for moral and emotional support. Both Titus and Bérénice urge their *confidents* to speak: far from being a silent presence or passive listeners, Paulin and Phénice must use their voices to allay protagonists' fears, and if they refuse to do so, their silence is ominous. As D. Maskell has shown, pauses and silences are an essential aspect of a character's performance as a listener.[422] In II.1 Bérénice's evocation of Titus's triumphal procession is punctuated by a brief command to Phénice to approve her sentiments:

---

[420] Hawcroft observes that the "predominance of real over artificial proof" is characteristic of *Britannicus* (*Word as Action*, p.107). The same is true of this speech of Paulin.

[421] See p.141.

[422] *Racine. A Theatrical Reading*, pp. 149-153.

> *Parle: peut-on le voir sans penser comme moi*
> *Qu'en quelque obscurité que le sort l'eût fait naître,*
> *Le monde en le voyant eût reconnu son maître?*
> (*ll. 314-6*)

No reply is forthcoming, but we may imagine a pause after the delivery of line 316, which gives the audience time to realise that Phénice may interpret the scene differently from Bérénice. The imperative "Parle" is again used in Bérénice's speech at the end of the act, when she is seeking to account for Titus's abrupt departure, but this time she hopes that Phénice may be able to furnish an explanation which she herself cannot uncover:

> *Mais tu nous entendais. Il ne faut rien me taire:*
> *Parle. N'ai-je rien dit qui lui puisse déplaire?*
> (*ll.635-6*)

It is Phénice's unbroken silence which helps us to appreciate Bérénice's mounting desperation before she finally seizes upon an erroneous explanation.[423]

A similar dynamic operates between Titus and Paulin in II.2, when Paulin is reluctant to pronounce the report which he knows Titus does not wish to hear. Maskell suggests we may suppose a brief pause as Titus invites Paulin to speak, followed by a harsher imperative:[424]

> *Voici le temps enfin qu'il faut que je m'explique.*
> *De la reine et de moi que dit la voix publique?*
> *Parlez: qu'entendez-vous?*
> (*ll.343-5*)

Paulin's response is a variation on Phénice's silence: an answer, but of the most general and evasive kind.[425] It is not until Titus has reminded Paulin of his duty to report the truth sincerely, and repeated the imperative "Parlez donc" (line 367) that Paulin embarks upon his long speech. These strategic silences of Racine's *confidents* are not the same as the silence that d'Aubignac would have enjoined upon the *suivantes*. Precisely because they must be bidden to speak - and even then may not reply - the *confidents* of *Bérénice* have a voice which both protagonists and audience wait to hear. The commands "Parle"/"Parlez" no longer belong exclusively to the domain of exchanges between main protagonists.[426]

---

[423] In lines 631-54 Bérénice speaks directly to Phénice, naming her twice, whereas in lines 655-662 she addresses the absent Titus as she elaborates her false hypothesis.

[424] *Racine. A Theatrical Reading*, pp. 151-2.

[425] "J'entends de tous côtés/ Publier vos vertus, Seigneur, et ses beautés." (ll.345-6).

[426] There are of course a number of occasions where main protagonists use the same command, pressing each other to speak (e.g. lines 183, 623, 704, 1153, and line 883 " Je veux que vous me parliez"): Phillips interprets these as signs of "the tension of utterance" (*Racine.*

It is not only the scenes in which *confidents* speak that provide evidence of
their strategic roles. In those in which they are apparently passive onlookers,
there are also occasions when they have a significant function. Phillips, like
Maskell, has drawn our attention to the role of the protagonist as listener in
Racine,[427] but we need to extend this analysis to focus on the *confident* in
particular. Racine has seized the chance of revitalising a particularly "tired"
area of the *confident*'s role. Of course, many earlier plays have a main
character calling to a *confident(e)* for support at a key moment.[428] But in
Bérénice such an appeal is made long before the dénouement. When Antiochus
delivers Titus's tragic message to Bérénice, the Queen's response is addressed
to Phénice, and it is the *confidente* who attempts to reason with her, while
Antiochus becomes the onlooker:

> BÉRÉNICE
> *Nous séparer! Hélas, Phénice!*
> PHÉNICE
>   *Eh bien, Madame?*
> *Il faut ici montrer la grandeur de votre âme.*
> *Ce coup sans doute est rude; il doit vous étonner.*
>   *(ll.903-5)*

On the printed page, Phénice's lines seem platitudinous, but I suspect that in
performance what matters is the degree of sympathy with which they are
spoken. The Queen and her *confidente* form a united front: Bérénice proceeds
to dismiss Antiochus quite brutally, and it is Phénice to whom she makes her
pathetic appeal.[429] This close relationship between Phénice and Bérénice is
recognised by Antiochus at the end of Act IV, imploring Titus to go to
Bérénice:

> *Qu'avez-vous fait, Seigneur? l'aimable Bérénice*
> *Va peut-être expirer dans les bras de Phénice.*
>   *(ll.1227-8)*

There seems to be a line from Andromaque/Céphise and Bérénice/Phénice, via
Monime/Phœdime to the special bond between Phèdre/Œnone. These
confidentes may argue with their mistresses for the duration of a scene, but their
loyalty is unswerving, their devotion calculated to heighten our pity for the

---

Language and Theatre, p.36). We might see the command to the *confidents* to speak as a
deliberate echo.

[427] *Racine. Language and Theatre*, pp. 52-65.

[428] A notable example is Cléopâtre's appeal to Laonice to escort her away, thus preserving
her dignity, at the end of *Rodogune* (ll.1827-30).

[429] Maskell suggests that Bérénice's address to Phénice is an example of the *apart dialogué*,
unheard by Antiochus (*Racine. A Theatrical Reading*, p.101).

heroines. We might see another such parallel in the close relationships between Oreste/Pylade and Antiochus/Arsace. It is in large measure Arsace's respect for Antiochus and concern for his suffering which persuade us that Antiochus shares in the tragedy of Titus and Bérénice.[430]

A second use of the silent *confident* is as a third-party to whom protagonists may appeal for solidarity. Racine had already exploited this device with particular skill in III.6 of *Andromaque*, where Andromaque and Pyrrhus addressed their *confidents* rather than each other at the start of the scene.[431] This scene had also exemplified how the command to the *confident* to accompany the protagonist offstage could be employed as a veiled threat to the other party.[432] Bérénice's "Allons Phénice" (line 1327), as she makes a move to leave Titus in V.5, has the same effect: Titus attempts to stop her departure. But an appeal to the silent *confident* can also be an admission of defeat, a signal that the protagonist seeks to withdraw from the fray. In this case the *confident*'s presence provides the protagonist with visible moral support, as in II.4 when Titus is constrained to break off his exchange with Bérénice. The fractured syntax which characterised his tortured attempts to address the Queen is suddenly replaced by the concise line to Paulin:

> Sortons, Paulin; je ne lui puis rien dire.
> (l.624)

It is as though the *confident* represents the certainty which Titus lacks.[433]

Scherer suggests that *confidents* generally have a shadowy existence: they are present in scenes in which they play no role and are such unobtrusive witnesses that protagonists need rarely dismiss them from their most intimate scenes.[434] While Scherer's observations may hold true for many tragedies of the period, I have found a substantial minority of counter-examples, among them *Bérénice*. Here, the dismissal of secondary characters takes on a significance at

---

[430] Dainard suggests that Antiochus's tragedy is that "although he is ready to talk, to declare his love, no-one really listens to him." ("The Power of the Spoken Word in *Bérénice*", p.161). I believe this statement needs to be refined: Antiochus's tragedy is that Bérénice and, to a lesser extent, Titus do not listen to him; but Arsace listens closely and this is essential to Antiochus's tragic dignity.

[431] Racine may well have been working from the model of a similar situation in Quinault's *Stratonice*, II.6.

[432] On Racine's use of the exit as the final blow in an argument, see Maskell, *Racine. A Theatrical Reading*, pp.55-56.

[433] Compare Néron summoning Narcisse when he takes his leave of Agrippine in V.5 of *Britannicus*.

[434] *La Dramaturgie classique*, pp.43-45.

several points.[435] In Act II, Titus makes the distinction between Paulin and the
rest of his *suite*, sending away all but his trusted adviser (line 338). Bérénice
recognises Paulin's special status when she expresses herself willing to speak
openly to Titus in his presence:

> *Mais Seigneur (car je sais que cet ami sincère*
> *Du secret de nos cœurs connaît tout le mystère)*
> (ll.563-4)

The surprising thing is that she should even need to comment on the presence
of a *confident*. In contrast, Titus gives the command to his *suite*, but surely
particularly to Paulin, not to follow him when he enters for his final meeting
with Bérénice in V.3.[436] Only now does he face Bérénice alone, without the
moral support of Paulin. Phénice is also dismissed from this scene when Titus
orders that Antiochus be fetched (line 1362). By this contrivance Racine has
engineered a unique dénouement, in which first two and then all three of the
protagonists are entirely alone on the stage without retinue. It is a fitting visual
image of such an intimate tragedy that not even the *confidents* should witness
the final separation. Only we, the audience, are afforded this privilege.

Arsace's silent presence is less marked than that of Paulin or Phénice, but
there is an important reference to it in Antiochus's "virtual monologue" which
originally constituted IV.9. In his depths of self-abasement, Antiochus
dismissed even his *confident*:

> *Désespéré, confus, à moi-même odieux,*
> *Laisse-moi; je me veux cacher même à tes yeux.*

Suppressed in 1676, probably for the negative, unheroic image it portrayed of
Antiochus,[437] the scene nonetheless confirms beyond doubt the separate identity
of the *confident*. No longer is this a protactic character, nor a silent "walk on-
walk off" role, but an essential component of the tragic structure, who has an
active role to play.

This shift did not go entirely unnoticed by Racine's contemporaries.
Whereas the earliest critics of *Andromaque* had generally passed over the
confidents, the Abbé de Villars commented on Arsace's extended role. For the
Abbé, the whole first act of *Bérénice* was misconceived in that it did not contrive
an early meeting between Titus and Bérénice.[438] In suggesting an alternative

---

[435] Compare Maskell's argument that "the discreet exit of a confidant <Phœnix> marks the
turning point in relations between Andromaque and Pyrrhus." (*Racine. A Theatrical Reading*,
p.56).
[436] "Demeurez: qu'on ne me suive pas." (l.1286).
[437] Maskell suggests it also posed the logistical problem of Antiochus's movements
between Acts IV and V (*Racine. A Theatrical Reading*, p.242).
[438] "Ses adieux <= Les adieux d'Arsace> à Bérénice sont de l'invention du Poete pour gagner
du temps, pour tricher et pour fournir un Acte" (Granet, *Recueil*, p.189).

opening to the play, de Villars imagines Arsace prompting Antiochus to win Bérénice, as he does in III.2 of Racine's version:

> *Le Confident eut pû lui inspirer de demander la Reine à l'Empereur.*[439]

De Villars would still allow Arsace to deliver the *récit* of Antiochus's heroic part in the siege of Jerusalem, albeit after a new scene between Titus and Antiochus. He outlines his alternative scene thus:

> *Son Confident refait la description du siege de Jerusalem (un peu poétiquement à la vérité, mais il n'est pas absolument contre le vraisemblable qu'un Confident soit Poete).*[440]

In his parenthesis which draws attention to the register of Arsace's speech, the Abbé demonstrates his awareness of the evolution Racine has brought to the *confident*'s role. Arsace not only relates essential expository material, but does so in a style which breaks down the division between the discourse of protagonists and of *confidents*. While de Villars is critical of Arsace's role later in the play,[441] his remark here is central, for it displays his awareness of a Racinian strategy which was to culminate in the celebrated and controversial *récit de Théramène*.

---

[439] *Ibid.*, p.190.

[440] *Ibid.*, p.192.

[441] Notably in the original IV.9, where he says that Arsace acts "fort humainement" but has a role that is nonetheless "inutile" (Granet, *Recueil*, p.195).

CHAPTER FIVE

THE *CONFIDENT* TURNED *CONSEILLER*

If the definition of the active *confident(e)* is that he or she should contribute significantly to the play's tragic mechanism through both speech and actions, the figure of the *confident* turned *conseiller*, an intermediary step between the lowliest *confident* and a main protagonist, is particularly well placed to fulfil this brief. Since seventeenth-century tragedy by definition revolves around high-ranking individuals, there is much scope for figures seeking to influence the ruler or prince. The evil counsellor is, even more than the neutral one, a recurrent figure. In Chapter 1, we saw the example of Euphorbe in *Cinna*, and in Chapter 4 Phædime in *Camma*. From the 1660s we might also cite Prédaspe, "capitaine des gardes" and adviser to the king Cambise in Mlle Desjardins's *Nitétis* (1663), who not only dispenses amoral counsel but even kills the king's brother with his own hands; or Araxe in Thomas Corneille's *La Mort d'Annibal* (1669), another "capitaine des gardes" and counsellor to Prusias, the king, who devises the machiavellian scheme whereby Annibal is captured by the Romans. In such cases, the *mauvais conseiller* makes a distinct contribution to the plot, but disappears from focus once his advice is enacted. The subject of this chapter, by contrast, will be those tragedies in which *conseillers* retain a high profile throughout.

Plays in which there are two or more *conseillers*, with the plot drawing upon rivalries or alliances between them, provide a particularly rich field of enquiry. Thematically and dramaturguically works within this group share a number of common features. First, many of them are based upon conspiracies and secret threats to the state, and the portrait of the ruler or prince is coloured by the influence the *conseillers* exert over him. Secondly, because such plays are broadly political, love interests are either subservient or yoked to affairs of state. Finally, the *conseiller* has no obvious female equivalent, unlike the correlation between the standard *confident/confidente*. In the political systems portrayed in French classical tragedies there are some memorable female rulers, but they are the exception rather than the rule; and although many female figures exert political influence by virtue of kinship or sexual passions, there are no cases of a woman wielding influence as a purely political *conseillère*.[442]

How are we to recognise these *confidents* turned *conseillers*? J. Truchet and his team of researchers devoted a thematic study to the figure of the *conseiller du prince*.[443] They found that the term *conseiller* is employed only once in the list of *dramatis personae* of seventeenth-century tragedies.[444] True, we have observed that the function of *confident* is borne by characters with a diverse range of nomenclatures,[445] but the term *confident(e)* is prominent among these. In the case of the *conseiller*, we not only face the problem of identifying which characters fulfil this function, but must also ask how far it is legitimate or helpful to impose the term on texts which do not use it, at least in the list of *dramatis personae*.[446] I would suggest that this term helps us to understand the evolution of the *confident*'s role by highlighting those tragedies which rely on this particular device. The example which springs immediately to mind is Racine's *Britannicus*, in which the struggle between Burrhus and Narcisse lies at the heart of the tragedy. Together with the renewal we have discussed of the *confident* tradition in *Andromaque* and *Bérénice*, the shift of focus towards the *conseiller* in the intermediate tragedy is a significant development in Racine's dramaturgy. Yet it is not always sufficiently stressed that Burrhus and Narcisse are part of a well-established tradition, with Racine refining rather than inventing the role. It follows that we need first to look back to the earlier *conseiller* tradition, of which Rotrou's *Cosroès* provides a memorable example. The most interesting experiments with *confidents/conseillers* in the following generation are those plays which draw on the Tacitean tradition in which advisers and conspirators loom large: namely Pierre Corneille's *Othon*, Gilbert's *Arie et Pétus* and Racine's *Britannicus*.

---

[442] Livie in *Cinna* uses the political vocabulary of a *conseiller* when she counsels Auguste in IV.3. However, the essential distinction is made at the end of the scene that she is speaking because of personal affections not because of political ambition ("AUGUSTE: C'est l'amour des grandeurs qui vous rend importune. LIVIE: J'aime votre personne et non votre fortune.", ll.1261-2).

[443] Truchet's team specifically excluded the "simple confident" from their enquiries (*Recherches de thématique théâtrale*, p.17). Thus where Truchet looked from the ruler downwards to define the *conseiller du prince*, I am concerned to look from the *confident* upwards to identify the "*confident* turned *conseiller*".

[444] In Montchrestien's *La Reine d'Ecosse* of 1608 (ed. J. Truchet, *Recherches de thématique théâtrale*, p.76). I have not found the term used in the cast lists of any other seventeenth-century tragedies I have consulted for this study.

[445] See p.14.

[446] But note the use of the term by a character in Poisson's comedy *L'Apres-Soupé* (1665) when discussing characters in Pierre Corneille's recent play *Othon*.

(i) THE LEGACY OF THE *CONSEILLER* UPON WHOM THE PLOT TURNS: ROTROU'S *COSROÈS*

Rotrou's *Cosroès* (1648) is essentially a political play.[447] The only love interest is restricted to the episodic role of Narsée, (who does not appear until III.4),[448] and Syra's relationship with Cosroès is dictated purely by ambitions for herself and her son, not by romantic passions. Rotrou has thus dispensed with one key aspect of the traditional *confident(e)* since none of the five main characters needs to discourse privately on love.[449] Instead all the secondary characters are used to contribute to either the political debate or the action of the play. Like many "conspiracy plays" of the 1640s, *Cosroès* has a relatively large number of secondary characters (one female and four male parts).[450] Yet this already represents a reduction from the seven satraps in Rotrou's source, the Latin play *Chosroès* (1630) by Père Louis Cellot.[451] While Artanasde and Hormisdate, the lower-ranked secondary characters (invented by Rotrou), contribute significantly to the evolution of the plot by defecting to the prince, neither has the status of a *conseiller*.[452] It is only the three secondary characters inherited from Cellot who take on this role. Sardarigue and Palmyras in particular significantly affect our perception of both the protagonists and the moral dilemmas they face.

---

[447] Although *Cosroès* did not achieve anything like the success of *Venceslas*, it is widely recognised as a source for Corneille's *Nicomède*, and more than one critic has suggested that Racine may have had it in mind when writing *Britannicus*. See D. Watts, introduction to his edition of *Cosroès* (1993), pp.VIII-IX.

[448] On the lack of integration of the role of Narsée and the debts to tragicomedy, see Watts' comments, *Cosroès*, pp.XVII-XVIII.

[449] It is at first sight surprising that the *jeune première* should not have a *confidente*, but as Watts points out (*Cosroès*, p.XXIV) Rotrou passes rapidly over the potential conflict arising from Narsée's divided loyalties (love versus filial duty).

[450] Compare for example the slightly earlier "conspiracy" play, *La Mort de Sénèque* (1645) by Tristan l'Hermite, in which there are four comparable male characters and one comparable female character. However, in *La Mort de Sénèque* none of them seeks to act as a *conseiller*; indeed, the Emperor Néron's only adviser, Tigillin, is silent throughout the play.

[451] For an exhaustive study of Rotrou's use of Cellot's play, see A.L. Stiefel, "Jean Rotrous *Cosroès* und seine Quellen" (1901). Rotrou's Palmyras, Pharnace and Sardarigue correspond to Cellot's Sarbaras, Pharnaces and Cardariga respectively.

[452] We should note, however, that in Hormisdate's single appearance (III.1) she argues vigorously with the queen, even referring to theories of revolution and popular reaction (ll.742-4).

In Cellot's play the satrap Cardariga remained a loyal follower of the king,[453] but in Rotrou Sardarigue defects to Syroès after in vain offering the king his frank advice (II.1). Separated from the protagonist whom he served as a *confident/conseiller*, Sardarigue's function changes in the remainder of the play. Although his declaration of his defection in II.4 contains advice for his new master (conveyed through an accumulation of declarative statements which are effectively disguised imperatives),[454] his specific counsel has no immediate effect. Furthermore the presence of Palmyras as the prince's established *confident/ conseiller* leaves little scope for Sardarigue to assume this capacity. Instead, Rotrou uses him in the remaining acts as the voice for a providential interpretation of the drama. In IV.2, Sardarigue's *récit* of the arrest of Cosroès and Mardesane (lines 1216-1236) concludes with an appeal for Syroès to recognise the workings of the gods:

> *Goustez mieux la faveur d'un changment si prompt,*
> *N'en soyez pas ingrat, aux Dieux, qui vous la font.*
>   *(ll.1239-40)*

Similarly, in his *récit* in the last scene of the play Sardarigue sees the hand of Providence in the deaths of Syra and Cosroès:

> *Hà Sire! malgré vous, le destin de la Perse,*
> *Vous protege, et detruit tout ce qui vous traverse.*
>   *(ll.1723-4)*

Here, Sardarigue's view is dramatically contrasted with Syroès's furious denunciation of the work of his ministers. In a conclusion which has been the subject of much critical debate, the prince upholds filial duty and thus, implicitly, the divine right of even a bad king, while the conspirators argue the necessity of the overthrow of tyranny.[455] By making Sardarigue speak for the conspirators in the last lines:

> *... Ses soins sont superflus,*
> *Le poison est trop prompt, le Tyran ne vit plus.*
>   *(ll.1741-2)*

Rotrou follows a tradition of realigning the prince with absolute moral and political order, while leaving a secondary character to draw a different conclusion based on expediency. Thus, although Sardarigue started the play as *confident/conseiller* to the king, his significance in Acts IV and V lies far less in

---

[453] Cardariga was imprisoned with the king, and executed in Act V.

[454] E.g. "Il est temps de paroistre." (l.695); "Il est temps d'arracher des mains d'une marastre ..." (l.701); "il n'est plus de respect, qui doive retenir ..." (l.703). In addition, Sardarigue uses three imperatives (lines 694, 698, 700).

[455] See for example D. Watts, *Cosroès*, p.XXV and p.XXIX; J. Morel, *Jean Rotrou*, p.155 and pp.178-9.

any practical advice he offers than in his expression of an alternative political philosophy.

From Cellot Rotrou also inherited two other satraps. Although retaining the earlier seventeenth-century predilection for pairs of secondary characters,[456] Rotrou distinguishes between them, giving Pharnace a minimal role and few lines, while Palmyras has a substantial role.[457] Significantly, Pharnace is silent in the majority of scenes in which he is present (5 out of 8), whereas Palmyras is rarely present without speaking (3 out of 12 scenes). In Pharnace's main scene (I.4) he is essentially a messenger, delivering a *récit* of the crowning of Mardesane. Pharnace's condemnation of Mardesane and Syra is unequivocal, but he does not give Syroès any advice - unlike Sardigue in IV.2. It is only in the last act (V.4 and V.6) that Pharnace assumes the voice of a *conseiller*, in several short remarks to Syroès. These largely echo the advice of Palmyras, and although we should not overlook the visual symbolism of the two satraps who have been present through the trials of Syra (V.2) and Mardesane (V.3), Rotrou chose to make only Palmyras a centre of dramatic interest.

Palmyras is an outstanding example of the importance of the *confident* as *conseiller*. Unlike the other secondary male characters, he is closely identified throughout with a single protagonist (Syroès) whom he seeks to influence. Of twelve scenes in which he appears, there are only two in which he is on stage without Syroès, and these (IV.4-5) are explained by the romanesque episode surrounding the revelation of Narsée's identity. It is true that this episode integrates Palmyras more closely in the plot through his relationship to her,[458] but the spectator is not given leisure to dwell upon the consequences. It is as *confident/conseiller* to Syroès that he crucially affects the spectator's appreciation of the tragedy. As the prime mover of the rebellion, responsible for urging Syroès to disown his stepmother, stepbrother and, most seriously, his father the king, Palmyras becomes effectively a scapegoat for Syroès's actions, allowing us to pity Syroès caught in a tragic dilemma not of his own making.[459] Critics agree that Syroès is a peculiarly passive hero. We are invited to believe that without his satraps, but above all without Palmyras, Syroès would have lacked the resolve both to accept the crown and to accomplish the defeat of his

---

[456] See Scherer, *La Dramaturgie classique*, p.36.

[457] Pharnace speaks 31 lines, Palmyras 195 lines.

[458] As the true father of Narsée, he is effectively about to become the father-in-law of the monarch!

[459] On the widespread use of secondary characters to make protagonists appear less guilty, see M. Baudin, "The Shifting of Responsibility in Seventeenth-Century French Tragic Drama" (1934).

enemies.[460] Other characters comment on the influence of Palmyras. Syroès, on accepting that he must take the throne, declares to Palmyras and Pharnace:

> *Fidelles confidents, je m'abandonne à vous.*
> *(l. 332)*

Syra and Cosroès both scornfully condemn Syroès's dependence on his advisers,[461] but Artanasde at the end of Act IV provides the most eloquent account of Palmyras's relationship to Syroès when he urges the satrap to confirm Syroès's sense of purpose:

> *En moins que d'un moment, il <Syroès> veut, et ne veut plus:*
> *Tous vos travaux sont vains, si réduit à ce terme,*
> *Son esprit ne reprend une assiette plus ferme;*
> *Et l'on n'attend, Seigneur, cet effort que de vous.*
> *(ll. 1344-7)*

Foreshadowing Racinian heroes, Syroès oscillates indecisively between opposing courses. The role of Palmyras is to listen and advise, and even to intervene to ensure acts are accomplished. Twice in the presence of the hesitant Syroès he gives orders: to have Syra led away (III.3), and to have Cosroès brought for trial (V.4).[462] His power is symbolised by the stage direction (l.1381) that he and Pharnace should sit for the trials of Syra and Mardesane. And at the end of the play it is Palmyras (like Pylade in Racine's *Andromaque*) who assumes control as he follows the grief-stricken and crazed Syroès from the stage with the words "Ne l'abandonnons point".

Unlike *Britannicus*, however, Rotrou's *Cosroès* does not show the making of a "monstre naissant" urged on by an evil genius. Rotrou had abandoned Cellot's characterisation of an increasingly cruel and despotic prince.[463] The conflict between Syroès and Palmyras is not that between good and evil but a morally more ambiguous struggle between indecision and resolution. It is epitomised by Palmyras's prayer in IV.5:

> *Sauve un Roy trop pieux, de sa propre foiblesse.*
> *(l.1349)*

Palmyras's role is the more interesting because initially Syroès does not heed - perhaps even does not hear - the advice of the satrap. Watts has suggested that the speech delivered by Syroès in I.3 *"resvant et se promenant"* (ll.176-202) is effectively a "monologue devant le confident".[464] However, the *confident/conseiller* responds to the "monologue" at great length (ll. 203-

---

[460] J. Van Baelen argues that this weakness is a fault common to both Cosroès and Syroès, who are paralysed by their consciences (*Rotrou. Le Héros tragique et la révolte*, 1965, p.198).

[461] Lines 883, 1640.

[462] Lines 892, 1586.

[463] See Stiefel, "Jean Rotrous *Cosroès*", p.131.

[464] *Cosroès*, p.84.

258), as though it had been addressed to himself. Syroès ended his speech by invoking the gods;[465] Palmyras instantly takes up Syroès's terms of reference to urge him to rely on political and military strength, not Providence. Thus Syroès is not allowed the hero's privilege of an unanswered soliloquy, for the *conseiller* contests his interpretation of circumstances.[466] We are aware from the first act that the satraps do not simply need to convince Syroès of their viewpoint, but more fundamentally must guard against his falling into a state of melancholic *furie* in which *all* reason goes unheard. Cosroès's madness in II.1 provides a sinister presage; Artanasde's report of Syroès's distress in IV.5 reminds us of the danger, and it is of course realised in the last scene when the stage-direction indicates that Syroès delivers his final speech *"furieux"* (1.1737). Morel concludes that in *Cosroès* tragedy ensues because Syroès did not heed the ruthless advice of his satraps.[467] Another perspective would allow us to say that *Cosroès* dramatically reveals the limitations of the *confident/conseiller*'s influence: however powerful his arguments and however forcefully they are presented, they are doomed to failure if the hero will not listen.

On the evidence of *Cosroès*, we can conclude that the role of the *confident/conseiller* grows in importance as certain qualities of the ruler/prince diminish. If Syroès were the resolute hero of some of the earlier tragedies of Corneille, he would not need a political adviser to fight his vacillations. *Cosroès* has traditionally been compared with *Nicomède*, yet this Cornelian tragedy has no *conseiller*. The contrast is instructive: both are political plays; both involve a plot centred on the heir apparent who could depose the king. However, where the interest in *Cosroès* lies precisely in Syroès's irresolutions, and therefore how far his *conseillers* can bring their influence to bear, in *Nicomède* the prince is his own master and the audience is invited to appreciate his spirit of *générosité* and actions which are undertaken independently of any advisers. It is a decade later that Corneille plumbs the depths of the monarch who allows himself to fall prey to his *conseillers*, and then his inspiration is no longer the record of noble Roman deeds offered by Justin, but the cynical histories of Tacitus.

(ii) TACITEAN TRAGEDIES: THE "ARCANA IMPERII" IN PIERRE CORNEILLE'S *OTHON*

In *Cosroès*, Rotrou may have exposed how an irresolute king is led by his strong-minded *conseillers*, but he was drawing on sources which subscribed to a Providentialist view of history. However morally dubious the advice given may

---

[465] "Vous, Dieux, qui presidez au sort des Diadesmes ..." (ll.198-202).

[466] In contrast in III.3 Syroès does have a short soliloquy (ll. 943-50) after the departure of Palmyras, in which he regrets the painful loss of "un repos bien plus calme, et plus pur".

[467] J. Morel, *Jean Rotrou*, p.100.

have been, higher powers were responsible for the ultimate resolution of the plot. In a world in which Providence is not seen to intervene, the relationship between a weak ruler and his powerful advisers becomes critical. Such is the case of Rome under Nero and Galba, as described by Tacitus. Although the rediscovery of Tacitus dates back to the late sixteenth century, and although the fascination of Tacitism had remained strong in the first half of the seventeenth century,[468] it was - ironically - as Louis XIV assumed personal control of state that, within a decade, the *Annals* and *Histories* provided the major source for three tragedies concerned with weak Emperors: Gilbert's *Arie et Pétus* (1659), Corneille's *Othon* (1664) and Racine's *Britannicus* (1669). All three plays are distinguished by having two or more *conseillers*, drawn largely from Tacitus, whose influence over the Emperor in question is highly significant. Tacitus's contempt for the decadence of Nero, the weakness of the aged Galba and the shameful accession of Otho is beyond doubt; what his writing also reveals is a piercing awareness of how such regimes spawn self-serving, ambitious courtiers who seek the Emperor's ear. For dramatists, the latter, if elevated into *conseillers*, provide a double focus of interest: both in their attempts to influence the Emperor, but also in the potential clash of interests between individual *conseillers*.

It is Corneille's *Othon* which offers the most unremittingly negative portrait of the amoral *conseiller*, for of Vinius, Lacus and Martian, the three characters who struggle to impose their will upon Galba, not one represents the voice of moral conscience. In his study of Corneille's use of Tacitus in his later tragedies, T. Allott underlines the paradox that a playwright "usually associated with a predominantly providentialist and moralistic treatment of political issues" should now, for the first time in his career, choose as his source the Roman historian "commonly denounced for his paganism, his corrosive anti-idealism and his political subversiveness".[469] Many other Cornelian scholars have also seen *Othon* as something of an enigma, not least because of the unheroic nature of all the male protagonists - a consequence, surely, of Corneille's reliance for the most part on the account of Tacitus. It is significant that Plautine and Camille, who show something closer to Cornelian *générosité* than their male counterparts, are largely Corneille's own invention. Approaching the play from the angle of the three *conseillers* helps to illuminate what Corneille has achieved. He himself indicates this direction to us in his particularly defensive preface. In arguing that his Othon does have "vertus" but that his vices (all too clearly detailed by Tacitus) are not hidden, Corneille says of the latter:

---

[468] See P. Burke's chapter "Tacitism", in *Tacitus*, ed. T.A. Dorey (1969). Various plays before 1650 draw loosely on Tacitus (often via Coëffeteau's *Histoire romaine*), including Tristan L'Hermite's *La Mort de Sénèque* (1645) and Cyrano de Bergerac's *La Mort d'Agrippine* (?1653).

[469] "Tacitus and some late plays of Corneille" (1980), p. 34.

> *et je me suis contenté de les attribuer à une politique de cour, où quand le*
> *souverain se plonge dans les débauches, et que sa faveur n'est qu'à ce prix, il y*
> *a presse à qui sera de la partie.*[470]

The prominence accorded to Galba's *conseillers* follows from this view: *Othon*
is not so much the dramatic story of the accession of the new Emperor, but
rather an exploration of the attempts of different factions to impose their will.[471]
We might note that *Othon* was published in the same year as the first edition of
that other merciless exposure of the forces of *intérêt* and *amour-propre*, La
Rochefoucauld's *Maximes*.

Vinius, Lacus and Martian are all certainly far more than just *confidents*, yet
each of them has power and each interests the audience precisely because they
retain their relationship of trusted *confident/conseiller* to the Emperor. In
contrast, Albin, Albiane and Flavie[472] are standard *confidents* who play a limited
role, accompanying their respective master/mistresses,[473] and, in the case of
Albiane and Flavie, serving as silent onlookers to a number of scenes. While
Flavie and Albiane have important roles as messengers,[474] and while Albin's
opening scene with Othon is essential to the exposition, these characters are
never a focus of dramatic interest in their own right. Vinius, Lacus and Martian,
on the other hand, straddle precisely the middle ground of the *conseiller*: they
can appear on stage without their master, but their status and existence are still
closely bound to the Emperor. Corneille exploits this limited degree of
independence to the full, in part to demonstrate the treachery of Lacus and
Martian. Galba appears in only two acts of the play: Acts III and V, and it is not
until the final act that we actually witness *conseillers* in dialogue with him. This
is a very different vision of the *conseiller* from that in Rotrou's *Cosroès* or
Racine's *Britannicus*. While V.2 shows a gripping battle for power as Vinius

---

[470] *Œuvres complètes*, vol. III, p.461.

[471] See M. Prigent's account of the importance accorded to "la cour" in *Othon: Le Héros et l'Etat*, pp. 421-6.

[472] In the wake of *Querelle de Sophonisbe* the previous year, however, Corneille avoids the terms *suivant(e)* or *confident(e)* and styles these characters "ami d'Othon", "sœur d'Albin, et dame d'honneur de Camille", and "amie de Plautine" respectively. Only Albin is drawn (in name, though not in function) from Tacitus; Albiane and Flavie are invented by Corneille (as of course is Camille, and even Plautine is renamed and developed far beyond the several lines accorded to Vinius's daughter in Tacitus).

[473] The one exception is Albin's presence in III.2, to inform Camille of Galba's imminent arrival.

[474] Flavie reports back to Plautine (II.1) on Othon's false declaration of love to Camille between Acts I and II, and bears the *récit* of Vinius's death at the end of the play (V.6); Albiane, informed by her brother Albin, can pass on to Camille information about Galba's intentions (III.1).

and Lacus vie to win Galba's support (a scene very closely modelled on speeches in Tacitus),[475] Martian never acts out his role of *conseiller* before our eyes. In V.4, he brings Atticus, the supposed assassin of Othon, before the Emperor, but speaks only two lines in Galba's presence. It is possible that Corneille recoiled from showing at first hand the depths to which the Roman Empire had sunk when an Emperor allowed himself to be influenced by his former slave; certainly he departs from Tacitus by having Martian's disgrace confirmed on stage as he is arrested in V.5.[476] Alternatively one might argue that the preceding four Acts had left the audience needing no further confirmation of Martian's power and base motives.

With Galba's entrance so significantly delayed until III.3, the audience's interest is initially focused on the two opposing power factions: Vinius and Othon versus Lacus and Martian. *Othon* is a play in which nothing happens on- or offstage for nearly three acts; it is only when Galba exits at the end of III.5 to announce to the army his choice of Piso as successor that a series of actions and counter-actions offstage carry the plot forward. Thus the first half of the play is dominated by what Corneille referred to in the preface with self-deprecating irony, as "<des> intrigues de cabinet qui se détruisent les unes les autres."[477] Stasis is avoided on account only of two sets of offstage consultations: Othon's (false) declaration of love to Camille, between Acts I and II, and various attempts to influence Galba's choice of successor and husband for Camille before and during Act II. In both cases we are aware that this is the deceitful, calculating world painted by Tacitus, in which even the more honourable characters are forced into acting a role.[478]

The influence of each of the three *conseillers* over Galba is commented upon, and it is verbs of speech which convey the axis of power. In I.2, Vinius summarises the configuration of interests to Othon:

> *Mais il <Galba> balance encor sur ce choix d'un époux,*
> *Et je ne puis, Seigneur, m'assurer que sur vous.*
> *J'ai donc pour ce grand choix vanté votre courage,*
> *Et Lacus à Pison a donné son suffrage;*
> *Martian n'a parlé qu'en termes ambigus,*
> *Mais sans doute il ira du côté de Lacus,*
> *Et l'unique remède est de gagner Camille,*
> *Si sa voix est pour nous, la leur est inutile.*
> (*Othon, 163-70*)

---

[475] Tacitus, *Histories*, I.32-33.

[476] In Tacitus Marcianus, as a *libertus Caesaris*, passed into Otho's household *after* the death of Galba, and was then publicly executed (*Histories* I.46).

[477] *Œuvres complètes*, vol. III, p.462.

[478] See the excellent discussion by G. Forestier, "De la politique, ou la stratégie du mensonge dans *Othon*", Introduction to *Othon*, ed. J. Sanchez, (1989), pp.LXIII-LXXXII.

The semantic cluster of terms denoting speech acts (*vanté, donné son suffrage, parlé, termes, voix*) is remarkable, and not an isolated occurrence in this play.[479] In Act II, all four main male characters speak to Galba, or are reported recently to have done so: we are told of Othon "Il lui parle à présent" (1.437); Lacus arrives fresh from talks with Galba to announce to Plautine that he has persuaded the Emperor to accept her mariage to Othon (ll.552-4); Martian answers Camille's anxious and revealing question "Parlez, qu'avez-vous dit à Galba l'un et l'autre?" (1.685) by reminding her that Galba has consulted himself, Lacus and Vinius on the choice of his successor. We might have expected Act III to open with Galba's own announcement of his decision to Camille, yet he is forestalled by the mere *confidente* Albiane, who relays the secret decision to Camille via her brother Albin. The opening line of the Act appears unexceptional:

> CAMILLE
> *Ton frère te l'a dit, Albiane?*
>
> ALBIANE
> *Oui, Madame;*
> *Galba choisit Pison, et vous êtes sa femme...*
> *(ll.757-8)*

But it reminds us that this is the world of spies and informers, so loathed by Tacitus, where a niece of the Emperor must depend for information and counsel on servants who will betray confidences.

The inversion of the master/servant relationship, a theme of *Othon* which Doubrovsky has examined in detail,[480] is a crucial element of Corneille's depiction of the three *conseillers*. The term *maître* is used more than twenty times. From the first scene of the play, Othon recognises the paradox that Galba is subject to his three *conseillers*; he is "Un Maître qui sans eux n'ose rien consentir" (1.64). The greatest irony, however, is generated by Martian's use of terms related to mastery and service, for he is the ex-slave who has the Emperor's confidence. If to Plautine Martian defines himself only as the first adviser to the Emperor,[481] it is clear when he is alone with Lacus that by his choice of alliance (with Vinius or with Lacus) Martian has the power to decide their new "master".[482] In III.1 Albiane gives Camille and the spectator a

---

[479] Compare the lexis of speech in Flavie's report to Plautine of Othon's declaration to Camille (ll.399-414).

[480] *Corneille et la dialectique du héros*, pp.378-381.

[481] "Galba m'écoute enfin, et c'est être aujourd"hui,/ Quoique sans ces grands noms, le premier d'après lui." (519-20).

[482] LACUS: "Quoi, vous nous donneriez vous-même Othon pour maître?" (1.601).

brutally accurate explanation of why Lacus and Martian have preferred to
support Pison, and goes so far as to apply the word *maître* to the *conseillers*:

> *Car comme il <Pison> n'a pour lui qu'une suite d'Ancêtres,*
> *Lacus et Martian vont être nos vrais maîtres,*
> *Et Pison ne sera qu'un idole sacré*
> *Qu'ils tiendront sur l'Autel pour répondre à leur gré.*
>   *(ll. 765-8)*

It can hardly have been to the taste of the Versailles audience who attended the
première of *Othon* to see the monarch as a mere figurehead or puppet!
However, Corneille is in no way glorifying the machinations and ambitions of
Lacus and Martian. For one thing, when Galba does appear in Act III, he proves
cleverer than any of the other characters had assumed he could be.
Furthermore, the scene when Lacus and Martian are left on stage alone (II.4)
demonstrates the depths to which their cynical self-interest will take them.

The scene is a long one - 103 lines - for two secondary characters, but
Corneille uses it to expose the dangers of machiavellian powerbroking.[483] It is
possible that Racine had this scene in mind when in the original version of
Britannicus he wrote a scene at a similar stage between Burrhus and Narcisse.
However, Racine removed the scene before the first edition of the play was
published, whereas its counterpart in *Othon* stands. The scenes are different in
that Racine's *conseillers* take opposing stances, whereas Corneille's are in
collusion in the pursuit of their amoral ends. The conflictual scene in
Britannicus was probably judged to be an inappropriately explicit illustration of
the differences between the *conseillers*, which contributed nothing to the play's
development. The meeting between Lacus and Martian does have a debate
(whether Martian will declare support for Lacus's candidate, Pison), but
interests us not so much on this level, but rather as a revelation of true motives.
Forestier has pointed out the irony that whereas the more virtuous characters of
Othon are seen to lie and act out roles, Lacus and Martian speak only the
truth.[484] I would perceive a further irony in that the *confidents/conseillers*, whose
function is usually to allow the main protagonists to disclose their true state of
mind and feeling, here reveal themselves. Galba, on the other hand, is given no
neutral interlocutor and no conventional *confident* scene. It is the *conseillers*,
not the ruler, whose motives must be laid bare to the audience. Racine allowed
his Narcisse one short soliloquy (II.8) to declare his base ambitions, yet
traditionally actors omit the lines as being too cynical. *Othon* would be severely
amputated were a similar censorship to prevail, for the political creed expressed
by Lacus is no less shocking, with lines such as:

---

[483] On the traditional association between Tacitean and Machiavellian ideas in the
seventeenth century, see T. Allott, "Tacitus and some late plays of Corneille", p.34, and J.
Sanchez, "Le choix de Tacite", introduction to his edition of *Othon*, pp. LI-LXII.

[484] Introduction to *Othon*, ed. J. Sanchez, pp. LXVII-LXXII.

> *Lui-même <Pison> il nous priera d'avoir soin de l'Empire,*
> *Et saura seulement ce qu'il nous plaira dire,*
> *Plus nous l'y tiendrons bas, plus il nous mettra haut,*
> *Et c'est là justement le maître qu'il nous faut.*
> *(ll.645-8)*

and

> *Et qu'importe à tous deux de Rome et de l'Etat?*
> *Qu'importe qu'on leur voie ou plus ou moins d'éclat?*
> *Faisons nos sûretés et moquons-nous du reste.*
> *Point, point de bien public, s'il nous devient funeste.*
> *(ll.651-4)*[485]

As S. Baker has demonstrated, the speech of Lacus in particular is regularly tainted by "the language of mercenary exchange and the reductive logic of Machiavellianism", while Martian, the ex-slave, views both power and love in terms of their relative price not as absolute values.[486]

In contrast with this, Vinius's manipulations to secure power, but also to ensure his own safety and that of his daughter, look lesser evils. He is equally concerned that Galba should choose a new "maître" (a term he also uses on a number of occasions) who will favour him; he is cynically prepared to see his daughter married to either Othon or Pison according to which is victorious;[487] but he never goes so far as to claim a total disregard for the good of the state.[488] In fact it is only the presence of Vinius which provides some check on the ascendancy of Martian and Lacus for, as the latter observes:

> *Et notre indépendance irait au dernier point,*
> *Si l'heureux Vinius ne la partageait point.*
> *(ll.627-8)*

If one looks to draw something positive from *Othon*, it may be that ambitious *conseillers* are doomed because others will never allow them to enjoy the spoils of power unchallenged.

With all the lexis of speech as power, the question remains, as it did for Rotrou's *Cosroès*, as to how far the *conseillers'* words achieve the results they desire. Lacus and Martian seem successful when Galba announces his adoption

---

[485] See M. Prigent's analysis of this passage as an example of "la politique de l'amour-propre": *Le Héros et l'état*, pp.432-3.

[486] *Dissonant Harmonies*, p.132.

[487] IV.4. A tactic scorned by Plautine: "Que votre Politique a d'étranges maximes!/ Mon amour, s'il l'osait, y trouverait des crimes." (ll.1329-30).

[488] For a positive reading of Vinius's role, see E. Ellington-Gunter, "The Function of Vinius in *Othon*"(1981). She contrast Vinius's active role with the passivity of Othon.

of Pison in Act III, but this is only one stage in a treacherous chain of events. Lacus and Vinius must then engage in an open showdown for control of Galba in V.2. Their smouldering exchanges should lead directly to the climax of the play; the spectator is riveted by the attempt of each in turn to prevail upon Galba. Yet the scene does not result in Galba coming down on one side or other. Instead, before Camille can respond fully to Galba's rather platitudinous remark on the trials facing a ruler, Plautine bursts in with the (false) news of Othon's death. The test of rhetorical skills is thus abandoned in favour of a dramatic *peripeteia*. The scene seems a showpiece for Corneille's close imitation of Tacitus,[489] but in fact the dramatist departs from his source at the end of it, for Tacitus's Emperor did act upon the conflicting advice: "Galba without further delay supported those whose plan would look best."[490] We might note the contrast with Racine's handling of parallel material: his *conseillers* are never called upon to argue their case out together before Néron, but rather in Act IV have successive private interviews with the Emperor. The construction of this act of *Britannicus* is, as we shall see shortly, the best proof of the performative power of the speech acts of Racine's *conseillers*. For Corneille, the dénouement of *Othon* provided instead an opportunity for a succession of the *coups de théâtre* which are integral to his drama. None of these derives from the persuasive powers of the three *conseillers*, although the device of the false report of Othon's death does rely on the words and performance of another secondary character, Atticus.[491] So we may conclude that in *Othon* the attempts of all three *conseillers* to impose their will on the Emperor come to nought; it is finally the role assumed by a soldier (a *miles ex machina*?) which resolves the stalemate. Allott has suggested that Louis XIV's courtiers may have appreciated the lesson of the failure of bickering advisers,[492] but given the subdued tone of the final scene and our knowledge from Tacitus and other sources that Otho's inglorious reign lasted a mere three months, it is hard not to see *Othon* as a bleak portrayal of Rome at its lowest ebb.[493] And it is fitting that the *conseillers* play a powerful yet ultimately fruitless role.

---

[489] In the preface Corneille says: "Les caractères de ceux que j'y fais parler y sont les mêmes que chez cet incomparable auteur, que j'ai traduit tant qu'il m'a été possible." (*Œuvres complètes*, vol. III, p.461).

[490] *Histories*, I.34.

[491] ATTICUS: "Et tout ce que j'ai dit n'était qu'un stratagème/ Pour livrer en ses mains <=les mains d'Othon> Lacus, et Galba même." (ll.1737-8).

[492] He indicates that the three *conseillers* were seen by some as allegories of Louis's quarrelsome ministers, Colbert, Louvois, Lionne: "Tacitus and some late plays of Corneille", p.38.

[493] I agree with critics like S. Baker who emphasise the negativity of the ending: "with its aborted marriages and missed suicides, the dénouement represents instead an ironic commentary on the futility of the preceding action." (*Dissonant Harmonies*, p.122).

(iii) TACITEAN TRAGEDIES: THE COURTIERS OF NERO IN GILBERT'S *ARIE ET PÉTUS* AND RACINE'S *BRITANNICUS*

Tacitus's report of the reign of Galba's predecessor, Nero, also offered dramatists great scope for presenting the shifting relations between ruler and those seeking to influence him, ranging from noble *conseillers* to infamous *pestes de cour*. One of the greatest problems a dramatist faced was determining a clear focus for a plot, given the evolving and often confused groupings of secondary characters. Tristan l'Hermite's *La Mort de Sénèque* (1645) demonstrates some of the pitfalls in following a complex episode of Tacitus, and although it is a play with conspirators rather than *conseillers*, and therefore strictly outside the scope of this chapter, it merits a brief word for the contrasts it affords with Gilbert's and Racine's tragedies. In *La Mort de Sénèque*, we are unsure whether the philosopher, who appears only in Acts I, II and V, or the Emperor and his consort Sabine (who appear in all except the second Act) are the true subject. This is different from Racine's famous claim that "ma tragédie n'est pas moins la disgrâce d'Agrippine que la mort de Britannicus", for Tristan does not consistently interweave the two strands of his plot. His Sénèque and Néron meet only once, in Act I, and by Act V the spectator's interest has shifted from the philosopher himself, however moving his death scene may be. In the intervening acts, we have witnessed the exposure of the conspiracy against the Emperor, involving substantial secondary parts for no fewer than seven characters. J. Madeleine may well be right in surmising that Néron's *confident*, Tigillin, has a non-speaking role because there would have been no experienced actors left in the troupe of the Illustre Théâtre to play his part![494] Whatever the philosophical interest of Tristan's play, and the undeniable dramatic quality of some individual scenes, his inclusion of so many secondary characters from Tacitus makes it difficult for the spectator to discern one principal, developing centre of interest. The problem lies in the fact that the conspirators and those who denounce them are presented not primarily in relation to Néron or Sénèque, but for their own interest.[495]

Corneille, for all his fascination with polymythic plots, achieved a much tighter concentration in *Othon* by portraying the influence of only three *conseillers*. It is illuminating that Piso, who must also be assumed to have influence over Galba, never appears on stage. The ability to create and maintain such a focus of attention is a priority to which Racine also subscribed, and which marks *Britannicus* out from Gilbert's *Arie et Pétus*, which had presented a similar episode from the reign of Nero some ten years earlier. Of the Tacitean

---

[494] See his edition of *La Mort de Sénèque* (1919), p.XI. He also suggests that three actors may each have played two minor roles, since there are sufficient intervals in each case between the appearances of the pairs of characters.

[495] For example, the heroic resistance of the *affranchie* Épicharis forms a vivid and tragic episode in its own right.

dramatisations, Corneille's is closest to the Roman historian's text. Gilbert and
Racine both take far more liberties with chronology, notably as far as
conseillers are concerned, but where in the first case this leads to a dispersal of
interest, in the latter it provides a tightly controlled plot. Given Racine's evident
if unacknowledged familiarity with Gilbert's tragedy, we should look to *Arie et
Pétus* to see what Racine may have learned from it about the role of the
conseillers, and to assess how far it contributed in its own right to the evolution
of this role.

From the cast list, *Arie et Pétus* gives a significant place to the
confident/conseiller, for Néron has two "Confidens", Pétrone and Tigillin, and
Pétus has two "Amis", Sénèque and Burrhus.[496] This symmetry contrasts with
the use of single *confidente* for Sabine (Ismène), and may be a late example of
the prevalence of pairs of secondary characters.[497] There are, however, marked
variations in the deployment of the four *confidents/ conseillers*. Whereas
Tigillin and Pétrone function in both Acts I and V as a pair, supporting each
other, Sénèque and Burrhus are never seen on stage together. Indeed, Burrhus is
present in only one scene of the play (II.1). If we look at the share of the
discourse apportioned to each character, there can be no doubt of the
cumulative importance of their roles:[498]

Burrhus speaks	59 lines	= 3.36%
Pétrone	137	= 7.80%
Sénèque	229	= 13.04%
Tigillin	78	= 4.44%

Together the four *conseillers* speak for 28.64% of the play; or, if we add the
share of the discourse of Ismène to arrive at a total for all *confidents/conseillers*
30.01%. This figure is quite unparalleled by the *confidents* of any play of
Pierre Corneille, and approximately matched in Racine's *œuvre* only by
Britannicus.[499]

We might expect from this that *Arie et Pétus* would be a play concerned
with the powerful influence of the *confidents/conseillers*, yet when we look

---

[496] E. Pellet points out that the playwright ignored history in keeping Pétrone, Sénèque and
Burrhus alive for this episode: *A Forgotten French Dramatist. Gabriel Gilbert (1620?-1680?)*
(1931), p.149.

[497] We should note that in Gilbert's earlier tragedy *Hypolite, ou le garçon insensible* (1647)
the heroine, Phædre, has a pair of *confidentes* (see p.207).

[498] Compare this with the very limited role of the *confidente*, Ismène, who has 23 lines, i.e.
1.31%.

[499] In the 1670 edition the *confidents/conseillers* (i.e. Burrhus, Narcisse and Albine) have
30.38% of the discourse. If we include the draft of (?) III.1, published by Louis Racine, this figure
rises to 33.42%.

more closely the four characters do not spend most of their time trying to
persuade either Néron or Pétus has two "Amis of the course of action to follow.
Burrhus's one scene (II.1) is largely taken up by a *récit* to Pétus has two "Amis
of the games which had just taken place. True, Burrhus's influence is attested
by the fact that he has prevailed upon Néron to allow Pétus to see Arie, but the
only example we witness of his counsel is the order to Pétus at the end of the
scene not to approach Arie until the Empress has departed (ll.471-2). Similarly,
in V.5 Sénèque's main speech contains a *récit* to Néron of the death of Arie
and Pétus has two "Amis; his short moral gloss goes unheeded by the
distraught Emperor. The longest scene involving both Sénèque and Pétrone
(I.3) is essentially a play within a play, arresting the action and having no real
effect upon Néron's course of action. It involves a philosophical debate
between Pétrone and Sénèque, designed and orchestrated by Néron. The scene
operates on two levels of persuasion: ostensibly Pétrone and Sénèque are each
trying to persuade the Emperor of the strength of their position. However, as
Pétrone and the spectators know from the previous scene, Néron will pretend to
be persuaded by Sénèque only so that the Stoic philosopher will in turn be
persuaded of the Emperor's reformed character and report this news to Arie. In
the event, the double deception does not achieve its end for this report cuts no
ice with the virtuous Arie. And the amplitude of the debate (lines 112-294) also
suggests that Gilbert has engineered a set piece in its own right. Statements on
morality and the role (or absence) of divine authority do feature in some
libertin plays of this period,[500] but Gilbert has stretched the convention of the
unity of action far beyond the norm. Why should he have included the scene
(for which there is no model in Tacitus)? I would suggest two reasons. First,
Sénèque and Pétrone embody the two extremes of (Stoic) morality and
(Epicurean) amorality at the court of Nero, mirroring the conflict between
Néron and Arie/Pétus. But secondly, the theatricality of the debate is the first of
a number of episodes, on and off-stage, which develop Tacitus's accounts of
acting and spectating/spying at the court of Nero.[501] Gilbert's baroque love of
disguise and pretence marries particularly harmoniously with the inglorious
deceits and lavish spectacles recorded by the historian. It is telling that Néron
derives obvious entertainment from directing the course of the debate.[502] What
Gilbert has shown us is Nero the inveterate actor, a character who is too taken
up with his role to be susceptible to moral persuasion from his former tutor and
conseiller.

---

[500] Compare Cyrano de Bergerac's *La Mort d'Agrippine*, which caused much controversy on
account of Séjanus's veiled scepticism.

[501] On the importance of this theme in Tacitus, see A. J. Woodman, "Amateur Dramatics at
the Court of Nero: *Annals* 15.48-74" (1993).

[502] E.g. his intervention to move the speakers on to the next subject at ll.221-2: "C'est
assez discourir des vices et des vertus,/ Parlez des Immortels et de leurs Sacrifices."

What of Tigillin and Pétrone? Are these corrupt courtiers shown to exert any greater influence over the Emperor? Scarcely, for when they are together their role is that of a chorus, approving the Emperor's whims and aiding him in his plans to achieve his ends. While the debate with Sénèque means that Pétrone is more fully-fleshed, and it is he who is chosen to act out Néron's little charade of feigning to court the Empress (IV.1), in the rest of the play he and Tigillin appear to be almost interchangeable.[503] There is for example none of the rivalry which characterised the alliance of Lacus and Martian in *Othon*. What is emphasised is the servility of both characters, whom Néron refers to as his "chers confidents" (l.33). However, Gilbert ensures that their immorality is punished at the end of the play, for the Emperor angrily dismisses both as "lasches courtisans ... cruels imposteurs" (l.1594) when he learns of Arie's death. For all that the audience would share Sénèque's righteous denunciation of their "mauvais conseil" (l.1606), we do not have the impression that Néron's conduct has in large part been dependent upon it. Pétrone and Tigillin could be seen as part of his troupe of actors, giving the performance Néron wished them to. When the Emperor - himself the playwright/director/actor - calls an abrupt halt to the spectacle, there is no role left for them.

*   *   *

What might Racine have intuited from Gilbert as far as *confidents/conseillers* are concerned?[504] Undoubtedly, the interest of putting such roles at the heart of a play. It cannot be coincidence that *Britannicus* and *Arie et Pétus* both give these figures such uncharacteristically large roles. Moreover, if Racine had any scruples about departing from Tacitus by keeping Narcissus alive beyond the beginning of Nero's reign,[505] Gilbert had provided ample precedent for the modification of history. The principle of using opposing secondary figures can also be traced to Gilbert's Pétrone/ Sénèque. Yet conflict is already a well-established constituent of Racinian drama, so the opposition of Burrhus-Narcisse is also a natural evolution of Racine's own practice. Barnwell has shown how his plots from *La Thébaïde* to *Andromaque* depend on a simplification of earlier French tragedies.[506] I think the same line of argument

---

[503] Indeed in the copy I have consulted of the play there is an intriguing confusion about the identity of Tigillin, whose name is replaced by "Othon" in the scene headings and before some of the speeches in Act V (despite the fact that no Othon is named in the list of *dramatis personae*). Perhaps Gilbert thought any corrupt associate of Nero's would serve his purpose, and originally chose Otho, forgetting to amend the name to Tigillin when the manuscript was printed.

[504] For a general discussion of the influence of other aspects of *Arie et Pétus* on *Britannicus*, see E. Pellet, *A Forgotten French Dramatist*, pp. 161-4.

[505] See *Annals* XIII.1.

[506] "From *La Thébaïde* to *Andromaque*" (1951).

illuminates Racine's use of Gilbert: the four *confidents/conseillers* are reduced to two, but the opposition between them is maintained.[507] Racine's own contribution is to make this conflict central to the development of his main character.

It is highly symbolic that when Racine's Néron first appears on stage (II.1), he is flanked by both Burrhus and Narcisse. With his finely tuned sense of dramatic tension, however, Racine has neither *conseiller* speak in this scene; indeed, it is not until the following scene, when Néron has dismissed Burrhus, that Narcisse reveals clearly his treacherous alliance with the Emperor. On the face of it, II.1 shows Néron's authority and decisisveness. The imperatives and jussive subjunctives addressed to Burrhus sound impressive; the tone is epitomised in the hemistich "Je le veux, je l'ordonne" (l.369). It seems unlikely that this is a play in which the *conseillers* are to have a major role. Yet Racine will show that a *conseiller*'s power relies precisely on his sense of when to speak and when to remain silent.[508] Burrhus's silence in II.1 can be read as his acquiesence to the Emperor's orders and he will later defend Néron's exiling of Pallas to Agrippine (ll. 823-6). Narcisse's silence, though, is more ominous: it is the silence of deceit.[509]

When we compare Burrhus's and Narcisse's roles, it is Burrhus who speaks more. Burrhus has 285 lines (15.94% of the play), Narcisse only 168 (9.41% of the play),[510] yet it is Narcisse whose influence ultimately prevails. Just as in *Andromaque*, the protagonist displays impatience when a *confident*'s advice does not please him. In Act III Burrhus tries to persuade Néron that he could easily overcome his passion for Junie; the Emperor denies Burrhus any authority to speak on the matter, and brusquely leaves him with the line:

> *Adieu. Je souffre trop, éloigné de Junie.*
> *(l.799)*

---

[507] Racine discusses his preference for Burrhus rather than Seneca in his preface of 1676. E. Pellet suggests that in excluding Seneca he may also have been seeking to mark out his distance from Gilbert (*A Forgotten French Dramatist*, p.104) - and, we might add, Tristan's *La Mort de Sénèque*. Equally plausible is P. Butler's suggestion (in the introduction to his critical edition of *Britannicus*, p.20) that Seneca's philosophical doctrines would have risked making the play too sententious by this date.

[508] In the draft scene in which Burrhus and Narcisse were alone (?original III.1: reproduced in P. Butler's edition of *Britannicus*), the contrast is remarkable: Burrhus speaks 73 lines, Narcisse only 9. Narcisse himself ironically tells Burrhus: "Vous pouvez tout, j'écoute, et garde le silence."

[509] Compare R. Albanese's analysis of Néron's use of silence as an ironic strategy in "Patterns of irony in *Britannicus*" (1977).

[510] I base my statistics on the original 1669 text. If we include in addition the scene from the start of Act III, which Louis Racine claims Boileau persuaded his father to remove, the contrast is even sharper: Burrhus would have 358 lines, i.e. 19.14%, Narcisse 177 lines, i.e. 9.47%.

Like Agrippine and Britannicus, Burrhus does not grasp that speaking out when the Emperor does not wish to listen is a futile strategy.[511] Narcisse, on the contrary, listens silently to Néron's *aveu* of his love for Junie (II.2), making only the briefest of interventions until he is explicitly ordered to respond:

> *Dis-moi: Britannicus l'aime-t-il?*
> *(l.427).*

Both Narcisse's preceding interventions and his reply to this demand all take the forms of questions.[512] Racine shows the clever *conseiller* holding his peace until the ruler has chosen to unfold the whole picture. Only when he is fully aware of what Néron wishes to hear does he employ his rhetorical skills to persuade Néron that he can win Junie and free himself from Agrippine. It is Narcisse who suggests the path that Néron will follow (divorce from Octavie, freedom from Agrippine's influence, the banishment of Pallas). His advice is heeded because it coincides with Néron's own instincts.

Yet to show the total dominance of Narcisse from Act II onwards would not make for good theatre. Like Rotrou in *Cosroès*, Racine appreciates the dramatic potential of a ruler torn between conflicting instincts. Even at the end of II.2 Néron's jealous passion for Junie makes him ignore some of Narcisse's pragmatic advice,[513] and in Act IV it is only after a struggle that Narcisse prevails. What is surprising is just how much influence is accorded to the *confidents/conseillers* in this crucial act. This is one of the clearest examples in French classical tragedy of not one but two *confidents* substantially affecting the development of the plot. M.-O. Sweetser has drawn convincing parallels between Narcisse's role and at least three of Pierre Corneille's unscrupulous *conseillers*,[514] but Racine's strategy is different in that it relies upon the contrast between the advice of the two *conseillers*. Each addresses the Emperor in successive scenes; each moves him to a different course of action. Burrhus persuades him to stay the execution of Britannicus; Narcisse, to revert to his criminal plan. On one level, the *conseillers* are almost the equals of Agrippine in this act in that all three affect the decisions Néron makes. Yet on another level there is a vital distinction, for the fate of Agrippine herself is of far more consequence to the spectator than that of any secondary character. We may be

---

[511] Compare Néron's warning to Britannicus in III.8: "Néron de vos discours commence à se lasser" (l.1054), and his ill-concealed impatience with Agrippine's *tirade* in Act IV.

[512] "Vous?" (l.382); "Vous l'aimez?" (l.385); "Quoi, Seigneur! croira-t-on/ Qu'elle ait pu si longtemps se cacher à Néron?" (ll.409-10); "Quoi! s'il l'aime,/ Seigneur?" (ll.428/9).

[513] Narcisse vainly urges him to banish Britannicus (l.521).

[514] Euphorbe in *Cinna*, Achillas in *La Mort de Pompée* and Vinius in *Othon*: "Racine rival de Corneille: 'innutrition' et innovation dans *Britannicus*" (1975).

moved by Burrhus's display of loyalty, kneeling to Néron, shedding tears and even offering up his own life, but still our primary interest lies in the effect he has upon Néron. The *confident/conseiller* must not detract from our focus upon the main protagonist.

Within this regulated framework, what we witness is a finely balanced duel between the influence of Burrhus and that of Narcisse. Scenes 3 and 4 of Act IV are almost the same length (86 and 90 lines respectively), and, more importantly, each *confident/conseiller* has an identical number of lines - 67. This parallel structure surely invites us to compare the two performances no less than we did those of Sénèque and Pétrone in their debate in *Arie et Pétus*, but whereas Gilbert's Néron was a *metteur en scène*, ironically aloof from the import of the debate, Burrhus and Narcisse must be judged on whether they change Néron's actions. Some of their strategies are opposed: Burrhus's instant expression of horror, Narcisse's apparent unwillingness to criticise;[515] Burrhus's tears, Narcisse's cold calculations. Yet they both use to telling effect a device which we identified in Chapter 4 as characteristic of Racinian *confidents*, the appropriation of another voice. Racine's Burrhus and Narcisse, like Gilbert's *conseillers*, and like the courtiers of Nero described by Tacitus, act out a part. In Burrhus's case, he dares to speak in Néron's voice, imagining the Emperor's delight if he could congratulate himself on winning the people's love not their fear.[516] Narcisse's counter-strategy is to adopt the hypothetical voice of Néron's critics.[517] By so doing, he can express unequivocally the arguments he knows will most wound Néron, but without alienating the Emperor by acknowledging them as his own. Narcisse's disguised barbs outweigh Burrhus's flattery; the latter's promise that Néron will be able to congratulate himself is cancelled out by Narcisse's image of the power to silence the dissenting voices he has just imitated:

> NARCISSE
> *Ah! ne voulez-vous pas les forcer à se taire?*
>
> NÉRON
> *Viens, Narcisse: allons voir ce que nous devons faire.*
> *(ll.1479-80)*

Ultimately it is the machiavellian strategy of imposing a reign of silence and fear which prevails.[518]

---

[515] Compare: "Non, quoi que vous disiez, cet horrible dessein/ Ne fut jamais, Seigneur, conçu dans votre sein." (ll.1325-6) and "Je me garderai bien de vous en détourner,/ Seigneur." (ll. 1401-2).

[516] Lines 1360-4.

[517] Lines 1468-78.

[518] For a full study of Racine's exploitation of other machiavellian elements in *Britannicus*, see A. Viala, "Péril, conseil et secret d'État" (1996).

If the *conseillers* have been pivotal to Act IV, one could theoretically imagine Act V of *Britannicus* without either Burrhus or Narcisse present. After all, neither is strictly material to the action, and the spectator's interest is centred upon each of the four main protagonists in turn. Yet Racine brings Burrhus and Narcisse on stage together for one last time, in V.6, thus underlining how far they are implicated in the catastrophe. Like II.1, the scene has a strong visual impact, but it shows how the allegiances of the *confidents/conseillers* have now changed. Narcisse enters and exits with Néron; Burrhus is present with Agrippine at the start of the scene, and remains on stage with her when the Emperor leaves. The final configuration reminds us of the political autonomy which the *conseiller*, unlike the simpler *confident(e)*, enjoys. Albine, for example, appears in a total of 7 scenes, always with Agrippine. Her relatively limited role in the play[519] is largely explained by the fact that her mistress turns instead to Burrhus to give vent to her thoughts and feelings. Burrhus has appeared in debate with both Néron and Agrippine, seeking to influence each in turn,[520] a double role that involves compromises in his position, as a number of critics have observed. Narcisse likewise has spoken alone with both Britannicus and Néron.[521] Indeed, in the draft of the scene between Burrhus and Narcisse, this is the basis for the first of Burrhus's major recriminations:

> *Quoi! Narcisse au palais obsédant l'Empereur,*
> *Laisse Britannicus en proie à sa fureur.*

By omitting the scene, Racine leaves the spectators to observe for themselves Narcisse's duplicity - highlighted by the number of scenes in which he plays the silent *confident* to Britannicus between his secret meetings with the Emperor.

Until V.6, Narcisse seems the epitome of the Tacitean spy and informer, frequently guarded in his speech to the point of being laconic. Yet in his final appearance he interrupts the dialogue between Néron and Agrippine, answering Agrippine on the Emperor's behalf, to justify the murder of Britannicus which Néron had been about to deny. Not only is this a breathtaking disregard for protocol,[522] but also apparently out of character. On the one hand, Racine may be completing his depiction of Narcisse's political *credo*: a defence of the right

---

[519] While Albine contributes to a particularly vigorous expository scene, her spoken role in the rest of the play is limited to 6 lines in III.4 and 47 lines (largely a *récit*) in V.8.

[520] He speaks to each in three scenes (albeit of differing length): to Agrippine in I.2, III.3, IV.1; to Néron in III.1, III.9, IV.3.

[521] He speaks to Britannicus in two scenes (I.4, III.6), but to Néron in four scenes (II.2, II.4, II.8, IV.4).

[522] But Racine's credentials here were less than perfect, as critics of *Andromaque* had pointed out. (See p.97.)

of might and a confidence in the pre-eminence of the security of the state. This is broadly in accordance with the tenor of Narcisse's advice throughout, deriving more from Machiavellian politics than from anything in Tacitus's account of the historical Narcissus.[523] But on the other hand, Racine may also be following established practice by lessening the audience's revulsion for the main character through casting some of the responsibility for his misdeeds onto his adviser. Narcisse's aside at the end of II.8 (ll.757-60) leaves us in little doubt that he sees his own fortunes inextricably bound up with those of Néron: in V.6, his defence of Néron is also a defence of his own interests. It is true that, unlike the *conseillers* of *Othon*, Narcisse expresses no ambitions to wield his power more overtly, yet this very fact makes him less assailable by rivals. Racine has shown perhaps an even more dangerous example of the court flatterer than either the powerbrokers of *Othon* or the cynical companions of Néron in *Arie et Pétus*. Of all these *conseillers*, it is Narcisse who contributes most clearly to the tragic dénouement, and who duly meets his nemesis, while perhaps allowing the audience to retain a vestige of pity for his master who is distinguished from him by the sufferings born of his passions.[524] The fact that the final line of the play is spoken by Burrhus may restore a sense of moral perspective; however it leaves the spectator with a sense of tragic inevitability. Once more, Burrhus's words will be no more than an empty wish. A *conseiller*, even more than a simple *confident*, must be judged not only on his words but on the actions which they bring forth.

(iv) AN EPILOGUE: THE *CONSEILLER* IN RACINE'S BIBLICAL TRAGEDIES

I suggested at the start of this chapter that *Britannicus* is the outstanding example of a play with *confidents/conseillers* at the heart of the plot, and it is chronologically the last play I shall examine in detail here. As far as other of Racine's strategies to revitalise the role of the *confident* are concerned, I have argued that contemporary playwrights were probably influenced by them, and that Racine himself reworked them in new forms in subsequent plays. Is the same true of the *confident/conseiller*? As Truchet's study (which continues into the eighteenth century) shows, the figure of the *conseiller du prince* does not disappear from tragedies after 1670. However, I would view *Britannicus* as the

---

[523] See P. Butler's comparison of the machiavellian policy of Narcisse and the Senecan line of Burrhus (introduction to his edition of *Britannicus*, pp.49-51). However I would not follow Butler in assuming that Narcisse's policies could be viewed as transparently relevant to Bourbon France.

[524] Racine's reference in his *Préface* of 1670 to Tacitus underlines the idea that Narcisse has "une conformité merveilleuse avec les vices du prince encore cachés." But this obscures the fact that his Néron is set apart from Narcisse by virtue of his love for Junie.

culmination of a traditional strategy, invested with new dynamism certainly, rather than a model easily assimilable in the changing climate of the 1670/1680s. As the fashion for *tragédies galantes* came to displace political tragedies, it was less likely that two or more *conseillers* would be the motive force of a plot. This did not mean, of course, that an individual *confident/conseiller* could not play a role, but the distinction is well demonstrated by, for example, Thomas Corneille's *Le Comte d'Essex* of 1678. On the face of it, this is a play heavily dependent on politics, in which Cécile, Elizabeth's adviser, has a leading role. Yet Thomas Corneille's adaptation of the historical material shifts the focus to Elizabeth's jealousy of Essex's love for La Duchesse d'Irton, and the attitude of the Duchesse and Essex have far more influence upon Elizabeth than the advice of Cécile.[525] We may be reminded of Voltaire's unfairly dimissive comment about Thomas Corneille's slightly earlier tragedy, *Ariane* (1672), in which Pirithoüs, adviser and *confident* to Thésée, appears less like a crown prince than a "valet". Such are the reordered priorities of *galanterie* and politics.

Did Racine's own later tragedies, which perhaps make fewer concessions to this shifting taste than do those of Thomas Corneille or Quinault, keep a role for the *confident/conseiller*? We saw in Chapter 4 how Paulin's advice (and indeed that of Philon in Pierre Corneille's *Tite et Bérénice*) is dictated by his political status. However, Paulin's and Philon's are single voices, not part of a Tacitean web of political conspiracies. Much closer to the mood of *Britannicus* is *Bajazet*, its opening scene evoking another context in which spying, plotting and machiavellianism are the order of the day. Acomat holds a central role, but he is a *confident/conseiller* who crosses the boundary to become a main protagonist, not least because he is himself drawn into the tangled web of passions and proposed marriages. I shall therefore return to *Bajazet* in Chapter 7. While Racine's subsequent three plays all have a character who might fall broadly within the category of *conseiller* - Arbate, Ulysse, Théramène - they draw little from the schema of *Britannicus*. Arbate and Théramène are not powerbrokers, while Ulysse, a wholly political character, is not in any sense a *confident*.

It is in fact Racine's biblical tragedies, written some twenty years after *Britannicus*, which might be thought to build upon the achievements of Burrhus and Narcisse. Perhaps it is unsurprising in that the *confident/conseiller* is associated with plays in which sexual passions are eclipsed by politics. In *Esther*, the fall of the *mauvais conseiller* is the centrepiece of the drama, but Aman is a

---

[525] Significantly, Cécile is absent from Acts III and IV, and reappears in Act V only to be reviled and dismissed by the distraught queen.

main protagonist in his own right, not to be compared with Burrhus or Narcisse. However, there are more interesting structural parallels between *Britannicus* and *Athalie*. The roles accorded to Abner and Mathan are the more striking because of the very low-key roles of the other two *confidents*. Abner and Mathan are conflicting voices, called upon to influence Athalie in her moment of irresolution. Their interests are clearly opposed, and in II.5 each strives to win the queen over to his side.[526] Both contribute significantly to the development of the plot: Mathan by encouraging Athalie in her desire to ensure her safety by destroying the Temple and Joas; Abner by his final, if unwitting, betrayal of the queen to Joad. Mathan is very close to Narcisse in his ruthlessly machiavellian maxims,[527] but he is exposed more brutally by Racine for his ambitions.[528] Like Narcisse, he meets bloody retribution at the hands of the crowd in the last Act,[529] but since he has not been present in either Act IV or V, his fate may seem peripheral. Furthermore, although Racine has chosen to elaborate upon the biblical character (simply named as a priest of Baal) by making him a renegade Levite, in the play itself Mathan plays an open role; no character entertains a moment's doubt as to his allegiance.[530]

Instead, in a reversal of the Burrhus/Narcisse paradigm, the double agent is Abner. The latter moves between Joad (with whom he opens the play) and Athalie, and his divided loyalties are epitomised in II.7 when, accompanying Athalie to see Joas, he makes two comments *à part* to Josabet.[531] *Athalie* offers no re-run of Act IV of *Britannicus*, but in Act V Abner's powers of persuasion are put to the test. As Athalie's envoy he must offer Joad a last chance to save the temple. Like Burrhus, he uses both rhetoric and gesture (kneeling, tears) to move his listener.[532] Joad, who has deliberately asked for his *conseil* (l.1588), appears won over:

> *Je me rends. Vous m'ouvrez un avis que j'embrasse.*
> *(l.1647)*

Yet this is not the successful intervention of the *conseiller* that it would appear, but rather the proof that Joad is immune to human persuasion. He is, of course, merely using Abner as the instrument to trick Athalie. Abner is both innocent

---

[526] A notable distinction from *Britannicus* being that both characters are shown together seeking to persuade Athalie, and even engaging with each other in argument (ll. 547-82).

[527] E.g. His arguments justifying the killing of Joas whatever his parentage (ll.562-570).

[528] Mathan is given a *confident* - a sign of his rank - to whom he reveals his cynical motives in III.2.

[529] "Mathan est égorgé" (l.1768).

[530] Compare *Othon*, in which the most corrupt characters are the only ones not *seen* to act out a role.

[531] "Princesse, assurez-vous, je les prends sous ma garde." (l.619) and "Je vous l"avais promis,/Je vous rends le dépôt que vous m'avez commis." (l.737-38).

[532] "Faut-il que je me mette à vos sacrés genoux?" (l.1633) and "Mais je vois que mes pleurs et que mes vains discours/ Pour vous persuader sont un faible secours." (ll.1641-2).

CHAPTER SIX

THE STRATEGIC EXCLUSION OF THE *CONFIDENT*

The development of the Racinian *confident* from *La Thébaïde* to *Bérénice* could be summarised briefly: first, an experiment in the eclipse of the *confident* (*La Thébaïde*, *Alexandre*); then a complete reversal of the strategy, with almost all protagonists accompanied by *confidents* with prominent roles (*Andromaque*, *Britannicus*, *Bérénice*). Yet for the next six years of Racine's career it is impossible to determine any such simple schema. *Phèdre* may look back to the second phase in which *confidents* are indispensable; or, perhaps more accurately, it extends that strategy in new directions, as I shall discuss in Chapter 8. But what of the three intervening tragedies? Why do *Bajazet*, *Mithridate* and *Iphigénie* accord the *confidents* a middling role, neither eclipsed, nor obviously pivotal? A quick answer would be to emphasise Racine's creative flexibility, to suggest that in his use of the *confident*, no less than in many other areas of his dramatic art, he did not choose to be bound to one formula, however successful it may have been. More precisely, however, we can identify two patterns which mark out his tragedies from 1672-1677: on the one hand, the strategic exclusion of one or more *confidents*; and on the other hand, the presence of a protagonist who is simultaneously another's *confident* and rival. Both strategies can be glimpsed in earlier plays: in *Britannicus*, Julie is bereft of a *confidente*; in *Bérénice*, Antiochus is Titus's *confident* and rival for Bérénice's affections. In Racine's subsequent tragedies, one or both of these devices is developed, and, as I shall argue here and in Chapter 7, is central to our perception of each play. What both devices have in common is their origin in tragicomedies and heroic novels, and the greatest challenge facing the tragedian was to assimilate them without threatening the dignity and solemnity of his genre.

The strategic omission of one *confident* is quite different from the eclipse of the role (discussed in Chapter 3) whereby playwrights contrived - contrary to common practice - to minimise the import of all secondary or *confident*-type characters. In plays in which there are some *confidents* with a significant function, a dramatist may achieve particular effects by leaving one or more protagonists to stand alone. We have seen that *Andromaque* and *Bérénice* were unusual precisely for their symmetrical pairing of the protagonists and *confidents*, whereas our survey of Corneille's tragedies from *Médée to*

Nicomède illustrated that it was standard practice to have at least one or two protagonists without a *confident*. We thus need to draw an initial distinction between the many plays in which one or two protagonists do not require a *confident*, and the more interesting cases in which the absence of a *confident* for a particular protagonist can be judged to be essential to the import of the play.

Not all dramatists necessarily weighed up the absence of secondary characters closely. We have seen from Tristan L'Hermite's *La Mort de Sénèque* that at times the resources of some troupes may have affected how playwrights could use *confidents*. And this practical consideration apart, there are many classical tragedies in which at least one protagonist is without a *confident(e)*, but the lack is of no consequence because the function is assumed by another protagonist, i.e. a *para-confident*. Boyer's *Oropaste* (1662) illustrates this pattern. In this long and complex play of mistaken identity, the only two secondary characters are essentially messengers rather than *confidents*,[534] while the seven protagonists are united by various degrees of kinship, or political or amorous alliance. The eponymous hero had a brother according to Boyer's main historical source (Herodotus). The playwright also introduces his father (not mentioned in the Greek historian),[535] with the effect that almost the whole of Act III can be sustained by exchanges between the three related characters. Furthermore, Boyer contrives a Cornelian symmetry by having a pair of conspiring Persian princes (whose meeting provides the opening scene of the exposition), each with a mistress. This "quadrille amoureux"[536] is exploited notably in I.3 and V.4-7, and the four characters are drawn closer together by the fact that Araminte (a character invented by Boyer) is made the sister of Darie, one of the princes. In short, no character in *Oropaste* is isolated for any length of time despite the absence of conventional *confidents*. It is indicative of this that the play has only two monologues, (Mégabise in III.1 and Oropaste in IV.3). Both are strategically placed to draw the spectator's attention to a momentary hesitation or dawning certainty, rather than to mark the hero's solitude.

For confirmation of the continuing role of unremarkable *para-confidents* throughout the 1660s, we can look to both Pierre and Thomas Corneille. The former's *Agésilas* seems to mark a radical departure after the *querelle de Sophonisbe* in dispensing with any *confidentes*. Whereas in earlier plays of Pierre Corneille heroes often had no *confidents*, heroines were regularly

---

[534] Cléone, who is listed as the "confidente d'Hermione", has no scene alone with her mistress. Her only substantial speech is her *récit* of the death of Prexaspe (V.4).

[535] See *Oropaste, ou le faux Tonaxare*, ed. C. Delmas and G. Forestier (1990), pp.36-37.

[536] As Delmas and Forestier describe it (*ibid.*, p.44).

accompanied by *confidentes*. Yet when we look more closely, *Agésilas* is no bold experiment, for the three heroines (all invented characters) have ready *para-confidentes*. Elpinice and Aglatide are sisters, a device enabling a smooth exposition in the opening scene as well as an exchange in II.7; Mandane is the sister of Spitridate (a "grand seigneur persan"), with whom she has two scenes alone (II.1, IV.2). If we add that Spitridate is depicted as a close friend of the other *jeune premier*, Cotys, and that they confide in each other (I.4), we can see how Corneille circumvented the need for *confidents* for five of his seven protagonists in a play which R. Knight has compared to a game of musical chairs.[537] It is effectively the same design that he refines to dispense with *confidents* altogether in *Pulchérie*.[538] In a similar way, though less elaborately, Thomas Corneille dispenses with a *confident* for the *jeune premier* in *Laodice* (1668), since Ariarate and one of the other protagonists, Phradate, swear an "amitié sincère" in I.3, which allows them to complete the exposition with a double exchange of confidences.

The absence of a *confident* in such plays is more than compensated for by the presence of a *para-confident*, and it is scarcely necessary to enumerate further examples here. Rather, I propose to concentrate on tragedies in which one or two characters are conspicuous by their unrelieved isolation, for it is these plays which are the most dramatically interesting. We shall see that the immediate effects achieved by the strategic omission of a *confident* can be strikingly varied, but ultimately the strategy works to one of two ends, increasing either the suspense or the spectators' sense of pity.

(i) HEIGHTENING SUSPENSE IN TRAGI-COMEDIES: THOMAS CORNEILLE'S *TIMOCRATE*

With the vogue for romanesque tragicomedies in the 1650s, the omission of one or more *confidents* becomes a vital mechanism for plots that rely upon creating suspense. Although this study is concerned essentially with the *confidents* of tragedy, it would be impossible to leave aside the influence of some of the strategies employed in tragicomedies. To give a character a *confident(e)* is potentially to expose his or her inner thoughts and feelings. Such transparency precludes deceptions which are designed to take in the spectator as well as other characters. It is of course possible for a skilful dramatist to engineer a *coup de théâtre* later in the play if a character's revelatory scenes with a *confident* are restricted to earlier acts: the dénouements of both *Rodogune* and *Camma* rely upon such an arrangement.[539] But for the

---

[537] *Corneille's Tragedies*, p.96.
[538] See Chapter 3.
[539] See p.103.

type of plays which revolve around disguise and hidden identity from start to finish, the playwright faces a simple choice: should the audience be privy to the deception or not? Given that the 1650s have the greatest number of plays involving disguise and false or mistaken identity, the question is particularly pertinent.[540] If the answer is yes, then an early scene between the disguised protagonist and *confident* permits the audience to appreciate the ensuing ironies. This is precisely the strategy followed by Magnon in his tragicomedy *Tite et Bérénice* (1660).[541] The play opens with a scene between Bérénice (disguised as the mysterious prince Cléobule) and her *confidente* Cléonte, in which the heroine's identity and motives are revealed. Thereafter, there are no further scenes between Bérénice and Cléonte.[542] In fact it is Bérénice who artfully exploits her disguise to receive the confidences of Tite and her rival, Mucie. As we shall see in Chapter 7, the Racinian strategy of the protagonist turned *(faux) confident* derives from the world of just such romanesque tragicomedies. The alternative of denying the spectator a privileged insight into the deception - that is to say by depriving the disguised protagonist of a true *confident* - yields other dramatic rewards. The most striking illustration must be Thomas Corneille's phenomenally successful *Timocrate* (1656).[543] The absence of a *confident* for its eponymous hero has rarely been discussed by critics of the play,[544] but I would contend that it is a vital structural device.

Timocrate ostensibly uses a structure similar to Thomas Corneille's later tragedy *Laodice*: Timocrate, disguised as Cléomène, has no *confident*, but in the first act finds a loyal friend in Nicandre. However, here friendship is not the harbinger of absolute confidence. While Nicandre is open with Cléomène, the hero deliberately witholds vital information from Nicandre (and the spectator). The main achievement of the play is to leave the spectator in suspense about the identity of Timocrate for four acts.[545] Thomas Corneille's patron, the Duc de Guise, of course solved the riddle in the first act, earning himself lavish praise:

> *Je me souviendray toûjours avec admiration de cette merveilleuse vivacité, qui*
> *vous fit découvrir d'abord les intérests les plus cachez de Cléomène, et*

[540] See the statistics compiled by G. Forestier, *Esthétique de l'identité dans le théâtre français (1550-1680)* (1988), p.24.

[541] For a fuller discussion of the rest of this play see Chapter 7.

[542] Instead, Cléonte acts as *confidente* to Bérénice's rival, Mucie, in IV.1.

[543] On the reception of *Timocrate*, see *Timocrate*, ed. Y. Giraud (1970), pp. 11-17.

[544] C. Gossip briefly alludes to the importance of the strategy in his excellent article "*Timocrate* reconsidered" (1973, p.27), but he does not develop the point.

[545] D. Collins argues that in this prolonged dependence on disguise, as well as in other features of the play, Thomas Corneille is heavily dependent on comic devices. See *Thomas Corneille. Protean Dramatist* (1966), p.60.

> *déveloper dès ses premiers sentiments le secret d'un noeud qui, pendant quatre Actes a laissé Timocrate inconnu presque à tout le monde.*

The playwright modestly forbears from claiming for himself the credit for planting ample clues to stimulate the Duke's "merveilleuse vivacité". Not least among these is the contrast between the ample use of *confidents* for the hero's rival, Nicandre, and for the Princesse.[546] This is certainly not a play in which Thomas Corneille is delivering a challenge to the traditional role of the *confidente*. The *jeune première* has, for example, a finely *précieux* scene of over a hundred lines in which she confesses her conflicting emotions to her *confidente* at the start of Act II. Act I had also opened with a conventional expository scene between Nicandre and his *confident,* Arcas. After a series of surprising twists and turns, Nicandre and Arcas have further scenes to close Act III and open Act IV. In these exchanges, Nicandre is totally open with his *confident*. The second of these scenes is particularly important to confirm Nicandre's heroic character in the eyes of the audience. When he is given the chance to serve his interests in love at the expense of his honour, he declares to Arcas:

> *Souffrons ce dur revers, plûtost que consentir*
> *Que ma vertu s'attire un honteux repentir.*
> *(l.1300-1)*

For Cléomène/Timocrate, on the other hand, the lack of a *confident* is sorely felt. He cannot prove his *générosité* until he reveals his true identity in the celebrated *coup de théâtre* at the end of Act IV.

Thomas Corneille adds a further strand to what is already an extremely complicated plot by establishing an initial bond of friendship between Cléomène and Nicandre. As the hero approaches, Nicandre refers to Cléomène as "un amy" (1.74). The embrace between the two men and warm exchange of compliments might seduce us into expecting a flat *para-confident* scene. At first sight, I.2 simply provides the excuse for Nicandre to deliver an account of the troubled relations between Crete and Argos.[547] The information is essential for the audience to follow the passions of love, hatred and vengeance which fuel the plot, but Cléomène's request seems a clumsy justification for the narrative:

> *Puis-je estre curieux sans perdre le respect,*
> *Seigneur? Tout me surprend, et j'ay peine à comprendre*
> *Ce qu'un bruit fort confus m'a voulu faire entendre.*
> *(ll.120-2)*

---

[546] Ériphile is in fact listed as having two *confidentes*, but the role of Dorine is minimal. She accompanies the Princess without speaking in a number of scenes, and acts as a messenger at the end of III.5 and in IV.2.

[547] In his edition of *Timocrate* (p.33) Y. Giraud points out Thomas Corneille's predilection for *récits* throughout the play.

However, an astute theatregoer like the Duc de Guise might have pricked up his ears at the repeated references earlier in the scene to what is known (forms of the verb *savoir* have occurred three times already), and what Cléomène cannot or will not say about the motives of his absence or return:

> *Ne me demandez point que je m'explique mieux*
> *Seigneur: un tel secret m'est de telle importance*
> *Que la Reyne elle-mesme excuse mon silence.*
>   *(ll. 104-6)*

Such a clearly-flagged mystery suggests that this *para-confident* scene must have a twist.

Thomas Corneille prolongs the irony in the last scene of Act I, when Cléomène confesses to Nicandre that he is his rival for the Princess's affections. Since Cléomène will soon declare his sentiments to Ériphile herself (II.4), this scene with a *para-confident* may seem unnecessary, and Nicandre himself suggests that Cléomène's confession is misplaced:

> *Certes, si vous aimez, l'exemple est assez rare*
> *Qu'en faveur d'un Rival un Amant se déclare.*
>   *(ll. 413-4)*

However, the scene works on two levels. It sets up an open but noble rivalry between Nicandre and Cléomène, which will determine Nicandre's conduct for the rest of the play. More subtly, it dupes both Nicandre and the innocent spectator into believing that Cléomène's relationship with Nicandre is transparent, like that with a *para-confident*. After all, Cléomène sighs, then admits his love in standard fashion. However, if the spectator is aware of the true identity of the hero, the scene takes on a different complexion: it is Cléomène's skilful deception of Nicandre which is striking. Following a pattern familiar in *confident* scenes, Cléomène gives his *para-confident* a commentary on his thoughts which had remained unvoiced in the previous scene. He claims to be repeating to Nicandre the exact words which passed through his mind, using the formula "disois-je en ma triste pensée" (l. 429), and quoting his reflections verbatim for eight lines. Yet there is a striking difference in comparison with standard *(para-)confident* scenes. Heroes do not deliberately deceive their *confidents*. The words which Cléomène repeats to Nicandre could have been his exact thoughts, but only if read with an ironic gloss. Nicandre of course suspects nothing, but the rather tortuous question which he addressed to Cléomène at the start of the scene:

> *De vous-mesme à vous-mesme enfin puis-je me plaindre?*
>   *(l. 373)*

was far nearer to the truth than he guessed.

Because Act I establishes this (deceptive) *para-confident* relationship between Cléomène and Nicandre, on a first or naive reading of the text we are not made aware that Cléomène lacks a *confident*-figure. On a subequent or informed reading, however, we realise that this absence is crucial to the workings of the plot. With every character, including Nicandre, Cléomène must be constantly acting a part. The real achievement of Thomas Corneille lies in the fact that the hero does not speak simply as Cléomène, but constantly uses ironic formulae which allow his words to apply simultaneously to his identity as Timocrate.[548] Only thus can he avoid losing our admiration, for as Cléomène himself says to the Queen in III.6:

> *Mais un cœur généreux hait des ruses semblables.*
> *(l. 1207)*

Cléomène has one other scene alone with Nicandre (IV.3), and it exploits to the full the hero's ability to talk in enigmatic double statements. By this point Nicandre is no longer a *para-confident*, but a jealous rival, and the tone of the scene is quite different from I.4. The sustained use of stichomythia effectively conveys the tension. As informed spectators we might feel that Cléomène is enjoying his intellectual and verbal dexterity which permits such gems as:

> NICANDRE
> *De ce que vous valez nous estions trop instruits.*
>
> CLÉOMÈNE
> *Pas tant, qu'il ne fallust montrer mieux qui je suis.*
> *(ll. 1381-2)*

However, we might also see hints that Cléomène suffers from the self-imposed isolation of his disguise, for he indicates that his double identity covers a genuine conflict. He is forced to accept less than his birth and military supremacy (as Timocrate) demand because under the guise of Cléomène he must remain subservient to his mistress's wishes. Four lines of his exchange with Nicandre are a genuine if enigmatic confession; it is simply that his *para-confident* is not in a position to understand them:

> NICANDRE
> *Timocrate sans vous auroit bravé sa haine.*
>
> CLÉOMÈNE
> *Timocrate avoit lieu de craindre Cléomène.*
>
> NICANDRE
> *Vous lui cachiez sans doute un dangereux Rival.*

---

[548] G. Forestier observes that *"Timocrate* est le type même de la pièce construite sur ce que nous appelons le *déguisement rhétorique"* (*Esthétique de l'identité*, p.274). T. Cave also draws attention to the way in which Thomas Corneille's preoccupation with the poetics of recognition is demonstrated through the lexis of the play (*Recognitions. A Study in Poetics*, 1988, p.294).

CLÉOMÈNE
Mon amour en effet luy peut estre fatal.
(ll. 1394-7)

Earlier in the play too there have been fleeting hints that playing the role of Cléomène causes Timocrate pain.[549] Yet because Thomas Corneille's priority is to maintain what he refers to in the *Au Lecteur* as "une suspension d'esprit si agréable", he cannot allow his hero either a monologue or a transparent *confident* scene to develop these sentiments. We might argue that it is only on a second, informed reading that we can perceive the potentially tragic resonances in the first four Acts. The playwright's achievement, as later in *Camma*, is to create suspense rather than pity.[550] However, the revelation of Cléomène/Timocrate's double identity at the end of Act IV does permit a greater focus upon the hero's state of mind and feeling in the final act.[551] For a brief while, he is the hero who stands alone, facing the prospect of death with fortitude if not total resignation. This is an alternative model of the hero without *confident* which is to be exploited by other playwights of the 1660s and 1670s.

(ii) THE CLIMATE OF DOUBT: QUINAULT'S *BELLÉROPHON*

Disguises and false identities are practically a *sine qua non* for heroic novels and tragicomedies of the decade 1650-1660. As the shift to "classical" tragedy was accomplished over the next twenty years, with the increased focus on the complexities of the inner mind and feelings rather than the deceptive appearances of outer reality, the glittering exploitation of the *invraisemblable* in a *Timocrate* or a *Tite* waned.[552] The tragic hero's or heroine's identity may still be at issue in such plays as Quinault's *Astrate*, Thomas Corneille's *Laodice* or Racine's *Iphigénie*, but it is a psychological climate of doubt which lies at the heart of such tragedies. The absence of a *confident* for Cléomène/Timocrate prevented the enigma of his identity being solved before it had run its course; in later tragedies in which protagonists are denied a *confident*, their thoughts and passions become the source of taxing, even agonising uncertainty both for other protagonists and the spectator.

As we saw in our discussion of *Pausanias*, much of the theatre of Quinault revolves precisely around the themes of knowledge, doubt and

---

[549] Notably in his enigmatic exchanges with Ériphile in II.4.

[550] See p.103.

[551] Some contemporaries condemned the fact that the play did not end at the recognition scene, but Thomas Corneille defended his final act in the *Au Lecteur*.

[552] Forestier estimates that where 10 out of 34 tragedies used disguises in the decade 1650-9, the proportion falls in the following two decades to 8 out of 43 (1660-9) and 11 out of 43 (1670-80): *L'Esthétique de l'identité*, p.25.

misunderstanding.[553] The ways in which these constitute the tragic dilemma is closely related to the presence or exclusion of *confidents*. In chapter 4 we observed that each of the four protagonists in *Pausanias* had a *confident*, an echo of the successful formula of *Andromaque*. Just over two years later, in January 1671, the Hôtel de Bourgogne staged *Bellérophon*, Quinault's last tragedy before he turned to writing the libretti for Lully's operas. Here, Quinault no longer adopts the symmetry of the Racinian model: the heroine Sténobée has a very active *confidente*, seen by many critics as a source for Phèdre's Œnone;[554] two other protagonists, Philonoé and Prœtus, have *confidents* whose role is essentially confined to the exposition;[555] and the titular hero stands alone. Bellérophon is not simply cast in the conventional mould of the male protagonist who does not require a *confident*. Rather, Quinault's design is to draw our attention to the doubts which the hero's isolation engenders in the other characters. For this reason, it is essential that Bellérophon should have no *confident*.

From Bellérophon's first appearance, in I.2, we are drawn into an atmosphere of uncertainty and mystery, in sharp contrast to the uncomplicated optimism of the expository scene between Prœtus and his *confident* Licas. Bellérophon first asks that Licas should leave them, in itself a sign of the gravity of the scene to come, and then presages the announcement of his departure by sighs and "regards troublez" (l.65). Given the high esteem in which Prœtus held their friendship in the opening scene (ll.39-54), we anticipate that Prœtus will act as a *para-confident*;[556] indeed, he himself expects the same, urging Bellérophon:

> *Bellérophon, expliquez-vous, parlez.*
> *Apprenez-moy quel trouble ainsi vous peut surprendre.*
> *(ll.66-67)*

His (and our) expectations are confounded, however, by the wall of silence which meets his questions: Bellérophon's speech is characterised by references to what cannot be said.[557] The scene is effective precisely because Quinault has

---

[553] See W. Brooks, "The Evolution of the Theatre of Quinault", chapter 5.

[554] For a detailed comparison of the similarities and differences between *Bellérophon* and *Phèdre*, see J. Émelina, "Racine et Quinault: de *Bellérophon* à *Phèdre*" (1979).

[555] The role of these two *confidents* is very limited: Licas has 12 lines (0.83% of the play) and Ladice 17 lines (1.18%). Even Mégare has only 69 lines (4.77%), so that in total the three *confidents* account for just 6.78% of the play.

[556] The example of *Astrate* would have provided a precedent for this. Although Astrate has no *confident* as such, Sichée acts as his *para-confident* in a number of scenes.

[557] Lines 68, 88, 90, 96, 100, 111-4. This aspect of Bellérophon's speech may well have provided a model for Racine's *Phèdre*.

built up expectations of an exposition with a *para-confident*, only to refuse to meet them. Nonetheless, the strategy carries an inherent danger, for Bellérophon's discreet silence makes him a particularly passive hero.[558] Unwilling to justify his conduct to Prœtus and bereft of a *confident* in whom to confide, he is unable to demonstrate that his conduct stems from noble motives.

In contrast, Sténobée's scene with her *confidente* at the end of the first act allows the spectator to comprehend the surprising hostility she has shown towards Bellérophon, for we learn that it masks her anguished doubts as to whether he loves her or her sister.[559] Even the manner in which Sténobée's doubts were born demonstrates how Quinault is exploiting the absence of a *confident* for Bellérophon. The plot hinges upon her discovery, before the start of the play, of the *tablettes* on which Bellérophon had written a declaration of love, but not named the object of his affections. Sténobée's *récit* of how she came upon the *tablettes* emphasises Bellérophon's solitude:

> *J'ay veu Bellérophon qui s'estoit endormy.*
> *Le trouvant à telle heure en cette solitude,*
> *J'ay jugé par mes soins de son inquiétude.*
>   *(ll.270-2)*

Bellérophon is here the archetypal suffering lover, communing only with nature, but the fact that he has no *confident* also accommodates the romanesque device of his confiding his secret passions in the fatal letter. Like Sténobée, we are aware of the depth of passions which Bellérophon experiences, but we do not yet know its object. Until the end of Act II, when he declares his love to Philonoé, he remains the most distanced and enigmatic of the four protagonists, whereas each of the others has already had a lengthy *confident* scene in which to reveal their true feelings.[560]

Because Bellérophon is present only in scenes with other protagonists - never having a monologue[561] - our interest is always divided between what he reveals about himself and how the other protagonists react to his words. Quinault is noticeably economic with the number of scenes in which his titular hero appears: except for Act IV, Bellérophon is present in only one scene in each Act.[562] In contrast, each of the other three main characters is present in a series of consecutive scenes in at least three acts. The effect is that we build up a fuller picture of Sténobée, Philonoé and Prœtus, while Bellérophon is perceived

---

[558] See the negative assessment of E. Gros: *Philippe Quinault*, pp.436-7.

[559] This rivalry between Sténobée and Philonoé is of Quinault's own invention. In the legend Philonoé's marriage to Bellérophon is arranged subsequent to the hero's killing of the monster.

[560] Prœtus and Licas in I.1, Sténobée and Mégare in I.4, and Philonoé and Ladice in II.3.

[561] W. Brooks notes that after *Stratonice* Quinault does not make use of monologues ("The Evolution of the Theatre of Quinault", pp.381-2).

[562] In Act IV he is present in three consecutive scenes (IV.4-6), but these are all brief, totalling 52 lines.

only in occasional cameo shots. Furthermore, Bellérophon is frequently the subject of discussion when he is not present, so that our perception of the hero is filtered through other characters' judgements as they seek to establish his passions and motives.

In particular, the image we form of Bellérophon relies on reports which are given at the beginning of Acts II and III of two offstage conversations with him. Mégare, charged by Sténobée with testing his reaction to a proposed marriage with Philonoé, returns to her mistress in II.1.[563] Sténobée is aware that she has entrusted her *confidente* with a critical task, not simply transmitting a verbal message but interpreting the unspoken signs which might reveal Bellérophon's true feelings:

> *Mais avec soin, Mégare, as-tu bien remarqué*
> *L'air, ou libre, ou contraint, dont il s'est expliqué?*
> *(ll.333-4)*

As in Racine's *Bérénice*,[564] the *confident*'s regular function of message-bearer has renewed significance. Both Sténobée and the spectator remain in some degree of doubt over the accuracy of Mégare's report. By providing only a *récit* rather than allowing us to witness the exchange between Mégare and Bellérophon, Quinault has increased the uncertainty. At the same time, his strategy focuses our attention on the heroine's reaction: we recognise that she wishes to believe that Bellérophon may indeed love herself not her sister.[565] And this is representative of Quinault's purpose throughout the tragedy. E. Gros argued that the major role is Sténobée's.[566] The statistics bear this out: she has 579 lines (40.04% of the play), compared to Prœtus's 302 (20.89%), Bellérophon's 226 (15.63%) and Philonoé's 169 (11.69%). Quinault's achievement is to show with fine precision Sténobée's doubts and illusory hopes, and then in the last two acts her thirst for revenge.[567]

Prœtus's report in III.1 of his offstage conversation with Bellérophon serves a similar end. His short account of why Bellérophon rejected the offer of Philonoé's hand fuels Sténobée's desire to believe she may still be the object of Bellérophon's love. However, the spectator, having witnessed Bellérophon's *précieux* declaration of love to Philonoé at the end of the previous act, now knows that Sténobée is in error. Yet we follow with pity and fear her elaboration

---

[563] Mégare's role here is in marked contrast to that of her counterpart, Corisbe, *confidente* to Élise in *Astrate*. Corisbe takes on additionally the role of *confidente* to Astrate in III.2, whereas Mégare is strictly Sténobée's messenger to Bellérophon.

[564] See p.113.

[565] See the analysis of W. Brooks and E. Campion in their edition of *Bellérophon*, p. XXII.

[566] *Philippe Quinault*, pp.376-7.

[567] Émelina draws our attention to Sténobée's "*succession* d'états d'âme contradictoires et non pas *coexistence*" ("Racine et Quinault", p.77). This is comparable to the development I outlined in Chapter 4 in respect of the character of Demarate in *Pausanias* (see p.106).

to Mégare (III.2) of her interpretation of Bellérophon's words to Prœtus. Precisely because of Sténobée's scene with her *confidente*, she becomes the focus of the spectators' attention. As a result, the single scene between herself and Bellérophon, which falls right in the middle of the play, is experienced primarily through Sténobée's eyes, a perspective which is sustained by her scene immediately afterwards with Mégare, in which the full force of her jealousy explodes.

The absence of a *confident* for Bellérophon in the first three acts thus initially sustains the enigma, and centres the spectator's attention on the passions of Sténobée. It is only in Act IV that Quinault allows us to dwell on how cruelly Bellérophon suffers from his isolation. In this Act there are no *confident* scenes. The other protagonists have no need of them for they provide a framework of support for each other. Bellérophon, in contrast, is brutally rebuffed when he seeks the support of Prœtus, whom he assumes still to be his *para-confident*. Prœtus and Philonoé have acted as reciprocal *para-confidents* in IV.1 and IV.3, before and after Sténobée's indictment of Bellérophon.[568] When the latter joins them, it is in the expectation that his mistress and friend will celebrate with him. Yet in an ironic reversal of the opening scenes of the play, Bellérophon's naive optimism is dashed by the rejection of first Philonoé and then Prœtus. Bellérophon must plead with them to listen to his explanations. His mistress departs before he can even begin to explain himself:

> BELLÉROPHON
> *Me quitter sans m'entendre!*
>
> PHILONOÉ
> *Et pour toute ma vie!*
> *(l. 1119)*

When Prœtus suffers Bellérophon to speak, Bellérophon appeals to their friendship and assumes at the outset that he is speaking openly to a *para-confident*, but he is then struck by Prœtus's hostility:

> *Que vois-je? ô justes Dieux! quelle fureur soudaine*
> *Dans vos yeux menaçans m'exprime tant de haine?*
> *(ll. 1139-40)*

Bellérophon's bewildered lament moves the spectator to pity him. His speech becomes not a dialogue with a *para-confident*, but a quasi-monologue, as Prœtus refuses all Bellérophon's attempts to engage his sympathy. When the act

---

[568] We might note that there is no compelling reason for bringing Philonoé and Prœtus together on stage at this juncture, and IV.1 in particular is an example of the kind of unmotivated and undramatic meeting between main protagonists which Racine avoids.

ends with Bellérophon's summary arrest, his isolation is physically highlighted as he walks off with Timante (the "capitaine des gardes"), a prisoner.[569] It is only for these brief scenes in Act IV that Quinault has used the absence of a *confident* to draw our attention to the hero's undeserved suffering.

The last act of the play restores Bellérophon's heroic status and his slaying of the monster dispels the previous impression of his passivity, but Bellérophon himself appears only in the final scene of this act, when the full facts have been revealed and the atmosphere has changed to something closer to a tragicomedy.[570] He may be the titular hero, but the play has been more about the reactions he has provoked in the other characters than his own sentiments or actions. To this extent, the strategic absence of a *confident* forced Quinault to keep his hero at a distance in order to achieve his main priority: maintaining a climate of doubt and misunderstanding throughout five acts.

(iii) THE CLIMATE OF SUSPICION: RACINE'S *MITHRIDATE* AND PIERRE CORNEILLE'S *SURÉNA*

A. Viala has demonstrated that in the 1670s the fascination of secrecy belonged equally to the domains of the novel and the theatre, and was even a subject of debate for *moralistes* such as Bouhours.[571] Of course, in the *roman précieux* and the tradition of *tragédies galantes* it was conventional for lovers to hide their passions. Molière's *précieuses ridicules* could not conceive of the idea that an *aveu* might be made in the first chapter, the first act - or the first meeting between real-life lovers! As we move into the 1670s, however, there is a noticeable increase in works, both of prose fiction and tragedy, which treat the theme of secrecy, particularly in affairs of the heart, in a more sombre manner. *La Princesse de Clèves* and *Phèdre* are generally recognised as the most powerful portrayals of this darker mood, but one might equally cite *Britannicus*, *Bajazet* or *Mithridate* in the case of Racine,[572] or *Suréna* in that of Pierre Corneille. What links these last two plays is the way in which both playwrights exploit the strategic exclusion of *confidents* as an essential constituent of the tragedy. An absence of trust, even in a secondary character, is symptomatic of the climate of secrecy and suspicion which prevails.

---

[569] Quinault resists the possibility of making Timante a *confident* for Bellérophon at this late stage. Timante is essentially a protactic character, used to deliver two *récits* in the final Act. His account (V.4) of Bellérophon's presumed death in the battle with the monster is particularly passionless and functional, especially in contrast with the *récit* which Théramène - anything but a protactic character - gives after Hippolyte's death.

[570] See J. Émelina, "Racine et Quinault", p.75.

[571] "Péril, conseil et secret d'État", pp.91-114.

[572] Compare A. Viala: "c'est à partir de *Britannicus* que le secret devient un motif dominant et central." (*ibid.*, p.103).

In *Bellérophon*, the one character without a *confident* is the hero whose
misfortunes are undeserved, and yet his role in the play is not pre-eminent. We
have seen that the strategy of his isolation is essential to the mechanism of the
play as a whole, but only briefly does the victim have the opportunity to take
centrestage, allowing us to focus on his solitude. Racine's handling of the
exclusion of the *confident* in *Mithridate* is very different. It is Mithridate
himself who is exposed without a *confident*: he is no simple victim but a
fearsome figure whose desire for cruel revenge knows almost no bounds, and
his self-willed isolation is essential to the spectator's perception of him. After
exploring the full dramatic and affective potential of the *confident* in
Andromaque, *Britannicus* and *Bérénice*, Racine showed in *Mithridate* the
effectiveness of the contrast achieved by leaving one character alone.[573] On a
smaller scale, the device had been employed in *Britannicus*, with Junie
repeatedly seeking to escape to Octavie, the ideal but unattainable *para-
confidente*. Junie, like Bellérophon, is portrayed as a victim; that she should find
no *confidente* is in accordance with the corruption of Nero's court. With
Mithridate, on the other hand, we are made to feel that if he lacks a *confident* it
is by his own choice, and it is a choice which creates a sinister atmosphere of
suspicion and fear.

It may seem surprising that I have described Mithridate as the character
without a *confident*, for according to the list of *dramatis personae* he is
accompanied by both Arbate "confident de Mithridate, et gouverneur de la
place de Nymphée" and Arcas "domestique de Mithridate", in addition to the
guards who symbolise the glory of his past military achievements. Arcas we
may quickly discount: he is a purely protactic character, brought on as a
messenger at the end of Act IV and again in Act V. He speaks a total of eight
lines, and his role is created in addition to that of Arbate only because in each
Act two successive messengers are required.[574] Arbate, however, is far more
interesting, for he becomes the *confident* of Xipharès from the opening scene
of the play. With his father presumed dead, Xipharès invites Arbate to declare
which brother he will serve:

> *Voilà tous les secrets que je voulais t'apprendre.*
> *C'est à toi de choisir quel parti tu dois prendre,*

---

[573] I shall return to the disposition of *confidents* in Racine's intervening tragedy, *Bajazet*, in
Chapter 7 since this play is dominated by the strategy of a protagonist acting as false *confident*.

[574] I find D. Moncond'huy's suggestion ("*Mithridate* ou la conquête du tombeau", 1995) that
Arcas may represent the ignoble side of Mithridate and Arbate his nobler side ingenious, but I
think he reads too great a moral significance into a very minor role. I prefer his initial
hypothesis that Racine used two secondary characters in successive scenes to heighten the drama
of the dénouement.

> *Qui des deux te paraît plus digne de ta foi,*
> *L'esclave des Romains, ou le fils de ton roi.*
>   *(ll.107-110)*

Arbate's choice to serve Xipharès is made in good faith, but on Mithridate's return it means that his loyalty to the prince puts him in a false position. I can think of no other tragedy in which a *confident* effectively becomes a double agent at the outset.[575] Thereafter Arbate is, as it were, the reverse of Narcisse; motivated by moral considerations, he secretly serves Xipharès, while outwardly retaining his position within Mithridate's suite. On two occasions Arbate deceives the king, to the advantage of Xipharès. Subjected to a ruthless inquisition about the state of affairs in Mithridate's absence, he denies that Xipharès loves Monime (ll.497-500), which is a blatant lie since Xipharès had confessed his passions to Arbate in I.1. In Act IV he is reported to have acted independently to save Xipharès, by warning him of what Mithridate knew:

> *Un mot même d'Arbate a confirmé ma crainte;*
> *Il a su m'aborder, et les larmes aux yeux:*
> *"On sait tout, m'a-t-il dit, sauvez-vous de ces lieux."*
>   *(ll.1196-8)*

That Xipharès should repeat Arbate's very words to Monime indicates the importance of the *confident*'s role, and the reference to Arbate's tears denotes his close bond with the prince.

However, it is not only the fact that Arbate serves Xipharès which leads me to argue that he is not Mithridate's *confident* other than in name. We have seen a number of other plays in which *confidents* take on a double role without relinquishing their original function.[576] Rather, Mithridate himself excludes Arbate from the role of *confident*, for he chooses to take no-one into his confidence. A character renowned, according to Racine in his 1676 Preface, for "sa finesse, sa dissimulation",[577] he does not trust his subordinates any more than his sons or mistress. There is only one scene between Mithridate and Arbate which comes close to a traditional *confident* scene: on his return, Mithridate dismisses his sons and speaks to Arbate alone (II.3). The fact that he delivers the récit of his last campaign to the "gouverneur de la place de Nymphée" is a device to complete the exposition. He could hardly have given this récit to Xipharès and Pharnace, whom he has just dismissed in peremptory

---

[575] In Racine's *Iphigénie*, for example, Arcas's betrayal of Agamemnon occurs in the middle of the play (III.5). In *Bajazet*, in contrast, Atalide has played the false *confidente* to Roxane before the play starts (see p.191).

[576] E.g. *Rodogune* (see p.40).

[577] Racine, *Théâtre complet*, p.447.

fashion, rebuking them for their presence in the palace; likewise, it would be
invraisemblable for Monime to listen to such a speech. However, Arbate is not
called upon to respond to the *récit*, and there is no attempt to move the listener
as, say, in Andromaque's *récit* to Céphise of the sack of Troy.[578] It is only when
Mithridate declares his continuing passion for Monime and his hostility towards
his sons that we witness something along the familiar lines of a *confident* scene.
Yet once Mithridate has (economically) made clear his feelings towards each of
the three, the dynamics of the scene change abruptly. Instead of the
conventional pattern of the protagonist exposing his viewpoint and the
confident responding, the scene turns into an inquisition in which Mithridate
fires a series of questions at Arbate.[579] It is true that these questions implicitly
reveal much about Mithridate's state of mind, but he is essentially seeking
information rather than consciously revealing it. Like Paulin in *Bérénice*,
Arbate is reluctant to answer, and again Racine exploits the tension of the
confident's utterance by Mithridate's repeated imperative "Parle".[580] As we
have seen, Arbate's refusal to betray Xipharès leads him to tell a lie, which
signals the disintegration of the normal *confident*/master relationship.
Mithridate for his part continues to question Arbate with the same hostile
mistrust with which he addresses other protagonists.

Our impression of Mithridate's strained relationship with his *confident* is all
the more striking in that this scene follows shortly after the first scene between
Monime and Phœdime (II.1). The spectator recognises their relationship as
intimate and open; Monime readily confesses her feelings, and Phœdime
understands even unspoken signs:

> *Malheureuse! comment paraîtrai-je à sa vue,*
> *Son diadème au front, et dans le fond du cœur,*
> *Phœdime .... Tu m'entends, et tu vois ma rougeur.*
> *(ll.392-4)*

A further contrast lies in the balance between interrogation and response. It is
Phœdime, another example of the active Racinian *confidente*, who takes the
initiative as the second Act opens, urging her mistress to prepare to meet
Mithridate. Her first lines contain a series of interrogatives:[581]

> *Quoi? vous êtes ici quand Mithridate arrive,*
> *Quand, pour le recevoir, chacun court sur la rive?*

---

[578] See p.1.

[579] M. Hawcroft examines the nature of inquisitional rhetoric in *Mithridate* with particular
reference to III.5 (*Word as Action*, pp.134-41). He concludes that Mithridate is the "most
effective of <Racine's> inquiring orators" (p.136).

[580] Lines 479 and 503. H. Phillips proposes that speech lies at the root of the conflict in
Mithridate, and provides a persuasive account of this thesis in *Mithridate* (Grant and Cutler
Critical Guides to French Texts, 1990), Chapter 3.

[581] Compare the opening speech of Albine in *Britannicus*.

> *Que faites-vous, Madame? et quel ressouvenir*
> *Tout à coup vous arrête, et vous fait revenir?*
>   *(ll.375-8)*

When Monime reveals her love for Xipharès, Phœdime continues to prompt the disclosure by more questions.[582] This is the reverse of the exchange between Mithridate and Arbate, in which the king asks twelve questions, but Arbate only one. Hereafter, Monime has two further long *confident* scenes with Phœdime, opening Acts IV and V. These scenes are crucial in evoking the spectators' pity for the heroine. Mithridate, however, has no more confidential scenes alone with Arbate.[583]

It is essential to the portrayal of Mithridate's character that he should be shown alone, without a *confident*. Even when he speaks to Monime immediately after interrogating Arbate, he takes care to dismiss his *confident*:

> *Arbate, c'est assez: qu'on me laisse avec elle.*
>   *(l.527)*

There are a number of scenes in Acts III and IV in which one might expect the king to be accompanied by a silent *confident*: his meeting with his sons (III.1), his subsequent interviews with Monime (III.5, IV.4). Yet in none of these is Arbate present. This has two effects. In these scenes themselves, we perceive Mithridate as a solitary and particularly menacing figure; in their aftermath, Mithridate has no witness of the preceding scene to whom he may open his heart. And this is precisely the point: Mithridate chooses not to open his heart or mind to any other character, for he is the master of deception. In his study of Racine's "Machiavellian" monarchs, A. Viala reminds us that Machiavelli observed that the prince "doit interroger sur chaque chose <mais> décider ensuite tout seul". For Viala, this leads to a "double logique du secret, la découverte du secret des autres et la préservation de ses propres secrets".[584] Viala applies his schema to Racine's main protagonists, but I would suggest that in *Mithridate* the second requirement is extended to the protagonist's relationship with his *confident*, traditionally the repository of the best kept secrets. This is not the world of Tacitus in which a monarch needs to fear betrayal at every step by unfaithful courtiers, but Mithridate is a man tormented by suspicions in both the political and personal domain. To have given him a *confident* in Arbate but then for the king not to have confided in him is a masterly way of confirming Mithridate's character.

---

[582] She asks six more questions in the dialogue between lines 390-408.

[583] Arbate is alone with Mithridate in IV.6 to deliver a *récit* of events offstage, but there is no confidential exchange. Even Mithridate's final exclamation against his sons (ll.1442-3) is an imprecation addressed directly to them, not a comment to Arbate.

[584] "Péril, conseil et secret d'État", p.102.

Is there not a price to pay for the absence of the *confident* at least as far as the audience's engagement with Mithridate is concerned? It is true that Pharnace also has no *confident*, but he is something of a functional character, disappearing after Act III, and never gaining the audience's sympathy. Some critics have argued that *Mithridate* is a difficult, even flawed, play because our interest and sympathies are divided between Xipharès/Monime and Mithridate.[585] What Racine does instead is to make full use of an alternative strategy: the monologue. At a time when monologues were used very sparingly if at all by other dramatists, he introduces three in *Mithridate* - all spoken by the titular hero. It is true that he had made significant use of monologues in *Bajazet*,[586] but what is strikingly different about *Mithridate* is that in each case the monologue falls where we might have expected a *confident* scene: in III.4 after Xipharès has failed to allay Mithridate's suspicions; in III.6 after he has tested Monime; and in IV.5 after Monime's *grande scène* in which she has defended herself so passionately. Furthermore, in the first of these, Mithridate's speech is structured by devices which might equally have belonged to an exchange with a *confident*. At the outset he speaks, as it were, in two voices, taking both his role and that of an interlocutor:

> *Je ne le <Xipharès> croirai point? Vain espoir qui me flatte!*
> *Tu ne le crois que trop, malheureux Mithridate!*
> *(ll.1007-8)*

He questions what he has heard (l.1009-10); offers alternative readings of the situation (ll.1016ff); persuades himself to reflect further (ll.1021-2). Why in this case has Racine resorted to the monologue, a form which ran the charge of *invraisemblance*?[587] It could be argued that Mithridate's decision to test Monime is too unheroic to be voiced to any other character, but additionally Racine's use of the monologue conveys the desperate isolation in which Mithridate has placed himself. When he asks:

> *... Mais par où commencer?*
> *Qui m'en éclaircira? quels témoins? quel indice?*
> *(ll.1022-3)*

he reveals that he can literally trust no-one.

The second monologue, at the end of Act III, is short (ll.1117-1126), and serves to confirm that as a result of what he has learned from Monime Mithridate has resolved to take revenge on Xipharès. It is dramatically

---

[585] See for example M. O'Regan, *The Mannerist Aesthetic. A Study of Racine's Mithridate,* (1980) pp.17-18.

[586] See p.193.

[587] There is one awkward moment in this monologue (almost akin to a comic aside?), where Mithridate answers his own desperate search for proof with the line: "Le ciel en ce moment m'inspire un artifice." (l.1024).

important, but not so clearly an alternative to a *confident* scene. His last monologue, however, is patently of a kind with that in III.4.[588] In each case he could have confided in Arbate, but Racine has shown him choosing isolation. In the monologues of Act III, though angered and anxious he was in control, deciding the next stage in the gameplan. In Act IV, Monime has refused to acquiesce to his will, and Mithridate is reduced - for the first time in the play - to a genuine state of indecision. In this, the scene might be seen as a parallel to Titus's monologue in IV.4 of *Bérénice*. But whereas Titus is arriving at a conclusion as Bérénice bursts in upon him, Mithridate, astonishingly, ends the scene no more decided than at the start. His final line:

> De ce trouble fatal par où dois-je sortir?
> (l.1421)

is a reflection of his state of mind, not a sign of how the play will move on. H. Phillips remarks that one of the weaknesses of Act IV is that it arrives at a stasis as far as the relations between Mithridate, Monime and Xipharès are concerned.[589] Technically I think he is right, but perhaps the monologue of IV.5 achieved exactly the balance between fear and *le pathétique* which its original audiences so appreciated. It is Arbate who breaks the stasis in IV.6 with the news that the troops, led by Pharnace, have revolted. Thus it is the reappearance of a *confident* who was not present to hear the protagonist voice his sufferings which finally advances the plot.

What makes *Mithridate* such an interesting play from our point of view is that it is not simply a play in which one character does not have a *confident*, but rather a play in which this character has a *confident* in theory, but relegates him to the sidelines. When we look at the tragedy in this light, our attention is drawn to the opportunities Racine had to introduce conventional *confident* scenes between Mithridate and Arbate, and the dramatic effect he achieves by denying our expectations. I would suggest that only a dramatist who had worked so closely on the full integration of the *confident* in his earlier plays could have perceived what he would achieve by the strategic exclusion here.

*   *   *

---

[588] Mithridate's speech in IV.5 has often been compared to Auguste's famous monologue in *Cinna* (IV.2). However Corneille structured his fourth act so that Livie appears (for the first time in the play) in the following scene, IV.3. She provides Auguste with moral support and good counsel, tempering the desperate sense of isolation he had just expressed in his monologue.

[589] *Mithridate*, p.24.

Pierre Corneille's last tragedy has some similarities with *Mithridate*, which preceded it by less than two years.[590] In particular, *Suréna* is another play in which we become aware that there is a critical absence of *confident* scenes at points where we would conventionally expect them. The main protagonists of *Suréna* are five in number, but Corneille uses only two *confidents*, and their role is circumscribed.[591] Since *Suréna* was staged at the Hôtel de Bourgogne, we cannot ascribe this economy to the limited resources of the troupe, as we did with *Pulchérie* before it.[592] Yet neither can we say that Corneille was seeking to eliminate the role of secondary characters altogether. The play opens with a long expository scene between Eurydice (a character invented by the playwright) and her *confidente*, in familiar Cornelian style.[593] Equally, Orode has a scene with a *confident*, his lieutenant Sillace, when he first appears in III.1.[594] Had Corneille been intent on minimising the role of *confidents*, the king might have disclosed his thoughts to Pacorus, his son, but instead Corneille affords the monarch and his Machiavellian adviser a substantial debate over what Sillace terms "la saine Politique" (line 728). If the roles of Ormène and Sillace show that Corneille was still convinced of the utility of some *confidents*, *Suréna* nonetheless leaves three main characters without any.

Like *Mithridate*, *Suréna* is dominated by a climate of suspicion, and it is important that there should be no proliferation of scenes with *confidents* which might provide moments of reprieve. A number of critics have pointed out the uncharacteristic economy with which Corneille has orchestrated the play: there are no surprising reversals in Acts I-IV; the only *coup de théâtre* is reserved for the final scene of the play; and the number of scenes is reduced to a mere 18.[595] The latter point draws our attention to the care with which Corneille has placed his *confident* scenes: one at the start of each of Acts I, III, IV (together with Ormène bringing the news of Suréna's death in the final scene of the play). In other words, once these acts have been initiated, they are carried forward only by exchanges between main protagonists. Corneille's dramaturgical control is further highlighted when we realise that each Act apart from Act IV has one

---

[590] *Suréna* is assumed to have been staged in December 1674: see J. Sanchez's introduction to his edition, *Suréna général des Parthes* (1970), pp. 31-33.

[591] Ormène speaks a total of 42 lines (2.42% of the play), Sillace only 26 lines (1.5%). Thus together the *confidents* account for no more than 3.92% of the discourse.

[592] See p.78.

[593] Corneille does not seek to give Ormène an active role on a par with Albine or Phœdime. She speaks only 19 of the 148 lines in the first scene, and Eurydice's desire to expound upon her thoughts and feelings gives the exchange its momentum with minimal contributions from Ormène.

[594] Sillace is a historical character, mentioned in Plutarch's *Life of Crassus*, a fact which lends justification to the political dimension of his role.

[595] See ed. J. Sanchez, *Suréna*, pp.61-2. Sanchez remarks briefly (here and p.82) upon the surprising economy of the *confidents'* roles.

character present throughout, whose perspective governs the act.[596] Thus we move successively from Eurydice (Act I) to Pacorus (Act II) to Orode (Act III) to Eurydice/Suréna (Act IV) and back to Eurydice (Act V).

In the Acts which are governed by Eurydice, the relative absence of *confidents* is less apparent, for several reasons. Eurydice herself can speak with Ormène, but in addition her relationship with Suréna is completely open. The lovers have nothing to hide from each other. There is thus no call for either Eurydice or Suréna to have recourse to a *confident* after their meetings in I.3 or V.2, for there are no concealed thoughts or intentions to be revealed. Furthermore, Eurydice has deliberately sought to make Suréna's sister, Palmis (another character invented by Corneille), her *para-confidente*, a strategy which she justifies to Ormène in I.1:

> N'osant voir Suréna qui règne en ma pensée
> Et qui me croit peut-être une âme intéressée,
> Tu vois quelle amitié j'ai faite avec sa sœur:
> Je crois le voir en elle, et c'est quelque douceur.
> (ll.125-8)

In the first scene between the two heroines (I.2), this permits a reciprocal exchange of confidences. The characteristically Cornelian symmetry is underlined by the repetition of the key terms *savoir* and *secret*,[597] as first Eurydice reveals her love for Suréna:

> EURYDICE
> Savez-vous mon secret?
>
> PALMIS
> Je sais celui d'un frère.
>
> EURYDICE
> Vous savez donc le mien. Fait-il ce qu'il doit faire?
> (ll.177-8)

and then Palmis hers for Pacorus:

> PALMIS
> Je sais votre secret, sachez aussi le mien.
> (l.200)

What seems at first simply another convenient use of *para-confidentes* to ensure two strands of the exposition (like that in *Pulchérie*)[598] is in fact an essential foundation of the plot. Because Palmis shares Eurydice's and Suréna's secret,

---

[596] It is notable that while Corneille respects the dramaturgical convention of the *liaison des scènes*, he makes little effort to ensure verisimilitude in the sucessive entrances of his characters. On a number of occasions, the character about to exit simply announces the simultaneous arrival of the next character (I.2/3, II.2/3, IV.2/3, IV.3/4).

[597] *Secret* becomes a leitmotif, used 16 times throughout the play.

[598] See p.79.

she possesses information which others desire. Her role as a trusted friend and sister, the ideal (para)-*confidente*, draws her ineluctably into the circle of suspicion.

By the end of Act I, the audience are fully apprised of the passions of Suréna, Eurydice and Palmis. In what follows we concentrate upon the uninformed characters' attempts to establish hidden truths. It is now that Corneille exploits the strategic absence of other *confidents*. Act II revolves around Pacorus, the only protagonist who has neither *confident* nor *para-confident*. Tellingly, Corneille has no exchanges between Pacorus and his father Orode. Although their respective personal and political interests are intertwined, Pacorus is never shown on stage with the one character who would have lent him moral support. The spectator soon perceives that Pacorus is governed by a cruel streak of jealousy and an obsessive desire to know the truth, like Racine's Mithridate. However as far as the absence of a *confident* is concerned, there is a crucial difference: Mithridate could have confided in Arbate, but chose not to; Pacorus is isolated against his will. He has no servant as a *confident*, but what he most desires is that one of Suréna or Eurydice or Palmis should become his *para-confident*. We can see him as a character vainly in search of a *confident*.

Critics have often drawn attention to the inquisitional tone of Acts II and III, as Pacorus and then Orode subject different protagonists in turn to their increasingly menacing demands to know the truth. What has not been discussed is how the absence of *confidents* and, in addition, the dangerous status of *para-confidents* contribute to the menacing atmosphere. Pacorus's exchange with Suréna in II.1 swiftly comes to resemble a scene in which a young hero confesses his doubts and asks his *confident* for enlightenment:

> *Cette Princesse donc, si belle, si parfaite,*
> *Je crains qu'elle n'ait pas ce que plus je souhaite,*
> *Qu'elle manque d'amour, ou plutôt, que ses vœux*
> *N'aillent pas tout à fait du côté que je veux.*
> *Vous qui l'avez tant vue, et qu'un devoir fidèle*
> *A tenu si longtemps près de son père et d'elle,*
> *Ne me déguisez point ce que dans cette cour*
> *Sur de pareils soupçons vous auriez eu de jour.*
> (*ll.373-80*)

Pacorus looks to Suréna to reassure him and to receive his confidences - unaware of the irony that he is addressing his rival. However the spectator recognises the trap in which Suréna is ensnared. The circumstances force him to adopt a less than heroic posture; he cannot avoid the duplicity of the role which Pacorus has assigned him. After a rather stilted attempt to avoid the task by pleading his lack of knowledge, he meets Pacorus's blunter demands with a *propos équivoque* (ll.401-6) quite worthy of Timocrate, and then several platitudinous reassurances which could have come out of the breviary of the archetypal *confident*![599] He can only dampen the fire of Pacorus's interrogations by prevarications, and the spectator is made to sense his relief when Eurydice's entrance provides the excuse for him to depart.

Having dismissed Suréna at the end of II.1, Pacorus is again isolated after the testing scene with Eurydice which follows. This is the point at which conventionally we would expect the anxious hero to unburden himself to his *confident*. However, Pacorus is not given the opportunity to take centrestage in this fashion; nor is he allowed a monologue. Despite the pathos of his situation, he does not win the spectators' pity because he must always appear with other, hostile protagonists: in other words, at his worst. Pacorus's meeting with Palmis (II.3) shows him at his most unheroic: threatening, yet impotent. Again, his wish is to secure himself a *confident*, and this time he is bitterly aware of his failure. Like Racine's Mithridate, he resorts to the unsavoury tactics of deception and blackmail. Palmis, in contrast, wins our respect and pity.[600] Pacorus's ironic dismissal of her contains just a hint of what might have furnished another dimension of the tragedy:

> *...Adieu, Madame.*
> *Je vous fais trop jouir des troubles de mon âme.*
> *(ll.689-90)*

Throughout the Act Pacorus has indeed exposed his sufferings, but neither Suréna, nor Eurydice nor Palmis has been willing to become the *confident* he sought, and he has been denied this resource to engage the audience's pity.

From Act III onwards, the role of the *confident*, real or projected, becomes central, and the recurrence of the terms *confident*, *confidence* and *confiance* underscores the theme. Orode, unlike Pacorus, does not seek a *confident* for himself, for he is preoccupied by politics not sexual passions.[601] Perhaps one reason why the king appears such a sinister figure is that we never see the face of the man behind the mask of the ruler. However, Orode is shown to be obsessed by the confidential relationships which exist between other characters, and the drama depends on both Suréna's and Palmis's attempts to resist his

---

[599] Lines 413-6 and 421-4. The reassuring use of the future tense in the last speech ("Tout cessera... Vous verrez ces chagrins") reads like a parody of the language of *confidents*.

[600] Although even she is not a model of absolute virtue, for she hints that were Pacorus to marry her, she might betray Eurydice's confidence (ll.653-8).

[601] See S. Doubrovsky's discussion of the *dédoublement* of Pacorus and Orode, and the distinction between them: *Corneille et la dialectique du héros*, pp.451-3.

pressure to make them break Eurydice's confidence. The focus thus shifts from
the *confident* Pacorus is denied to the web of *confidence* which protects
Eurydice. Mistrustful from the outset of his overpowerful subject, Orode's
suspicions of Suréna are heightened towards the end of their interview in III.2
when Suréna implies that he knows Eurydice's private thoughts:

> SURÉNA
> *Et si je puis vous dire avec quels sentiments*
> *Elle attend à demain l'effet de vos serments,*
> *Elle aime ailleurs.*
>
> ORODE
> *Et qui?*
>
> SURÉNA
> *C'est ce qu'elle aime à taire.*
> *(ll.931-3)*

By defining himself as the *confident* of Eurydice, Suréna awakens the king's
darkest suspicions. Together with his inference some twenty lines later that he
too has a secret passion which he cannot reveal, he has provided the information
which will condemn the lovers. Orode may accept for the present that neither
Suréna nor Palmis will break their silence, but in the following Act, Pacorus
displays none of the restraint of his father.

In the prince's exchanges first with Eurydice and then with Suréna (IV.2-3),
the status of the *confident* becomes explicitly linked to the impending
tragedy.[602] As the palace is surrounded by guards and the tension rises, Pacorus
threatens not Eurydice's unknown lover, but the person who holds her secret:

> *Si je n'en sais l'objet, j'en sais le confident.*
> *Il est le plus coupable, un amant peut se taire,*
> *Mais d'un sujet au Roy, c'est crime qu'un mystère.*
> *(ll.1172-4)*

His argument is rational: to withold a secret from the ruler is a criminal offence.
Yet his attack is motivated by the suspicion that Suréna may be more than just
the *confident*, a suspicion strengthened as Eurydice betrays her concern:

> *Mais ce trouble, Madame, et cette émotion*
> *N'ont-ils rien de plus fort que la compassion?*
> ....
> *Un si cher confident ne fait-il point douter*
> *De l'amant, ou de lui, qui les peut exciter?*
> *(ll.1183-88)*

Eurydice does not give Pacorus the satisfaction of either confirming or denying
his suspicions. Instead she takes pleasure in threatening him in turn, reminding

---

[602] The word *confident* is used 5 times in IV.2 and *confidence* 3 times.

him that he cannot control her love. While we both admire her and fear for her, we may also now feel some degree of pity for Pacorus in his isolation. Again he stands alone: denied the love of Eurydice, mistrusted, and without even a personal *confident* to whom he might confess his thoughts at the end of this tumultuous scene. There is much irony in Eurydice's parting shot as she leaves Pacorus with Suréna:

> *Je vous laisse achever avec mon confident.*
> *(l.1268)*

She utters the line to taunt Pacorus over her ambiguous relationship with Suréna, but the prince's words in the following scene reminds us that Suréna had also been Pacorus's trusted *para-confident*:

> *Et j'attendais de vous plus de sincérité,*
> *Moi qui mettais en vous ma confiance entière,*
> *Et ne voulais souffrir aucune autre lumière.*
> *(ll.1272-4)*

Unlike the earlier scene between Pacorus and Suréna (II.1), the last scene of Act IV does not emulate a *confident* scene; Suréna is no longer playing any role. But what should we make of Pacorus's final advice to Suréna to obey the king, prefaced by a declaration of friendship:

> *Recevez cet avis d'une amitié fidèle.*
> *(l.1373)*

Is Pacorus speaking honestly or with irony? On one level, it does not matter, for Suréna will disregard the advice and thus seal his fate. Yet as spectators we might wish to know whether Pacorus's last words in the play were sincere or cynical. Without a *confident* scene for Pacorus at the close of Act IV, we have no means of deciding, and will probably judge him the worse, sharing Suréna's pessimistic assessment (ll.1650-54) that he is condemned because of the threat he poses to the crown, irrespective of his love for Eurydice.

A similar enigma applies, *a fortiori*, in respect of the final appearance of Orode. As the pressure of the impending dénouement mounts, Corneille does not temporise by allowing Orode another scene with Sillace to open Act V. From III.1 we were aware both that Orode had contemplated the possibility of Suréna's death and that he was still appalled at the moral consequences of taking such a step.[603] We have no means of knowing to what extent the king's position has shifted before his interview with Eurydice in V.1. They fence with such verbal dexterity that it is impossible to extrapolate from their barbed

---

[603] Lines 737-44.

exchanges the king's true intentions.[604] Is he still offering an honourable compromise to save both Eurydice and Suréna? Or is he only suffering "L'impétuosité de cette grandeur d'âme;/ Cette noble fierté que rien ne peut dompter" (ll.1466-7) in the belief that Eurydice will condemn herself and Suréna unequivocally? Orode's final words give nothing away:

> Nous ferons voir, Madame, en cette extrémité
> Comme il faut obéir à la nécessité.
> (ll.1503-4)

When Eurydice is left alone with Suréna, the following scene resolves what may have been ambiguous in her responses to Orode. She explains the strategy she adopted with Orode as openly to her lover as she might have done to her confidente:

> Et l'unique bonheur que j'y puis espérer
> C'est de toujours promettre, et toujours différer.
> (ll.1559-60)

Of Orode's private thoughts, however, we know nothing, and, exceptionally, the dénouement deliberately maintains the obfuscation. Suréna's death is delivered "d'une main inconnue" (l.1714). The spectator may presume that this is the act of a king who declared in V.1:

> Le soupçon m'est plus doux que la vérité sûre,
> L'obscurité m'en plaît, et j'aime à n'écouter
> Que ce qui laisse encor liberté d'en douter.
> (ll.1382-4)

But not even Thomas Corneille, the master of dramas of suspense, had dared to close a tragedy on an unsolved crime. It is because Pacorus never has a scene with a confident, and Orode none after III.1, that their part in the dénouement can remain so tantalisingly unconfirmed.

Many Cornelian scholars have seen the unheroic ending of Suréna as indicative of Corneille's disillusionment with the politics of power.[605] Set within the context of tragedies of the early 1670s, we may also see it is as a penetrating exploration of the climate of suspicion in which to be a confident is to endanger one's life, and to be without a confident, like Pacorus, is to be condemned to mistrust all other protagonists. The playwright whose unimaginative use of confidentes in Sophonisbe had sparked the Querelle du confident shows in his final play a uniquely controlled understanding of the dramatic value of the role. We may have credited Racine with the most dynamic reinterpretation of

---

[604] Compare S. Doubrovsky's observation that throughout the play characters avoid making definite statements: "Suréna est, par excellence, la pièce du flou." (Corneille et la dialectique du héros, p.456.)

[605] M. Prigent, Le Héros et l'état, pp.495-8; (ed.) J. Sanchez, Suréna, pp.86-7; A. Stegmann, L'Héroïsme cornélien, p.650.

confidential strategies from *Andromaque* onwards, but Corneille must take the credit for conceiving how the theme of *confidence* could sustain a whole tragedy.

I have suggested at various points in this chapter that there are some strong resemblances between *Mithridate* and *Suréna* in tone, themes and dramaturgy. Recent criticism has been anxious to identify "Racinian" qualities in Corneille's last play, yet for the original audiences it seems that *Suréna* was viewed as a poor relation of *Le Cid* or *Cinna*. Why should *Mithridate* have won such public acclaim when *Suréna* patently failed to find favour? Should this lead us to ask whether *Suréna* is in some ways closer to tragedies like *Bellérophon*? I would suggest that one answer lies in the fact that the strategy of excluding *confidents* raises obstacles in all these three plays which *Mithridate* alone overcomes. Quinault and Corneille keep doubt and mystery at the centre of their tragedies; as a result, the characters denied *confidents* (Bellérophon, Pacorus, and - in Act V - Orode) cannot engage the audience's sympathy. Racine adopted quite a different perspective: much of *Mithridate* is focused precisely on the isolation of the character without a *confident*. It is the unfashionable recourse to the form of the monologue which achieves this. By balancing the vision of the king as victim and tyrant Racine evokes our pity in the same way as the sensitive use of a *confident* might have done. I suspect that *Bellérophon* and *Suréna* retain an intellectual fascination for the modern reader attracted by problems of hermeneutics, whereas the evocation of passions and solitude in *Mithridate* provided the less cerebral, more moving theatrical experience, favoured by Louis XIV and his court.

CHAPTER SEVEN

CROSSING BOUNDARIES: PROTAGONISTS ACTING AS *CONFIDENT(E)S*

Racine was ironically dismissive of heroic novels in several of his prefaces. As early as his first Préface to *Alexandre* (1666), he inveighed against:

> *ceux qui blâment Alexandre de rétablir Porus en présence de Cléofile. C'est assez pour moi que ce qui passe pour une faute auprès de ces esprits qui n'ont lu l'histoire que dans les romans ... a reçu des louanges de ceux qui, étant eux-mêmes de grands héros, ont droit de juger de la vertu de leurs pareils.*[606]

Similarly, in the first preface to *Andromaque* (1668) he rose to the defence of Pyrrhus with the rejoinder:

> *Mais que faire? Pyrrhus n'avait pas lu tous nos romans... et tous les héros ne sont pas faits pour être des Céladons.*[607]

Yet there is no doubt that he and his audiences were more familiar than they might have cared to admit with the intrigues of Céladon, Clélie and their ilk. Authors of tragicomedies enjoyed relative freedom to borrow incidents and characters from both prose fiction and history; those who wrote tragedies were far more careful to conceal any debts to the former source. The names of some invented characters in tragedies may suggest that they had their predecessors in novels,[608] but the romanesque world of fast-moving, improbable adventures, sustained by coincidences and intricate deceptions, was scarcely deemed compatible with the serious purpose of tragedy.[609] In the novels of the 1640-60s, heroes and heroines could be expected to take on disguises and false identities and to play a succession of roles. Gender reversals, changes in social status raised the pulse rather than the eyebrows of those accustomed to such works. Tragicomedies, as G. Forestier has shown, also accommodated such

---

[606] *Théâtre complet*, pp.71-72.

[607] *Théâtre complet.*, p.130.

[608] For example, Axiane in Racine's *Alexandre*. See R. Knight, *Racine et la Grèce*, p.264.

[609] Recent criticism has emphasised the complex and fruitful (if unacknowledged) interchanges between romance and neo-classical tragedies. See for example T. Cave's discussion of *Timocrate* (*Recognitions*, pp.292-95).

extravagant devices with ease.[610] Thomas Corneille's Timocrate could conceal his royal birth when he appeared as Cléomène, and Bérénice, the heroine of Magnon's *Tite*, disguised herself as the mysterious prince Cléobule. In Chapter 6, I suggested that from the 1660s onwards authors of tragedies concentrated on psychological rather than physical manifestations of disguise and deception, yet there is one situation which remains common to novels and tragedies: the protagonist who plays the role of false *confident* to another protagonist. This device, which has its roots in novels and tragicomedies, and is also used in comedies,[611] is deployed by Racine in three tragedies, *Bérénice*, *Bajazet* and *Iphigénie*, and he is imitated in turn by both Thomas Corneille in his *Ariane* (1672) and Pradon in his *Phèdre et Hippolyte* (1677).

How can we account for the interest of the protagonist acting as a false *confident* in the tragedies of the 1670s? First, it provided a much needed variation on the eternal love triangle. To show one of the two rivals for the affections of a third protagonist as the trusted but false *confident(e)* of the other injected fresh suspense and irony. According to the playwright's handling of the device, it might in addition allow the exploration of diverse emotional responses: heroic self-abnegation, guilt, or the throes of furious jealousy upon the discovery of betrayal. Secondly it was a strategy which lent itself ideally to dramatic exploitation, for it required the protagonist acting as *confident* to take on a role. For the audience, much of the pleasure derives from observing how well this role is performed, and whether there are any fatal slips in the performance. Protagonists acting out roles are, of course, commonplace in the comic tradition, but it required a bold hand to transpose them to the domain of tragedy without compromising the dignity of the tragic emotions.

We may also see this strategy as another stage in the metamorphosis of the *confident*, or rather as a final confirmation of the new-found dramatic value of the role. At its most interesting, it requires the protagonist to cross the boundary and take on the identity of a *confident*: not simply as a neutral *para-confident*, but as a false *confident* whose performance may decide the whole course of the tragedy. We have caught a glimpse of the pressure such a mechanism exerts in Corneille's *Suréna*.[612] Here it is only in Act IV that the issue of the protagonist acting as *confident* is articulated, as we witness both Pacorus's jealous obsession with the identity of Eurydice's *confident*, and Suréna briefly adopting the role of *confident* to Pacorus in order to allay the latter's suspicions. In the tragedies which we shall consider in this chapter, the protagonist acting as false *confident*

---

[610] See *Esthétique de l'identité*, pp.417-76.

[611] A celebrated example being Arnolphe's relationship with Horace in *L'École des Femmes*.

[612] In *Cinna* Maxime had briefly used his friendship with Cinna to receive his confidences (III.2). However, in this earlier play Corneille did not explore any further the dramatic possibilities of the *faux confident* as rival.

lies at the heart of the plays. In this, unlike *Suréna*, they draw heavily on tragicomic and romanesque traditions.

(i) THE MODEL OF TRAGI-COMEDIES: MAGNON'S *TITE*

If we return briefly to Magnon's *Tite*,[613] we find a prime example of a practised author of tragicomedies structuring the first two Acts of his work around the ironies afforded by the heroine's role as a false *confidente*. An analysis of ways in which Magnon exploits the device will highlight some of the strategies which writers of tragedies were soon also to develop. We have seen in Chapter 6 that in the opening scene with her *confidente*, Bérénice initiated the spectators into the secret of her disguise, The references to her performance as Cléobule alert us to the dramatic interest of her role-playing, and her *confidente* suggests that Titus's failure to see through her disguise has been due in part to her skilled performance:

> *Joignez à ces raisons les travaux d'un voyage,*
> *Un changement d'habit, et de cheveux, et d'âge,*
> *Mesme un desguisement d'actions et de voix ...*
> *(ll.85-87)*

Such is her success, indeed, that both Tite and her rival, Mucie, choose to confide in her, a fact which Magnon highlights by Bérénice/Cléobule's successive scenes with Mucie and Tite in I.2-3. Mucie appeals to Cléobule with the words:

> *Mon secret confident, ne me déguisez rien.*
> *(l.131)*

and this is echoed by Tite's exclamation in the following scene:

> *Arreste, Cléobule.*
> *Ah! de ma passion unique confident ...*
> *(ll.231-2)*

It is the ironies of the situation which Magnon delights in exploiting in Act I, even allowing Cléobule to tell Mucie that were "he" Bérénice "he" would come to Tite's court in disguise (ll.201-4)! But how does Bérénice's role as disguised *confident* contribute to the development of the play? And what responses are evoked in the audience?

With Mucie, in Act I Bérénice exploits her disguise unmercifully in order to learn the true thoughts and feelings of her ambitious rival. The spectators enjoy their complicity with Bérénice, and need feel no real sympathy for a deceived character who has already declared:

> *L'amour est toujours beau pour les ames communes,*

---

[613] See p.150.

> *Mais pour moy ces ardeurs sont tousjours importunes;*
> *La seule ambition emporte mes désirs,*
> *Et fournit de soy-mesme à d'éternels plaisirs.*[614]
> *(ll.177-80)*

With Tite, on the other hand, Bérénice takes a secret delight in prompting him to recall his love for his absent mistress.[615] The scene is delicately touching, our pleasure threatened only when Tite announces at the end his intention of marrying "Cléobule" to Mucie. Technically the relationship between the Emperor Tite and Cléobule is such that Bérénice's disguise draws on what Forestier identifies as the "approche servile", popular in tragicomedies earlier in the period, in which the heroine would disguise herself as a page in the household of the hero.[616] However, as Forestier is the first to recognise, Magnon handles the strategy in such a way that he does not allow Bérénice's position to detract from her tragic dignity.[617]

From Act II the tone of *Tite* changes significantly, for it now appears that Tite will fulfil his promise to marry Mucie, and the perils facing Bérénice inspire pity and fear in the audience. Thus from resembling a *comédie galante* the play turns into a (quasi-)historical tragedy, until, in true tragicomic fashion, the catastrophe is averted at the very end of Act V. Bérénice's role as a disguised/ false *confidente* remains central to Act II, and I would agree with H. Bell that this act probably suggested to Racine some of the directions in which he developed the strategy in his *Bérénice*.[618] Magnon repeats the structure of Act I in that Bérénice/Cléobule again has successive scenes with Mucie and Tite (II.3-4). That with Tite is the less interesting here, since Magnon does not focus on the role of the false *confident*. Bérénice's scene with Mucie, however, introduces a major development in the device of the false *confidente*, for the report Bérénice chooses to give Mucie of her interview with Tite in Act I arouses Mucie's suspicions. "Cléobule" informs Mucie very directly of Tite's preference for Bérénice. Twice Mucie upbraids "Cléobule", accusing "him" of being an unworthy *confident*:

> *Indigne confident, et plus indigne Amant.*
> *(l.619)*

---

[614] The similarity with Domitie in Corneille's *Tite et Bérénice* is obvious.

[615] Eight times she need speak no more than half a line or a single line to prompt Tite to continue his declaration of love.

[616] *Esthétique de l'identité*, pp.449-453.

[617] *Ibid.*, pp. 457-61.

[618] See H. Bell's edition of Magnon's *Tite* (p.34).

and

> *Est-ce ainsi qu'on me sert, orgueilleux, imprudent,*
> *Vous, Amant temeraire, et lasche confident?*
>   *(ll.663-4)*

Mucie is assuming that "Cléobule" has allowed his own desire to marry her (his role as "Amant") to intrude upon his duties as her *confident*. The parallel with the situation of Bérénice and Antiochus in Racine's *Bérénice* is striking. Moreover, such is Mucie's anger at the idea that "Cléobule" might be taking Bérénice's side for his own ends, that she makes violent threats against both Bérénice and "Cléobule" himself:

> *Que ne la <=Bérénice> tiens-je icy, ni vous, ni son Amant*
> *Ne l'arracheriez pas à mon ressentiment.*
> *Vous, si vous estiez tel que vous paroissez estre*
> *Je vous ferois perir aux yeux de vostre Maistre.*
>   *(ll.635-8)*

Might we see here, in embryonic form at least, the situation which Racine will work out fully in *Bajazet* as the wronged Sultana plans the death of her rival and false *confidente*?

Bérénice's confidential relationship with Mucie is effectively broken at the end of this scene;[619] Mucie henceforth distrusts her and actively conspires in her downfall. But in their two encounters Magnon has led us through the essential stages in one version of the role of protagonist as false *confident(e)*: the *confident(e)* exploiting the deception to her own advantage, and then awakening the distrust of the other protagonist who vows revenge. Moreover in the second scene between Bérénice and Mucie, he has proved that the device need not be restricted to the comic register. Racine's reworking of the story of Titus and Berenice may be different in many respects, but Magnon had illustrated the dramatic interest of the protagonist acting as a false *confident*, a strategy which is also central to Racine's version.

(ii) THE PROTAGONIST AS UNWILLING FALSE *CONFIDENT(E)*: RACINE'S *BÉRÉNICE* AND THOMAS CORNEILLE'S *ARIANE*

In both comedy and tragicomedy protagonists are usually free to choose which disguises and deceits to adopt. True, they may sometimes react to the pressure of circumstances, like Molière's Dom Juan who dons a "habit de campagne" to make good his escape at the start of the third Act, but frequently the disguise has been carefully premeditated. In tragedies, however, it is far more likely that protagonists will be victims of circumstances, coerced against

---

[619] "Vous de mes sentimens infidele interprete,/ Sortez de cette Cour, je veux votre retraite." (ll.694-5).

their will into any role involving feint. This is particularly true of the protagonist acting as false *confident*. Magnon's Bérénice followed a noble line of heroines of novels and tragicomedies who sought to restore their amorous fortunes by freely adopting a different *persona*; she chose to use her new identity in order to gain the trust of both her rival and her lover. In contrast, Racine's Antiochus, Atalide and Ériphile, Thomas Corneille's Phèdre and Pradon's Aricie are not shown as choosing the false position in which their *confidence* with their rivals places them. We may, however, draw a broad distinction between those tragic protagonists for whom the false *confidence* is perceived as an additional cause of suffering (Antiochus, Phèdre), and those who seek to exploit it (Atalide, Ériphile, Aricie). The former situation lends itself more easily to the exploration of heroic sentiments (self-denial, loyalty), whereas the latter tends towards a darker portrayal of human motives. *Amitié* may temper the claims of *amour*, at least briefly, in the first case, while in the second the passions alone dictate the course of action.

We established in Chapter 4 that Racine makes exceptional use of the full complement of lower-ranked *confidents* in *Bérénice*, but he also promotes *confidence* into a theme in its own right by making Antiochus Titus's *confident*. In *Bérénice*, as in most of the plays under discussion in this chapter, one protagonist is not called upon to act as *confident* because another protagonist lacks a lower-ranking character to fulfil this function. Instead, the second protagonist has a conventional *confident*, but in addition chooses to confide in the first protagonist as a trusted friend. It is this which makes the position of the false *confident* and rival so ironic and poignant. It could be argued that Racine's conception of Antiochus's double role - not suggested by any of his sources as far as we know - was in part a solution to a dramaturgical problem. With only three main characters, Racine was particularly pressed to satisfy the rules of verisimilitude in contriving meetings between them. We have already seen that for this reason the lower-ranked *confidents* take on a vital role as messengers.[620] As an additional *confident* to Titus, Antiochus has privileged access to both the Emperor and Bérénice, and is charged with communicating between them. Does this detract from the tragic dignity of Antiochus's role, reducing him effectively to the level of a messenger?

Not all critics have been kind about the role of Antiochus, but it can be argued that Racine orchestrated the dénouement in such a way that Antiochus should participate fully in the tragedy.[621] One aspect of this dénouement has received little attention, yet seems to me surprising: namely the fact that it is only in the last scene that Titus is disabused as to Antiochus's true status. Titus specifically invites Antiochus to be present at his final farewell to Bérénice:

---

[620] See p.113.
[621] See the discussion by R. Parish, *Racine: the limits of tragedy*, pp.62-63.

> *Venez, Prince, venez, je vous ai fait chercher.*
> *Soyez ici témoin de toute ma faiblesse;*
> *Voyez si c'est aimer avec peu de tendresse;*
> *Jugez-nous.*
>   *(ll.1426-29)*

It is at this point that Antiochus discloses the truth to Titus. Two details of the revelation are particularly interesting. First, Antiochus reminds Titus that he was an unwilling but totally faithful *confident*:

> *Vous m'avez, malgré moi, confié l'un et l'autre,*
> *La reine, son amour, et vous, seigneur, le vôtre.*
> *La reine, qui m'entend, peut me désavouer:*
> *Elle m'a vu toujours ardent à vous louer,*
> *Répondre par mes soins à votre confidence.*
>   *(ll.1435-39)*

Antiochus, no less than Titus and Bérénice, thus merits our respect. My second observation is rather different: the language in which Antiochus prepares Titus for the truth and delivers the fateful news could equally belong to a tragicomedy of disguised identity. He calls upon the Emperor to recognise him, using the loaded verb *connaître*:

> *Mais connaissez vous-même un prince malheureux*
>   *(l.1430)*

He warns Titus that what he is about to hear will seem unbelievable:

> *Mais le pourriez-vous croire en ce moment fatal,*
> *Qu'un ami si fidèle était votre rival?*
>   *(ll.1441-42)*

The *coup de grâce* delivered, he then explains the disguise, using another key verb of recognition scenes in tragicomedies, *éclaircir*:

> *Il est temps que je vous éclaircisse.*
>   *(l.1443)*

However, the emotions Antiochus's revelation provokes are far from the surprised relief and general rejoicing which greet, for example, Bérénice's disclosure of her identity at the end of Magnon's *Tite*. Racine's fusion of a tragicomic device with an uncompromisingly tragic situation risks a hiatus. He resolves it by something of a compromise. Titus's only response to the revelation is the exclamation "Mon rival!" (l.1443); these are his last words in the play.[622] After Antiochus's speech, the focus is then swiftly transferred to Bérénice, whose momentous decision to depart raises the tragedy to a new level

---

[622] Compare in contrast the last scene of Magnon's *Tite*, in which the Emperor resumes the initiative. His speech which closes the play contains four imperatives as he dictates the fates of the other protagonists (ll.1868-76).

of intensity. In the rapid movement of a stage performance, we may not notice
that we never learn Titus's exact reaction to Antiochus's deception, but when
one re-reads the play reflectively, it is hard to avoid the impression that Racine
faced a dilemma in the dénouement. He could scarcely fail to reveal
Antiochus's false identity, yet equally he could not allow it to be played out at
full length without detracting from the moment of supreme tragedy, Bérénice's
renunciation. It is noticeable that in his two subsequent tragedies which employ
the device of a protagonist acting as a false *confident*, the revelation occurs far
earlier, and is fully integrated into the workings of the plot.

If the disclosure of Antiochus's false identity is not the centrepiece of the
dénouement, we may ask how effective the strategy proves throughout the rest
of *Bérénice*. Apart from its dramaturgical purpose of facilitating exchanges
between major characters, does the situation contribute in any significant way to
the tragedy, particularly to its emotional appeal? I would suggest that it is
essential to our perception of Antiochus's suffering, as well as to the tragic
irony with which the play is loaded. For Antiochus, the pain of unrequited love
is compounded by the fact that Bérénice will suffer his presence only because
he is a substitute for Titus. In I.4 Antiochus recognises that Bérénice listens
more attentively to his *récit* when he has just mentioned Titus's part in the
siege:

> *Je vois que l'on m'écoute avec moins de regret,*
> *Et que trop attentive à ce récit funeste,*
> *En faveur de Titus vous pardonnez le reste.*
> *(ll.226-28)*

Bérénice herself cruelly confirms that this is why she has sought him out as a
"témoin de ma joie":

> *Cent fois je me suis fait une douceur extrême*
> *D'entretenir Titus dans un autre lui-même.*[623]
> *(ll.271-2)*

Bérénice is treating Antiochus as though he were no more than a *confident*,
charged with conveying Titus's words, present when Titus cannot be. What she
overlooks is that, unlike a simple *confident*, he has an independent emotional
reaction. Both in I.4 and, even more so, in III.3, we may be shocked by
Bérénice's disregard for Antiochus's suffering. Yet he himself has in part
invited her blindness, for he has allowed herself and Titus to be deceived:

---

[623] Compare line 698 of Magnon's *Tite*.

> *Un voile d'amitié vous trompa l'un et l'autre,*
> *Et mon amour devint le confident du vôtre.*
> *(ll.243-44)*

As Antiochus attempts to take his leave of Bérénice he particularly evokes our pity, for he seeks to escape the intolerable situation of being present without being truly seen:

> *Que vous dirai-je enfin? Je fuis des yeux distraits,*
> *Qui me voyant toujours ne me voyaient jamais.*
> *(ll.277-8)*

His lines give an exact description of how protagonists traditionally view *confidents*, but when the *confident* is a protagonist acting a role, we are made to realise the pain of this shadowy existence.

The tragic irony of the protagonist-*confident*'s situation is even sharper in III.3, the centripetal scene in which Bérénice learns from Antiochus that Titus has resolved to leave her. On the one hand, Antiochus enters with false hopes (raised by Arsace) that his thankless task as *confident* may finally serve his passions. Bérénice, on the other hand, waits only to hear what message he brings from Titus. The audience watches Bérénice closely as she hears the fatal news; yet, unlike Bérénice, we also perceive Antiochus's suffering. Once he has reluctantly delivered Titus's words, he is again of no consequence whatsoever to Bérénice; it is as though she does not see him. Her use of the device of *interruptio* (line 913) prevents him from even completing his attempted explanation, and, having dismissed him brutally, it is to Phénice - her true *confidente* - that Bérénice turns for emotional support.[624] Racine was obviously concerned to heighten the spectator's pity for Antiochus as well as for the queen, for it is Antiochus who is left on stage with Arsace, and on whose sufferings the Act closes. As he resolves for a second time to leave Rome, he expresses his sense of injustice. It is his personal tragedy that he is fated to be only a substitute for Titus in Bérénice's eyes, his own emotions, like those of a lowly *confident*, of no significance to her. There is further irony in the fact that Bérénice chooses not to trust Antiochus in his role. Her reaction in III.3 is born of passion, not reason; the wish to believe that Titus could not have said what Antiochus conveyed. Yet Antiochus has not betrayed the bond of friendship.[625] However, the final two acts of the play demonstrate that *amitié* can be no substitute for love. When Antiochus throws off the mantle of the *confident* in the final scene it is fitting that he is included in Bérénice's celebrated formula as an example of "l'*amour* la plus tendre et la plus malheureuse"(line 1503).

---

[624] See p.117.

[625] Indeed, he claims to Arsace that he represented Titus's love as stronger than it was (ll.939-40).

He was never other than an unwilling *confident*, accepting his charge in the vain attempt to serve his passion.

Thomas Corneille is far more preoccupied than Racine with fine distinctions between different manifestations of *amour* and with the relationship between *amour* and *amitié*. For Racine's Antiochus, the potential conflict between his friendship for Titus and his love for Bérénice is not developed; the tragedy depends on the conflict between what he desires and Bérénice's refusal to accept his love. Versed in the subtleties of the *Carte de Tendre* and the *questions d'amour* which had preoccupied salons for more than a decade, Thomas Corneille distinguishes the characters in *Ariane* - arguably the most Racinian of his tragedies[626] - by the gradations of their passions. The eponymous heroine, played by La Champmeslé, won the most resounding praise and has continued to dominate interpretations of the play,[627] but we need to remember that the full force of her violent passion (*Amour-Inclination*, in the language of the *Carte de Tendre*) relies in part on the contrast afforded by the other characters. Œnarus, who in many ways resembles Racine's Antiochus, hopes to the end that *Amour-Estime* may finally win him Ariane's hand. Unlike Antiochus, however, he is no secret *confident* to his rival.[628] Nor does he need to be, for Thésée has a *para-confident* already, his legendary friend Pirithoüs, whose high rank allows him to move freely between all the main protagonists[629] and whose fidelity to his friend affords Thomas Corneille opportunities to explore the relationship between *amour* and *amitié* with a sense of discrimination reminiscent of La Rochefoucauld. But it is the relationship between Ariane and her sister Phèdre which crucially opposes *amour* and *amitié*, precisely in the context of a protagonist acting as a false *confidente*.[630]

---

[626] See J. Truchet's *notice* to *Ariane* in *Théâtre du XVIIe siècle*, vol.II, ed. J. Scherer et J. Truchet (1986), p.1525.

[627] See Truchet's summary of those critics from Madame de Sévigné and Voltaire onwards who have been exclusively concerned with the role of Ariane (*Théâtre du XVIIe siècle*, vol. II, p.1527).

[628] He nobly confesses his passions to Thésée at almost the first opportunity (II.3).

[629] Dramaturgically, it is Pirithoüs who holds the play together, advising Thésée in Act I, interceding with Ariane in Acts II and III, consulting with Phèdre in Act III, and finally bearing the rumour of Thésée's departure to Ariane in Act V.

[630] Since Ariane already has a low-ranking *confidente* (Nérine), Phèdre's role as a *para-confidente* is not dramaturgically necessary. Rather, Thomas Corneille exploits the thematic and affective resonances of the relationship between the sisters.

Although the episode of Theseus's abandonment of Ariadne is familiar from classical sources,[631] the role of Phædra as her accomplice and then rival is not. M. Bertaud reminds us that early in the seventeenth-century (?1610-20) Alexandre Hardy had used a version of the legend involving both sisters in his tragicomedy *Ariane ravie*.[632] However, it is only in Act II of Hardy's play that Theseus's decision to seduce Phædra is announced; Phædra learns of Theseus's desires via his *confident* in Act III, and thereafter she never reappears on stage. In other words, Hardy does not give his Phædra any opportunity to act as *confidente* (false or otherwise) to Ariadne; this is Thomas Corneille's invention.[633]

In a play which critics have suggested relies heavily on a situation rather than the development of a plot, it should be noted that the role of Thomas Corneille's Phèdre as false *confidente* is essential in driving the action towards the dénouement. It is precisely because she is made privy (in IV.3) to Ariane's secret decision to kill her rival that Phèdre warns Thésée and finally consents to depart with him (IV.5). But the interest of Phèdre's role extends beyond her contribution to the action: her divided loyalties evoke the audience's pity both for herself and for Ariane, and the way in which she is obliged to *act* her part generates irony and suspense no less surely than the device of hidden identity had done in *Timocrate*. Thomas Corneille is economic with meetings between the sisters, reserving them for key dramatic moments.[634] In addition, the audience is reminded of their confidential relationship by the comments of both heroines to other characters. Before Ariane appears on stage, Phèdre has argued that Ariane's *amitié* for her prevents her from accepting Thésée's love:

> *J'aurais de ces combats affranchi votre cœur*
> *Si j'eusse eu pour rivale une autre qu'une sœur,*
> *Mais trahir l'amitié dont on la voit sans cesse ...*
> *Non, Thésée, elle m'aime avec trop de tendresse.*
> *(ll.323-6)*

Phèdre's dilemma, divided between a love she cannot deny and a loyalty she cannot renounce, provides the main emotional focus of Act I. Although Ariane's passions come to dominate the rest of the play, particularly Act V,

---

[631] Thomas Corneille had himself recently translated Ovid's *Heroides*, in which it constitutes the basis of the Xth letter.

[632] "Deux *Ariane* au XVII siècle: Alexandre Hardy et Thomas Corneille" (1997), p.146.

[633] J. Truchet discusses at length the vexed question of whether Thomas Corneille was familiar with Racine's *Bajazet* (staged early January 1672) when he wrote *Ariane* (staged 26 February, 1672, according to Truchet). Although Truchet cites several parallels in the use of the protagonist as false *confident* (*Théâtre du XVIIe siècle*, vol. II, p.1534), the evidence of direct imitation is not conclusive.

[634] They have two long scenes alone together (II.7 and IV.3) and one shorter one at which Pirithoüs is also present (III.2).

Thomas Corneille has taken care to portray his second heroine sympathetically before she is seen to act out her morally compromising role.[635]

Yet once Ariane is present on stage, Phèdre is necessarily involved in duplicity. Ariane's only complaint about Phèdre, when speaking to her *confidente* Nérine at the start of the second Act, alerts us to the fact that Phèdre must constantly act a role to conceal her true feelings:

> *J'aime Phèdre; tu sais combien elle m'est chère;*
> *Si quelque chose en elle a de quoi me déplaire,*
> *C'est de voir son esprit, de froideur combattu,*
> *Négliger entre nous de louer sa <= de Thésée > vertu.*
>   *(ll.425-8)*

Nérine explains Phèdre's "indifférence" (l.434) as a consequence of not having experienced love herself. In this, Nérine has accurately defined the *confidente*-persona Phèdre projects, but failed to see beneath it. Phèdre is first called upon to counsel and comfort Ariane at the end of Act II. Were we not aware of Phèdre's double role, we too might interpret her stilted responses and her lack of emotion in comparison with Ariane as the behaviour of the indifferent *confidente*. Phèdre's condolences to her sister are impersonal, formulaic:

> *Un revers si cruel vous rend sans doute à plaindre;*
> *Et vous voyant souffrir ce qu'on n'a pas dû craindre,*
> *On conçoit aisément jusqu'où le désespoir...*
>   *(ll.709-11)*

This is the kind of cold discourse which d'Aubignac had derided in the *Querelle de Sophonisbe*, and, like a banal prototype of the *confidente*, Phèdre takes a minimal role in the scene, speaking only five and a half lines to Ariane's fifty-seven and a half. Ariane is too distressed to remark on Phèdre's aloofness, but she perpetuates the impression of her sister as a *confidente* by giving her precise instructions on how to speak to Thésée on her behalf.[636] It is the spectators who recognises the full irony of Ariane's assumption that Phèdre will be an inadequate emissary because she lacks the experience of love.

Thomas Corneille does not stage the scene in which Phèdre interecedes with Thésée on behalf of Ariane.[637] Instead, with the touch still of a tragicomic author, Thomas Corneille cannot resist drawing out the irony of Ariane's

---

[635] For a fuller refutation of unjustifiably hostile criticisms of Phèdre (notably by Reynier), see D. Collins, *Thomas Corneille*, pp.149-157.

[636] Compare the prominence of the theme of voice substitution in Racine's *Bérénice* (see p.113).

[637] Compare Racine's omission of two similar moments of duplicity: Bajazet's reconciliation with Roxane (between Acts II and III of *Bajazet*) and Œnone's calomny of Hippolyte (just before Act IV of *Phèdre*).

misreading of the situation as she subsequently reproaches her sister for not
having played her role of messenger convincingly enough:

> *Vous avez oublié de bien marquer l'horreur*
> *Du fatal désespoir qui règne dans mon cœur.*
> *Vous avez oublié, pour bien peindre ma rage,*
> *D'assembler tous les maux dont on connaît l'image.*
>   *(ll.839-42)*

It is again Phèdre's *performance* as *confidente* which is brought to the fore.[638]
She is permitted to slip back into obscurity as Pirithoüs replaces her as
counsellor, and she departs, obeying Ariane's orders to fetch Thésée, just as a
confidente would. But the last scene between the sisters tests Phèdre's role-
playing to its limit.

Act IV is constructed around a series of ironical reversals of knowledge,
with role-play, and therefore control, moving from Phèdre to Ariane and then
back to Phèdre again. Having sought Œnarus's protection for Ariane at the start
of the Act, Phèdre maintains her role as the conventional *confidente* when she is
a silent witness to her sister's long scene with the king (IV.2). Ariane's apparent
acceptance of Œnarus, however, is a feint to facilitate her revenge, a deceit
which she reveals to Phèdre in IV.3. It is revealing to chart the shift in Phèdre's
language in this scene from the familiar responses of the *confidente* to the point
at which her own voice breaks through. Initially, as she prompts her sister to
explain her change of heart, she speaks as a *confidente* would, pressing for
more information, objecting to an improbable course of action. When Ariane
reveals her determination to discover the identity of her rival, however, we sense
more urgency in Phèdre's questioning, prefaced by a cautiously conventional
acknowledgement of Ariane's distress:

> *Ce revers est sensible, il faut le confesser.*
> *Mais quand vous connaîtrez celle qu'il vous préfère,*
> *Pour venger votre amour, que prétendez-vous faire?*
>   *(ll.1320-2)*

Finally, as Ariane's furious desire for revenge is unleashed, Phèdre is forced
into a totally defensive position. She cannot prevent herself from indirectly
defending the rival whose bloody death Ariane has just planned:

---

[638] Compare Bérénice's anxieties about her *confidente*, Phénice's, performance to Titus (see
p.114).

> Mais sans l'autoriser à vous être infidèle,
> Cette rivale a pu le voir brûler pour elle;
> Elle a peine à ses vœux peut-être à consentir.
>   (ll.1333-5)

It is the ultimate irony that when Phèdre finally speaks in her own voice, Ariane fails to recognise her rival. La Champmeslé's performance as Ariane may have left spectators like Madame de Sévigné overpowered by Ariane's passions. The irony of Phèdre's position throughout the scene also bears witness, though, to the skill of Thomas Corneille's writing. We can recognise her hidden anxieties precisely because her discourse so closely resembles that which we know as characteristic of a *confidente*, and as a result any departure from the *persona* stands out in relief.

By closing Act IV on a scene between Phèdre and Thésée (the first since I.3), the playwright exposes fully the ambiguities of Phèdre's position, before devoting the whole of the final Act to Ariane's frenzied grief. Since Phèdre has no *confidente*, it is only in her scenes with Thésée (and to a lesser extent Pirithoüs) that she can be open. IV.5 leaves us with a final impression of a heroine whose crime costs her conscience dear.[639] In her distress at learning herself abandoned in Act V, Ariane assumes the worst of her sister, believing that Phèdre enjoyed her false role:

> La perfide, abusant de ma tendre amitié,
> Montrait de ma disgrâce une fausse pitié,
> Et jouissant des maux que j'aimais à lui peindre,
> Elle en était la cause, et feignait de me plaindre.
>   (ll.1649-52)

The spectator, though moved to pity Ariane's sense of betrayal, can recognise that her judgement is partial, obscured by her jealousy. The interest of Thomas Corneille's Phèdre has lain precisely in the fact that she hesitated so long to sacrifice *amitié* to *amour*, and for this reason alone continued to play the part of a false *confidente*. Had La Champmeslé taken the part of Phèdre, one wonders whether its tragic resonances might have been more striking. That the protagonist as false *confidente* could be cast in the main role had, after all, just been demonstrated at the same Hôtel de Bourgogne with Racine's *Bajazet*: in this play, the great actress had played Atalide.[640]

---

[639] H.C. Lancaster has suggested, not without reason, that we can see Thomas Corneille's Phèdre as a "preliminary sketch for Racine's Phèdre, a woman who feels that she is doing wrong, yet, once started on her course, finds that it is too late to turn back." (*A History of French Dramatic Literature*, Part III, vol. II, p.601).

[640] M. McGowan comments in her edition of *Bajazet* (1968): "It is also possible that Racine wished to create, with his character Atalide, a particular kind of part for his mistress La Champmeslé, who would not only make us think but also feel deeply." (p.26).

(iii) OVERPLAYING THE ROLE OF FALSE *CONFIDENTE*: RACINE'S *BAJAZET* COMPARED WITH PRADON'S *PHÈDRE ET HIPPOLYTE*

For an actress who had already won acclaim playing Hermione (since 1670), the role of Atalide gave a new opportunity for interpreting the passions of the younger heroine. Both Atalide and Roxane have extremely demanding parts, but in the first three Acts of *Bajazet* Roxane is not adopting a false persona. Her passion for Bajazet is already known to him as well as to Atalide and Acomat; she also apprises each of them of her bold plan to marry Bajazet. The part of Atalide, on the other hand, demands that the actress adopt two different identities: she is the devoted lover when alone with Bajazet, but to both Roxane and Acomat she is the trusted *confidente* of the Sultana. Even more than Thomas Corneille's *Ariane*, *Bajazet* is a play which draws our attention to the heroine's *performance* of her false role: not because Atalide underperforms, as Ariane suspected in the case of Phèdre, but because her passions lead her to the opposite error of overacting, and thus arousing Roxane's suspicions.

The emphasis given to the protagonist acting as false *confidente* is not entirely of Racine's invention. It sounds romanesque, and it indeed corresponds broadly to an episode in a work of prose fiction. But did Racine borrow it directly from *Floridon*, one of the stories in Segrais's *Nouvelles Françaises*, which had appeared in 1656?[641] The sources of *Bajazet* have been a subject of debate, with Racine declaring at the start of his original preface to the play: "Quoique le sujet de cette tragédie ne soit encore dans aucune histoire imprimée, il est pourtant très véritable."[642] He claims to have based it on a second-hand oral source: the chevalier de Nantouillet, who had heard it from the French ambassador at Constantinople, the comte de Césy. Yet some close resemblances between *Floridon* and *Bajazet* give pause for thought. Nantouillet's oral account and *Floridon* probably both derive from Césy, but did Racine know only the first, or both? Lancaster suggests that Nantouillet's report may have sent Racine back to Segrais.[643] If this is the case, the playwright is less than honest in covering up his debt to Segrais at the start of his preface. However, we must remember that such was the dubious status of prose fiction that Racine also says nothing of an obvious classical model, Heliodorus's *Theagenes and Chariclea*. W. G. Moore, on the other hand, reminds us that Césy and Nantouillet were both known to embellish anecdotes, while he judges that Segrais had limited powers of invention. He concludes that Segrais would have inherited a ready-made story from Césy, and Racine would have received

---

[641] See *Floridon* in Jean Regnault de Segrais, *Les Nouvelles Françaises* (ed. R. Guichemerre, 1990-2, vol. II, pp.479-539).

[642] *Théâtre complet*, p.381.

[643] *History of French Dramatic Literature*, vol. IV, p.78.

romanesque details from Nantouillet without needing to look at Segrais.[644] Moore's argument is helpful in directing our attention to these romanesque elements which Racine indubitably exploits, from whichever source he may have obtained them. Personally, I find the echoes of *Floridon* striking enough to accept the judgement of R. Knight, who claimed "Que Racine ait tenu, ou non, le récit de la mort de Bajazet de ce Nantouillet ... il est évident qu'il connut aussi une nouvelle de Segrais, *Floridon*."[645] In what follows I shall therefore examine the relationship between *Floridon* and *Bajazet* as though Racine knew Segrais's tale, but with the reservation that if *Floridon* were not an actual source it would still be valubale as the closest approximation we can have to the récit which Racine heard.

I suggested at the start of this chapter that the protagonist playing the role of false *confidente* is one of the disguises of identity common in the world of romances. *Floridon* illustrates the device well. But the short story also reminds us of the need for the playwright to adapt prose fiction to suit the *bienséances* of the theatre in general, and the dignity of tragedy in particular. Floridon, the heroine of Segrais's tale,[646] is a slave who has risen to power and riches as the favourite of the Sultana. It is only after Bajazet has begun his liaison with the Sultana (mother, not wife, of the reigning Sultan) that he and Floridon are drawn together. Even once their affair is discovered, Segrais's young lovers do not abandon their deceit of the Sultana: when she has forgiven them, allowing them to continue to meet once a week, they again betray her trust. Racine makes his Atalide incomparably more noble: she is of royal birth; her love for Bajazet existed for many years before Roxane's; and, once discovered, she and Bajazet make no sordid attempts to prolong the deceit. However, Racine does retain the duplicitous situation of the false *confidente*, and moreover Atalide's exploitation of her position (unlike Floridon's) is not tempered by any debt of gratitude to the Sultana. In *Bajazet* we are made acutely aware that how well Atalide plays her role as false *confidente* will shape the course of the plot.

In *Bérénice*, we saw that the full disclosure of Antiochus's false role was delayed until the last scene and then rapidly passed over. In *Ariane*, the discovery of Phèdre's betrayal is seminal, but the structure of Thomas Corneille's tragedy does not allow the wronged heroine to confront her false *confidente*; the situations of deceiver and deceived are presented successively. The great structural achievement of *Bajazet* - which, to my mind, makes it the most satisfying exploitation of the device of the protagonist as false

---

[644] "Le *Bajazet* de Racine: étude de genèse" (1949).

[645] *Racine et la Grèce*, p.290.

[646] No critic has yet accounted for the change of name to Atalide in Racine's play.

confident(e) - is to place the discovery of the betrayal exactly at the centre of the play, and to wring the full drama and pathos from it. Acts I-III depend on Atalide's performance; in Act IV, while she is still striving to play her role, Roxane tests her beyond endurance, and in Act V Atalide becomes her victim, denied a role in a drama of which she is deliberately kept ignorant.

A lesser, but significant structural twist is to ensure the audience witness Atalide playing her role before their suspicions are confirmed.[647] In this Racine achieves a subtlety not present in Segrais.[648] The long first scene between a protagonist and *confident* (Acomat and Osmin) may appear routine, but with hindsight it is important not only in establishing the background to an unfamiliar story, but also because it conveys several misapprehensions on the part of the Vizir. In particular, the latter assumes that Roxane and Bajazet are bound by mutual love (ll.161-2), and that Atalide is a decoy preventing others from suspecting their affair:

> *Atalide a prêté son nom à cet amour*
> ....
> *Du Prince en apparence elle reçoit les vœux,*
> *Mais elle les reçoit pour les rendre à Roxane,*
> *Et veut bien sous son nom qu'il aime la sultane.*
>   *(ll.168-74)*

This seems like the exposition of a convoluted tragicomedy: we might think of the role of Fédéric as decoy for Alexandre's love in Rotrou's *Venceslas*.[649] What the audience cannot know at this stage is that "en apparence" (l.172) does not provide the full clue here. Nor would we see anything untoward in the Vizir's ironic reference to "sa chère Atalide" as Roxane arrives accompanied by Atalide:

> *Et ... Mais on vient. C'est elle, et sa chère Atalide.*
>   *(l.210)*

But this is perhaps the most deadly ironic of Racine's tragedies, in which even conventional devices like an expository scene with a *confident* are not what they seem. R. Picard defined *Bajazet* as the "tragédie du mensonge",[650] and Acomat's own role is in part that of a deceitful *confident/conseiller*.[651] He is the one character in whom Bajazet - deprived of a *confident* - confides, yet, like

---

[647] M. Hawcroft observes that this is an exception to Racine's usual practice of letting the audience "know beforehand what a character's persuasive aim will be and what mask, if any, will be worn." (*Word as Action*, p.117).

[648] Compare *Floridon*, p.500-2.

[649] See p.72.

[650] Racine, *Œuvres*, Bibliothèque de la Pléiade, p.543.

[651] Racine has developed Acomat significantly beyond the character in Segrais. The latter was simply a eunuch, privy to the Sultana's passions, but with no political ambitions of his own.

many a *conseiller*, his loyalty to his protégé is a means to secure his own advancement. However, for all the machiavellian plans which Acomat exposed in the first scene, he cannot see through the deception which Atalide is practising before his eyes.

How soon does Racine sow the seeds of doubt in our minds as to Atalide's role? Not in I.2, the scene between Roxane and Acomat, to which Atalide is no more than the silent witness we expect a *confidente* to be. But in I.3 there are direct and indirect indications. First, Atalide is a very active *confidente*, far more so than Thomas Corneille's Phèdre, meeting Roxane's hesitations and doubts with vigorous counter-arguments.[652] We might initially see her in the mould of Céphise, Albine, or Phénice, engaging in temporary conflict with her mistress, but we could notice that twice she provides not one but a sequence of arguments or illustrations to persuade Roxane of her opinion. Why should she argue so strongly, unless she feels insecure? Secondly, Roxane herself alerts the spectator to the disjuncture between how Atalide represents Bajazet and how he speaks himself:

> *Pourquoi faut-il au moins que pour me consoler,*
> *L'ingrat ne parle pas comme on le fait parler?*
> ....
> *Je ne retrouvais point ce trouble, cette ardeur*
> *Que m'avait tant promis un discours trop flatteur.*
> *(ll.275-84)*

As H. Phillips has shown, this is a play in which there is an exceptional concentration on voice substitution.[653] Atalide is more than simply the *confidente* who listens to Roxane; she is also the messenger entrusted with bringing her the words of Bajazet.[654] The precarious situation can be maintained only as long as she can intervene between Roxane and Bajazet and construct the message Roxane wishes to hear. Atalide's own performance is skilful, conveying a lover's "trouble" and "ardeur". As she herself recognises when she is alone with Zaïre in the following scene, however, Bajazet does not share her ability to deceive.[655]

---

[652] In contrast, Roxane's slave Zatime is silent in this scene. She in fact has no lines until the end of Act III, and her spoken part is confined in the main to the end of Act IV and Act V, i.e. once Roxane has ceased to confide in Atalide. Even then Zatime has the reticence of a slave addressing a feared mistress (e.g. line 1282-4).

[653] *Racine: Language and Theatre*, pp.73-76.

[654] A modification of Segrais, in which it is letters rather than verbal messages that Floridon transmits.

[655] Lines 391-2. Zaïre's role is almost identical in length to Zatime's, but her scenes with Atalide are spaced more regularly through the play, at the points where Racine wishes to reveal the troubled thoughts and feelings of Atalide. Her speech is less obviously that of a fearful slave, and closer to a conventional *confidente*.

Yet it is not just Bajazet's reluctance or inability to act which undeceives
Roxane; rather, it is the contrast with Atalide's overperformance of her role.
Between Acts II and III Bajazet's (offstage) interview with Roxane sufficed to
reassure the Sultane.[656] Even his "sombre accueil" and "discours glacé"
(l.1035) when he then sees her in the presence of Atalide in III.5 cause her only
to ask desperate questions about her own perceptions of both meetings. It is
Atalide's excessive zeal in acting as *confidente* which fans Roxane's suspicions.
In *Ariane*, Phèdre avoids giving herself away by laconic impassivity; Racine
depicts his false *confidente* as too distressed for the safety of her lover to
exercise such self-control. Her fatal response to Roxane's menacing
questions[657] rings untrue for a *confidente* because of the accumulation of
excuses:

> Madame, ce chagrin n'a point frappé ma vue.
> Il m'a de vos bontés longtemps entretenue;
> Il en était tout plein quand je l'ai rencontré,
> J'ai cru le voir sortir tel qu'il était entré.
> Mais, Madame, après tout, faut-il être surprise
> Que, tout prêt d'achever cette grande entreprise,
> Bajazet s'inquiète, et qu'il laisse échapper
> Quelque marque des soins qui doivent l'occuper?
> (ll.1049-56)

A *confidente* could well have spoken either the first quatrain or the second to
reassure her mistress, but the succession of the two quatrains,[658] and the awkward
repetition of "Madame", are just sufficient to expose the counterfeit. Although
in the monologue which follows Roxane will oscillate between believing and
doubting the evidence, from this point her trust in Atalide is broken. It is
symbolic that she excludes Atalide at the end of III.6 in a way she would not
have done a passive *confidente*:

> J'ai, comme Bajazet, mon chagrin et mes soins,
> Et je veux un moment y penser sans témoins.
> (ll.1063-4)

---

[656] Roxane's words make it clear that she wished to believe in Bajazet's love, and was a
generous audience to his weak performance: "J'ai cru dans son désordre entrevoir sa tendresse"
(l.1025).

[657] Roxane in this scene and Act IV has rightly been compared to Mithridate with his
inquisitions and traps.

[658] Even in lines 1049-52 the parataxis betrays a desperation to accumulate proofs.

In Segrais's *Floridon*, the Sultana had originally trusted her favourite to the extent of allowing her to remain in the room while she received her lover;[659] Roxane - like Mithridate after her - now seeks only solitude. She thus denies Atalide the opportunity to prolong her performance.

What is striking in the subsequent confrontation between Roxane and Atalide is that Atalide is no longer afforded the *confidente*'s privilege of listening rather than speaking. Roxane's speeches are no longer than one or two lines; no fewer than fourteen times, Atalide must respond to a terse comment or interrogation. Again, she adopts some of the conventional strategies of the *confidente*'s discourse in her attempt to bluff: short exclamations of surprise, universal statements of compassion.[660] When she reads Amurat's order for Bajazet's death, she is spurred on to a last attempt to move Roxane, with the counter arguments that a *confidente* who was close to her mistress might have used:

> *Il <Amurat> poursuit son dessein parricide.*
> *Mais il pense proscrire un prince sans appui:*
> *Il ne sait pas l'amour qui vous parle pour lui,*
> *Que vous et Bajazet vous ne faites qu'une âme,*
> *Que plutôt, s'il le faut, vous mourrez ...*
> *(ll.1194-8)*

Yet as in III.6, her passions betray her: the speech is too vigorous, the accumulation of arguments too rapid for a true *confidente*. Finally, when Roxane announces that she has ordered Bajazet's death, Atalide faints, and beyond any shadow of a doubt establishes in Roxane's eyes that she is a protagonist in her own right. Racine's *confidentes* may, exceptionally, shed tears, but no *confidente* in seventeenth-century tragedy faints. Atalide has definitively crossed the boundary between *confidente* and protagonist.

In contrast to Segrais's Sultana, Roxane expends little emotion on Atalide's betrayal itself.[661] Yet with consummate irony, Racine creates a last scene between the rivals (V.6), in which Atalide finally drops her mask. There is a fascinating inversion of the roles of protagonist-*confidente* for the greater part of the scene. Atalide has sought out Roxane (ll. 1568-9); she speaks of her own role, her emotions, at great length, uninterrupted. In her 48 lines, she uses the pronoun *je* 16 times. Roxane listens, apparently imperturbable, as a *confidente* might. But finally it takes the Sultana a mere six lines to reassert her authority. There are

---

[659] Segrais suggests that "par un goût bizarre" the Sultana may even have taken pleasure in this voyeurism on the part of her favourite (*Floridon*, p.500).

[660] E.g. lines 1177-8.

[661] Compare, for example, the Sultana's outburst blaming Floridon for her ingratitude in Segrais: "Et quel outrage as-tu fait à mon amitié! Déloyale fille, esclave née pour la perte de mon repos! As-tu aisément mis en oubli combien je t'aimais, et est-ce ainsi que tu m'as aimée?" (*Floridon*, p.505).

various other layers of irony to this scene. Atalide has dropped one mask, that of the *confidente*, but she now plays - consciously or otherwise - a different role. She takes upon herself all the blame for her affair with Bajazet, claiming that once she is dead he will be reconciled with Roxane. Whether manipulating the voice of Bajazet or modulating her own, Atalide performs roles to the end in order to save her lover. Yet it is, of course, too late, for the fatal "Sortez" has already been uttered. Atalide has been unable to control the circle of passion under the guise of either a *confidente* or a heroically self-sacrificing lover.

The dénouement of *Bajazet* holds the bleakest irony of all: the discovery that it was Amurat who had decided the deaths of Bajazet and Roxane, irrespective of the other characters' actions. Low-ranking *confidents* have occupied a very limited place in such a world, and even a protagonist acting as *confidente* was denied the power which she assumed that her discourse gave her. Yet Atalide's performance, if ultimately futile, was riveting. Just how effectively Racine turned a strategy of prose fiction and tragicomedies into the centrepiece of his tragedy is brought out by the contrast with the imitation of it in Pradon's *Phèdre et Hippolyte*. This latter, conceived precisely to rival Racine's *Phèdre*,[662] clearly borrowed the device of the protagonist as false *confidente*/rival from *Bajazet* (with several debts to Thomas Corneille's *Ariane*, for good measure).[663] Like Quinault's *Pausanias*,[664] it is a useful indicator of the respect in which Racine's handling of confidential strategies was held. What we can observe in Pradon, however, is a mechanical transposition, which does not expoit the aspects of performance so central to Racine's play.

*   *   *

O. Classe has shown that statistically Pradon's Aricie is more prominent than her counterpart in Racine's *Phèdre*: Pradon's character has 16% of the discourse, Racine's only 8%. This shift in balance is explained largely by the absence of a *nourrice* for Pradon's Phèdre;[665] Aricie, acts as Phèdre's false

---

[662] Pradon's play was staged two days àfter the première of Racine's (January 1677). See Pradon, *Phèdre et Hippolyte* (ed. O. Classe, 1987), pp. XII-XVI.

[663] Critics have looked closely at the resemblances between Pradon's play and *Bajazet*, and also at his possible debts to Quinault's *Bellérophon* and to Bidar and Gilbert (Lancaster, *A History of French Dramatic Literature*, Part IV, vol. I, p.114). Parallels with *Ariane* deserve further analysis.

[664] See Chapter 4.

[665] There is a "femme de la suite de Phèdre", Mégiste, but her role is that of a messenger (comparable to Panope in Racine), speaking only in V.4.

confidente in Acts I-III. From the first scene between Aricie and Hippolyte
(I.2), we learn that Aricie resembles Thomas Corneille's Phèdre rather than
Racine's Atalide, for it is by feigning detachment that she has concealed her
passion from Phèdre:

> *Que j'endurois, Seigneur, une dure contrainte,*
> *Quand luy cachant mes feux sous une injuste feinte*
> *Elle me reprochoit alors avecque ardeur*
> *Que je parlois de vous avec trop de froideur.*
>   *(ll.197-200)*

We might note that in II.1 she recommends that Hippolyte should adopt the
same deceptive strategy of "un air d'indifférence" and "une feinte froideur"
(ll.410-2). Pradon gives Aricie not one but two scenes to act out her role of
false *confidente* to Phèdre before the deceit is suspected.[666] In both scenes her
performance is the same: she produces counter-arguments to try to persuade
Phèdre to adopt a different course of action, but she remains controlled and
collected. In particular, unlike Atalide, she develops only one single argument
in each intervention. For example, after the *coup de théâtre* in which Phèdre has
revealed to Aricie her love for Hippolyte, Aricie first uses the counter-argument
that Phèdre should love Thésée rather than his son (ll.273-6), and then awaits
Phèdre's response before producing a second, different argument based on
Hippolyte's reputation for chastity (ll.289-96). The audience is aware of the
tension and irony generated by Atalide's deceit, but her words themselves do
not develop a sense of imminent danger.[667]

Where Racine used successive scenes between Atalide and Roxane to build
up our expectation that Atalide's over-performance must become suspect,
Pradon is content to replay the same device with no change of pitch, and no
development of the situation. Nor is the evolution of the plot dependent upon
the conflict between the *amitié* which binds Aricie to Phèdre and the *amour*
both feel for Hippolyte, as it was in *Ariane*. Instead, Pradon uses an external
event, Thésée's unexpected return, to resolve the stasis. With his predilection for
sudden, dramatic shifts and *grandes scènes*,[668] he accomplishes the exposure of
Aricie's deception with little warning. We have seen that Racine constructed his
play so that the unmasking of Atalide was carefully prepared and followed
through. Pradon, in contrast, has his Aricie still playing the cool and collected
confidente at the start of III.1. Her advice to Phèdre to forget Hippolyte and
love Thésée is identical to that which she had offered in II.3. Even more

---

[666] Aricie is also present as a *confidente*/silent witness to Phèdre's and Hippolyte's exchange
in II.2. In this scene Aricie contributes only one line.

[667] Only once is there an instance of *correctio* which suggests that Aricie might have
betrayed herself, but it is not developed. Indeed, it is not even clear what the words were which
she cuts short ("Et je tremble pour vous ... enfin, pour vostre amour", l.331).

[668] See (ed) O. Classe, p.XL.

significantly, in a counter-argument of twelve lines (ll.721-32), she shows the same reasoned control as in the two earlier acts; there is nothing in either her logic or syntax to indicate the pressure under which she is performing. Pradon has failed to prepare the spectator at all for the sudden reversal when, using the device of *interruptio*, she betrays herself even more completely than Atalide had done:

> *Ah! chérissez plutôt un Héros qui vous aime,*
> *Vous perdrez Hippolyte, et vous perdrez vous-mesme,*
> *Pour luy tous vos soupirs seront empoisonnez,*
> *Et songez en l'aimant que vous l'assassinez ...*
> *Que deviendrois-je helas! si cet Amant si tendre*
> *Perissoit ... Oüy, Madame, et vous devez m'entendre,*
> *J'y prens sans y penser mesme interest que vous,*
> *Songez encore un coup que Thesée est jaloux.*
> *(ll.749-56)*

Pradon's Aricie does not simply overperform her role here; rather, she slips from this fault in the first quatrain to forgetting her role altogether within two lines. On the level of the plot, Pradon achieves a similar effect to Racine: the jealous heroine's suspicions are alerted and she will test the truth of them.[669] However, the build-up to the crucial moment has been far less interesting. Nor does Pradon pursue the strategy in Acts IV and V with the relentless ferocity and irony of *Bajazet*. His Aricie is absent for the remainder of Act III and the whole of Act IV, and the final scene between Phèdre and Aricie (V.1) owes nothing to confidential strategies. For in Act V Pradon's has moved into a very different vein: the tragedy of misinterpretation.[670] The comparison between his Aricie and Racine's Atalide acting as false *confidentes* illustrates that other playwrights had learned from Racine (and Thomas Corneille) the dramaturgical value of the strategy, but that Racine alone fully exploited the possibilities afforded by the theme of performance.

(iv) REJECTING THE ROLE OF THE FALSE *CONFIDENTE: RACINE'S IPHIGÉNIE*

In *Bérénice* and *Bajazet*, Racine had exploited two remarkably different variations on the role of the protagonist as false *confident*. Although deception and falsehood are integral to *Mithridate*, the device of the protagonist as false *confident* is not employed,[671] but in *Iphigénie* Racine again returns to it, for the

---

[669] Albeit with a variation in that she lays her trap for Hippolyte (IV.4) not Aricie.

[670] In Acts III-V, Pradon is closer thematically to the preoccupations of Quinault than of Racine.

[671] But Arbate's betrayal of Mithridate is a striking example of the simple *confident* acting falsely (see Ch.6).

last time. It forms an essential aspect of his integration of the invented episode
of Ériphile within the framework of the classical plot. Racine's preface reminds
us how much importance he attached to this episode, calling his character
"l'heureux personnage d'Ériphile, sans lequel je n'aurais jamais osé
entreprendre cette tragédie."[672] She it is who allows Racine to conceive of an
Iphigénie which departs significantly from those of Euripides or Rotrou.[673]
Ériphile's part is romanesque in the extreme: she adopts the *persona* of false
confidente to Iphigénie; the mystery of her identity is quite worthy of
Quinault's *Astrate*; and her name is the same as that of the heroine of Thomas
Corneille's *Timocrate*.[674] However, Racine once again adapts a romanesque/
tragicomic strategy to suit his tragic design. The difference this time is that
Ériphile, far from giving the over-zealous performance of an Atalide, fights
against the role in which she has been cast.

Many critics have seen *Iphigénie* as marking a new stage in Racine's
dramatic art, not least in his return to the source of Greek myths and
tragedies.[675] Certainly it belies the thesis that Racine sought an ever greater
simplicity, for there are no fewer than 10 characters, and 37 scenes - in the same
year that Corneille achieved the economy of 7 characters and 18 scenes in
Suréna. As far as the exploitation of the *confidents* is concerned, I would see
Iphigénie drawing selectively upon a number of successful strategies in which
Racine was now well versed. In particular, Doris is the active *confidente* shown
in vigorous temporary conflict with her mistress (both characters invented);
Arcas is the faithful older *confident/ conseiller*, whose conscience ultimately
causes him to betray Agamemnon (both characters drawn from Euripides); and
lastly Ériphile is the protagonist acting as false *confidente*. The low-ranked
confidents of *Iphigénie* (Doris, Arcas, Eurybate and Ægine - the latter two with
minor roles) speak for only 9.42% of the play. By the standards of
Andromaque, *Bérénice* or *Bajazet*, this is limited, but it is broadly in line with
the strategies characteristic of *Bajazet* and *Mithridate*. In addition, the presence
of Ulysse,[676] and the family bonds between Agamemnon, Clytemnestre and
Iphigénie facilitate a higher proportion of *para-confident* scenes than in any
other Racinian tragedy. Both conventional *confident* and *para-confident* scenes

---

[672] *Théâtre complet*, p.510.

[673] Nor is there any equivalent to Ériphile in the *Iphigénie* of Leclerc and Coras, staged in
May 1675.

[674] On the invention of Ériphile and Racine's very thin debt to classical sources, see R.
Knight, *Racine et la Grèce*, pp. 306, 317-8. It has also been suggested that Racine chose
Ériphile's name for the ironic association of its Greek etymology (see the discussion by R.
Pfohl, *Racine's Iphigénie: Literary Rehearsal and Tragic Recognition*, 1974, pp.166-8).

[675] See for example R. Knight, *Racine et la Grèce*, p.298.

[676] Ulysse was also present in Rotrou's *Iphigénie*. However, as Knight points out, Racine
dispensed with the classical role of Ménélas, which Rotrou had inherited from Euripides (*Racine
et la Grèce*, p.316).

are invested with the dramatic interest characteristic of Racine, but it is the relationship between Iphigénie and Ériphile which particularly fascinates the spectator, for the original audience could not have known how Racine would develop the situation he had constructed.

Drawing attention to the problems of focus which result from Racine's introduction of a second heroine, R. Parish describes Ériphile's role as "juxtapositional" to the main Iphigenia myth.[677] In Act I there is no suggestion of a particularly close bond between the two heroines. However, this Act is centred on the perspective of Agamemnon; not one of the three main female characters is present.[678] With the shift to the female perspective in Act II, we may think we are on familiar ground. Doris's reference to Iphigénie's *amitié* for Ériphile leads us to expect a relationship similar to that between Thomas Corneille's Ariane and Phèdre:

> *Maintenant tout vous rit: l'aimable Iphigénie*
> *D'une amitié sincère avec vous est unie;*
> *Elle vous plaint, vous voit avec des yeux de sœur.*
> *(ll.409-11)*

But Racine's Ériphile wants only to reject a role which does not fit. She has come on stage precisely to escape from Iphigénie and Clytemnestre.[679] Nor is she prepared to accept the *confidente*'s part of silent witness, excluded from the passions of the protagonists:

> *Hé quoi! te semble-t-il que la triste Ériphile*
> *Doive être de leur joie un témoin si tranquille?*
> *Crois-tu que mes chagrins doivent s'évanouir*
> *A l'aspect d'un bonheur dont je ne puis jouir?*
> *(ll.417-20)*

Her *aveu* to Doris of her love for Achille and of her jealousy towards Iphigénie allows the audience to understand her motivation. Significantly, before we witness Ériphile with Iphigénie, we know of Ériphile's malevolence:[680]

> *Iphigénie en vain s'offre à me protéger*
> ....
> *Je n'accepte la main qu'elle m'a présentée*
> *Que pour m'armer contre elle, et sans me découvrir,*
> *Traverser son bonheur que je ne puis souffrir.*
> *(ll.503-8)*

---

[677] *Racine: the Limits of Tragedy*, p.58.

[678] Lancaster reminds us that the introduction of a third main female role was unprecedented in Racine, and probably a consequence of la Beauval joining the Hôtel de Bourgogne: *A History of French Dramatic Literature*, Part IV, vol. I, p.92.

[679] "Ne les contraignons point, Doris, retirons-nous." (line 395).

[680] In contrast to Atalide, who played the role of false *confidente* to Roxane before we learned of her true motivation.

Her false *persona* is adopted with reluctance, only as a temporary expedient to serve her quest for revenge.

With this in mind, we are aware of the irony of Ériphile's presence at Agamemnon's cold reception of Iphigénie in II.2. Unlike protagonists who play the false *confidente* in other tragedies, she makes no attempt to perform her role adequately when she and Iphigénie are left alone. The departures from the conventions of a *confidente*'s role are instructive: Ériphile dismissively belittles Iphigénie's sufferings (ll.583-4), before arguing that her own situation is far worse. This might seem to be a variation on a Cornelian struggle of *générosité*,[681] but Ériphile's petulant refusal to acknowledge Iphigénie's pain is a rejection of the *amitié* which is supposed to underlie their confidential relationship. Iphigénie may ignore the deviation here (II.3), and go on to deliver a long confession of her passion to the unresponsive Ériphile,[682] but as soon as Clytemnestre has suggested that Ériphile may be the cause of Achille's supposed infidelity, Iphigénie holds Ériphile's poor performance of her role as *confidente* in II.5 against her :

> *Déjà plus d'une fois, dans vos plaintes forcées,*
> *J'ai dû voir, et j'ai vu, le fond de vos pensées.*
> *(ll.685-86)*

Since Iphigénie appears disabused, we might expect that Ériphile will be relieved of the role of false *confidente* at this early stage in the play - far earlier than any of her counterparts in other tragedies. Certainly she makes no attempt to placate Iphigénie.[683] Yet her response to Iphigénie's jealous outburst stops short of revealing her true sentiments. Hiding behind half-statements, Ériphile maintains for herself the only advantage she can hope for: that of adopting the *confidente*'s privilege of allowing others to act while she waits and observes.[684]

The inconclusive shifts in Ériphile's position in Act II are the first of a sequence. Rather than moving in a linear fashion towards the exposure of the false *confidente* as he did in *Bajazet*, Racine alternately raises and frustrates our expectations. In each of the remaining three acts Ériphile oscillates between assuming and rejecting her role. Our expectation that the mystery of her identity will be resolved rises each time she appears to cast off her false *persona*,

---

[681] For example, Sabine and Camille's debate over whose suffering is the greater in *Horace* III.4.

[682] Iphigénie speaks for 32 lines without Ériphile making any reply.

[683] The wounding tone in which her reply should be delivered is indicated by Iphigénie's comment on it: "Vous triomphez, cruelle, et bravez ma douleur." (l.711).

[684] At the end of the Act she draws attention to her role as observer ("J'ai des yeux", l.761). On Ériphile's "spectatorial role", see R. Parish, *Racine: the Limits of Tragedy*, p.62.

yet we are disappointed as the evolution of the plot forces her to resume her unwelcome role. The tensions of Ériphile's status are conveyed in Acts III and IV by her alternate presence alongside Iphigénie (as false *confidente*) and alone (as protagonist seeking her own identity). After the bitter exchanges of II.5 we may be surprised that at Iphigénie's next appearance (III.4), she is still accompanied by Ériphile. However, although Ériphile leaves with Clytemnestre after Arcas's dramatic betrayal of Agamemnon (III.5), she does not re-enter with the Queen two scenes later. Her absence from Iphigénie's side at the end of Act III may pass unremarked in the drama of the moment,[685] but it foretells the dénouement. The first scene of Act IV is a virtual *reprise* of II.1: Ériphile alone with Doris in order to escape the sight of her rival.[686] As the tragic weight of Act IV then tilts towards Iphigénie, Agamemnon and Achille, Ériphile makes one last appearance as a silent *confidente* before she prepares to throw off the mantle. In IV.10, she and Doris simply accompany Iphigénie: however, her choice not to exit with Iphigénie implies that a resolution is near. As she departs to find Calchas, she is finally independent of Iphigénie, no longer condemned to the passive inaction of a *confidente*.[687]

In one of the many ironies of focus in *Iphigénie*, it is in the course of the last Act that Ériphile crosses the boundary to be recognised as a full protagonist, and yet she does not appear on stage once in this act. Instead, the opening of Act V leaves us with the impression that Iphigénie has again upstaged Ériphile. The heroine's decision to offer herself as sacrificial victim once more relegates Ériphile to the role of spectator. She does not accompany Iphigénie in V.1 as a *confidente* might have done (the irony would have been too black perhaps), but Ulysse reports that she was a witness to the impending sacrifice:

> Ainsi parle Calchas. Tout le camp immobile
> L'écoute avec frayeur, et regarde Ériphile.
> Elle était à l'autel, et peut-être en son cœur
> Du fatal sacrifice accusait la lenteur.
>   (ll.1757-60)

When her true identity is revealed by Calchas, Ériphile takes centrestage - yet only in Ulysse's *récit*. Eclipsed from view, blackened by her treachery, she cannot summon up the depth of tragic pity in the spectator that her namesake

---

[685] That the other characters do not spare a thought for Ériphile in the rest of the Act is also characteristic of the traditional role of the *confidente*.

[686] Again, it is her role as witness not protagonist which has made Ériphile flee (ll.1090-1).

[687] On the significance of the stage movements at the end of Act IV, see D. Maskell, *Racine*, p.56.

would have done. Perhaps it was as a gesture towards pathos that Racine had Ulysse report how his heroine wept for her:

> *Tout s'empresse, tout part. La seule Iphigénie*
> *Dans ce commun bonheur pleure son ennemie.*
>   *(ll.1785-86)*

But we might also attribute this to Racine's fascination with the symmetry of Iphigénie's and Ériphile's roles. Finally, Ériphile has become a protagonist, assured of her own identity, speaking in her own voice (ll.1768-70), and watched by the crowd. In contrast, Iphigénie has accepted the role of spectator and silent witness, but also of *confidente* who alone of those present empathises with the fate of the heroine. Forestier suggests that Iphigénie's grief is due to the fact that she is "bien consciente qu'elle est morte à travers son double", and his reading is psychologically convincing.[688] In addition, he draws out many of the strands of the "dédoublement du même personnage" which have operated throughout the tragedy. I think we need to add to them the inversion of the roles of *confidente* and protagonist. Racine's control of the dramaturgical device of a protagonist acting as false *confidente* had enabled him to create a tragedy of mistaken identity which was quite unlike its many romanesque and tragicomic predecessors.

---

[688] *Esthétique de l'identité*, p.586

CHAPTER EIGHT

CONCLUSIONS

Our survey of tragedies from 1635 to 1677 has, first of all, confirmed that the *confident* remains a device used in nearly every work. In this respect we can still echo Scherer's view: "il est toujours là. On ne saurait se passer de lui."[689] What has become clear, however, is that the role admits enormous variations, and that far from dramatists merely seeing the *confident* as a necessary evil, some exploit the full dramatic potential of the role. To what extent, in conclusion, is it valid to discern some broad chronological evolutions?

(i) EVALUATING THE EVOLUTION OF THE *CONFIDENT*'S ROLE

We started out in Chapter 1 by looking at Scherer's bipartite model for the use of the *confident*: "après le confident triomphant, le confident honteux". At the conclusion of this study, I would propose instead a tripartite summary. First, a widespread and relatively untrammeled use of *confidents* in the first decade of the emergence of French classical tragedy, approximately 1635-45. For this I accept Scherer's dates for "le confident triomphant",[690] although I would not go so far as to describe this as a "triumph"; rather, the generous use of *confidents* is one of the manifestations of earlier playwrights' tendency to introduce a large number of secondary roles, whether as *confidents*, conspirators, messengers or attendants.

Secondly, there is a period of some unease over the *confident*'s role, culminating in the *Querelle du confident* of 1663 and Racine's first experiments with the eclipse of the role. This second stage covers approximately twenty years (c.1645-65), and embraces a wide range of reactions. Some playwrights, like Pierre Corneille in his plays from 1648-52, Rotrou in *Venceslas*, or Racine in *La Thébaïde* and *Alexandre* minimise the speaking part of any *confident*, relying on alternative strategies (*para-confidents*, monologues, asides). Alternatively, as *vraisemblance* becomes a central preoccupation of playwrights and critics alike, plays which do use

---

[689] *La Dramaturgie classique*, p.47.
[690] *La Dramaturgie classique*, p.46.

confidents display a growing tendency for these characters either to justify the close relationship they enjoy with a protagonist, or to accept the role of the silent listener. Another common solution is the creation of fictional characters who act as *para-confidents*, thus avoiding some of the problems of *vraisemblance* associated with a lower-ranked *confident*, but not necessarily resolving the obstacle of holding the audience's interest. Yet we should not suggest that there is a monolithic evolution in these twenty years, and Scherer's category of "le confident honteux" should be taken as no more than an indicator of *one* significant trend. For we can equally name works from 1645-65 in which *confidents* continue to enjoy prominence, and these include *Timocrate*, *Arie et Pétus* and *Camma*. In fact it is often such works as these, in which *confidents* are fully exploited, in which the role seems least problematic. Playwrights like Thomas Corneille perhaps had an innate sense of how to marry a conventional device to the creation of exciting drama.

Finally, in the decade from *Andromaque* to *Phèdre*, we have observed what I termed the rebirth of the active *confident*. Again, the phenomenon is not universal; there are of course still plays in which *confidents* have limited roles and others in which their roles are flatly conventional. But there is a marked tendency for the *confident* to become an essential component of the successful playwright's armoury, and, as I have argued in chapters 4-7, this means that our appreciation of many of the best tragedies from this period is significantly enhanced by our understanding of the ways in which they exploit confidential strategies. The reasons for this upturn in the *confident*'s fortunes in the late 1660s and the 1670s are, as we have seen, several. The *Querelle du confident* had brought the subject to the forefront of debate and invited playwrights to reflect on a device which they might previously have employed more mechanically. The models offered by Racine and Thomas Corneille, in particular, offered a new vision of how the *confident* could participate in lively, conflictual dialogues. And the increasing taste for *tragédies galantes* put the analysis of sentiments and passions at the centre of drama, with the *confident* serving as a prime agent to evoke the audience's emotional response.

I have chosen to end this study with Racine's *Phèdre*, not because 1677 marks the end of the road for the *confident*, but because a survey of a range of tragedies from the later years of the reign of Louis XIV has led me to the conclusion that in general they do not show new or very imaginative handling of the device. In part, this may be the result of a change of generation. By 1677 the prestige of tragedy was severely threatened by the rise of opera, at least as far as court audiences were concerned. Pierre Corneille, Gilbert and Quinault were no longer writing tragedies; Boyer and Thomas Corneille would produce only one more play each.[691] Of the "old guard" Racine alone returned to

---

[691] See p.144 on Thomas Corneille's *Le Comte d'Essex* (1678).

tragedy, with *Esther* (1689) and *Athalie* (1691). What other tragedies of the 1680s and 1690s - those of Catherine Bernard, Campistron, Pradon and their generation - demonstrate is that the role of the *confident* is still a viable dramaturgical device. However, like many other conventions of French classical dramaturgy,[692] it rarely prompts searching scrutiny or creative innovation.

In the Introduction I argued that it is above all in the works of Racine that we can discern the most interesting and successful experiments with confidential strategies. Throughout this study I have sought to balance an analysis of the evolution of the *confident* in his tragedies with detailed discussions of the contributions of other playwrights. Racine is both a model for contemporaries but also himself borrows or adapts structures from earlier works. Thus if *Andromaque* provided the example for the prominent use of four *confidents* in Quinault's *Pausanias*, or if *Bajazet* was the inspiration for Pradon to introduce the protagonist as false *confidente* in *Phèdre et Hippolyte*, we should not forget that Racine found the opposing *conseillers* of *Britannicus* in Gilbert's *Arie et Pétus*, and that his Œnone has undoubted similarities with Mégare in Quinault's *Bellérophon*. What distinguishes Racine from his contemporaries is that the exploitation of confidential strategies is germane to the conception of every one of his tragedies. There may be striking variations between, say, the minimal presence of *confidents* in *La Thébaïde* and their central role in *Andromaque*, or between the powerful *conseillers* of *Britannicus* and the king's rejection of his *confident* in *Mithridate*, but in no play has Racine assumed that the *confident* is simply a static dramaturgical convention. Critics have long acknowledged that Racine's handling of the unities contributes to the power of his tragedies; I would contend that the same is equally true of his vision of the *confident*. In none of his works is this more apparent than in *Phèdre*, and I have reserved this play for the concluding section as a final illustration of the way in which our appreciation of confidential strategies may shed new light on even the most familiar of French classical tragedies.

(ii) A FINAL TEST OF CONFIDENTIAL STRATEGIES: RACINE'S *PHÈDRE*

For Racine, *Phèdre* was a test on many levels. His version of the play would have to stand comparison with that of Euripides (whose influence he proclaimed in his preface), as well as with the tragedies of Seneca and of three

---

[692] See the discussion in *Le Théâtre du XVIIe siècle*, ed. J. Truchet et A. Blanc, vol. III (1992), p.XVIII.

earlier seventeenth-century playwrights (La Pinelière's *Hippolyte*, 1635; Gilbert's *Hypolite, ou le garçon insensible*, 1647; Bidar's *Hippolyte*, 1675).[693] His subject also begged obvious comparisons with Thomas Corneille's successful *Ariane* and Quinault's *Bellérophon*, and, in the months before *Phèdre* was staged, Pradon was commissioned by Racine's enemies to steal his thunder.[694] As far as secondary characters were concerned, the classical models both gave significant but rather different roles to Phædra's nurse, and both relied upon a secondary male character (a messenger) to deliver a long, poetic *récit* to Theseus of his son's fate. The other four French versions of the Phædra myth in turn all employed secondary characters to accompany Phædra and Hippolytus, but with marked variations in their status and the importance of their roles. When we measure Racine's *Phèdre* against these, it is at once apparent that he is closer to his classical models, especially to Euripides, in his conception of the roles of Œnone and Théramène, and in the significance he attributes to them. Before examining how his *confidents* contribute to the tragic design of *Phèdre*, it is instructive to note the comparative figures for the use of *confidents*/secondary characters in each of the tragedies on the theme:[695]

EURIPIDES

Nurse of Phædra	232/1466 lines	= 15.83%
An old servant of Hippolytus	18/—	= 1.23%
Messenger (servant of Hippolytus)	97/—	= 6.62%
TOTAL		= 23.68%

SENECA

Nurse of Phædra	244/1280 lines	= 19.06%
Messenger	121/—	= 9.45%
TOTAL		= 28.51%

---

[693] Of his debts to these Latin and French precursors, Racine said nothing in his Preface. For a full comparison of the relationship between Racine's play and its predecessors, see: W. Newton, *Le Thème de Phèdre et d'Hippolyte dans la littérature française* (1939). Newton concludes (p.156) that it is impossible to be sure whether Racine was familiar with the earlier French plays on the theme. More recently, critics have tended to assume that Racine did have some acquaintance with them (e.g. A.G. Wood, *Le Mythe de Phèdre*, 1996, p.13). From our point of view, some comparisons with Racine's predecessors are interesting as an indication of what makes Racine's treatment of the myth so memorable, whether or not he was consciously imitating or rejecting previous treatments.

[694] In the event, the rival *Phèdre et Hippolyte* opened two days after Racine's. See O. Classe's edition of Pradon, *Phèdre et Hippolyte* (1987), pp. XII-XXII.

[695] I take into account only those characters who have a speaking role, not silent attendants.

LA PINELIÈRE[696]

Athys (lieutenant des chasses d'Hippolyte)	133/1446 lines	= 9.2%
Capitaine des gardes	10/ —	= 0.69%
Hésione (fille d'honneur de Phèdre)	40/ —	= 2.77%
Lycrate (courtisan de Thésée)	64/ —	= 4.43%
Procris (fille d'honneur de Phèdre)	13/ —	= 0.9%
SUBTOTAL		=17.99%
Nourrice de la Reyne[697]	280/1446	=19.36%
TOTAL (including Nourrice)		=37.35%

GILBERT

Achrise (confidente de Phædre)	170/1634 lines	= 10.4%
Aristée (chasseur, ami d'Hypolite)	134/ —	= 8.2%
Omphale (suivante)	7/ —	= 0.43%
Pasithée (confidente de Phædre)	59/ —	= 3.61%
Tecmènes (confident de Thésée)	19/ —	= 1.16%
SUBTOTAL		= 23.8%
Pithée (aieul d'Hypolite)[698]	50/1634 lines	= 3.06%
TOTAL (including Pithée)		= 26.86%

BIDAR

Arbate (Athenien confident d'Hippolyte)	109/1688 lines	= 6.46%
Barsine (confidente de Phèdre)	99/ —	= 5.86%
Mégare (confidente de Cyane)	5/ —	= 0.3%
TOTAL		= 12.62%

PRADON

Arcas (confident de Thésée)	12/1738 lines	= 0.69%
Cléone (confidente d'Aricie)	11/ —	= 0.63%
Idas (gouverneur d'Hippolyte)	125/ —	= 7.19%
Mégiste (femme de la suite de Phèdre)	2/ —	= 0.12%[699]
TOTAL		= 8.63%

---

[696] For La Pinelière, Gilbert and Bidar, I base my figures on the critical editions in A. G. Wood, *Le Mythe de Phèdre*.

[697] A. G. Wood does not view the Nourrice as a secondary character (*Le Mythe de Phèdre*, p.43). Given the Senecan nature and proportions of her role, I would judge her status to be on the borderline between main and secondary characters.

[698] Although Pithée is a *para-confident* rather than a *confident* by virtue of his rank, his role is strictly limited to receiving and responding to confidences.

[699] Pradon's Aricie is a protagonist acting as false *confidente* to Phèdre (see p.195). This is a major reason for Mégiste's role being so limited.

RACINE

Ismène (confidente d'Aricie)	32/1654 lines	= 1.93%
Œnone (nourrice et confidente de Phèdre)	212/ —	= 12.82%
Panope (femme de la suite de Phèdre)	37/ —	= 2.24%
Théramène (gouverneur d'Hippolyte)	181/ —	= 10.94%
TOTAL		= 27.93%

Abandoning the "middling role" accorded to confidents in his three most recent tragedies (*Bajazet, Mithridate* and *Iphigénie*), in *Phèdre* Racine once again exploits the strategy of the active, prominent confident which he had developed in *Andromaque, Britannicus* and *Bérénice*. When we look at the overall share of confidents' discourse, there is a particularly striking contrast if we compare *Phèdre* (27.93%) with the other two versions of the 1670s, Bidar's (12.62%) and Pradon's (8.63%). It is not that either Bidar or Pradon have sought to eliminate confidents on any major scale; the total percentage of discourse by their confidents is within the normal parameters for the period. Rather, Racine's *Phèdre* stands out as the exception, appearing to hark back to the patterns of La Pinelière and Gilbert some thirty to forty years earlier. Comparing Racine and La Pinelière is in fact of limited interest, both because the latter follows Seneca so closely, and also because the whole mode of his tragedy is far closer to the static, lyrical vein of Garnier and late Renaissance playwrights. Gilbert provides a far more illuminating contrast. We have seen that Racine had derived the basis for some of his confidential strategies in *Britannicus* from Gilbert's *Arie et Pétus*, transforming them in the process; there is a similar relationship between *Phèdre* and Gilbert's *Hypolite*. I suspect that the latter provided a model which encouraged Racine to rely heavily on confidents, especially in the first half of the play, but in place of the dialectical arguments of Gilbert's protagonists and confidents Racine substitutes scenes in which attempts at persuasion are intimately linked to the workings of the passions.

If we ask what is original about Racine's conception of the roles of his *confidents* in *Phèdre*, and to what extent his confidential strategies contribute significantly to the tragedy, his Preface suggests one direction in which we should look. His Phèdre is inspired by Euripides' character, but his Hippolyte is different, for the death of the classical Hippolytus provoked "beaucoup plus d'indignation que de pitié".[700] Racine wants both his young hero and the mature heroine to appeal to the audience's sense of pity. The result is that the first two acts are structured around the parallels between the confessions of

---

[700] *Théâtre complet*, p.577.

Hippolyte's and Phèdre's passions. Within this framework the roles of Théramène and Œnone are, as Barthes recognised,[701] essential and complementary. This is quite different from the structure governing the equivalent roles in either Euripides or Seneca. Both classical tragedians accorded a prominent role to the Nurse before the arrival of Theseus, but in neither did Hippolytus have a corresponding confidant. The band of servants/ huntsmen who accompany him early in Euripides's play address Artemis not Hippolytus, and the old servant who engages in dialogue with the prince has an adversarial role, cautioning Hippolytus not to slight Aphrodite. This servant is, furthermore, a protactic character, who never reappears. Seneca's play opens with Hippolytus assigning duties for the hunt to his band of followers, but none of them is named or speaks. Racine signals his allegiance to classical tradition by opening his play with Hippolyte - La Pinelière, Gilbert and Bidar had all opened with Phèdre - but he also marks out his difference from Euripides and Seneca in the long exposition between Hippolyte and Théramène.

Opening scenes between protagonist and *confident* are, from *Andromaque* onwards, a standard feature of Racine's tragedies. The first scene of *Phèdre* is vital both for us to understand how Racine is adapting the classical myth by having a hero with "quelque faiblesse" (his passion for Aricie), and also to ensure that Hippolyte engages our sympathies before Phèdre appears. Théramène's role contributes to both of these ends. He resembles Euripides's Old Huntsman only in so far as his age is concerned. Like Gilbert, who gave Hypolite both an "ayeul" (Pithée) and a younger "amy" (Aristée), Racine senses the need to balance his Hippolyte's youth against the *confident*'s experience.[702] But Gilbert's Pithée appeared only once, in II.2, to recall to Hypolite his father's example; it was the young Aristée who in the following scene (II.3) listened to Hypolite's confidential revelations, including the confession of his love for Phædre. As in his adaptation of *Arie et Pétus* for *Britannicus*, Racine shies away from Gilbert's preference for pairs of secondary characters.[703] Instead, Théramène combines the experience and *gravitas* of an *ayeul* with the bond of affection of an Aristée. From the outset he is portrayed as an active *confident*: he has undertaken an extensive search for Thésée at Hippolyte's behest, and Théramène's enumeration of his efforts on the prince's behalf makes it clear that he is engaged in the unfolding of the plot:

---

[701] *Sur Racine*, p.111.

[702] Théramène is quite different from the young companions of Hippolyte who are the equivalent of *confidents* in La Pinelière and Bidar. Athys in *La Pinelière* appears only once before the dénouement, in II.2, simply to receive Hippolyte's orders for the hunt. Bidar's Arbate fulfils the function of messenger in II.3 and IV.6, and resembles a *confident* only in V.3-7 when he delivers a récit of Hippolyte's death and listens to Thésée's expressions of grief.

[703] Gilbert's Phædre also has two *confidentes*, Achrise and Pasithée.

> *J'ai couru les deux mers que sépare Corinthe;*
> *J'ai demandé Thésée aux peuples de ces bords*
> *Où l'on voit l'Achéron se perdre chez les morts;*
> *J'ai visité l'Élide ...*
> *(ll.10-13)*

In addition, his affection for Hippolyte is shown to rest on solid foundations. When Hippolyte is about to confess his love for Aricie, he prefaces his speech to Théramène by recalling the *gouverneur*'s role in his childhood:

> *Ami, qu'oses-tu dire?*
> *Toi qui connais mon cœur depuis que je respire...*
> *(ll.65-66)*

and

> *Attaché près de moi par un zèle sincère,*
> *Tu me contais alors l'histoire de mon père.*
> *(ll.73-74)*

Théramène is, as it were, *in loco parentis*. In the past he replaced the absent Thésée by his *récits*; now, he again stands in for the father in his close relationship with Hippolyte. In a play which will depend on the gravest misunderstanding between father and son, Racine draws an implicit contrast through the alternative pairing of Hippolyte and Théramène, a contrast which will be evoked again in the final act.[704]

The reference to Théramène's presence since Hippolyte's birth can be construed as a deliberate parallel with the relationship between Phèdre and Œnone. Euripides and Seneca have the Nurse stress her maternal affection for Phædra in order to make her appeals to her mistress more eloquent. Racine's Œnone, seeking to prevent Phèdre from dying, demands in I.3:

> *Songez-vous qu'en naissant mes bras vous ont reçue?*
> *(line 234)*

In Théramène, Racine created her male counterpart. When Théramène responds to Hippolyte's confession of love by arguing that such a passion is no cause for shame, his arguments in fact resemble those used by Seneca's Nurse to Hippolytus (*Hippolytus*, ll.461-82). Parallels betwen Racine's Théramène and Œnone are the more striking because the two *confident* scenes of Act I follow in quick succession. Only the briefest transitional scene separates Hippolyte's confession to Théramène (I.1) from Phèdre's to Œnone (I.3). This structure, which cannot be traced to any of Racine's precursors, has several consequences. First, it allows Racine to postpone the *grande scène* between Hippolyte and Phèdre until II.5. Gilbert likewise had no scenes between any main protagonists

---

[704] Compare Aristotle's recommendation that the most moving tragedies are those which concern kinship (*Poetics*, chapter 14).

until his Phædre and Hypolite met in Act III scene 2, but he devoted the whole of his first Act to exchanges between Phædre and her *confidentes* and then the whole of the second Act to Hypolite and secondary characters. Racine in contrast moves swiftly to establish a symmetry between Phèdre and Hippolyte in the first act. The second consequence of the parallel confessions is to establish one of the seams of tragic irony which will run throughout the play: unsuspected by Phèdre, Hippolyte is, like her, in thrall to a passion he considers shameful. On one level, we may be more struck by the differences than the similarities between I.1 and I.3: Phèdre's confession is laborious and anguished, her passivity and reliance on Œnone quite unlike Hippolyte's determination to take his fate into his own hands by leaving Trœzen. Yet both scenes provoke in the audience a deep sense of pity for characters who will fall victim to the ironies of fate. And both herald the symmetrical scenes of confession which balance Act II, Hippolyte's declaration of love to Aricie (II.2) and Phèdre's to Hippolyte (II.5).

The close balance of the roles of Hippolyte and Phèdre, and of Théramène and Œnone, shapes the first two acts. Thereafter the symmetry is less precise, with Œnone's role far greater in Acts III and IV, Théramène's in Act V. Even so, there is evidence that Racine still considered the *confidents* essential to his tragic design, for there is a *confident* scene not only to open but also to close each of Acts I-IV. Placing *confident* scenes at the end of acts is rare among most seventeenth-century tragedians,[705] but Racine had already done so in Acts I-IV of both *Britannicus* and *Bérénice*. In *Phèdre*, there is a striking contrast between Théramène's role at the end of Acts II and III and Œnone's at the end of Acts I and IV. Théramène is present in II.6 and III.6 to allow Hippolyte to express his shocked reaction to Phèdre's confession and to his initial meeting with Thésée. The *gouverneur* does not influence Hippolyte's conduct in either scene; indeed, in III.6 he is a silent listener. In contrast, Œnone has a material effect upon Phèdre's conduct. Such is the significance of the *confidente*'s influence that Racine draws attention to it in the preface, claiming that he has made Œnone more guilty in order to make Phèdre "un peu moins odieuse qu'elle n'est dans les tragédies des Anciens".[706] The most important interventions of Œnone, proposing that Phèdre should accuse Hippolyte (III.4) and she herself should bear false witness to Thésée (IV.1), derive not so much

[705] Compare Corneille's *Suréna*, in which, with the exception of the last scene of the play, *confidents* are deployed only in the opening scene of an act. See p.166.
[706] *Théâtre complet*, p.577.

from Seneca's Nurse[707] as from Phædre's *confidente*, Achrise, in Gilbert's *Hypolite*. In this latter play, however, Achrise's accusation of Hypolite is unplanned; it is only after Phædre has nearly betrayed herself and exited leaving Thésée bewildered that Achrise, without consulting her mistress, tells a blatant lie (which is supported in front of Hypolite by Phædre's other servants in the following scene).[708] Similarly, in Quinault's *Bellérophon*, another probable model for *Phèdre*, when the heroine's *confidente* Mégare lies to insinuate that Bellérophon sought to dishonour the queen, the calumny is unplanned and made without reference to Sténobée.[709] In contrast, Racine builds up with meticulous care to the false denunciation. His Phèdre is "ni tout à fait coupable, ni tout à fait innocente". In III.3 she is made aware of the lie Œnone proposes to tell, and recognises the immorality of the action,[710] yet lacks the strength to oppose it. Phèdre's appeal to the audience is based precisely upon this fragile balance.[711]

When we look closely at the relationship between Phèdre and Œnone in III.4 and its aftermath, what becomes clear is that Racine has based his *confidente*'s role on the figure of the *conseiller*, adapting it to the personal rather than political domain. Like the hero of Rotrou's *Cosroès*, Phèdre is relieved of the full burden of her guilt because she is portrayed as weak, and subject to the blandishments of an amoral adviser. Five times Racine has Phèdre refer to Œnone's "conseils",[712] and as early as Act III her advice is associated with the negative epithet "flatteurs".[713] When Phèdre finally disowns Œnone at the end of Act IV, in a scene equal in power to any exchange between main protagonists, she explicitly compares her *confidente* to the sycophantic *conseillers* of princes:[714]

> *Et puisse ton supplice à jamais effrayer*
> *Tous ceux qui, comme toi, par de lâches adresses,*
> *Des princes malheureux nourrissent les faiblesses,*
> *Les poussent au penchant où leur cœur est enclin,*
> *Et leur osent du crime aplanir le chemin!*

---

[707] In Seneca the Nurse shouts to the listening attendants that Hippolytus has tried to rape Phædra (*Hippolytus*, ll.725-30), but it is Phædra herself who maintains the lie before Theseus by showing him Hippolytus's sword (ll.996-7).

[708] *Hypolite*, IV.3, ll.1053-62; IV.4, ll.1225-27.

[709] *Bellérophon* IV.2.

[710] "Moi, que j'ose opprimer et noircir l'innocence!" (l.893).

[711] M. Hawcroft, analysing the difference between Phèdre's and Œnone's persuasive strategies in III.3, argues that the contrast increases our pity for Phèdre: *Word as Action*, p.182.

[712] Lines 363, 771, 791, 838, 1307.

[713] "Par tes conseils flatteurs tu m'as su ranimer" (l.771).

[714] Although the final scene of Act IV is based on the scene in Euripides in which Phædra reviles her Nurse, Racine has moved beyond his Greek source in associating Œnone with the favourites of princes.

> *Détestables flatteurs, présent le plus funeste*
> *Que puisse faire aux rois la colère céleste.*
>   (Phèdre, *ll.1320-6)*

Even in her final confession to Thésée in the last scene of the play, Phèdre still invites us to perceive Œnone as sharing the traits of a Narcisse:

> *La détestable Œnone a conduit tout le reste*
> ....
> *La perfide, abusant de ma faiblesse extrême,*
> *S'est hâtée à vos yeux de l'accuser lui-même.*
>   (Phèdre, *ll.1626-30)*

And like the worst of *mauvais conseillers*, Œnone pays the price with her own life. Whereas *confidents* in seventeenth-century French tragedy do not die, *conseillers*, who are on the borderline between *confidents* and protagonists, may risk their lives. For Phèdre fully to win the spectators' pity, she must convince us in the course of her performance that her responsibility is mitigated by Œnone's actions. Yet in his preface, Racine stood back and weighed Œnone's role more objectively, speaking of "une nourrice ... qui néanmoins n'entreprend cette fausse accusation, que pour sauver la vie et l'honneur de sa maîtresse."[715] Again, Racine has brought together ancient and seventeenth-century traditions to shape our response to the tragedy: the Euripidean Nurse whose deep love for her mistress awakens the audience's pity for the heroine is lent the language, strategies and even the fate of the political *conseiller*.

Just how far Théramène and Œnone are essential and innovatory figures is made clearer by the contrast with Aricie's *confidente*, Ismène. The flexibility with which Racine handles the *confident* in his last secular tragedy is underlined by the fact that he does not feel constrained to give Aricie and Thésée *confidents* of similar stature. The symmetry of four protagonists and four *confidents* is no longer appropriate. Aricie's *confidente* speaks in only one scene;[716] Thésée is strategically isolated, with no *confident*. Because Aricie is an invented character, it is imperative that Racine should present her to us in a neutral *confident* scene before we see her engaged in dialogue with Hippolyte. With skill, he disguises the transmission of information beneath deliberative rhetoric.[717] However, Ismène is not an individualised character. She may convey

---

[715] *Théâtre complet*, p.577.

[716] The character who is the counterpart to Aricie in Bidar's *Hippolyte* also has only one scene alone with her *confidente* (III.4), and it is far shorter than II.1 of *Phèdre*.

[717] Aricie uses the phrase "Tu sais" to Ismène three times (lines 427, 431, 433). She is repeating information about her past conduct which is familiar to her *confidente*, but framing it within the argument that her love for Hippolyte has transformed her.

her report of reactions to Thésée's death in a lively manner; she may even engage in a temporary conflict with her mistress about the behaviour of Hippolyte, but there is no sense of Ismène sharing with her mistress the intimate bonds which link Théramène and Hippolyte or Phèdre and Œnone. Tellingly, there is no further scene between Aricie and Ismène in the play; hereafter Ismène is only a silent attendant.

For Thésée the absence of a *confident* is both in accordance with the classical models, and also a means of highlighting the king's isolation. Whereas La Pinelière and Gilbert have Thésée accompanied by a *confident* with whom he has a long scene upon his return (IV.1 in both plays), Racine exploits the strategy we examined in Chapter 6, the selective exclusion of the *confident*. He allows no rational, moderating voice which could stay the king's anger in Act IV; neither is there any familiar friend or servant to share the tormented doubts Thésée expresses in his monologue of V.4. It is in front of his son's *confident*, Théramène, that the king expresses his anguish in Act V. In their common grief the two father figures remain divided, even antagonistic. Thésée implies his reproach to Théramène as soon as the latter arrives on stage, while acknowledging that the *gouverneur* replaced (or displaced) him:

> *Théramène, est-ce toi? Qu'as-tu fait de mon fils?*
> *Je te l'ai confié dès l'âge le plus tendre.*
> *(ll.1488-89)*

Théramène concludes his *récit* of Hippolyte's death by faithfully reporting Hippolyte's dying message to Thésée, but he gestures towards the contrast between himself and Thésée:

> *A ce mot, ce héros expiré*
> *N'a laissé dans mes bras qu'un corps défiguré,*
> *Triste objet, où des dieux triomphe la colère,*
> *Et que méconnaîtrait l'œil même de son père.*
> *(ll.1567-70)*

It was Théramène's arms, not Thésée's, which held the dying Hippolyte,[718] and Théramène claims that the father would not even recognise his son's dead body. This is not simply Racine finding a euphemistic paraphrase for the gory horror of the death so memorably evoked by Seneca.[719] The opposition between Théramène and Thésée is, rather, an echo of that between the messenger and Theseus at the same point in Euripides' version, for the messenger dared to defend Hippolytus and ask Theseus's leave to have the dying prince brought in. Racine's Théramène prefaced his *récit* in a similar manner:

---

[718] Compare line 234 in which Œnone referred to receiving Phèdre in her arms at her birth.

[719] There is nothing equivalent to line 1570 in Euripides, Seneca, La Pinelière, Gilbert or Bidar.

J'ai vu des mortels périr le plus aimable,
Et j'ose dire encor, Seigneur, le moins coupable.
                    (ll.1493-94)

Yet again, Racine shows that he has learned the most important lesson from Greek tragedy: that conflict can bring to life scenes between protagonists and secondary characters. To that he has added his awareness that the bonds between protagonist and *confident* - in *Phèdre* bonds which for two characters are quasi-parental - are an essential means of generating the pity which tragedy should evoke. Far from the *confident* being a mere fixed device, in Racine's hands confidential strategies are an essential thread in the fabric of the tragic design. *Phèdre* is unthinkable without either Œnone or Théramène, and this is the ultimate test of the significance of the Racinian *confident*.

APPENDICES

NOTE

Plays are listed according to the probable order in which they were performed. All statistics relate to the first printed edition of each play (see date in brackets). I have drawn this data from the editions of Pierre Corneille and Racine listed below (using the Tables of variants to establish the text of the first printed edition where appropriate):

Pierre Corneille, *Œuvres complètes*, ed. G. Couton, 3 vols. Bibliothèque de la Pléiade, Gallimard, Paris, 1980-87.

Jean Racine, *Théâtre complet*, ed. J. Morel et A. Viala, Classiques Garnier, Paris, 1995.

For the number of lines spoken by a particular character in a scene, I have rounded up or down (as appropriate) to the nearest whole alexandrine. Calculations involving percentages are given to two decimal places.

I discuss in Chapter 1 my general criteria for deciding which characters are considered as *confident(e)s* (see p.14). When using the Appendices readers may wish to consult the discussion of individual plays via the Index.

APPENDIX ONE.

THE USE OF *CONFIDENTS*/EQUIVALENT CHARACTERS IN CORNEILLE'S TRAGEDIES AND RELATED GENRES

Play	Character	Present in play			Present but silent		Speaks			
		Scenes	Lines	%age of play present	Scenes	Lines	Scenes	Lines	%age lines spoken by character	%age lines spoken in whole play
Médée	Cléone	7	438	26.32%	4	250	3	26	13.83%	1.56%
(1639)	Nérine	9	696	41.83%	3	398	6	127	42.62%	7.63%
	Pollux	3	264	15.87%	0	0	3	82	31.06%	4.93%
	All three characters									14.12%
Le Cid	Elvire	13	757	40.57%	5	329	8	97	22.66%	5.20%
(1636)	Léonor	6	318	17.04%	3	127	3	62	32.46%	3.32%
	Both characters									8.52%
Horace	Julie	7	636	35.77%	1	172	6	128	27.59%	7.20%
(1641)										
Cinna	Euphorbe	2	130	7.30%	0	0	2	62	47.69%	3.48%
(1643)	Fulvie	9	827	46.46%	6	681	3	49	33.56%	2.75%
	Both characters									6.23%
Polyeucte	Albin	9	592	32.64%	4	269	5	84	26.00%	4.63%
(1643)	Fabian	6	431	23.76%	4	255	2	37	21.02%	2.04%
	Stratonice	10	662	36.49%	7	401	3	124	47.51%	6.84%
	All three characters									13.51%
La Mort de	Charmion	12	813	44.87%	9	592	3	31	14.03%	1.71%
Pompée	Philippe	4	303	16.72%	3	199	1	51	49.04%	2.81%
(1644)	Both characters									4.52%
Théodore	Paulin	19	968	51.43%	11	429	8	173	32.10%	9.19%
(1646)	Stéphanie	16	860	45.70%	10	640	6	80	36.36%	4.25%
	Both characters									13.44%
Rodogune	Laonice	12	1115	60.47%	6	710	6	215	53.09%	11.66%
(1647)	Timagène	5	538	29.18%	1	104	4	69	15.90%	3.74%
	Both characters									15.40%
Héraclius	Amintas	6	299	15.61%	4	254	2	33	73.33%	1.72%
(1647)										
Don Sanche	Blanche	11	926	50.60%	7	691	4	92	39.15%	5.03%
(1650)										
Nicomède	Araspe	10	768	41.42%	7	561	3	36	17.39%	1.94%
(1651)	Cléone	9	416	22.44%	7	322	2	13	13.83%	0.70%
	Both characters									2.64%

Play	Character	Present in play			Present but silent		Speaks			
		Scenes	Lines	%age of play present	Scenes	Lines	Scenes	Lines	%age lines spoken by character	%age lines spoken in whole play
Œdipe	Cléante	6	444	22.09%	5	380	1	5	7.81%	0.25%
(1659)	Dymas	3	157	7.81%	0	0	3	61	38.85%	3.03%
	Mégare	6	600	29.85%	3	320	3	30	10.71%	1.49%
	Nérine	7	500	24.88%	5	343	2	86	54.78%	4.28%
	All four characters									9.05%
Sertorius	Arcas	7	299	15.57%	6	260	1	13	33.33%	0.68%
(1662)	Aufide	6	352	18.33%	1	50	5	89	29.47%	4.64%
	Celsus	2	60	3.13%	1	48	1	3	25.00%	0.16%
	Thamire	12	756	39.38%	8	563	4	68	35.23%	3.54%
	All four characters									9.02%
Sophonisbe	Barcée	12	804	44.13%	11	672	1	19	14.39%	1.04%
(1663)	Bocchar	2	174	9.55%	1	140	1	30	88.24%	1.65%
	Herminie	16	1031	56.59%	13	814	3	42	19.35%	2.31%
	Mézétulle	12	623	34.19%	9	439	3	40	21.74%	2.20%
	All four characters									7.20%
Othon	Albiane	13	795	43.40%	11	701	2	63	67.02%	3.43%
(1665)	Albin	5	208	11.35%	2	156	3	22	42.31%	1.21%
	Flavie	5	262	14.30%	3	141	2	88	72.73%	4.80%
	All three characters									9.44%
Agésilas	Cléon	4	208	9.80%	3	142	1	13	19.70%	0.61%
(1666)	Xenoclès	12	778	36.67%	8	599	4	64	35.75%	3.02%
	Both characters									3.63%
Attila	Flavie	6	365	20.41%	3	222	3	65	45.45%	3.64%
(1667)	Octar	13	1043	58.33%	8	762	5	122	43.42%	6.82%
	Both characters									10.46%
Tite et Bérénice	Albin	9	764	43.07%	7	630	2	88	65.67%	4.96%
	Flavian	10	742	41.83%	6	539	4	50	24.63%	2.82%
(1671)	Philon	11	674	37.99%	9	564	2	61	55.45%	3.44%
	Plautine	7	559	31.51%	5	341	2	39	17.89%	2.20%
	All four characters									13.42%
Suréna	Ormène	6	481	27.68%	3	285	3	42	21.43%	2.42%
(1675)	Silace	1	89	5.12%	0	0	1	26	29.21%	1.50%
	Both characters									3.92%

APPENDIX TWO

THE USE OF *CONFIDENTS*/EQUIVALENT CHARACTERS IN RACINE'S TRAGEDIES

Play	Character	Present in play			Present but silent		Speaks			
		Scenes	Lines	%age of play present	Scenes	Lines	Scenes	Lines	%age lines spoken by character	%age lines spoken in whole play
La Thébaïde	Attale	7	368	22.22%	2	160	5	30	14.42%	1.81%
(1664)	Olympe	11	648	39.13%	5	300	6	49	14.08%	2.96%
	Both characters									4.77%
Andromaque	Céphise	8	505	29.85%	4	291	4	48	22.43%	2.84%
(1668)	Cléone	10	608	35.93%	5	390	5	83	38.07%	4.91%
	Phœnix	8	521	30.79%	4	364	4	38	24.20%	2.25%
	Pylade	3	304	17.97%	0	0	3	127	41.78%	7.51%
	All four characters									17.51%
Britannicus	Albine	7	474	26.51%	4	271	3	90	44.33%	5.03%
(1670)	Burrhus	15	587	32.83%	4	91	11	285	57.46%	15.94%
	Narcisse	14	525	29.36%	7	132	7	168	42.75%	9.41%
	All three characters									30.38%
Bérénice	Arsace	13	480	31.62%	7	234	6	130	52.85%	8.56%
(1671)	Paulin	8	360	23.72%	2	82	6	104	37.41%	6.85%
	Phénice	7	452	29.78%	3	278	4	26	14.94%	1.71%
	All three characters									17.12%
Bajazet	Osmin	5	406	23.11%	2	83	3	111	34.37%	6.32%
(1672)	Zaïre	12	554	31.53%	6	300	6	47	18.51%	2.68%
	Zatime	13	348	19.81%	6	145	7	54	26.60%	3.07%
	All three characters									12.07%
Mithridate	Arbate	8	436	25.50%	3	78	5	151	42.18%	8.83%
(1673)	Arcas	4	100	5.85%	1	60	3	8	20%	0.47%
	Phædime	10	454	26.55%	4	255	6	62	31.16%	3.63%
	All three characters									12.93%
Iphigénie	Ægine	11	510	28.40%	9	454	2	7	12.50%	0.39%
(1675)	Arcas	4	309	17.12%	1	77	3	75	32.33%	4.18%
	Doris	13	554	30.85%	10	352	3	52	25.74%	2.90%
	Eurybate	4	120	6.68%	1	18	3	35	34.31%	1.95%
	All four characters									9.42%
Phèdre	Ismène	5	295	17.84%	4	199	1	32	33.33%	1.93%
(1677)	Œnone	10	678	40.99%	1	8	9	212	31.64%	12.82%
	Panope	3	108	6.53%	0	0	3	37	34.26%	2.24%
	Théramène	10	451	27.27%	6	164	4	181	63.07%	10.94%
	All four characters									27.93%

Note on Britannicus

If we take account of the draft of ?III.1, published by Louis Racine – see P. Butler's edition of *Britannicus* – the statistics for the play would be as follows:

Play	Character	Present in play			Present but silent		Speaks			
		Scenes	Lines	%age of play present	Scenes	Lines	Scenes	Lines	%age lines spoken by character	%age lines spoken in whole play
Britannicus	Albine	7	474	25.35%	4	271	3	90	44.33%	4.81%
(1670)	Burrhus	16	669	35.78%	4	91	12	358	61.94%	19.14%
	Narcisse	15	607	32.46%	7	132	8	177	37.26%	9.47%
All three characters										33.42%

BIBLIOGRAPHY

I list only those works directly referred to or cited in the text.

PRIMARY TEXTS

AUBIGNAC, François Hédelin, Abbé d', *Dissertations contre Corneille*, ed. N. Hammond and M. Hawcroft, University of Exeter Press, 1995

——, *La Pratique du théâtre*, ed. P. Martino, Algiers-Paris, 1927

BIDAR, Mathieu, *Hippolyte* in (ed) A. Wood, *Le Mythe de Phèdre. Les Hippolyte français du dix-septième siècle*, Honoré Champion, Paris, 1996

BOYER, Claude, *Oropaste, ou le faux Tonaxare*, ed. C. Delmas and G. Forestier, Droz, Geneva, 1990

CORNEILLE, Pierre, *Œuvres complètes*, ed. G. Couton, 3 vols., Bibliothèque de la Pléiade, Gallimard, Paris, 1980-7

——, *Le Cid 1637*-60, ed. G. Forestier, Paris, *Société des textes français modernes*, 1992

——, *Médée*, ed. A. de Leyssac, *Textes littéraires français*, Droz, Geneva, 1978

——, *Othon*, ed. J. Sanchez, Mugron, 1989

——, *Suréna général des Parthes*, ed. J. Sanchez, Ducros, Bordeaux, 1970

CORNEILLE, Thomas, *Théâtre complet*, ed. E. Thierry, Paris, 1881

——, *Camma*, ed. D. Watts, University of Exeter Press, 1977

——, *Stratonice*, ed. E. Dubois, University of Exeter Press, 1987

——, *Timocrate*, ed. Y. Giraud, *Textes littéraires français*, Droz, Geneva, 1970

CYRANO DE BERGÉRAC, Savinien, *La Mort d'Agrippine*, ed. C. Gossip, University of Exeter Press, 1982

DESJARDINS, Marie-Catherine (Madame de Villedieu), *Manlius*, Claude Barbin, Paris, 1662

——, *Nitétis*, Chez la veuve de Claude Barbin, Paris, 1702

EURIPIDES, *Andromache*, ed. D. Kovacs, Loeb Classical Library (*Euripides*, vol. II), Harvard University Press, 1995

——, *Hippolytus*, ed. D. Kovacs, Loeb Classical Library (*Euripides*, vol. II), Harvard University Press, 1995

GILBERT, Gabriel, *Arie et Pétus ou les amours de Néron*, Guillaume de Luyne, Paris, 1660

——, *Hypolite, ou le garçon insensible*, in (ed) A. Wood, *Le Mythe de Phèdre. Les Hippolyte français du dix-septième siècle*, Honoré Champion, Paris, 1996

GRANET, François, *Recueil de dissertations sur plusieurs tragédies de Corneille et de Racine*, 2 vols., Paris, 1739

LA PINELIÈRE, Guérin de, *Hippolyte* in (ed) A. Wood, *Le Mythe de Phèdre. Les Hippolyte français du dix-septième siècle*, Honoré Champion, Paris, 1996

MAGNON, Jean, *Tite: tragi-comédie*, ed. H. Bell, John Hopkins Press, 1936

PRADON, Nicolas, *Phèdre et Hippolyte*, ed. O. Classe, University of Exeter Press, 1987

QUINAULT, Philippe, *Théâtre*, Paris, 1739

——, *Astrate*, ed. E. Campion, University of Exeter Press, 1980

——, *Bellérophon*, ed. W. Brooks and E. Campion, *Textes littéraires français*, Droz, Geneva, 1990

RACINE, Jean, *Œuvres*, ed. P. Mesnard, Paris, 8 vols, 1923 (1st ed. 1865-73)

——, *Œuvres complètes*, ed. R. Picard, Gallimard, Bibliothèque de la Pléiade, Paris, 2 vols, 1966

——, *Théâtre complet*, ed. J. Morel and A. Viala, Classiques Garnier, Paris, 1995 (1st ed. 1980)

——, *Alexandre le Grand*, ed. M. Hawcroft and V. Worth, University of Exeter Press, 1990

——, *Andromaque*, ed. R.C. Knight and H. T. Barnwell, *Textes littéraires français*, Droz, Geneva, 1977

——, *Bajazet*, ed. M. McGowan, University of London Press, 1968

——, *Britannicus*, ed. P. Butler, Cambridge University Press, 1967

RACINE, Louis, *Œuvres*, Paris, 1808

ROTROU, Jean, *Cosroès*, ed. D. Watts, University of Exeter Press, 1983

——, *Venceslas,* ed. D. Watts, University of Exeter Press, 1990

SAINT-EVREMOND, Charles de Marguetel de Saint-Denis, *Œuvres en prose*, ed. R. Ternois, *Société des textes français modernes*, Paris, 1962-69

SEGRAIS, Jean Regnault de, *Les Nouvelles françaises*, ed. R. Guichemerre, 2 vols., Paris, 1990-2.

SENECA, *Tragedies*, ed. F. Miller, Loeb Classical Library, London, 1960

SOPHOCLES, *Sophocles*, ed. H. Lloyd-Jones, Loeb Classical Library, Harvard University Press, 1994-6

SUBLIGNY, Adrien Perdou de, *La Folle Querelle*, Paris, 1668

TACITUS, *Annales* and *Historiæ*, ed. J. Jackson and C. H. Moore, Loeb Classical Library, Harvard University Press, 1968-70

TALLEMANT DES RÉAUX, Gédéon, *Historiettes*, ed. A. Adam, 2 vols., Gallimard, Paris, 1960-61

Théâtre du XVIIe siècle, ed. J. Schérer, J. Truchet, A. Blanc, Bibliothèque de la Pléiade, Gallimard, Paris, 3 vols., 1975-92

TRISTAN L'HERMITE, François, *La Mort de Sénèque*, ed. J. Madeleine, *Société des textes français modernes*, Paris, 1919

VILLARS, Nicolas-Pierre-Henri, Abbé de, *La Critique de Bérénice*, in Granet, *Recueil* (q.v.)

VISÉ, Jean Donneau de, *Nouvelles nouvelles*, 3 vols., Paris, 1663

——, *Deffense de la Sophonisbe de Monsieur de Corneille*, in Granet, Recueil (q.v.)

——, *Deffense du Sertorius de Monsieur de Corneille*, in Granet, Recueil (q.v.)

VOLTAIRE, François-Marie Arouet de, *Œuvres complètes*, Firmin-Didot, Paris, 1876

SECONDARY WORKS

(i) WORKS ON PIERRE CORNEILLE

ALLOTT, T., "Tacitus and some late plays of Corneille", *Journal of European Studies*, 10 (1980), 33-45

AUTRAND, M., "Stratégie du personnage secondaire dans l'*Attila* de Corneille. Étude dramatique", in *Pierre Corneille. Actes du Colloque tenu à Rouen du 2 au 6 octobre 1984*, ed. A. Niderst, PUF, Paris, 1985

BAKER, S., *Dissonant Harmonies: Drama and Ideology in Five Neglected Plays of Pierre Corneille*, G. Narr, Tübingen, 1990

BARNWELL, H.T., *The Tragic Drama of Corneille and Racine. An Old Parallel Revisited*, Clarendon Press, Oxford, 1982

CLARKE, D., *Pierre Corneille. Poetics and Political Drama under Louis XIII*, Cambridge University Press, 1992

COUTON, G., *La Vieillesse de Corneille (1658-84)*, Maloine, Paris, 1949

DAVISON, H. M. , "La vraisemblance chez d'Aubignac et Corneille: quelques réflexions disciplinaires" in *L'Art du Théâtre. Mélanges en hommage à Robert Garapon*, textes réunis et publiés par Y. Bellenger et al., PUF, Paris, 1992, 91-100

DESCOTES, M., *Dix Promenades dans le cimetière cornélien*, Pensée Universelle, Paris, 1983

DESFOUGERÈS, A.-M., "L'échec de *Pertharite*" in *Pierre Corneille. Actes du Colloque organisé par l'Université de Rouen (1984)*, PUF, Paris, 1985, 501-6

DESMOND, S., "Les confident(e)s dans le théâtre comique de Corneille", *Papers on French Seventeenth-Century Literature*, XXV-48 (1998), 167-175

DOUBROVSKY, S., *Corneille et la dialectique du héros*, Gallimard, Paris, 1963

ELLINGTON-GUNTER, E., "The Function of Vinius in *Othon*", *French Review*, 55-1 (October 1981), 188-92

FORESTIER, G., *Essai de génétique théâtrale. Corneille à l'œuvre*, Klinksieck, Paris, 1996

——, "Une Dramaturgie de gageure", *Revue d'histoire littéraire de la France*, 85-5 (1985)

GOSSIP, C., "*Tite et Bérénice*: a coherent *comédie héroique?*" in *Form and Meaning: aesthetic coherence in seventeenth-century French drama. Studies presented to Harry Barnwell*, Avebury, 1982, 115-126

HARWOOD-GORDON, S., *The Poetic Style of Corneille's Tragedies: an aesthetic interpretation*, Mellen, Lewiston, 1989

KNIGHT, R.C., *Corneille's Tragedies. The Role of the Unexpected*, Cardiff, University of Wales Press, 1991

PRIGENT, M., *Le Héros et l'État dans la tragédie de Pierre Corneille*, PUF, Paris, 1986

SCOTT, J.W., "*Pertharite*: a re-examination", *Forum for Modern Language Studies*, (1965-4), 352-7

STEGMANN, A., *L'Héroïsme cornélien: genèse et signification*, 2 vols., A. Colin, Paris, 1968

SWEETSER, M.-O., "Racine rival de Corneille: 'innutrition' et innovation dans *Britannicus*", *Romanic Review*, 66 (1975), 13-31

(ii) WORKS ON JEAN RACINE

ALBANESE, R., "Patterns of irony in *Britannicus*", *Australian Journal of French Studies*, 14-5 (1977), 233-49

BARNWELL, H.T., "From *La Thébaïde* to *Andromaque*. A View of Racine's Early Dramatic Techniques", *French Studies*, 5 (1951), 30-35

——, *The Tragic Drama of Corneille and Racine. An Old Parallel Revisited*, Clarendon Press, Oxford, 1982

BARTHES, R., *Sur Racine*, Éditions du Seuil, Paris, 1963

CLAUDEL, P., *Conversation sur Jean Racine*, Gallimard, Paris, 1956

DAINARD, J., "The Power of the Spoken Word in *Bérénice*", *Romanic Review*, 67-3 (1976), 157-171

EDWARDS, M., *La Tragédie racinienne*, Paris, La Pensée Universelle 1972

EKSTEIN, N., *Dramatic Narrative: Racine's récits*, Peter Lang, Frankfurt, 1986

ÉMELINA, J., "Racine et Quinault: de *Bellérophon* à *Phèdre*", in *Hommage à Jean Onimus (Annales de la Faculté de lettres et de sciences humaines de Nice, no. 38)*, Nice, 1979, 71-81

HAWCROFT, M., *Word as Action. Racine, Rhetoric, and Theatrical Language*, Clarendon Press, Oxford, 1992

HEYNDELS, I., *Le Conflit racinien*, Éditions de l'Université de Bruxelles, 1985

KNIGHT, R., *Racine et la Grèce*, Nizet, Paris, 1974 (1st ed. 1951)

LAPP, J., *Aspects of Racinian Tragedy*, University of Toronto Press, 1955

LE BIDOIS, G., *La Vie dans la tragédie de Racine*, J. de Gigord, Paris, 6th ed., 1929 (1st ed. 1900)

MASKELL, D., *Racine. A Theatrical Reading*, Clarendon Press, Oxford, 1991

McFARLANE, I., "Reflections on the variants in *Andromaque*", in *Form and Meaning: aesthetic coherence in seventeenth-century French Drama. Studies presented to Harry Barnwell*, Avebury, 1982, 99-113

MONACO, M., "Racine's naming of 'Greek' confidantes and handmaidens", *Romanic Review* 52 (April 1961), 99-115

MONCOND'HUY, D., "*Mithridate* ou la conquête du tombeau" in *Racine et Rome: "Britannicus", "Bérénice", "Mithridate"*, ed. S. Guellouz, Orléans, 1995, 187-97

MOURGUES, O. de., *Racine or the Triumph of Relevance*, Cambridge University Press, 1967

NURSE, P., "Towards a definition of *le tragique racinien*", *Symposium*, 21-3 (1967), 197-221

OLGA, M., "Vers une esthétique du confident racinien", *Jeunesse de Racine* (Jan.-March 1964), 1-12

O'REGAN, M., *The Mannerist Aesthetic. A Study of Racine's Mithridate*, University of Bristol, 1980

PARISH, R., *Racine: the Limits of Tragedy*, Biblio 17, Paris, 1993

PHILLIPS, H., *Racine: Language and Theatre*, University of Durham, 1994

——, *Racine: Mithridate, Grant and Cutler Critical Guides to French Texts*, London, 1990

PICARD, R., *La Carrière de Jean Racine*, Gallimard, Paris, 1961 (1st ed 1954)

PFOHL, R., *Racine's Iphigénie: Literary Rehearsal and Tragic Recognition*, Droz, Geneva, 1974

PROPHÈTE, J., *Les Para-personnages dans les tragédies de Racine*, Nizet, Paris, 1981

ROSSI, H., "*Les détours obscurs*". *Le Annotazioni di Racine alle tragedie greche*, Schena, Fasano, 1985

SCHRAMMEN, G., "Zur Funktion des *confident* bei Racine", *Germanisch-Romanische Monatsschrift*, 20 (1970), 384-97

SPENCER, C., *La Tragédie du prince: étude du personnage médiateur dans le théâtre tragique de Racine*, Paris-Seattle-Tübingen, 1987

STONE, J. A., *Sophocles and Racine*, Droz, Geneva, 1964

SWEETSER, M.-O., "Racine rival de Corneille: 'innutrition' et innovation dans *Britannicus*", *Romanic Review*, 66 (1975), 13-31

TOBIN, R., *Racine and Seneca*, University of North Carolina Press, 1971

VIALA, A., "Péril, conseil et secret d'État", *Littératures classiques*, 26 (1996), 91-113

WORTH, V., "La querelle du confident et la structure dramaturgique des premières pièces de Racine", *Littératures classiques*, 16 (1992), 229-46

(iii) OTHER WORKS

BAUDIN, M., "The Shifting of Responsibility in Seventeenth-Century French Tragic Drama", *Modern Language Notes*, 49 (1934), 152-58

BERTAUD, M., "Deux *Ariane* au XVII siècle: Alexandre Hardy et Thomas Corneille", *Seventeenth-Century French Studies*, 19 (1997), 135-148

BROOKS, W., "The Evolution of the Theatre of Quinault", unpublished Ph.D. thesis, University of Newcastle-upon-Tyne, 1968

BURTON, R., *The Chorus in Sophocles' Tragedies*, Clarendon Press, Oxford, 1980

CAVE, T., *Recognitions. A Study in Poetics*, Clarendon Press, Oxford, 1988

COLLINS, D., *Thomas Corneille. Protean Dramatist*, Mouton, The Hague, 1966

DAVISON, H.M.., "La vraisemblance chez d'Aubignac et Corneille: quelques réflexions disciplinaires" in *L'Art du Théâtre. Mélanges en hommage à Robert Garapon*, textes réunis et publiés par Y. Bellenger (etc.), PUF, Paris, 1992, 91-100

DEIERKAUF-HOLSBOER, S.W., *Le Théâtre du Marais*, vol. II, Nizet, Paris, 1958

——, *Le Théâtre de l'Hôtel de Bourgogne*, vol. II, Nizet, Paris, 1970

(ed) DOREY, T., *Tacitus*, Routledge and Kegan Paul, London, 1969

ÉMELINA, J., *Les Valets et les servantes dans le théâtre comique en France de 1610 à 1700*, CEL-PUG, Cannes-Grenoble, 1975

FERMAUD, J., "*Défense du confident*", *Romanic Review*, 31 (1940), 334-40

FORESTIER, G., *L'Esthétique de l'identité dans le théâtre français (1550-1680)*, Droz, Geneva, 1988

GARAPON, R., "Rotrou et Corneille", *Revue d'histoire littéraire de la France*, 50 (1950), 385-94

GOLDMANN, L., *Le Dieu caché*, Gallimard, Paris, 1959

GOSSIP, C., "*Timocrate* reconsidered", *Studi Francesi*, 50, XVII-2, (1973), 222-37

——, "The Language of *confidence* in French Classical Tragedy", in *Voices in the Air. French dramatists and the resources of language. Essays in honour of Charles Chadwick*, ed. J. Dunkley and W. Kirton, University of Glasgow, 1992, 14-28

GROS, E., *Philippe Quinault: sa vie, ses tragédies et ses tragi-comédies*, H.J. Paris, Amsterdam, 1928

HILGAR, M.- F., *La Mode des stances dans le théâtre tragique français, 1610-87*, Nizet, Paris, 1984

LANCASTER, H.C., *Actors' Roles at the Comédie Française*, Baltimore, 1953

——, *A History of French Dramatic Literature*, John Hopkins University Press, 1929-42

LAWTON, H., "The Confidant in and before French Classical Tragedy", *Modern Languages Review*, 38 (1943), 18-31

LOCKERT, L., *Studies in French Classical Tragedy*, Nashville, 1958

MOREL, J., *Jean Rotrou dramaturge de l'ambiguïté*, Paris, 1968

NEWTON, W., *Le Thème de Phèdre et d'Hippolyte dans la littérature française*, Paris, E. Droz, 1939

PELLET, E., *A Forgotten French Dramatist. Gabriel Gilbert (1620?-1680?),* John Hopkins Press, Baltimore, 1931

SCHERER, J., *La Dramaturgie classique en France*, Nizet, Paris, 1948

STIEFEL, A., "Jean Rotrous *Cosroès* und seine Quellen", *Zeitschrift fur französische Spräche und Literatur*, 23 (1901), 69-188

(ed.) TRUCHET, J., *Recherches de thématique théâtrale: l'exemple des conseillers des rois dans la tragédie classique*, *Études littéraires françaises 8*, G. Narr, Tübingen-Paris, 1981

VAN BAELEN, J., *Rotrou. Le Héros tragique et la révolte*, Paris, 1965

WOODMAN, A., "Amateur Dramatics at the Court of Nero: *Annals* 15. 48-74", in *Tacitus and the Tacitean Tradition* (ed. T. Luce and A. Woodman), Princeton University Press, 1993, 104-28

INDEXES

Index of Plays

Aeschylus
  Chœphori, 96
Bidar, Mathieu,
  Hippolyte, 206, 207, 208, 209, 213
Boyer, Claude
  Oropaste, 67, 148
Cellot, Père Louis
  Chosroès, 123
Corneille, Pierre
  Agésilas, 77, 78, 107, 148
  Andromède, 14
  Attila, 77, 78, 90, 107-108, 111
  Cinna, 14, 15, 19, 24, 25, 26, 27,
    28, 29, 30, 35, 38-40, 43, 121,
    122, 140, 165, 173, 176
  Don Sanche, 14, 15, 20, 21, 25, 27,
    28, 29, 33, 34, 68
  Héraclius, 15, 19, 20, 22, 25, 27, 29,
    43, 68, 69
  Horace, 15, 16, 18, 24-29, 33, 34-35,
    36, 42, 43, 176, 200
  La Mort de Pompée, 15, 23, 25-26,
    27, 30, 76, 140
  La Suivante, 2
  Le Cid, 15, 18, 25, 26, 27, 28, 29,
    32-35, 41, 43, 63, 67, 173
  Médée, 8, 13, 15-17, 19, 21, 25, 26,
    27, 28, 29, 35, 36, 38, 41, 49, 77,
    96, 147
  Nicomède, 8, 13, 15, 16, 21, 22-23,
    25, 27, 28, 29, 37-38, 43, 68, 69,
    70, 73, 90, 123, 127, 148
  Œdipe, 53, 54, 56, 77
  Othon, 77, 78, 122, 128-135, 138,
    140, 143, 145
  Pertharite, 6, 14, 16, 20, 29, 35, 36,
    67, 68, 73-77, 79, 81, 90, 91
  Polyeucte, 15, 16, 21, 23, 24, 25, 26,
    27, 28, 29, 43
  Psyché, 78

  Pulchérie, 6, 43, 67, 77, 78, 79-81,
    87, 91, 149, 166, 167
  Rodogune, 15, 16, 19-21, 25, 26, 27,
    28, 29, 38, 40, 42, 43, 47, 52, 90,
    99, 108, 117, 149, 161
  Sertorius, 53-54, 56, 57, 78
  Sophonisbe, 8, 13, 17, 20, 22, 26,
    31, 35, 47-60, 61, 63, 68, 77, 78,
    81, 82, 83, 85, 87, 89, 93, 94, 97,
    129, 148, 172, 186
  Suréna, 76, 77, 78, 159, 166-173,
    176, 198, 211
  Théodore, 15, 16, 22, 25, 27, 28, 29,
    31, 47, 69, 71, 72, 73
  Tite et Bérénice, 15, 67, 77, 78, 94,
    99, 106, 108-112, 144, 178
Corneille, Thomas
  Ariane, 144, 176, 184-188, 189, 190,
    193, 195, 196, 199, 206
  Camma, 94, 101-103, 106, 108, 121,
    149, 154, 204
  La Mort d'Annibal, 121
  Laodice, 21, 22, 38, 149, 150, 154
  Le Comte d'Essex, 144, 204
  Maximian, 94
  Timocrate, 150-154, 169, 175, 176,
    185, 198, 204
Cyrano de Bergerac, Savinien de
  La Mort d'Agrippine, 93, 94, 128,
    137
Desjardins, Catherine
  Manlius, 47, 56, 60-63, 108
  Nitétis, 121
Euripides
  Andromache, 94, 97, 98
  Hippolytus, 206, 208, 210, 212, 214
  Iphigenia, 199
  Medea, 17
  Orestes, 96
  Phœnician Women, 82, 83, 85, 86

Gilbert, Gabriel
   Arie et Pétus, 111, 122, 128, 135-138, 141, 143, 204, 205, 208, 209
   Hypolite, 136, 206, 207, 208, 209, 211, 212
Hardy, Alexandre
   Ariane ravie, 185
La Pinelière, Guérin de,
   Hippolyte, 206, 207, 208, 209
Lucan
   Pharsalia, 23
Magnon, Jean
   Tite, 150, 154, 181, 182
Molière (Jean-Baptiste Poquelin)
   Dom Juan, 179
   George Dandin, 107
   Le Misanthrope, 75
   Les Fourberies de Scapin, 2
Montchrestien, Antoine de
   La Reine d'Écosse, 122
Pradon, Nicolas
   Phèdre et Hippolyte, 176, 195, 205, 206
Quinault, Philippe
   Astrate, 105, 154, 155, 157, 198
   Bellérophon, 155-160, 173, 195, 205, 206, 212
   Pausanias, 94, 103-106, 112, 154, 157, 195, 205
   Stratonice, 15, 25, 27, 28, 29, 94, 104, 118, 156
Racine, Jean
   Alexandre, 8, 23, 67, 69, 70, 71, 72, 73, 77, 78, 81, 83, 87-91, 93, 98, 147, 175, 185, 191, 203
   Andromaque, 1, 7, 8, 9, 15, 73, 74, 75, 78, 79, 82, 93, 94-101, 103, 104, 105, 106, 107, 109, 110, 111, 113, 114, 117, 118, 119, 122, 126, 138, 139, 142, 147, 155, 160, 162, 173, 175, 198, 204, 205, 208, 209
   Athalie, 8, 145, 205
   Bajazet, 9, 81, 110, 144, 147, 159, 160, 161, 164, 176, 179, 185, 186, 188, 189-195, 197, 198, 200, 205, 208

Bérénice, 9, 16, 67, 77, 81, 82, 94, 106, 108, 110, 111, 112-120, 122, 147, 150, 157, 160, 162, 165, 176, 177, 178, 179, 180, 181, 182, 183, 184, 186, 187, 190, 197, 198, 208, 211
Britannicus, 9, 42, 76, 78, 94, 107, 115, 118, 122, 123, 126, 128, 129, 132, 134, 135, 136, 138-143, 144, 145, 147, 159, 160, 162, 205, 208, 209, 211
Esther, 144, 205
Iphigénie, 4, 9, 68, 78, 82, 147, 154, 161, 176, 197-202, 208
Iphigénie en Tauride (prose draft of), 4
La Thébaïde, 8, 68, 77, 81-87, 89, 90, 91, 98, 138, 147, 203, 205
Les Plaideurs, 94
Mithridate, 9, 78, 83, 147, 159-165, 166, 168, 169, 173, 193, 194, 197, 198, 205, 208
Phèdre, 1, 3, 9, 67, 80, 82, 86, 117, 147, 155, 159, 176, 180, 184, 185, 186, 187, 188, 189, 190, 192, 193, 195, 196, 197, 199, 204, 205-215
Rotrou, Jean
   Cosroès, 68, 76, 122, 123-127, 129, 133, 140, 212
   Venceslas, 22, 68-73, 74, 81, 89, 90, 91, 123, 191, 203
Segrais, Jean Regnault de
   Floridon, 189, 190, 191, 192, 194
Seneca
   Hippolytus, 206, 208, 210, 212, 214
   Medea, 17
   Phœnissæ, 83, 85
   Troades, 94
Sophocles
   Electra, 85, 96, 99, 101
Subligny, Adrien Perdou de
   La Folle Querelle, 93, 97
Tristan L'Hermite
   La Mariamne, 24
   La Mort de Sénèque, 123, 128, 135, 139, 148

Index of Characters

Abner (J. Racine, *Athalie*), 145

Achillas (P. Corneille, *La Mort de Pompée*), 23, 140

Achille (J. Racine, *Iphigénie*), 96, 199, 200, 201

Achrise (G. Gilbert, *Hypolite*), 207, 209, 212

Acomat (J. Racine, *Bajazet*), 110, 144, 189, 191, 192

Ægine (J. Racine, *Iphigénie*), 198

Agamemnon (J. Racine, *Iphigénie*), 161, 198, 199, 200, 201

Agenor (P. Quinault, *Astrate*), 105

Aglatide (P. Corneille, *Agésilas*), 149

Agrippine (J. Racine, *Britannicus*), 115, 118, 135, 139, 140, 142

Albiane (P. Corneille, *Othon*), 77, 129, 131

Albin (P. Corneille, *Othon*), 129, 131

— (P. Corneille, *Polyeucte*), 15, 22, 24, 25, 26, 29

— (P. Corneille, *Tite et Bérénice*), 77, 109, 110, 111, 112

Albine (J. Racine, *Britannicus*), 136, 142, 162, 166, 192

Alexandre (J. Racine, *Alexandre*), 88, 89, 90, 91, 175, 185

— (J. Rotrou, *Venceslas*), 69, 70, 71, 72, 191

Aman (J. Racine, *Esther*), 144

Amyntas (P. Corneille, *Héraclius*), 15, 25, 27, 29

Andromaque (J. Racine, *Andromaque*), 1, 95, 96, 97, 98, 100, 101, 110, 117, 119, 162

Annibal (T. Corneille, *La Mort d'Annibal*), 121

Antiochus (P. Corneille, *Rodogune*), 20, 42

Antiochus (J. Racine, *Bérénice* 113, 114, 115, 117, 118, 119, 120, 147, 179, 180, 181, 182, 183, 184, 190

Araminte (C. Boyer, *Oropaste*), 148

Araspe (P. Corneille, *Nicomède*), 15, 22, 25, 27, 28, 29, 37, 38, 39

Araxe (T. Corneille, *La Mort d'Annibal*), 121

Arbate (J. Racine, *Mithridate*), 144, 160, 161, 163, 165, 168, 197

— (M. Bidar, *Hippolyte*), 207, 209

Arcas (P. Corneille, *Sertorius*), 56

— (T. Corneille, *Timocrate*), 151

— (N. Pradon, *Phèdre et Hippolyte*), 207

— (J. Racine, *Iphigénie*), 198, 201

— (J. Racine, *Mithridate*), 160, 161

Ardaric (P. Corneille, *Attila*), 107, 108

Ariane (T. Corneille, *Ariane*), 184, 185, 186, 187, 188, 199

Ariarate (T. Corneille, *Laodice*), 149

Aricie (J. Racine, *Phèdre*), 1, 180, 195, 196, 197, 207, 208, 209, 210, 211, 213

Arie (G. Gilbert, *Arie et Pétus*), 138

Aristée (G. Gilbert, *Hypolite*), 207, 209

Aristide (P. Quinault, *Pausanias*), 104

Arsace (J. Racine, *Bérénice*), 113, 114, 118, 119, 120, 183

Arsinoé (P. Corneille, *Nicomède*), 22, 23, 38, 75

Artanasde (J. Rotrou, *Cosroès*), 123, 126, 127

Aspar (P. Corneille, *Pulchérie*), 79, 80

Astrate (P. Quinault, *Astrate*), 105, 155, 157

Atalide (J. Racine, *Bajazet*), 110, 161, 180, 188, 189, 190, 191, 192, 193, 194, 195, 196, 197, 198, 199

Athys (G de La Pinelière, *Hippolyte*), 207, 209

Attale (J. Racine, *La Thébaïde*), 38, 83, 84, 85, 86, 88

Atticus (P. Corneille, *Othon*), 130, 134

Attila (P. Corneille, *Attila*), 107

Aufide (P. Corneille, *Sertorius*), 56

Auguste (P. Corneille, *Cinna*), 14, 24, 26, 35, 39, 40, 122, 165

Axiane (J. Racine, *Alexandre*), 89, 90,
  91, 175
Bajazet (J. Racine, *Bajazet*), 186, 190,
  191, 192, 193, 194, 195
Barcée (P. Corneille, *Sophonisbe*), 49,
  51, 54, 57, 58, 59
Barsine (M. Bidar, *Hippolyte*), 207
Bellérophon (P. Quinault, *Bellérophon*),
  155, 156, 157, 158, 159
Bérénice (P. Corneille, *Tite et Bérénice*),
  108, 110, 111, 112
— (J. Magnon, *Tite*), 150, 176, 177,
  178, 179
— (J. Racine, *Bérénice),* 113, 114, 115,
  116, 117, 118, 119, 180, 181, 182,
  183, 184, 187
Blanche (P. Corneille, *Don Sanche*), 15,
  25, 27, 28, 29
Bocchar (P. Corneille, *Sophonisbe*), 50,
  58, 59, 63
Burrhus (G. Gilbert, *Arie et Pétus*), 136,
  137
— (J. Racine, *Britannicus*), 3, 9, 111,
  115, 122, 132, 139, 140, 141, 142,
  143, 144, 145
Cambise (C. Desjardins, *Nitétis*), 121
Camille (P. Corneille, *Horace*), 15, 35,
  36, 42, 43, 200
— (C. Desjardins, *Manlius*), 60, 61, 62,
  63
— (P. Corneille, *Othon*), 128, 129,
  130, 131, 134
Camma (T. Corneille, *Camma*), 102,
  103
Cassandre (J. Rotrou, *Venceslas*), 69, 71,
  72
Cécile (T. Corneille, *Le Comte d'Essex*),
  144
Celsus (P. Corneille, *Sertorius*), 56
Céphise (J. Racine, *Andromaque*), 1, 74,
  95, 97, 98, 99, 100, 103, 104, 117,
  162, 192
Charile (P. Quinault, *Pausanias*), 104,
  105, 106
Charmion (P. Corneille, *La Mort de
  Pompée*), 15, 25, 26, 27, 28, 29
Chimène (P. Corneille, *Le Cid*), 18, 33,
  34, 41, 42
Cinna (P. Corneille, *Cinna*), 14, 24, 25,
  27, 28, 29, 43

Cléante (P. Corneille, *Oedipe*), 56
Cléobule (P. Corneille, *Théodore*), 16,
  22, 43
— <=Bérénice> (J. Magnon, *Tite*), 150,
  176, 177, 178, 179
Cléofile (J. Racine, *Alexandre*), 88, 89,
  90, 91, 175
Cléomène <= Timocrate> (T. Corneille,
  Timocrate), 150, 151, 152, 153, 154,
  176
Cléon (P. Corneille, *Agésilas*), 77
— (P. Corneille, *Polyeucte*), 14
Cléone (C. Boyer, *Oropaste),*148
— (P. Corneille, *Médée*), 15, 27, 29
— (P. Corneille, *Nicomède*), 15, 22,
  23, 25, 27, 29
— (N. Pradon, *Phèdre et Hippolyte*),
  207
— (J. Racine, *Andromaque*), 7, 75, 95,
  97, 98, 100, 101, 104, 106, 114
Cléonice (P. Quinault, *Pausanias*), 104,
  105
Cléonte (J. Magnon, *Tite*), 150
Cléopâtre (P. Corneille, *Rodogune*), 20,
  26, 40, 52, 117
Clytemnestre (J. Racine, *Iphigénie*), 198,
  199, 200, 201
Corisbe (P. Quinault, *Astrate*), 157
Cornélie (P. Corneille, *La Mort de
  Pompée*), 30
Cosroès (J. Rotrou, *Cosroès*), 124, 126,
  127
Cotys (P. Corneille, *Agésilas*), 149
Créon (J. Racine, *La Thébaïde*), 83, 84,
  86, 90
Crispe (P. Corneille, *Héraclius*), 20, 21
Darie (C. Boyer, *Oropaste*), 148
Demarate (P. Quinault, *Pausanias*), 104,
  105, 106, 157
Dircé (P. Corneille, *Oedipe*), 54
Domitian (P. Corneille, *Tite et
  Bérénice*), 109, 110, 111, 112
Domitie (P. Corneille, *Tite et Bérénice*),
  109, 110, 111, 112, 178
Don Diègue (P. Corneille, *Le Cid*), 43
Don Gomès (P. Corneille, *Le Cid*), 18
Dorine (T. Corneille, *Timocrate*), 151
Doris (J. Racine, *Iphigénie*), 198, 199,
  201
Dymas (P. Corneille, *Oedipe*), 56

Édüige (P.Corneille, *Pertharite*), 74, 75, 76

Élise (P.Quinault, *Astrate*), 157

Elpinice (P. Corneille, *Agésilas*), 149

Elvire (P. Corneille, *Le Cid*), 15, 18, 25, 26, 27, 28, 29, 33, 34, 41, 42, 59

Émilie (P. Corneille, *Cinna*), 24, 39

Ephestion (J. Racine, *Alexandre*), 72, 88

Épicharis (Tristan l'Hermite, *La Mort de Sénèque*), 135

Ériphile (J. Racine, *Iphigénie*), 180, 198, 199, 200, 201, 202

— (T. Corneille, *Timocrate*), 151, 152, 154

Éryxe (P. Corneille, *Sophonisbe*), 49, 51, 52, 53, 57, 58, 59

Essex (T. Corneille, *Le Comte d'Essex*), 144

Étéocle (J. Racine, *La Thébaïde*), 3, 87

Euphorbe (P. Corneille, *Cinna*), 15, 25, 26, 29, 39, 40, 121, 140

Eurianax (P. Quinault, *Pausanias*), 104, 105

Eurybate (J. Racine, *Iphigénie*), 198

Eurydice (P. Corneille, *Suréna*), 166, 167, 168, 169, 170, 171, 172, 176

Évandre (P.Corneille, *Cinna*), 14

Exupère (P. Corneille, *Héraclius*), 20, 25

Fabian (P. Corneille, *Polyeucte*), 14, 25, 26, 27, 29

Fédéric (J. Rotrou, *Venceslas*), 72, 191

Félix (P. Corneille, *Polyeucte*), 14, 15, 22, 26

Flavian (P. Corneille, *Tite et Bérénice*), 77, 109, 110, 112

Flavie (P. Corneille, *Attila*), 31, 77, 107, 111

— (P. Corneille, *Othon*), 129, 131

Fulvie (P. Corneille, *Cinna*), 15, 24, 25, 27, 28, 29

Garibalde (P. Corneille, *Pertharite*), 35, 75, 76

Grimoald (P. Corneille, *Pertharite*), 74, 75, 76

Hémon (J. Racine, *La Thébaïde*), 85, 86

Héraclius (P. Corneille, *Héraclius*), 25, 29, 43

Herminie (P. Corneille, *Sophonisbe*), 49, 51, 54, 56, 57, 58, 59

Hermione (C. Boyer, *Oropaste*), 148

Hermione (J. Racine, *Andromaque*), 1, 7, 75, 95, 97, 98, 100, 101, 102, 104, 106, 110, 114, 189

Hésione (G. de La Pinelière, *Hippolyte*), 207

Hésione (T. Corneille, *Camma*), 102, 207

Hippolyte (N. Pradon, *Phèdre et Hippolyte*), 196, 197

Hippolyte (J. Racine, *Phèdre*), 1, 39, 101, 159, 186, 207, 208, 209, 210, 211, 213, 214

Honorie (P. Corneille, *Attila*), 107

Horace (P. Corneille, *Horace*), 25, 27, 28, 29, 34, 43, 176

Hormisdate (J. Rotrou, *Cosroès*), 123

Hypolite (G. Gilbert, *Hypolite*), 207, 209, 211

Idas (N. Pradon, *Phèdre et Hippolyte*), 207

Ildione (P. Corneille, *Attila*), 108

Iphigénie (J. Racine, *Iphigénie*), 199, 200, 201, 202

Irène (P. Corneille, *Pulchérie*), 79, 80

Ismène (G. Gilbert, *Arie et Pétus*), 136,

— (J. Racine, *Phèdre*), 3, 208, 213

Iunius (C. Desjardins, *Manlius*), 60, 62, 63

Jason (P. Corneille, *Médée*), 16, 17, 41, 43

Jocaste (J. Racine, *La Thébaïde*), 83, 84, 86, 87

Julie (P. Corneille, *Horace*), 15, 16, 18, 24, 25, 26, 27, 28, 29, 34, 35, 36, 42, 59, 147

Junie (J. Racine, *Britannicus*), 42, 139, 140, 143, 160

Justine (P. Corneille, *Pulchérie*), 79, 80, 81

L'Infante (P.Corneille, *Le Cid*), 33, 34, 35, 69

La Duchesse d'Irton (T. Corneille, *Le Comte d'Essex*), 144

Lacus (P. Corneille, *Othon*), 128, 129, 130, 131, 132, 133, 134, 138

Ladice (P. Quinault, *Bellérophon*), 155, 156

Ladislas (J. Rotrou, *Venceslas*), 68, 69, 70, 71, 72

Laodice (P. Corneille, *Nicomède*), 21, 22, 38

Laonice (P. Corneille, *Rodogune*), 15, 19, 20, 21, 25, 26, 27, 28, 29, 39, 40, 42, 52, 70, 117

Léon (P. Corneille, *Pulchérie*), 79, 80, 81

Léonor (P. Corneille, *Le Cid*), 15, 25, 26, 29, 33, 34

— (J. Rotrou, *Venceslas*), 69, 72

Lépide (P. Corneille, *Sophonisbe*), 58

Licas (P. Quinault, *Bellérophon*), 155, 156

Lycrate (G. de La Pinelière, *Hippolyte*), 207

Mandane (P. Corneille, *Agésilas*), 149

Manlius (C. Desjardins, *Manlius*), 60, 61, 62, 63

Marcelle (P. Corneille, *Théodore*), 31, 32

Mardesane (J. Rotrou, *Cosroès*), 124, 125, 126

Martian (P. Corneille, *Othon*), 128, 129, 130, 131, 132, 133, 138

— (P. Corneille, *Pulchérie*), 79, 80, 81,

Massinisse (P. Corneille, *Sophonisbe*), 52, 53, 57, 59

Mathan (J. Racine, *Athalie*), 145

Maxime (P. Corneille, *Cinna*), 26, 39, 43, 176

Mégabise (C. Boyer, *Oropaste*), 148

Mégare (M. Bidar, *Hippolyte*), 205, 207, 212

— (P. Corneille, *Œdipe*), 54, 55, 56

— (P. Quinault, *Bellérophon*), 155, 156, 157, 158

Mégiste (N. Pradon, *Phèdre et Hippolyte*), 195, 207

Ménélas (J. Rotrou, *Iphigénie*), 198

Mézétulle (P. Corneille, *Sophonisbe*), 51, 57, 58, 59, 63

Mithridate (J. Racine, *Mithridate*), 160, 161, 162, 163, 164, 165, 168, 169, 193, 194, 197

Mucie (J. Magnon, *Tite*), 150, 177, 178, 179

Narcisse (J. Racine, *Britannicus*), 1, 9, 38, 111, 115, 118, 122, 132, 136, 139, 140, 141, 142, 143, 144, 145, 161, 213

Narsée (J. Rotrou, *Cosroès*), 123, 125

Néarque (P. Corneille, *Polyeucte*), 15, 16, 21, 25, 43

Nérine (P. Corneille, *Médée*), 15, 25, 26, 27, 28, 29, 36, 38, 41

— (P. Corneille, *Œdipe*), 54, 55, 56, 59

— (T. Corneille, *Ariane*), 184, 186

Néron (J. Racine, *Britannicus*), 42, 63, 115, 118, 123, 134, 135, 136, 137, 138, 139, 140, 141, 142, 143

Nicandre (T. Corneille, *Timocrate*), 150, 151, 152, 153

Nicomède (P. Corneille, *Nicomède*), 21, 22, 23, 25, 27, 28, 29, 37, 38, 43

Nourrice de la Reyne (G. de La Pinelière, *Hippolyte*), 207

Octar (P. Corneille, *Attila*), 77, 107, 108, 111

Octave (J. Rotrou, *Venceslas*), 69

Œdipe (P. Corneille, *Œdipe*), 54

Œnarus (T. Corneille, *Ariane*), 184, 187

Œnone (J. Racine, *Phèdre*), 1, 9, 39, 86, 101, 117, 155, 186, 205, 206, 208, 209, 210, 211, 212, 213, 214, 215

Olympe (J. Racine, *La Thébaïde*), 82, 83, 84, 85, 86, 88, 89, 98

Omphale (C. Desjardins, *Manlius*), 60, 61, 62, 63, 207

Oreste (J. Racine, *Andromaque*), 1, 3, 7, 75, 90, 95, 96, 97, 98, 100, 101, 104, 106, 118

Ormène (P. Corneille, *Suréna*), 77, 166, 167

Orode (P. Corneille, *Suréna*), 166, 167, 168, 169, 170, 171, 172, 173

Oropaste (C. Boyer, *Oropaste*), 148

Osmin (J. Racine, *Bajazet*), 191

Othon (P. Corneille, *Othon*), 129, 130, 131, 133, 134, 138

Pacorus (P. Corneille, *Suréna*), 166, 167, 168, 169, 170, 171, 172, 173, 176

Palmis (P. Corneille, *Suréna*), 167, 168, 169, 170

Palmyras (J. Rotrou, *Cosroès*), 123, 124, 125, 126, 127

Panope (J. Racine, *Phèdre*), 195, 208

Pasithée (G. Gilbert, *Hypolite*), 207, 209

Paulin (P. Corneille, *Théodore*), 15, 25, 27, 28, 29

— (J. Racine, *Bérénice*), 3, 110, 113, 114, 115, 116, 118, 119, 144, 162

Pauline (P. Corneille, *Polyeucte*), 15, 22

Pausanias (P. Quinault, *Pausanias*), 104, 105

Pertharite (P. Corneille, *Pertharite*), 74, 75, 76

Pétrone (G. Gilbert, *Arie et Pétus*), 136, 137, 138, 141

Pétus (G. Gilbert, *Arie et Pétus*), 136, 137

Phædime (T. Corneille, *Camma*), 102, 103, 121

Phædre (G. Gilbert, *Hypolite*), 136, 207, 209, 211, 212

Pharnace (J. Racine, *Mithridate*), 3, 161, 164, 165

— (J. Rotrou, *Cosroès*), 123, 125, 126,

Phèdre (T. Corneille, *Ariane*), 180, 184, 185, 186, 187, 188, 189, 190, 192, 193, 199

— (N. Pradon, *Phèdre et Hippolyte*), 195, 196, 197

— (J. Racine, *Phèdre*), 1, 86, 117, 155, 207, 208, 210, 211, 212, 213, 214

Phénice (C. Desjardins, *Manlius*), 60, 61, 63

— (J. Racine, *Bérénice*), 103, 114, 115, 116, 117, 118, 119, 183, 187, 192

Phénice (T. Corneille, *Camma*), 102

Philippe (P. Corneille, *La Mort de Pompée*), 25, 27, 29, 30, 94, 156, 157

Philon (P. Corneille, *Tite et Bérénice*), 77, 108, 114, 115, 144

Philonoé (P. Quinault, *Bellérophon*), 155, 156, 157, 158

Phocas (P. Corneille, *Héraclius*), 20, 21

Phœdime (J. Racine, *Mithridate*), 117, 162, 163, 166

Phœnix (J. Racine, *Andromaque*), 95, 96, 98, 99, 100, 104, 105, 106, 110, 112, 119

Photin (P. Corneille, *La Mort de Pompée*), 23, 76

Phradate (T. Corneille, *Laodice*), 149

Pirithoüs (T. Corneille, *Ariane*), 144, 184, 185, 187, 188

Pison (C. Desjardins, *Manlius*), 60, 61, 63, 130, 131, 132, 133, 134

Pithée (G. Gilbert, *Hypolite*), 207, 209

Placide (P. Corneille, *Théodore*), 16, 22, 31, 43

Plautine (P. Corneille, *Othon*), 128, 129, 131, 133, 134

— (P. Corneille, *Tite et Bérénice*), 77, 109, 111, 112

Pollux (P. Corneille, *Médée*), 16, 17, 21, 25, 26, 29, 43, 49, 77

Polyclète (P. Corneille, *Cinna*), 14

Polyeucte (P. Corneille, *Polyeucte*), 16, 21, 25, 27, 28, 29, 43

Polynice (J. Racine, *La Thébaïde*), 87

Porus (J. Racine, *Alexandre*), 87, 88, 90, 91, 175

Prédaspe (C. Desjardins, *Nitétis*), 121

Procris (G. de La Pinelière, *Hippolyte*), 207

Prœtus (P. Quinault, *Bellérophon*), 155, 156, 157, 158

Prusias (P. Corneille, *Nicomède*), 22, 37, 38, 121

Ptolomée (P. Corneille, *La Mort de Pompée*), 23

Pulchérie (P. Corneille, *Héraclius*), 43,

— (P. Corneille, *Pulchérie*), 79, 80, 81

Pylade (J. Racine, *Andromaque*), 95, 96, 97, 98, 101, 104, 118, 126

Pyrrhus (J. Racine, *Andromaque*), 1, 95, 96, 97, 98, 99, 100, 101, 105, 106, 110, 114, 118, 119, 175

Rodelinde (P. Corneille, *Pertharite*), 74, 75, 76, 90

Rodrigue (P. Corneille, *Le Cid*), 26, 33, 34, 41, 42, 43

Rutile (J. Racine, *Bérénice*), 81, 113

Sabine (P. Corneille, *Horace*), 15, 16, 18, 24, 34, 35, 42, 200

— (G. Gilbert, *Arie et Pétus*), 136

— (Tristan L'Hermite, *La Mort de Sénèque*), 135

Sardarigue (J. Rotrou, *Cosroès*), 123, 124

Séjanus (Cyrano de Bergerac, *La Mort d'Agrippine*), 137

Séleucus (P. Corneille, *Rodogune*), 20

Sénèque (G. Gilbert, *Arie et Pétus*), 136, 137, 138, 141

Septime (P. Corneille, *La Mort de Pompée*), 23

Sertorius (P. Corneille, *Sertorius*), 53

Sévère (P. Corneille, *Polyeucte*), 14, 15, 22, 24, 26

Sichée (P. Quinault, *Astrate*), 155

Sillace (P. Corneille, *Suréna*), 77, 166, 171

Sinorix (T. Corneille, *Camma*), 102, 103

Sophane (P. Quinault, *Pausanias*), 104, 105

Sophonisbe (P. Corneille, *Sophonisbe*), 52, 57, 58, 59

Sosime (T. Corneille, *Camma*), 102

Sostrate (T. Corneille, *Camma*), 102

Spitridate (P. Corneille, *Agésilas*), 149

Sténobée (P. Quinault, *Bellérophon*), 155, 156, 157, 158, 212

Stéphanie (P. Corneille, *Théodore*), 15, 25, 27, 28, 29, 31, 32

Stratonice (P. Corneille, *Polyeucte*), 15, 25, 27, 28, 29

Suréna (P. Corneille, *Suréna*), 167, 168, 169, 170, 171, 172

Syphax (P. Corneille, *Sophonisbe*), 58, 59

Syra (J. Rotrou, *Cosroès*), 123, 124, 125, 126

Syroès (J. Rotrou, *Cosroès*), 124, 125, 126, 127

Taxile (J. Racine, *Alexandre*), 87, 88, 89, 90, 91

Tecmènes (G. Gilbert, *Hypolite*), 207

Thamire (P. Corneille, *Sertorius*), 53, 54, 56

Théodore (J. Rotrou, *Venceslas*), 25, 27, 28, 29, 31, 69, 71, 72, 73

Théramène (J. Racine, *Phèdre*), 120, 144, 159, 206, 208, 209, 210, 211, 213, 214, 215

Thésée (P. Corneille, *Œdipe*), 54

— (T. Corneille, *Ariane*), 144, 184, 185, 186, 187, 188,

— (G. Gilbert, *Hypolite*), 207

— (G. de la Pinelière, *Hippolyte*), 207

— (N. Pradon, *Phèdre et Hippolyte*), 196, 209

— (J. Racine, *Phèdre*), 1

Tigillin (G. Gilbert, *Arie et Pétus*), 135, 136, 138

— (Tristan L'Hermite, *La Mort de Sénèque*), 123

Timagène (P. Corneille, *Rodogune*), 15, 19, 20, 25, 26, 29, 42

Timocrate (T. Corneille, *Timocrate*), 151, 153, 154, 169, 176

Tite (P. Corneille, *Tite et Bérénice*), 109, 110, 111, 112

Tite (J. Magnon, *Tite*), 177, 178

Titus (J. Racine, *Bérénice*), 113, 114, 115, 116, 117, 118, 119, 120, 147, 165, 177, 179, 180, 181, 182, 183, 184, 187

Torquatus (C. Desjardins, *Manlius*), 60, 61, 62, 63

Ulysse (J. Racine, *Iphigénie*), 3, 144, 198, 201

Unulphe (P. Corneille, *Pertharite*), 74, 76

Valamir (P. Corneille, *Attila*), 107, 108

Vinius (P. Corneille, *Othon*), 128, 129, 130, 131, 133, 134, 140

Viriate (P. Corneille, *Sertorius*), 53, 54

Xénoclès (P. Corneille, *Agésilas*), 77

Xipharès (J. Racine, *Mithridate*), 160, 161, 163, 164, 165

Zaïre (J. Racine, *Bajazet*), 192

Zatime (J. Racine, *Bajazet*), 192

General Index

Albanese, R., 139
Allott, T., 128, 132, 134
ami(e)s, 15, 16, 17, 21, 22, 43, 60, 77,
    96, 104, 119, 129, 136, 137, 181,
    207, 210
amitié, 104, 149, 167, 171, 180, 183,
    184, 185, 188, 194, 196, 199, 200
apostrophe, use of, 18, 24, 36
apprendre, 19, 24, 104, 160
Aristotle
    Poetics, 210
asides, use of, 63, 69, 70, 71, 73, 79,
    143, 164, 203
Baker, S., 133, 134
Barnwell, H., 24, 45, 46, 51, 73, 81, 82,
    87, 138
Barthes, R., 7, 42, 114, 209
Baudin, M., 125
Bell, H., 178
Bernard, Catherine, 205
Bertaud, M., 185
bienséance, 8, 26, 28, 47, 60
Blanc, A., 205
Brooks, W., 104, 106, 155, 156, 157
Burke, P., 128
Burton, R., 85, 98, 99
Butler, P., 139, 143
Campion, E., 157
Campistron, Jean-Galbert de, 205
capitaine des gardes, 15, 37, 102, 121,
    159, 207
Carte de Tendre, 184
Cave, T., 153, 175
Césy, Comte de, 189
chorus, 5, 9, 83, 85, 86, 94, 98, 99,
    101, 138
Clarke, D., xi, 42, 70
Classe, O., 195, 196, 206
Claudel, P., 1, 6
Coëffeteau, Nicolas
    Histoire romaine, 128
Collins, D., 150, 186
Comédie Française, 2, 68
comédie galante, 178

comédie héroïque, 14, 21, 67, 78, 106,
    110, 111
comedy, 1, 14, 19, 41, 47, 69, 70, 94,
    109, 122, 179
confidents
    absence of, 8, 43, 62, 63, 71, 74, 75,
        77, 78, 81, 91, 94, 148, 149, 150,
        152, 153, 154, 156, 158, 159,
        161, 164, 166, 167, 168, 195,
        201, 214
    advice offered, 16, 21, 37, 52, 61, 96,
        97, 101, 102, 109, 110, 111, 112,
        121, 124, 125, 126, 127, 134,
        139, 140, 143, 144, 196, 212
    and exposition, 1, 16, 17, 18, 19, 20,
        21, 22, 23, 24, 25, 26, 27, 38, 47,
        50, 58, 62, 69, 70, 74, 79, 80, 87,
        89, 92, 96, 99, 106, 129, 148,
        149, 155, 156, 161, 167, 191, 209
    and opposition to main characters, 7,
        98, 138, 214
    and revelation of main characters'
        thoughts and feelings, 7, 16, 29,
        30, 31, 33, 35, 38, 51, 53, 57, 59,
        69, 79, 80, 91, 95, 102, 103, 104,
        123, 142, 143, 144, 149, 151,
        154, 156, 157, 158, 159, 161,
        162, 166, 168, 169, 173, 177,
        180, 183, 184, 185, 186, 188,
        192, 194, 199, 204, 208, 209
    argumentative strategies, 7, 57, 105
    as passive listeners, 17, 18, 19, 29,
        32, 52, 83, 89, 97, 104, 108, 109,
        115, 117, 125, 145, 156, 162,
        193, 201, 204, 211
    discourse of, 4, 18, 28, 35, 37, 51,
        99, 102, 106, 107, 112, 113, 120,
        123, 136, 166, 186, 188, 194,
        195, 208
    elimination of (see also absence of),
        8, 63, 68, 73, 81, 91, 93
    faux confident, 38, 39, 40, 41, 160,
        161, 176, 177, 178, 179, 180,
        182, 184, 185, 188, 189, 190,

193, 195, 196, 197, 198, 200,
202, 205, 207
in opening scenes, 16, 19, 24, 158,
209
messages delivered, 16, 41, 72, 113,
192
narrating offstage events, 15, 16, 35,
39, 55, 57, 59, 83, 90, 114, 118,
157, 163, 193
nomenclatures, 14, 53, 122
performance of, 3, 114, 115, 117,
138, 176, 177, 182, 187, 188,
189, 191, 192, 193, 194, 195,
196, 197, 198, 200
receiving confidences, 60, 69, 96,
207, 214
secrets disclosed to, 40, 51, 75, 160,
163
status of, 1, 29, 36, 37, 60, 76, 77,
95, 96, 97, 104, 108, 113, 119,
123, 129, 144, 159, 168, 170,
175, 180, 189, 201, 206, 207
strategic exclusion of, 9, 147, 159,
165
conflict, 7, 22, 24, 34, 57, 61, 63, 70,
81, 83, 84, 86, 89, 96, 98, 106, 108,
109, 123, 126, 137, 138, 153, 162,
184, 192, 196, 198, 214, 215
connaître/connaissez/connais, 54, 89,
181, 187, 210
conspiracy plays, 123
conspirators, 24, 67, 122, 124, 135, 203
Corneille, Pierre
Examens, 20, 24, 45, 47
council scenes, 23
Couton, G., xii, 23, 48, 60, 107, 217
d'Aubignac, Abbé, 2, 4, 8, 13, 18, 20,
22, 23, 26, 31, 45, 46, 47, 48, 49,
50, 51, 52, 53, 54, 55, 56, 57, 58,
59, 60, 61, 62, 68, 70, 72, 73, 77,
83, 84, 87, 88, 89, 97, 100, 103,
107, 116, 186
Dissertations contre Corneille, 4, 45,
46, 48, 49, 50, 53, 54, 55, 57, 58,
59, 81
La Pratique du théâtre, 23, 46, 87,
221
dame d'honneur, 15, 26, 54, 129
Davison, H., 46

deception (theme of), 39, 63, 101, 106,
150, 152, 163, 169, 176, 179, 182,
192, 196, 197
Deierkauf-Holsboer, S.W., 2
deliberative rhetoric, 18, 24, 32, 62, 74,
89, 102, 115, 213
Delmas, C., 148
demonstrative language, 18
Descotes, M., 80
Desfougères, A.-M., 73, 74
disguised identity/disguise, 52, 97, 137,
150, 153, 176, 177, 178, 179, 181
domestique, 14, 25, 160
Donneau de Visé, Jean, 41, 48, 51, 52,
53, 54, 55, 57, 58, 61, 62
Dosmond, S., 14
Doubrovsky, S., 15, 36, 51, 73, 110,
131, 169, 172
doubt (climate of), 72, 74, 105, 145,
154, 156, 157, 159, 168, 173, 192,
dramatic illusion, 8, 44, 72
éclaircir/éclaircissez, 181
Edwards, M., 86, 97
Ekstein, N., 4
Émelina, J., 41, 47, 67, 107
entrances, 4, 20, 71, 130, 167, 169
Euripides
Racine's annotations on, 4, 82, 84,
85, 96
exclamations, use of, 87, 194
exits, 4, 70, 118, 119, 130, 142, 167,
201
exposition – confidents' role in, 1, 6, 16,
17, 18, 19, 20, 21, 22, 23, 24, 25,
26, 27, 38, 47, 50, 58, 62, 69, 70,
74, 79, 80, 87, 89, 92, 96, 99, 106,
129, 148, 149, 155, 156, 161, 167,
191, 209
fainting, 194
female confidentes/servants, 1, 2, 3, 6,
13, 14, 15, 16, 18, 19, 21, 23, 24,
25, 26, 28, 30, 31, 32, 33, 34, 35,
36, 37, 39, 40, 41, 42, 44, 45, 47,
51, 52, 53, 54, 55, 56, 57, 58, 61,
62, 63, 67, 69, 71, 72, 74, 75, 77,
80, 83, 84, 85, 86, 88, 90, 91, 94,
97, 100, 103, 105, 106, 107, 108,
109, 111, 114, 115, 117, 121, 123,
131, 136, 147, 148, 150, 151, 155,
156, 157, 158, 160, 161, 162, 166,

168, 172, 177, 178, 179, 183, 184,
185, 186, 187, 188, 189, 190, 192,
193, 194, 195, 196, 197, 198, 199,
200, 201, 202, 205, 206, 207, 208,
209, 211, 212, 213, 214
Fermaud, J., 5, 6
fille d'honneur, 54, 207
forensic oratory, 23
Forestier, G., 3, 9, 18, 77, 78, 130, 132,
148, 150, 153, 154, 175, 178, 202
galanterie, 87, 144
Garapon, R., 68
Garnier, Robert, xii, 208, 217
genetic criticism, 3
gestures, 70, 145, 146, 202, 214
Giraud, Y., 150, 151
Gossip, C., 6, 67, 94, 106, 150
gouverneur, 15, 42, 69, 96, 100, 160,
161, 207, 208, 210, 211, 214
Gros, E., 94, 156, 157
Guichemerre, R., 189
Hammond, N., 4, 45, 46
Harwood-Gordon, S., 18, 23
Hawcroft, M., xi, 4, 7, 23, 26, 45, 46,
57, 81, 87, 88, 89, 91, 99, 100, 115,
162, 191, 212
Heliodorus, 189
Herodotus, 148
heroic romances/novels, 97, 147, 154,
159, 175, 180
heroines, discourse of, 24, 31, 32, 33,
34, 35, 41, 51, 55, 57, 59, 60, 61,
63, 74, 75, 88, 90, 91, 97, 98, 102,
106, 108, 111, 115, 117, 136, 148,
150, 154, 155, 157, 163, 167, 175,
177, 178, 180, 184, 185, 186, 188,
189, 190, 197, 198, 199, 201, 202,
208, 212, 213
Heyndels, I., 86
Hilgar, M.-F., 4, 67
Hôtel de Bourgogne, 2, 78, 103, 155,
166, 188, 199
imperatives, use of, 19, 21, 22, 32, 41,
59, 74, 79, 89, 100, 102, 109, 112,
116, 124, 139, 162, 181, 213
inquisitional rhetoric, 162
interrogatives, use of, 162
interruptio, 32, 57, 96, 105, 183, 197
Knight, R., 4, 73, 79, 82, 83, 96, 97,
149, 175, 190, 198

La Champmeslé (Marie Desmares), 184,
188
Lancaster, H.C., 2, 188, 189, 195, 199
Lapp, J., 5, 7
Lawton, H., 5, 6
Le Bidois, G., 6, 7, 32, 112
Le Mercure Galant, 48
*Lettre sur les remarques ... sur la
Sophonisbe*, 52
Leyssac, A. de, 17
liaison des scènes, 8, 34, 167
libertin plays/playwrights, 93, 137
Lockert, L., 1, 68
Louis XIV, 128, 134, 173, 204
Machiavelli, 163
machiavellian characters, 37, 76, 84,
102, 121, 132, 141, 143, 145, 192
Madeleine, J., 135
Mairet, Jean, 5
male *confidents*/servants, xi, 1, 2, 3, 4,
5, 6, 7, 8, 9, 13, 14, 15, 16, 17, 19,
20, 22, 23, 24, 25, 26, 27, 28, 29,
30, 32, 33, 34, 35, 36, 37, 38, 39,
40, 41, 42, 43, 45, 46, 47, 51, 52,
53, 54, 55, 56, 57, 58, 59, 60, 61,
62, 63, 67, 68, 69, 70, 71, 72, 73,
74, 75, 76, 77, 78, 79, 80, 81, 82,
83, 84, 85, 86, 87, 88, 89, 90, 91,
93, 94, 95, 96, 97, 98, 99, 100, 101,
102, 103, 104, 105, 106, 107, 108,
109, 110, 111, 112, 113, 114, 115,
116, 117, 118, 119, 120, 121, 122,
123, 124, 125, 126, 127, 129, 132,
135, 136, 138, 139, 140, 141, 142,
143, 144, 145, 146, 147, 148, 149,
150, 151, 152, 154, 155, 156, 157,
158, 159, 160, 161, 162, 163, 164,
165, 166, 167, 168, 169, 170, 171,
172, 173, 176, 177, 178, 179, 180,
181, 182, 183, 184, 185, 191, 195,
197, 198, 203, 204, 205, 206, 207,
208, 209, 210, 211, 213, 214, 215,
217
Martino, P., 46, 55
Maskell, D., xi, 26, 70, 86, 115, 116,
117, 118, 119, 201
McGowan, M., 188
Mesnard, P., 3, 83, 85, 96, 101
messengers, 14, 20, 25, 29, 35, 51, 58,
59, 62, 63, 69, 83, 85, 88, 89, 102,

113, 114, 125, 129, 148, 151, 157,
160, 180, 187, 192, 195, 203, 206,
209, 214
mistaken identity (plays of), 148, 150,
202
mistrust, climate of (in plays), 69, 71,
162, 172
Molière (Jean-Baptiste Poquelin), 2, 21,
45, 107, 159, 179
his troupe, 68, 77
Monaco, M., 6
monologues, 4, 24, 30, 32, 33, 34, 35,
36, 37, 38, 39, 41, 43, 60, 61, 63,
67, 71, 73, 75, 76, 79, 83, 90, 102,
114, 119, 126, 127, 132, 148, 154,
156, 164, 165, 169, 173, 193, 203,
214
Moore, W., 189
Morel, J., xii, 72, 124, 127, 217
Mourgues, O. de, 7
Nantouillet, Chevalier de, 189
Newton, W., 206
nourrice, 14, 109, 195, 208, 213
Nurse, P., 1, 17, 97, 206, 209, 210,
212, 213
O'Regan, M., 164
offstage action, 4, 15, 16, 34, 35, 39,
55, 57, 60, 70, 83, 90, 114, 118,
130, 157, 163, 193
opera, 204
Ovid, 185
Palais-Royal, 78
para-confident(e)s, 29, 35, 43, 67, 72,
79, 80, 87, 88, 90, 92, 108, 113,
114, 148, 149, 151, 152, 153, 155,
156, 158, 160, 167, 168, 171, 176,
184, 198, 203, 207
Parish, R., 180, 199, 200
parler/parle/parlez, 36, 40, 50, 85, 100,
110, 112, 115, 116, 131, 134, 137,
155, 162, 192, 194, 201
Paul the Deacon, *Historia
Langobardorum*, 75, 76
Pellet, E., 136, 138, 139
peripeteia, 39, 74, 103, 134, 149, 151,
166, 196
Pfohl, R., 198
Phillips, H., 4, 6, 100, 113, 116, 117,
162, 165, 192
Picard, R., 93, 191

Plutarch, 102, 166
polymythie/polymythic plots, 54, 74,
81, 135
préciosité, 61, 62, 114, 151, 157, 159
Prigent, M., 129, 133, 172
Prophète, J., 29
protactic characters, 17, 20, 49, 58, 96,
119, 159, 160, 209
Querelle de Sophonisbe, 8, 13, 17, 20,
22, 31, 35, 68, 77, 81, 85, 93, 97,
129, 186
Querelle des Imaginaires, 93
Querelle du Cid, 8
Querelle du confident, 6, 8, 51, 53, 55,
67, 82, 94, 172, 203, 204
Quinault, Philippe, 10, 41, 87, 94, 103,
104, 105, 106, 118, 144, 154, 155,
156, 157, 158, 159, 173, 195, 197,
198, 204, 205, 206, 212
Racine, Jean
and the 'active' *confident*, 9, 61, 112,
121, 155, 192, 198, 204, 209
annotations on Euripides and
Sophocles, 4, 82, 84, 85, 96
récits, 4, 16, 17, 19, 20, 21, 22, 23, 24,
30, 39, 41, 46, 47, 49, 54, 58, 76,
83, 86, 88, 109, 120, 124, 125, 129,
137, 142, 148, 151, 156, 157, 159,
161, 163, 182, 190, 201, 206, 209,
210, 214
revenge (theme of), 34, 36, 75, 103,
106, 157, 160, 164, 179, 187, 200
rhetorical questions, use of, 24, 33, 41,
59, 74, 79, 87, 89, 105
romanesque devices, 9, 156
Rossi, H., 82
Saint-Evremond, Charles de Marguetel de
Saint-Denis de, 51
Sanchez, J., 130, 132, 166, 172
savoir/sachez/sache, 43, 152, 167
Scherer, J., 2, 4, 5, 6, 14, 15, 16, 17,
19, 24, 26, 29, 33, 36, 39, 67, 73,
118, 125, 184, 203, 204
Schrammen, G., 7, 98, 105
Scott, J., 74
Scudéry, George de, 8
secrecy, climate of, 69, 159
Sévigné, Mme de, 184, 188
silence, uses of, 2, 36, 61, 98, 100, 106,
115, 116, 139, 141, 152, 155, 170

silent attendants, 206
Sophocles
    Racine's annotations on, 4, 82, 84,
        85, 96
speech acts, 131, 134
Spencer, C., 91
stances, 4, 33, 67, 69, 74, 83, 84, 132
Stegmann, A., 14, 75, 76, 79, 80, 172
stichomythia., 153
Stiefel, A., 123, 126
Stone, J., 82
suivant(e)s, 14, 15, 18, 36, 48, 49, 50,
    51, 52, 53, 54, 55, 60, 61, 63, 69,
    88, 97, 116, 129, 207
suspense (plays of), 52, 73, 103, 149,
    150, 154, 172, 176, 185
Sweetser, M.-O., 140
symmetry - and structure of plays, 15,
    40, 76, 78, 80, 93, 94, 98, 104, 106,
    107, 108, 136, 148, 155, 167, 202,
    211, 213
Tacitus, 127, 128, 129, 130, 131, 132,
    134, 135, 137, 138, 141, 143, 163
    and Tacitism, 128
    Annals, 128, 137, 138
    Histories, 128, 130, 134
tears, 86, 98, 141, 145, 161, 194
Théâtre du Marais, 2
tragédie galante, 144, 159, 204
tragédie-ballet, 78

tragicomédie, 68, 70, 123, 150, 159,
    179, 181, 185, 191
tragicomic, 177, 178, 181, 186, 198,
    202
troupes, 2, 35, 47, 77, 78, 97, 132, 135,
    137, 138, 148, 166, 188, 189
Truchet, J., 37, 38, 39, 99, 122, 143,
    184, 185, 205
Unities, 49, 205
    Unity of action, 54, 84, 137
    Unity of place, 47
    Unity of time, 8
Van Baelen, J., 126
vengeance, theme of (see under revenge),
    24, 30, 42, 103, 106, 151
verisimilitude (see also dramatic
    illusion), 46, 47, 49, 50, 51, 54, 55,
    57, 60, 61, 70, 72, 81, 86, 91, 97,
    167, 180
Viala, A., xii, 141, 159, 163, 217
Villars, Abbé de
    La Critique de Bérénice, 109
virtual monologues, 30, 32, 61, 119
voice substitution, 100, 186, 192
Voltaire, François-Marie Arouet, 1, 30,
    36, 37, 39, 40, 58, 144, 184
Watts, D., 68, 69, 71, 72, 102, 123,
    124, 126
Wood, A., 206, 207
Woodman, A., 137

IMPRIME
RIE MEDE
CINE m+h
HYGIENE

mars–1999